BROADMAN COMMENTS 1994-95

# 52 Ready-To-Teach Bible Study Lessons

BROADMAN COMMENTS 1994-95

# 52 Ready-To-Teach Bible Study Lessons

DONALD F. ACKLAND
ROBERT J. DEAN

Based on the International Sunday School Lessons

Each Plan Includes These Sections: Studying the Bible
Applying the Bible Teaching the Bible

Nashville, Tennessee

4217-27
ISBN: 0-8054-1727-3



Dewey Decimal Classification: 268.61
Subject Heading: SUNDAY SCHOOL LESSONS—COMMENTARIES

Library of Congress Catalog Card Number: 45-437
Printed in the United States of America

## ABBREVIATIONS AND TRANSLATIONS

**KJV** *King James Version*

**NASB** From the *New American Standard Bible.* © The Lockman Foundation, 1960, 1962, 1963, 1968, 1971, 1972, 1973, 1975, 1977. Used by permission.

**NIV** From the Holy Bible, *New International Version,* copyright © 1973, 1978, 1984 by International Bible Society. Used by permission.

**NEB** From *The New English Bible.* Copyright © The Delegates of the Oxford University Press and the Syndics of the Cambridge University Press, 1961, 1970. Reprinted by permission.

**NRSV** From the *New Revised Standard Version Bible* copyright © 1989, by the Division of Christian Education of the National Council of Churches of Christ in the United States of America, and used by permission.

# Donald F. Ackland:
## A Man to Remember

Don Ackland is a man to remember. All those who knew him and knew of his contribution to Bible teaching in the churches, particularly Southern Baptist churches, will remember him with gratitude and even some awe. His contributions to Southern Baptists spanned nearly a half century. If you include the years he spent in England as writer, teacher, and servant of our Lord, his was a seventy-year ministry.

Don Ackland had many titles and filled a variety of positions, but each of them had as its focus the interpretation of Scripture. The driving force of his ministry is best explained with the words of Paul in Colossians 1:28: "We proclaim him, admonishing and teaching everyone with all wisdom, so that we may present everyone perfect in Christ. To this end I labor, struggling with all his energy which so powerfully works in me" (NIV). His was a ministry of proclamation, admonition, and teaching, always with the integrity of Scripture of his foundation. Because of the long hours of studying, praying, thinking, and writing it can be truly said that he taught with "all wisdom."

From 1949 until his death in 1994, Don Ackland influenced Southern Baptist Bible study materials and the quality of teaching through his work. He helped to encourage use of Scripture as the basis of personal worship through the design and early years of editing *Open Windows.* He exacted the highest standards from designers, writers, and editors of adult Bible study materials. New and experienced editors came often to his office asking for help in biblical interpretation. Though he never formally studied Greek and Hebrew, he used resources that enabled him to test translations and interpretations by their meanings in the original languages. Editors learned from him through his thorough and sometimes tough evaluation of their manuscripts. His commitment to the authority of Scripture was never in question. His desire to make the Bible truths applicable to life was a lifetime commitment.

January Bible Study was a favorite of his, and he was a popular teacher and speaker each year as churches used the materials he helped to design, edit, and—sometimes—write. He was the moving force in designing and producing the Bible Survey Series because he believed lay teachers were capable of discerning meaning of difficult texts if they were given appropriate training and resources. Thousands upon thousands of Sunday School teachers benefited from his work on these materials.

Don Ackland was a man who combined excellence in biblical scholarship, clarity of expression, evangelistic warmth, and humor to make clear the truths of the Bible. He had a grasp not only of individual texts but of the whole Scripture. In spite of his ability and excellence he never forgot that a "student is not above his teacher, but everyone who is fully trained will be like his teacher (Luke 6:40, NIV). Truly Don Ackland was like his Teacher. And for that we shall remember him and thank God upon every remembrance.

Harry Piland, Director
Bible Teaching and Reaching Division

# Contents

## THIRD QUARTER – Christian Living in Community



## FOURTH QUARTER – A Nation Turns from God

# From the Conquest to the Kingdom

**Books from BROADMAN & HOLMAN for Studying and Teaching**

*Layman's Bible Book Commentary,* Volumes 4,5,6
*Broadman Bible Commentary,* Volumes 2,3
*The Teacher's Bible Commentary,* Paschall and Hobbs
*Old Testament Survey,* Paul R. House
*The Heart of Hebrew History,* H. I. Hester
*Holman Bible Dictionary,* Trent C. Butler, ed.
*Atlas of the Bible Lands,* Harry Thomas Frank, ed.
*Learning to Study the Bible,* Earl P. McQuay
*Getting to Know Your Bible,* Julia Rippy Boone
*How to Interpret the Bible,* Robert L. Cate
*Holman Bible Handbook,* David S. Dockery, ed.

## INTRODUCTION

This quarter, we will take a series of giant steps through the Old Testament, beginning with the crossing of the Jordan, and the entry of the Israelites into their land of promise, Canaan.

In **Unit I**, "The Conquest of the Land," we will take account of events that culminated in the fall of the walls of Jericho, an important victory that opened up the land to the advancing Israelites. Details of the campaign that followed will be passed over that we may listen to Joshua's farewell speech in which he reviewed God's mighty works and called for loyalty to Him.

**Unit II**, "The Rule of the Judges," provides information on the period of the judges, considers their function, and focuses on the achievements of one of them, Gideon.

**Unit III**, "The Beginning of the Kingdom," deals with Samuel's leadership, and the demand of the people for a king. The answer came in the appointment of Saul, son of Kish, to be Israel's first king. In two lessons we consider the hopeful beginning of his reign and his subsequent failure to conform to the will of the Lord.

**Unit IV**, "The Kingdom Under David and Solomon," reveals the strengths and weaknesses of these two kings, leading up to the division of the kingdom after Solomon's death. In four lessons we shall be challenged to face up to the subtleties of Satan and make full commitment of ourselves to God.

September
4
1994

# Spying Out Jericho

**Basic Passage:** Joshua 1:1—2:24
**Focal Passages:** Joshua 2:1,8-14,22-24

The loss of a leader can be a devastating blow to any group. For the past thirteen weeks, our studies have majored on the man Moses, raised up by God to bring deliverance to His people, and start them on their journey to the promised land. He was a larger-than-life personality, successful in a difficult mission and enjoying an exalted status among his people that continues to the present day. Who could take the place of such a man? God had a successor in preparation, not a duplicate of Moses, but a man with abilities suited to the new circumstances. His name was Joshua, which means "God is salvation," with the revered name "Jesus" as the New Testament equivalent. The old adage, "God buries His workmen but carries on His work," is well illustrated in the stories of these two men, Moses and Joshua. There are always places to fill in the ranks of the Lord's servants, and divine help is always available to those who fill the gaps. Sometimes He makes surprising choices.

**Study Aim:** *To learn how God can use unworthy and unlikely people in kingdom service*

## STUDYING THE BIBLE

The events recorded in Deuteronomy took place in "the plains of Moab . . . over against Jericho" (Deut. 34:1). Moses had brought the Israelites to a point where only the waters of Jordan separated them from their destination, the land of Canaan. There, on a mountaintop, Moses died and God buried him "in a valley in the land of Moab" (vv. 5-6).

### I. Joshua Succeeds Moses (Josh. 1:1-9)

Joshua is described as "Moses' minister," that is, his helper, ready to carry out any duty assigned to him. He is introduced into the Old Testament narrative without statement of his background (Ex. 17:8–16). The journeying Israelites were attacked by Amalekites, and Moses called on him to select men who would resist this enemy. As Moses held high his hand, Joshua's small army prospered against the Amalekites, who were routed. He, with Caleb, withstood the evil report of ten other spies and encouraged trust in God for victory (Num. 14:6-9). Under divine instruction, Moses publicly announced Joshua's future leadership (27:15-23). We may be sure that Moses provided opportunities for the younger man to gain experience in preparation for the important task that awaited him. On the death of Moses, Joshua was ready to take over.

### II. Spies in Jericho (Josh. 2:1-7)

The city that lay across the Jordan from the encamped Israelites was possibly the oldest walled city in the world. It was strategically placed near a trade route that crossed the Jordan nearby. Jericho was one of a number of city-states, each with its own king, that stood in the path of the advancing Israelites. Its history goes back from eight to ten thousand years, and the city of Joshua's time was one of many that had stood on that site. This fact accounts for the problems archaeologists have met in seeking to identify the Old Testament location. The Jericho of our Lord's day was several miles distant.

> 1 And Joshua the son of Nun sent out of Shittim two men to spy secretly, saying, Go view the land, even Jericho. And they went, and came into an harlot's house, named Rahab, and lodged there.

Attempts have been made to make Rahab an innkeeper and not a prostitute. This ignores the true meaning of the Hebrew noun used to describe her, and minimizes the grace of God in receiving her into the family of faith. Her profession helped conceal the identity of the two strange men in her house, who were really Israelitish spies. The reality of her professed belief in "the Lord your God" (vv. 9-11) is attested to by subsequent references to her in Scripture. She is included in the honor roll of faith (Heb. 11:31). Also in Matthew's genealogy of our Lord where she is recognized as the wife of Salmon, therefore mother of Boaz who married Ruth (Matt. 1:5).

### III. Confession of Faith (Josh. 2:8-14)

The record does not conceal or excuse the lie that Rahab told to protect the spies. She told the king's men that she did not know the identity of the two men who had come and gone "about the time of shutting of the gate, when it was dark" (v. 5). There is an ethical problem here with which good people have always struggled: Is it permissible, in any circumstance, to tell an untruth? We are dealing, of course, with a pagan woman, of low moral character, in whom a Godward faith was only just awakening. The two Israelites had not fled but had been hidden under bundles of flax on the flat roof of Rahab's house.

> 8 And before they were laid down, she came up unto them upon the roof;
>
> 9 And she said unto the men, I know that the Lord hath given you the land, and that your terror is fallen upon us, and that all the inhabitants of the land faint because of you.
>
> 10 For we have heard how the Lord dried up the water of the Red Sea for you, when ye came out of Egypt; and what ye did unto the two kings of the Amorites, that were on the other side Jordan, Sihon and Og, whom ye utterly destroyed.

11 And as soon as we had heard these things, our hearts did melt, neither did there remain anymore courage in any man, because of you: for the Lord your God, he is God in heaven above, and in earth beneath.

12 Now therefore, I pray you, swear unto me by the Lord, since I have showed you kindness, that ye will also show kindness unto my father's house, and give me a true token:

13 And that ye will save alive my father, and my mother, and my brethren, and my sisters, and all that they have, and deliver our lives from death.

14 And the men answered her, Our life for yours, if ye utter not this our business. And it shall be, when the Lord hath given us the land, that we will deal kindly and truly with thee.

**1. Fear acknowledged (vv. 8-11).**—In her kind of business, Rahab learned much about happenings in the world outside of Jericho. Her visitors would bring news of the advancing Israelites, and the victories gained over their enemies. Rahab acknowledged to the spies that the whole city was in fear of the approaching host. The most recent victories were over two Amorite kings, Sihon and Og, who were "utterly destroyed" (see Deut. 4:46-49). For Jericho, this was too near to be comfortable. Rahab went further. She attributed these victories to Israel's God. It was He who divided the Red Sea and gave success to Israel's armies. Her acknowledgment was also a confession of faith in Yahweh, "God in heaven above, and in earth beneath."

**2. Protection requested (vv. 12-14).**—Anticipating the occupation of Jericho, Rahab asked for protection for herself and family. Her concern for various members, beginning with father and mother, sheds light on her character. While seeking to preserve her own life, family ties caused her to include these others in her request of Jericho's conquerors. The spies gave her the promise she wanted.

### IV. The Scarlet Cord (Josh. 2:15-21)

Whether the "crimson cord" (v. 18, NRSV) and the rope by which the spies were let down the wall were the same, is questionable. Different words are used in the Hebrew.

**1. The escape (vv. 15-16).**—Rahab's house is described as "upon the town wall." A literal reading is, "in the wall of the wall," a description that fits the facts, for there was a double wall around Jericho. Heavy timbers were laid from wall to wall, and on these, homes were built. Rahab's home extended over the outer wall, and through one of its windows she provided escape for the two spies, letting them down with a rope. Her instructions to them were to hide in the hillsides, where caves abounded, for three days. The soldiers of Jericho's king were already out looking for them, so they must not take the risk of an immediate return to the ford of the river over which they could reach Joshua's encampment.

**2. The plan (vv. 17-21).**—Rahab was to tie a scarlet cord to the window by which the spies made their escape. This would identify her home from others on the wall. Another condition was that no member of the family should leave the house during the attack. If anyone was foolhardy enough to ignore this, "his blood shall be upon his head" (v. 19). There is reminder here of the conditions of the Passover night, when God brought His people out of Egypt. There was safety for those who stayed in their houses, under the protective blood of a slain lamb (Ex. 12). The shed blood of the Savior avails for us.

### V. Reporting to Joshua (Josh. 2:22-24)

The report brought to Joshua by the two spies differed greatly from that brought to Moses at Kirjath-jearim (Num. 13). Echoing the words of Rahab, they told how all Jericho was in fear of the Israelites and gave credit to God for the coming victory.

> 22 And they went, and came unto the mountain, and abode there three days, until the pursuers were returned: and the pursuers sought them throughout all the way, but found them not.
>
> 23 So the two men returned, and descended from the mountain, and passed over, and came to Joshua the son of Nun, and told him all things that befell them:
>
> 24 And they said unto Joshua, Truly the Lord hath delivered into our hands all the land; for even all the inhabitants of the country do faint because of us.

Having successfully evaded their pursuers, the two left their hiding places, descended to the Jordan valley, crossed the river, and safely arrived at the Israelites' camp. There they told of their adventure, with special reference to the part played by Rahab and the promise they had given her. The fulfillment of that promise may be found in 6:23-25, which begins, "And the young men that were spies went in, and brought out Rahab, and her father, and her mother, and her brethren, and all that she had; and they brought out all her kindred, and left them without the camp of Israel." The concluding statement indicates that, because these people were non-Israelites, they were not allowed into the camp until after a period of purification. That they were ultimately accepted is evident from the statement, "She dwelleth in Israel even unto this day" (v. 25), a statement revised to read, "Her family has lived in Israel ever since" (NRSV).

## APPLYING THE BIBLE

**The people God uses.**—Look through the Bible and you will be amazed at the people God has used: Abraham, Jacob, and Peter were liars; Moses was a murderer; David was a murderer and an adulterer; and Rahab was a prostitute. Perhaps you have heard it said by preachers whose zeal has outrun their knowledge: "God can't use a crooked stick!" The truth is, God can use any kind of stick—a long one, a short one, a big one, a little one, a straight one, a crooked one—but He certainly prefers a clean and straight stick. Put no limit on God, for if He can use a prostitute in His divine scheme of things, He can use anyone—including you and me.

**The one thing everybody needs.**—Copernicus and Rahab made the same discovery.

Copernicus revolutionized our concept of the universe. As he lay dying in May 1543, his famous treatise "The Revolution of the Heavenly Bodies" came off the press and was laid in his arms. He discovered and developed the theory that the earth is a moving planet and in so doing he revolutionized astronomy. However, for all his greatness Copernicus thought of himself only as a poor sinner saved by the grace of God. But his greatest discovery, to which he testified, was the forgiveness of his sins through the grace of God. This discovery he and the prostitute Rahab held in common.

On his headstone at Frauenburg, Poland (now Frombork), one can read the epitaph he wrote for himself: "I do not seek a kindness equal to that given to Paul; nor do I ask the grace granted to Peter; but that forgiveness which thou didst give to the robber—that I earnestly pray."

**Dedication to the task.**—Few men have lived as meaningfully as did Dr. Albert Schweitzer. A brilliant German philosopher, physician, musician, missionary, theologian, organist, and authority on Bach, Schweitzer was in every sense of the word a genius. Probably all of us have read about his abandoning a brilliant musical, medical, or university career to bury his life at Lambarene, French Equatorial Africa.

Schweitzer's dedication to his calling as a teacher, doctor, and musician was so compelling that many nights as he studied during his formative years he would keep his feet in cold water to stay awake. He referred to those early years as a period of "continual struggle with fatigue."

But Schweitzer never lost sight of his main goal. When he passed the medical examination in October 1911, he gave a year to his work as an intern and then applied to the Paris Missionary Society to become a medical missionary in Africa. There Schweitzer served sacrificially for Jesus' sake. It was this kind of dedication to God and His will that encouraged the two faithful spies to bring back their positive report to Joshua. Whole-soul dedication nerved the arm of Joshua as he assumed the mantle of Moses and led the Israelites into Canaan. And the same thing drove Rahab to lay her life on the line for God's people and God's work.

**The curse of lukewarmness.**—Lukewarmness has been a hindrance to the work of the kingdom of God since the beginning of time. But there was nothing lukewarm about the two spies when they returned from their mission and gave to Joshua their report and the promise of

God based on faith: "Truly the Lord hath delivered into our hands all the land; for even all the inhabitants of the country do faint because of us" (Josh. 2:24).

The movers and shakers of history are people who are passionate about their work. Take, for example, Arturo Toscanini who, no doubt, was the greatest musical conductor who ever lived.

Conductor of the New York Philharmonic Orchestra (1926-1936), Toscanini was also director of the NBC Symphony Orchestra. A native of Italy, Europe was clamoring to hear Toscanini in the 1930s when he started out on a tour with his New York orchestra. In twenty-three cities he and his orchestra were a magnificent triumph. In 1933, Hitler came to power. Toscanini gave a staunch "no" to the invitation to conduct music in Hitler's Germany. Even Hitler himself appealed to Toscanini, but that only made the maestro more determined not to conduct in Germany. He declined, he said, because his feelings had been wounded "as a man and as an artist" by the events that had taken place under Hitler. Toscanini said about his convictions: "I burn or I freeze, but I cannot be lukewarm."

Indeed! And how can we be lukewarm who have the gospel the dying world so desperately needs?

## TEACHING THE BIBLE

▶ *Main Idea*: The Israelites' spying out Jericho demonstrates that God uses unworthy and unlikely people in kingdom service.
▶ *Suggested Teaching Aim*: To lead adults to describe how the Israelites spied out Jericho, and to discover how God can use unworthy and unlikely people in His service.

### Introduce the Bible Study

Ask: What makes a person eligible to be used in God's service? What criteria does a person have to meet before God can use that person in kingdom service? Let members respond and list their responses on a chalkboard or a large sheet of paper. You will use these responses at the end of the lesson. Point out this session begins a unit on Joshua titled, "The Conquest of the Land." Make a unit poster with lesson titles and Scriptures for this unit. Cut an arrow from colored paper and use it each week to indicate the lesson being studied. A map of the conquest will be helpful.

### Search for Biblical Truth

Set the context by locating Shittim [SHIT im] or Acacia [uh KAY she uh] and Jericho on a map. Acacia is directly opposite Jericho and about eight miles east of the Jordan [HBD, 1273]. Point out that Joshua sent two men to spy out the city of Jericho in preparation for an attack, and they went to Rahab's house in Jericho.

## A TEACHING OUTLINE

*1. Introduce the quarter's study.*
*2. Set the context.*
*3. Explore the actions of the spies and Rahab.*
*4. Identify how God can use class members today.*

For a Bible search, ask half the class to look for information about the spies and half to look for information about Rahab. Give the following questions without the answers to each group. Allow six to eight minutes for study and then call for reports.

**Group 1—The spies**

1. What was the purpose of the spies' mission? *(spy out the city of Jericho)*

2. Why did the spies go to Rahab's house? *(your response but consider: may have felt they would not attract as much attention there and that Rahab would have heard information from other travelers)*

3. How wise do you think this was? *(your response)*

4. What agreement did the spies make with Rahab? *(to save her and her family if she would not betray them)*

5. How did the spies escape? *(Rahab let them down over the wall; they hid for three days before crossing the Jordan.)*

6. What did the spies report to Joshua? *(The Lord had delivered Jericho into their hands.)*

**Group 2—Rahab**

1. What was Rahab's occupation? *(prostitute)*

2. What information did Rahab give the spies? *(All the city was afraid because they had heard what God had done in Egypt and on the east side of Jordan.)*

3. To what did Rahab credit the Israelites' previous victories? *(God's leadership)*

4. What made Rahab befriend the spies? *(your response)*

5. What did Rahab's concern for her family reveal about her? *(family was important to her)*

6. How did Rahab fit into the genealogy of Jesus? *(mother of Boaz, who was David's great grandfather)*

### Give the Truth a Personal Focus

Refer to the list compiled in Introduce the Bible Study. *Ask:* How many of these criteria did Rahab meet? What enabled God to use her in service of His kingdom?

Distribute paper and pencils to members. Ask them to list the aspects of their life that would appear to make them unworthy and unlikely prospects for kingdom service. Then ask, What do you need to do before God can use you in His service? Answers will vary but be sure that willingness and openness to God's leadership are mentioned.

# Acting on Faith

**Basic Passage:** Joshua 3:1—4:24
**Focal Passage:** Joshua 3:7-17

The Jordan River has been, and still remains, a great divider. It flows through what has been described as "the deepest ditch in the world." The river has its eastern source in a spring, one of which flows from a cave near Caesarea Philippi, where Jesus asked His disciples, "But whom say ye that I am?" (Matt. 16:13-20). There the infant river is 1,200 feet *above* sea level. It flows eventually into the Dead Sea, the same distance *below* sea level. On the eastern bank of the Jordan the Israelites, under Joshua, were encamped, its waters an effective barrier for an army possessed of no vehicular means of making the crossing. But in this river John the Baptist would do his baptizing, immersing, among others, the Lord Jesus Himself (Matt. 3:13-17). And today, these same waters separate territory claimed by Israel, the disputed West Bank, and the Arab kingdom of Jordan. Gospel songsters have seen the Jordan as a symbol of death, through which all must pass to enter heaven. But the crossing of the river for Joshua and his following provided no entry into everlasting rest and peace. For on the other side lay Jericho, the first of many obstacles to be overcome before Canaan could be occupied and settled.

**Study Aim:** *To recognize and rejoice in a God whose powers of deliverance reach from generation to generation*

## STUDYING THE BIBLE

We should not miss the statement that "Joshua rose early in the morning" (3:1). The two spies had reported to him that the inhabitants of Jericho "faint because of us" (2:24). He was eager to take advantage of the situation by a prompt advance. There were tremendous difficulties ahead, but Joshua's faith was in God (1:9). He had already assured his followers of a safe crossing of the Jordan and had ordered them to prepare for the event (vv. 10-11).

### I. Joshua's Leadership Confirmed (Josh. 3:7-8)

"Can I fill this man's shoes?" Joshua must often have asked himself this question. To be successor to Moses was a tremendous undertaking from which any normal person might shrink. "Can Joshua fill Moses' shoes?" is a question that others must have asked. So, on both Joshua's part and that of the people, doubts must have existed as to his ability to assume leadership of the Israelites. The Lord recognized this when, after the death of Moses, He said to Joshua, "As I was with Moses, so I will be with thee: I will not fail thee, nor forsake thee" (1:5). To read the verses that follow is to realize that God knew the need of Joshua for strong reassurance. Hence, "Only be thou strong and very courageous . . . be not afraid, neither be thou dismayed: for the Lord thy God is with thee withersoever thou goest" (vv. 7-9). But what of the people? A special demonstration of divine power, similar to that exercised by Moses, would help them understand that though a great leader had died, God would continue to fulfill His purposes through a worthy successor, Joshua.

> 7 And the Lord said unto Joshua, This day will I begin to magnify thee in the sight of all Israel, that they may know that, as I was with Moses, so I will be with thee.
> 8 And thou shalt command the priests that bear the ark of the covenant, saying, When ye are come to the brink of the water of Jordan, ye shall stand still in Jordan.

Soon after the exodus from Egypt, the Lord demonstrated His own power and endorsed the leadership of Moses at the same time, by the dividing of the waters of the Red Sea (see earlier lesson for June 26). Now He would again exercise the power of creatorship to enable His people to cross the last natural barrier between them and Canaan, the river Jordan. That God intended this miracle to be an expression of approval for Joshua is clear from verse 7. But it is also clear from verse 8 that there should be no escaping the fact that the phenomenon about to be witnessed was the work of God Himself. The ark of the covenant would be the symbol of His presence in behalf of His people.

## II. Following the Ark (Josh. 3:9-13)

One of the perils of leadership is self-centeredness. An effective leader is tempted to take credit to himself for everything good that happens. Joshua is outstanding for his determination to recognize God as the real miracle worker in behalf of His people. In many ways, he was an exemplary person. The Bible "gives the impression of a man who was single-minded in his duty toward God. Consequently he rose above the shabby things that mar the records of others, some more famous than he, to gain a place of renown in the annals of his people. At most, one error of judgment is the worst we know about him [9:3-27]."[1]

> 9 And Joshua said unto the children of Israel, Come hither, and hear the words of the Lord your God.
> 10 And Joshua said, Hereby ye shall know that the living God is among you, and that he will without fail drive out from before you the Canaanites, and the Hittites, and the Hivites, and the Perizzites, and the Girgashites, and the Amorites, and the Jebusites.
> 11 Behold, the ark of the covenant of the Lord of all the earth passeth over before you into Jordan.

12 Now therefore take you twelve men out of the tribes of
Israel, out of every tribe a man.
13 And it shall come to pass, as soon as the soles of the feet
of the priests that bear the ark of the Lord, the Lord of all the
earth, shall rest in the waters of Jordan, that the waters of
Jordan shall be cut off from the waters that come down from
above; and they shall stand upon an heap.

**1. Canaan's occupants (vv. 9-10).**—A famous scholar wrote, a hundred years ago, "Palestine has never belonged to one nation, and probably never will."[2] It is reasonable to suppose that Canaan was occupied by Canaanites, but verse 10 lists other tribes, one, the Hittites, from as far away as modern Turkey. Philistines had not yet arrived on the scene. But "five kings of the Amorites" (10:5) later fought against Joshua. And the Jebusites remained in control of the Jerusalem area until David's time (2 Sam. 5:6-9).

**2. Representative dozen (vv. 11-13).**—The task of the twelve men, one from each tribe, is not explained until the following chapter. That they were chosen in advance indicates the orderliness and thoroughness with which this crossing of the river took place. There was nothing haphazard or accidental.

## III. Crossing the Jordan (Josh. 3:14-17)

The ark of the covenant is described in detail in Exodus 25. It was made of shittim (acacia) wood, overlaid with gold, and had four gold rings, one at each corner, through which staves were inserted by which it could be carried. It represented the presence of God among His people. The priests who carried it were not guarantors of Israel's safety. They were the bearers and custodians of that sacred box which was the visible evidence of the fulfillment of the promise given to Joshua, "The Lord thy God is with thee whithersoever thou goest" (1:9). What happened to the ark after the sacking of Jerusalem by the Babylonians, nobody knows. It has its substitute in Jewish places of worship today in chests of various sizes and forms of embellishment, that contain the scrolls of the Law.

14 And it came to pass, when the people removed from their
tents, to pass over Jordan, and the priests bearing the ark of the
covenant before the people;
15 And as they that bare the ark were come unto Jordan, and
the feet of the priests that bare the ark were dipped in the brim
of the water, (for Jordan overfloweth all his banks all the time
of harvest,)
16 That the waters which came down from above stood and
rose up upon an heap very far from the city Adam, that is beside
Zaretan: and those that came down toward the sea of the plain,
even the salt sea, failed, and were cut off: and the people passed
over right against Jericho.

17 And the priests that bare the ark of the covenant of the Lord stood firm on dry ground in the midst of Jordan, and all the Israelites passed over on dry ground, until all the people were passed clean over Jordan.

**1. Waters held back (vv. 14-16).**—What happened that day to the waters of Jordan? That God performed a miracle in behalf of His people is not to be doubted. When a phenomenon of nature happens at a specific time, to serve a crucial purpose, that is a miracle. It reveals God in command of the dynamics which He created. Landslides have been recorded that damned up the waters of the Jordan. One of these occurred as recently as 1927 when the flow of the river was stopped for twenty-one hours. But, by whatever means employed, the Lord provided for His people a safe and dry pathway through the river that stood between them and their destination.

**2. Safety assured (v. 17).**—So long as the custodians of the ark stood their ground, the people were able to cross from the east to the west bank of the river. The power was not in the priests but in the presence of God represented in the sacred object in their charge. That the ark no longer exists is commentary on the fact that His people no longer look to symbols of His presence for their assurance, for they have His presence individually in the indwelling Holy Spirit.

## IV. The Event Memorialized (Josh. 4:1-9, 19-24)

Our assigned Scripture includes chapter 4 in which is recorded the setting up of monuments to keep bright the memory of God's undertaking that day as His people looked across Jordan to Jericho. The Lord knows our human forgetfulness and again and again, in Scripture, He provided means for jogging our memories of things important to remember. However, the two memorials in this chapter had another purpose, namely, to stimulate inquiry and thus ensure that God's mighty deeds were known to future generations. They were to be a "memorial unto the children of Israel forever" (v. 7).

**1. Monument at Gilgal (vv. 1-8, 19-20).**—The twelve men were each to carry a stone from the bed of the river and deposit them at their first campsite in Canaan, identified as Gilgal. These stones were to be a reminder, not only to Israel, but also "all the people of the earth" that they might know "the hand of the Lord, that it is mighty: that ye might fear the Lord your God for ever" (v. 24).

**2. Another in Jordan (v. 9).**—A second cairn of stones seems to have been erected in the bed of the river, "in the place where the feet of the priests . . . stood." The crossing took place at the "time of harvest" when the "Jordan overfloweth all his banks" (3:15). Evidently in dry seasons the water was shallow, exposing the memorial in the river. The statement of 4:9 concerning these stones, "They are there unto this day," attests the early authorship of the record.

## APPLYING THE BIBLE

**What God told George Washington Carver.**—When Moses died and was succeeded by Joshua, he surely felt greatly humbled in trying to fill Moses' sandals. That kind of humility is well expressed by Dr. George Washington Carver, the magnificent, humble Negro scientist who did so much for Southern agriculture.

Carver once said that when he was a young man he asked God to reveal to him the mystery of the universe. But God replied, "That knowledge is reserved for me alone." So Carver said he prayed, "God, tell me the mystery of the peanut." And the Lord replied, "Well, George, that's more nearly your size."

"And he told me," Carver humbly confessed.[3]

God can use a humble man such as Carver, Moses, or Joshua. But we know He "resisteth the proud" (1 Pet. 5:5).

**Keeping life's windows clean.**—Ole Bull (1810-1880) was a world-renowned Norwegian violinist. After he had played once for his king, the king asked: "Where did you hear the sounds of the music you just played?"

With a smile, Old Bull answered that he had heard the sounds in the mountains of Norway as he listened to the mating calls of the birds, and he had caught those sounds in his strings. He said he had listened to the little brooks tumbling down the mountainsides, and he had caught those sounds. He had listened to the leaves clap their hands in the evening breeze, and he had caught those sounds. He said he had listened from the safety of his home as the storms rolled up out of the sea and as the lightning flashed and the thunder crashed, and he had caught those sounds in his violin.

In telling the story, the late Roy Angell said that through our windows we look out over the world and we see the glorious, humorous, and tragic things that take place that make up life. But to see life as it is and enjoy it to the fullest, we must keep our life's windows clean.[4]

Joshua obeyed God and told the people: "Sanctify yourselves: for tomorrow the Lord will do wonders among you" (3:5). God was telling them to make sure they kept life's windows clean so they could see God and His mighty works. We keep life's windows clean by daily availing ourselves of the divine forgiveness and cleansing.

**Surrounded by God's love.**—The late R. L. Middleton told about an Englishman who had a beautiful estate on the Yorkshire coast from which one could see a great distance in every direction.

One day the man and his daughter climbed to a summit on the estate and the man said, intending to teach his little daughter a lesson: "Look up." "Look down." "Look out." "Now turn and look behind you." He then added, "Dorothy, just so high, so deep, so wide, and so broad is the love of God."

She learned a lesson she would never forget, but she also taught her daddy one that he never forgot. "Daddy," she said, "If God's love is so high, so wide, so deep, and so broad, then we are living in the middle of it."[5]

For all her history, through the good and bad, Israel had lived surrounded by the love of God.

**"Abide with me."**—The late, well-known Methodist minister William Stidger told about hearing the Royal Welsh Male Chorus and Quartet sing in the summer of 1916. He said he was surprised when they closed their secular concert with the hymn, "Abide with Me."

When Stidger asked the director why they had chosen to close their program with a hymn, the director replied that they always closed their program that way. "It's almost a ritual with us," he said.

Then the director told the rest of the story. When the Cunard Line passenger ship *Lusitania* was torpedoed and sank off the coast of Ireland on May 7, 1915, there were 1,924 people on board. Of that number, 1,198 lost their lives.

He said the members of the quartet were Christians and when someone suggested they sing a well-known hymn from their lifeboat in the dark ocean, they sang "Abide with Me."

"From that time on," the director continued, "We have been singing the hymn that saved our lives"[6]

This was Israel's heart hymn as she entered Canaan. God promised to abide with them and this is exactly what He did.

## TEACHING THE BIBLE

▶ *Main Idea*: Israel's crossing into the promised land demonstrates that God blesses those who in faith obey His commands.

▶ *Suggested Teaching Aim*: To lead adults to examine the events surrounding Israel's crossing into the promised land, and to identify how they can respond in faith to God's leadership in their lives.

### Introduce the Bible Study

Read the following: The morning service was a mixed blessing. During the invitation, Tom, a young high school student, came forward and said he felt that God was calling him to preach, and he wanted to make that decision public. After the invitation was over, Brother Perry, who had served the church for thirty two years, announced that he was retiring.

Point out that seldom does the retirement and the call of God's ministers come in the same service, but nonetheless, God is still at work in both. He continues to bless men and women who respond in faith to His commands.

### Search for Biblical Truth

Locate the title of this lesson on the unit poster you prepared last week. Locate Jericho on a map of the conquest.

Ask members to read Joshua 3:7-8. Ask, Which required greater faith: for Joshua to believe God was with him as He had been with Moses or for the priests to march into a flooded stream carrying the ark?

Ask members to look at 3:9-17. Write the following on a large sheet of paper without the answers:

CROSSING THE JORDAN

God's Acts: *(commanded Joshua; stopped the water; will drive out inhabitants of land)*

Joshua's Acts: *(believed God; commanded priests to march and people to select twelve men)*

Priests' Acts: *(believed Joshua enough to step in water)*

Israel's Acts: *(trusted enough to cross the dry river bed with the ark of the covenant)*

Our Acts:

Ask members to suggest answers to the first four lines. As members answer "God's Acts," use *Studying the Bible* to explain briefly who occupied the land. Locate on a map of the conquest the cities of Adam and Zaretan [ZER uh tan] and explain how the water may have been stopped. Be certain you portray the act as a miracle. Even if a natural explanation can be found, the real miracle was in God's timing.

As members suggest answers to "Joshua's Acts," refer to chapter 4 to explain what the 12 men did.

As members suggest answers to "Priests' Acts," describe the ark of the covenant and its role in Israel's history.

As members suggest answers to "Israel's Acts," emphasize the faith it took to walk into a riverbed that should have been running bank to bank.

---

## A TEACHING OUTLINE

*1. Introduce the session and share the case study.*
*2. List varying responses involved in crossing the Jordan.*
*3. Identify a class response of faith.*
*4. Identify a personal response of faith.*

---

**Give the Truth a Personal Focus**

To apply this lesson, distribute pieces of paper and pencils. Ask members to make two columns. Head the columns *Class* and *Personal.* Ask members to share challenges they feel God is leading them to take as a class. List these beside "Our Acts." This may be a ministry project, more concentrated study, an outreach project, or some other challenge to which they need to respond in faith. Then ask them to list on the paper at least one challenge to which they feel God has called them personally to take. Below that, ask them to suggest two steps they need to take to begin or accomplish this challenge.

Remind them that the same God who led Israel is still in charge of the world today. Ask them to write in bold letters across the front of the paper, *God still moves!*

---

1. Donald F Ackland, *Persons Who Shaped Israel* (Nashville: Convention Press, 1975), 53.
2. George Adam Smith, *Historical Geography of the Holy Land* (London: Hodder & Stoughton, 1894), 58.
3. Adapted from Rackham Holt, *George Washington Carver* (Garden City: Doubleday, 1934), 226-27.
4. Adapted from Roy Angell, *Iron Shoes* (Nashville: Broadman Press, 1953), 87.
5. Adapted from R. L. Middleton, *My Cup Runneth Over* (Nashville: Broadman Press, 1951), 60.
6. Adapted from William L. Stidger, *There Are Sermons in Stories* (New York, Nashville: Abingdon-Cokesbury Press, 1942), 72.

# Winning the Battle

September
18
1994

**Basic Passage:** Joshua 6
**Focal Passages:** Joshua 6:1, 15-20

War is ugly, and as recent years have proved, often causes more problems than it solves. The people called Israel were to experience this. By the invasion of Canaan they occupied for themselves a long-promised homeland. But they also started an endless series of conflicts that have lasted to the present day. This series of lessons will introduce us to highs and lows in the history of Israel, a story so confused as to raise the question, "What went wrong?" That the initial struggle to gain possession of the land, beginning at Jericho, was planned and ordered by God is firmly established in today's study. That He also purposed a noble future for Israel is also obvious from multiple promises, beginning with those given to Abraham, "Thou shalt be a blessing . . . and in thee shall all families of the earth be blessed" (Gen. 12:2-3). Disobedience and open rebellion repeatedly threatened the fulfillment of these divine plans, which survived, however, so that "in the fullness of the time . . . God sent forth his Son" (Gal. 4:4), born in the land that was entered at Jericho and to the people who made the invasion.

**Study Aim:** *To acknowledge God as the Lord of history who directs events toward the fulfillment of His redemptive purposes*

## STUDYING THE BIBLE

While the Old Testament is rich in heroes of the faith who receive their New Testament salute in Hebrews 11 (Joshua's triumph at Jericho is mentioned in v. 30), the real hero of the record is God Himself. The story of Israel, though often told in human terms, is the story of the outworking of a divine purpose. The Lord was in charge of events as He worked toward an ultimate goal, the redemption of our race by the life, death, and resurrection of His Son.

### I. Divine Commander

There is an important preface to Joshua 6 in chapter 5. It tells of the difference a day made in the fortunes of God's people and establishes the truth that in the fall of Jericho, and following events, the Lord was in command and victories were gained by following His leadership.

**1. Passover and after (5:10).**—Appropriately, before beginning the occupation of Canaan, the people engaged in a memorial meal that recalled their deliverance from Egypt. They needed the reminder that they were where they were because of the mercies of God. He who had opened the gates of freedom to them after 400 years of Egyptian slavery, was about to provide entrance into the promised land.

**2. Food supplies (vv. 11-12).**—In one day, their diet changed. They had been dependent on the miraculous gift of manna throughout their wilderness wanderings. With the crossing of Jordan behind them, they would feed on the bounty of their new homeland, "the fruit of the land of Canaan."

**3. Worship offered (vv. 13-15).**—The picture is suggested of Joshua viewing the walls of Jericho as he made plans for the assault of the city. His reverie was interrupted by the sudden appearance of "a man . . . with his sword drawn in his hand." Surprised by the event, Joshua demanded to know of the stranger whether he was friend or foe. The answer was an exalted claim, "As captain of the host of the Lord am I now come." Realizing that he was in the presence of God Himself, Joshua fell on his face in worship. He would go into battle in the strong conviction that the God whom he served would be with him to provide victory.

## II. Marching Around Jericho (Josh. 6:1-5, 10-11)

The scenes that followed have gripped the imagination of songwriters and poets and encouraged countless numbers to believe in the fulfillment of their hopes. Jericho was a strategic fortress that blocked the way into Canaan and, once conquered, opened up the way into the rest of the country.

> 1 Now Jericho was straitly shut up because of the children of Israel: none went out, and none came in.
>
> 2 And the Lord said unto Joshua, See, I have given into thine hand Jericho, and the king thereof, and the mighty men of valor.
>
> 3 And ye shall compass the city, all ye men of war, and go round about the city once. Thus shalt thou do six days.
>
> 4 And seven priests shall bear before the ark seven trumpets of rams' horns: and the seventh day ye shall compass the city seven times, and the priests shall blow with the trumpets.
>
> 5 And it shall come to pass, that when they make a long blast with the ram's horn, and when ye hear the sound of the trumpet, all the people shall shout with a great shout; and the wall of the city shall fall down flat, and the people shall ascend up every man straight before him.

**1. Conditions in Jericho (v. 1).**—Although no attack had begun, Jericho behaved as though in a state of siege. Rahab had reported to the spies that "your terror is fallen upon us" (2:9). The gates of the city were shut and no traffic passed through them either way. The phrase, "straitly shut up" is better rendered,"shut up inside and out" (NRSV).

**2. Instructions from God (vv. 2-5).**—The result of the assault on Jericho was given in advance. God would give His people victory. The assurance was doubtless needed because of the uniqueness of the strategy employed. A procession composed of a group of armed men, followed by seven priests with rams' horns, then the ark of the covenant, with another group of armed men as a rear guard. As the priests blew the rams' horns the whole procession was to encircle the walls of Jericho once, and then return to their camp. The distance covered has not been established with historical accuracy.

**3. Silent marchers (vv. 10-11).**—The occupants of Jericho would be alarmed by some of the features of the Israelitish daily march. The trumpets were not musical instruments, but rams' horns, used in religious and festival events, and making a loud blasting sound. The ark itself would doubtless have created perplexity while regarded as a religious symbol. The recurring number seven, conveying the idea of perfection to the Hebrews, would mystify pagan Canaanites. In addition, the silence of the marchers through their six-day routine had disturbing significance for those within the walls. As a whole, the daily march was calculated to demoralize the enemy.

### III. "The Walls Came Tumbling Down" (Josh. 6:15-20)

On the seventh day, matters were obviously reaching their climax. The silence of the marchers was broken as, this time, they encircled Jericho seven times. What with the blasts on the rams' horns and the shouts of the marchers, the people within the walls must have been prepared for the worst.

> 15 And it came to pass on the seventh day, that they rose early about the dawning of the day, and compassed the city after the same manner seven times: only on that day they compassed the city seven times.
>
> 16 And it came to pass at the seventh time, when the priests blew with the trumpets, Joshua said unto the people, Shout; for the Lord hath given you the city.
>
> 17 And the city shall be accursed, even it, and all that are therein, to the Lord: only Rahab the harlot shall live, she and all that are with her in the house, because she hid the messengers that we sent.
>
> 18 And ye, in any wise keep yourselves from the accursed thing, lest ye make yourselves accursed, when ye take of the accursed thing, and make the camp of Israel a curse, and trouble it.
>
> 19 But all the silver, and gold, and vessels of brass and iron, are consecrated unto the Lord: they shall come into the treasury of the Lord.
>
> 20 So the people shouted when the priests blew with the trumpets: and it came to pass, when the people heard the sound of the trumpet, and the people shouted with a great shout, that the wall fell down flat, so that the people went up into the city, every man straight before him, and they took the city.

**1. Spoils of war (vv. 17-19).**—The word"accursed" can be rendered, "devoted to the Lord" (NRSV). The Hebrew word is *cherem* (ban) and signifies that the spoils of war belong to God alone. They are not to become loot that any participant in battle can appropriate and make his own. Since God gives the victory, He alone has the right to benefit from the engagement. An example of the consequences of ignoring this principle of "holy war" is given in chapter 7 where Achan and his family were put to death for taking "a beautiful mantle from Shiner, and two hundred shekels of silver, and a bar of gold weighing fifty shekels" (v. 21, NRSV) from Jericho. The practice of gaining personal profit from war was a practice of ancient people. Unfortunately, many modern fortunes have been made by manufacturing and selling arms indiscriminately.

**2. Cause and effect (v. 20).**—What made the walls of Jericho fall down so as to give the advancing Israelites unopposed entry into the land of Canaan? The answer, of course, is that this was an act of God. But it is legitimate to ask whether God could have used an earthquake to fulfill His purpose. The geological structure of the Jordan valley has caused many earthquakes in the area. But, as in the crossing of Jordan (see previous lesson), the timing of the occurrence is evidence that it was the handiwork of the God who promised victory to His people.

### IV. Mercy Amid Destruction (Josh. 6:21-27)

These verses are included in our background material and merit our attention. These points may be noted.

**1. Jericho destroyed (v. 21).**—The slaughter described arouses questions for the Christian reader. We need to be reminded of the utter degradation of Canaanite religion, and the threat it offered to Israel if allowed to survive. However, for us, the words of our Lord must provide direction for personal relationships, "Love your enemies, bless them that curse you, and do good to them that hate you" (Matt. 5:44).

**2. Rahab spared (vv. 22-23,25).**—To complete the story of Rahab, these verses were considered in our previous lesson. Their context is, however, important since it provides example of divine mercy prevailing in the midst of judgment.

**3. Joshua's reputation (vv. 26-27).**—According to 1 Kings 16:34, Joshua's curse on Jericho was ignored by Hiel the Bethelite, who rebuilt the city "at the cost of" (NRSV) his two sons. As for Joshua, the fall of Jericho established his reputation "throughout all the country."

## APPLYING THE BIBLE

**Remembering our heritage.**—We will never get where we ought to be in life if we forget where we have been or who we are. Sir Walter Scott, in his "Old Mortality," told about the old schoolmaster who went to the cemetery on summer evenings to walk among the tombstones. Here was one that bore the effigy of a knight in his armor.

And over there was one of a bishop holding his pastoral staff. One evening, the schoolmaster heard the clink-clank of a hammer, and going nearer the sound he saw an old man seated upon one of the monuments using his chisel and hammer to deepen the inscriptions on the old timeworn headstones. Scott said he was none other than "Old Mortality" who haunted the remote cemeteries of Scotland, renewing the ancient writing on the half-defaced inscriptions of those who had died for their faith and their cause.[1]

It's a good therapy in which wise people engage. In Joshua 5:10, Joshua led the children of Israel to renew their heritage as, camped at Gilgal, they celebrated the Passover. It was after the celebration of their spiritual heritage that God appeared to Joshua and gave him the promise of victory at Jericho.

In this busy, mad day in which we live, we ought to pause frequently to remember our spiritual heritage. In so doing we will find guidance for tomorrow's challenges and demands.

**"Keepers of the baggage."**—Not everyone can be a Moses or a Joshua and not everybody can march in the front ranks or occupy the lofty positions. Some must shun the limelight and do the menial work and do the menial tasks if God's work is to move forward. It was so when Israel marched across the Jordan and attacked formidable Jericho which stood in their way, and it has been so in God's work and among God's people through history.

A striking reminder of this is the San Jacinto Monument, that hallowed place where Texas's freedom was won. On the monument are the words "Keepers of Baggage" and the following inscription: "Obeying the instructions of General Houston, the following officers and men remained April 21, 1836, as the camp of the Texas army established opposite Harrisburg (Houston). There the six were attended by their comrades who also guarded the baggage and acted as rear guard of the main army."

**"The uncut pages of life."**—A teen-age boy asked his father for a car. A secondhand Ford would be fine. "Wouldn't you rather have a new Ford?" his father asked.

The next night, the boy's father brought in a book and handed it to his son. "You will see that it is a new book and many pages have not yet been cut," he said. "But read it all and read it carefully," he added.

A week went by and the boy again timidly approached his father about the car. "Have you read the book?" the father asked. When the boy confessed he had read only about half of it, his father encouraged him to finish reading it.

As the time approached for the boy to go to college, he complained, "Dad, I don't have a car to drive." Asking his son to get the book, the boy was told to cut the remaining pages that were uncut. And as he did, a check for a new car fell out on the floor!

As the boy confessed he didn't deserve the car, his father said, "The car has been waiting for you a month, full of gas and oil, ready to run.

All you had to do was do what I told you, and it would have been yours."

In our lesson today, again and again obedience is stressed. There were certain things Israel had to do before victory over Jericho could be theirs. But when they obeyed, they received the blessing.[2]

**Lincoln's faith.**—Richard Oglesby, three-times governor of Illinois, was at one time very much discouraged during the war between the states. After the Union army had suffered several humiliating defeats, Oglesby wrote the president that it seemed all was lost. On reading Oglesby's pessimistic analysis of things, Lincoln wired back to the capitol at Springfield: "Dear Dick: Read Exodus 14:13: `Fear ye not, stand still, and see the salvation of the Lord.'—Abraham Lincoln."

Israel's faith had been sorely tried through their long stay in Egypt, the wilderness wanderings, and the well-protected fort of Jericho that stood immediately before them. But Joshua was there, and when their faith faltered he had the right word from the Lord to spur them on.

## TEACHING THE BIBLE

▶ *Main Idea*: The Israelites' winning the battle over Jericho demonstrates that God directs events to fulfill His redemptive purpose.
▶ *Suggested Teaching Aim*: To lead adults to describe how the Israelites won the battle over Jericho, and to identify how God is working out His redemptive purpose in their life.

### A TEACHING OUTLINE

1. *Use the map to set the context.*
2. *Organize the class in three groups and make assignments.*
3. *Call for reports.*
4. *Identify ways God is working out His redemptive purpose in their life.*

**Introduce the Bible Study**

Point out the lesson on the unit poster. Locate the city of Jericho and the possible location of Gilgal [GILL gal] on the map of the conquest. Point out that Gilgal was the first camp established by the Israelites in Canaan.

**Search for Biblical Truth**

Organize the class in three groups and make the following assignments. Group 1 and group 2 can have only one person in them if your class is small. Allow eight minutes for preparation. Presentation time will vary depending on the number of people you have present. Be careful not to run out of time for group 3 to report.

**Group 1–**

Read Joshua 6:1-5, 15-20. Pretend that you are a newspaper reporter for the *Jerusalem Herald.* Write an article or articles that describe what happened in Jericho. If you have several in your group, you might assign articles similar to the following: the destruction of the walls; the strange behavior of the Israelites in marching around the city; an interview with Joshua; the reputation of the Israelites from their previous encounters before crossing the Jordan; the strong defense of the city. You will have eight minutes to prepare your assignment and four minutes to read it to the class.

**Group 2–**

Read Joshua 6:1-5, 15-20. Pretend you are a resident of Jericho. Write a diary entry describing your reaction to the Israelites' actions. Begin your entries a week or so before the Israelites' first march around Jericho. You will have eight minutes to prepare your assignments and four minutes to read them to the class.

**Group 3–**

Read Joshua 6:1-5, 15-20. Pretend you are an eyewitness news television reporter for station WJER in Jerusalem. You are to interview both Israelites and those from Jericho about their reaction to the strange events. You will have eight minutes to prepare your assignment and eight minutes to present it to the class. You may interview such persons as the following:

**Israelite Soldier:** Would you explain what you have been doing here the past two days? What do you hope to accomplish against such a well-fortified city? Why have you even attacked Jericho? What did the city do to you? What are your plans for the future? What would you do if you could get in the city? Why would your God command you to do this?

**Jericho Resident:** Would you explain what has happened here the past couple of days? How have the Israelites' actions affected you? What do you expect to happen? Are the rumors true that Israelite spies entered the city? What do you think about the Israelites' God?

After groups have had time for study, call for reports.

**Give the Truth a Personal Focus**

Distribute paper and pencils to all members. Ask them to think about how God is working out His redemptive purpose in their life. Then ask them to write a headline that would describe how God is working this purpose out. Point out that our faithfulness to God will help us to win the battles we face. Close in prayer.

---

1. Adapted from Clarence McCartney, *McCartney's Illustrations* (New York, Nashville: Abingdon-Cokesbury Press, 1965), 261.
2. Adapted from Roy Angell, *Iron Shoes* (Nashville: Broadman Press, 1953), 11.

September
25
1994

# Choosing to Serve God

**Basic Passage:** Joshua 24
**Focal Passages:** Joshua 24:1-2,11-16

Decision making is one of the skills for which leaders of industry receive generous pay. Yet decision making is an activity in which all of us have to engage in one way or another. From the moment we rise at the beginning of each new day, to when we retire to sleep, we are faced with choices. Some are of minor importance, others may be significant both in the needed action and the continuing consequences. Before he died, Joshua faced the people of Israel with a decision beside which all others pale into insignificance. "Choose you this day whom ye will serve," he said, adding evidence of the decision he had already made, "as for me and my house, we will serve the Lord" (Josh. 24:15). These words continue to confront the world with a choice, a commitment, that has eternal consequences. They are repeated throughout the Bible and have major appeal on the lips of Jesus as He says, "Follow me" (Matt. 4:19). A major purpose of Sunday School is to echo this call to decision and action and so recruit new followers of Christ and new members of His church.

**Study Aim:** *To recognize our indebtedness to God and respond with commitment of life to His will*

## STUDYING THE BIBLE

The relationship of Joshua 23 and 24 is a matter of scholarly discussion. Both chapters appear to refer to the same event, a ceremony of covenant renewal that took place toward the end of Joshua's life. Many scholars believe that the original manuscript ended with chapter 23 and that a chapter was added to elaborate on what happened that day at Shechem. Whatever the explanation, we can be grateful for the inclusion of 24:15, with its challenging call, "Choose you this day whom ye will serve."

### I. Gathering at Shechem (Josh. 24:1-2)

The choice of Shechem for this important gathering recalled the long association of the place with early Hebrew history. It is the first place in Canaan mentioned in Abraham's story ("Sichem," Gen. 12:6). Jacob returned to Shechem after his long stay in Padan-aram, and there purchased land for an altar (33:18-20). The bones of Joseph, brought out of Egypt (Ex. 13:19), were buried in this plot of land (Josh. 24:32). The New Testament "Sychar" (John 4:5) was probably on the site of Shechem.

**1 And Joshua gathered all the tribes of Israel to Shechem,**

and called for the elders of Israel, and for their heads, and for their judges, and for their officers; and they presented themselves before God.

2 And Joshua said unto all the people, Thus saith the Lord . . .

Joshua went back to the beginning of the story of God's call to and choice of Israel to be His peculiar people. The family of Abraham, headed by his father Terah, lived in pagan territory, "beyond the Euphrates" (NRSV), where they "served other gods." The true God revealed Himself to Abraham, an act of divine grace, and called him to exercise faith by leaving home and kindred for an unnamed destination. This proved to be Canaan where Abraham's descendants were now assembled after taking possession of the land.

### II. Review of Events (Josh. 24:3-10)

History is a great teacher. This is specially true of Bible history whose recorded events are the basis for our present faith and source of hope for the future. In taking farewell of the people Israel, Joshua knew that the remembrance of God's dealings in the past would be important in the years and centuries to come. So he reminded them of highlights in their story, beginning with the call of Abraham (v. 3). The course of events had not been smooth for there had been centuries of slavery in Egypt. But God raised up Moses to lead them out of Egypt. They had crossed the Red Sea in safety, while their enemies were drowned (vv. 5-7). Passing over the years of wilderness wandering, Joshua picked up the story prior to the destruction of Jericho when first the Amorites (Num. 21) and then the Moabites (chap. 22) tried to prevent the advance of the Israelites, but failed.

### III. Call to Commitment (Josh. 24:11-16)

Most of the things rehearsed in the above verses happened before Joshua's listeners were born, with the exception of Caleb who alone, with Joshua, survived the wilderness wanderings and entered the promised land (Num. 14:35-38). So Joshua proceeded to speak of events that were more recent and within the memory of those who heard him.

11 And ye went over Jordan, and came unto Jericho: and the men of Jericho fought against you, the Amorites, and the Perizzites, and the Canaanites, and the Hittites, and the Girgashites, the Hivites, and the Jebusites; and I delivered them unto your hand.

12 And I sent the hornet before you, which drove them out from before you, even the two kings of the Amorites; but not with thy sword, nor with thy bow.

13 And I have given you a land for which ye did not labor, and cities which ye built not, and ye dwell in them; of the vineyards and oliveyards which ye planted not do ye eat.

14 Now therefore fear the Lord, and serve him in sincerity
and in truth: and put away the gods which your fathers served
on the other side of the flood, and in Egypt; and serve ye the Lord.
15 And if it seem evil unto you to serve the Lord, choose you
this day whom ye will serve; whether the gods which your
fathers served that were on the other side of the flood, or the
gods of the Amorites, in whose land ye dwell: but as for me and
my house, we will serve the Lord.
16 And the people answered and said, God forbid that we
should forsake the Lord, to serve other gods;

**1. God's promises kept (vv. 11-13).**—In verse 12, "the hornet," a large and vicious wasp-like insect, appears to be used figuratively and is understood by some to represent the terror caused by the Israelites and mentioned by Rahab (2:9). There is no mention of actual hornets in the biblical record of the conquest of Canaan. The point made, of course, is that Israel's victory was provided by the Lord, and was not achieved by their martial efforts. God kept His promise, given to Abraham and others, that He would provide for His people a land of their own. This was not empty, undeveloped territory, but replete with homes and harvests.

**2. Loyalty demanded (vv. 14-16).**—The seductive influence of idolatry was to be the future downfall of Israel. This was in spite of repeated exhortations and warnings by people like Joshua and the later prophets. Abraham was called out of a culture in which people, including his own family, "served other gods" (v. 2). The long sojourn in Egypt meant exposure to other idolatrous practices to which at least some were attracted (v. 14). In the future, they would have neighbors who practiced some of the most degraded forms of paganism. A firm stand against idols was the only hope for a continued loyalty to the true God, to whom they were so heavily obligated. Joshua not only called for this, but also offered the example of himself and his family, "As for me and my house, we will serve the Lord" (v. 15). The people responded with a pledge to be loyal to God.

## IV. Sincerity Questioned and Affirmed (Josh. 24:17-25)

The concept of "making a decision" is deeply rooted in the conversion theology of evangelical Christians. Many worship services conclude with an appeal for decision and an opportunity to make public the resolve to accept Christ as Savior and follow Him as Lord. Warning is sometimes necessary against taking this step too lightly, without full consideration of its meaning and consequences. Joshua showed this concern as he continued his farewell message to the people of Israel.

22 And Joshua said unto the people, Ye are witnesses against
yourselves that ye have chosen you the Lord, to serve him. And

they said, We are witnesses.
23 Now therefore put away, said he, the strange gods which are among you, and incline your heart unto the Lord God of Israel.
24 And the people said unto Joshua, The Lord our God will we serve, and his voice will we obey.
25 So Joshua made a covenant with the people that day, and set them a statute and an ordinance in Shechem.

**1. Obligation acknowledged (vv. 17-18).**—Continuing their response, begun in verse 16, Joshua's listeners acknowledged their indebtedness to the Lord. They spoke of deliverance from Egyptian bondage by "great signs" and divine protection and preservation throughout their wilderness journey. Echoing Joshua's own message, they brought their gratitude up to date by giving credit to the Lord for the conquest of Canaan,"therefore" they said, "will we also serve the Lord; for he is our God" (v. 18).

**2. Commitment questioned (vv. 19-20).**—Joshua's reply did not question their sincerity but was spoken as a warning against unfulfilled promises. The danger confronting Israel would be the pressure from "strange gods" (v. 20), and history would reveal that this eventually caused their downfall. Joshua could never forget what happened while he was the companion of Moses at the giving of the law, on Mount Sinai (Ex. 32). In their absence, the people, led by Aaron, made and worshiped a golden calf.

**3. Repeated affirmations (vv. 21-25).**—"Nay; but we will serve the Lord" (v. 21), was the people's reply. Thereupon, Joshua called them to add action to their words. At that very time, apparently, there were false gods in their possession, brought with them, perhaps, out of Egypt, or taken from Canaanites during the occupation. When the people agreed to put these away and serve God alone, Joshua sealed their decision in a written covenant and by the erection of a memorial stone (vv. 26-27).

## V. Death of Joshua (Josh. 24:29-31)

His obituary describes him as "the servant of the Lord," words previously used about Moses (1:1). He had worthily worn the mantle of the great Lawgiver and had progressed from being "Moses' minister" (1:1) to being leader of his people in the conquest and settlement of Canaan. He is credited with dividing the country among the twelve tribes, the record of that accomplishment occupying much of the book that bears his name (chaps. 13—22). To Joshua himself was assigned "Tinnath-serah in the hill country of Ephraim; he rebuilt the town and settled in it" (19:50, NRSV). There he lived until he was 110 years old. This good man's influence lasted beyond his death. "Israel served the Lord all the days of Joshua, and all the days of the elders who outlived Joshua and had known all the work that the Lord did for Israel" (v. 31, NRSV). So our study of Unit I, "The Conquest of the Land," ends on a high note, not to be sustained, unfortunately, in the Book of Judges that follows, with its sad and oft-repeated refrain, "the children of Israel did evil again in the sight of the Lord" (3:12).

## APPLYING THE BIBLE

**Rescued from paganism.**—As Joshua reviewed Israel's history to them at Shechem, he reminded them that Abraham, was saved out of paganism by the grace of God (24:3). We, too, live in a pagan world. For example: In the United States there are two million Hindus with 700 million worldwide. In the United States there are three million Buddhists with 300 million worldwide. Islam claims 4 million adherents in the United States, but there are 1 billion worldwide. And some groups that go under the guise of Christianity, but are not Christian in reality, also claim a lot of adherents. And this only begins to describe the paganism that surrounds us.

But we have a message for them and it is the message of Joshua 24:15.

**A heritage worth reviewing.**—Standing at Shechem, the place first mentioned in Canaan in the story of Abraham, Joshua talked to the people about their sacred heritage. He was coming near the end of his days, and did not want Israel to forget her past. Understanding and appreciating her past was the key to her future greatness.

As Americans, we must not forget our heritage for which so many have died. Perhaps more than any other symbol, the Liberty Bell symbolizes that heritage. Cast in England in 1752, around the top of the bell is carved a passage from Leviticus 25:10: "Proclaim liberty through-out all the land unto all the inhabitants thereof." The bell weighs two thousand and eighty pounds and was first rung on July 8, 1776, to announce to Philadelphians that the Declaration of Independence had been signed. It was rung every July 8 until 1835 when it cracked as it was tolling the funeral dirge for Chief Justice John Marshall.[1]

As Joshua reminded Israel of her heritage, so we who are Christian Americans must often be reminded of our heritage.

**Life's most important choice.**—Jonathan Edwards, the Puritan pastor/evangelist, was one of America's most effective preachers, Edwards said: "I go out to preach with two propositions in mind. First, every person ought to give his life to Christ. Second, whether or not anyone else gives Him his life, I will give Him mine."

This is what Joshua is calling the people to do in today's lesson: "Choose you this day whom you will serve" (24:15). But it is a personal choice, and no one can make it for you. To be a son or daughter of God you must make the choice yourself.

**The choice that counts.**—In his book *Thirteen Days to Glory* author Lon Tinkle tells about Colonel Jim Bowie and the brave defenders of the Alamo. That sacred Texas shrine had only 183 defenders against the hordes of Santa Anna and the Mexican government. On March 3, 1836, two hours before dusk the Mexican guns quit firing and William Travis lined his men up in a single line inside the Alamo and told them no reinforcements were coming and that their destiny was sealed. "Our doom is certain," Travis told the weary men. Travis then pulled his sword from its sheath and drew a line in the dirt floor in front of them and asked every man who was determined to stay in the Alamo and die to cross the line.

Topley Holland was the first man across the line. Others quickly followed— Daniel Cloud, Micajah Utry, Davy Crockett. Colonel Jim Bowie was sick and unable to cross the line so he called for help and four men sprang to the side of his cot and lifted him over the line as the other men cheered.

On March 6 the Alamo fell and the brave defenders within her walls died. They made the choice that counted most and the Republic of Texas was born out of their shed blood.

Joshua called upon Israel to make the choice that counts most—the choice to serve God and be faithful to Him.

## TEACHING THE BIBLE

▶ *Main Idea*: Joshua's call for the people to serve only God demonstrates that each of us must commit our life to Him.
▶ *Suggested Teaching Aim*: To lead adults to examine Joshua's call to the Israelites to serve God, and to commit their life to God's will.

**Introduce the Bible Study**

Ask: What decision have you made that affected your life the most? How has it affected it? Let several share their comments.

**Search for Biblical Truth**

In advance, prepare strip posters with the following outline points on separate strips; place the heading on the focal wall before class begins:

CHOOSING TO SERVE GOD

Gathering at Schechem (Josh. 24:1-2)
Review of Events (Josh. 24:3-10)
Call to Commitment (Josh. 24:11-16)
Sincerity Questioned and Affirmed (Josh. 24:17-25)
Death of Joshua (Josh. 24:29-31)

Place the first outline strip on the focal wall and ask members to read silently Joshua 24:1-2. Present a brief lecture in which you: locate Shechem on the map of the conquest and briefly tell its importance; identify all those Joshua called together for the covenant renewal; definc *flood* (v.2) based on modern translations; describe the pagan worship of Abraham's ancestors.

## A TEACHING OUTLINE

*1. To identify decisions that affect members' lives.*
*2. To describe the gathering at Shechem.*
*3. To examine Joshua's call of commitment.*
*4. Lead in a covenant renewal service.*

DISCUSSION QUESTION: How important is it to believers' faith to have a time periodically in which they renew their covenant with God?

Place the second outline strip on the focal wall and briefly summarize Israel's history as seen in Abraham and Moses based on *Studying the Bible.* Keep this section brief (1-2 min.) since it is not in the focal passage.

Place the third outline strip on the focal wall. Ask members to scan Joshua 24:11-16. Present a brief lecture on these verses in which you include the following:

24:11—Mention the seven tribes that occupied the land; emphasize that God was the One who delivered them.

24:12—Explain the use of *hornet* in this context and what the hornets symbolized.

24:13—Describe how God provided not an undeveloped land but one with vineyards and olive groves to provide for the people.

24:14-16—Use the information in the section "Loyalty demanded" in *Studying the Bible* to explain these verses.

DISCUSSION QUESTION: Why is it not possible to choose to worship both God and objects God has created?

Place the fourth and fifth outline strips on the focal wall. Briefly summarize these verses since they are not focal.

### Give the Truth a Personal Focus

Lead a covenant renewal service in which members can renew their covenant with God or decide for the first time to follow Him. On a chalkboard or a large sheet of paper write *Choose you this day whom you will serve.* Challenge your members to remove from their life any object, action, or person they place before God. Sing or read the words to the hymn, "Have Thine Own Way, Lord" (No. 294, *The Baptist Hymnal,* 1991). Allow a time of silence for members to consider their commitment. Close in a prayer for a renewal of faith.

---

1. Adapted from J. B. Fowler Jr., *Illustrated Sermons for Special Occasions* (Nashville: Broadman Press, 1988), 34-35.

# Israel's Tragic Pattern of Life

**Basic Passage:** Judges 2:6—3:6
**Focal Passage:** Judges 2:11-19

The words *environment* and *environmental* are buzz words these days. They are on every politicians lips and are featured prominently in the popular press. There is widespread opinion that they should also be on every preacher's lips since Christians live in the same world as other people, a world that is threatened by the abuse and wastage of natural resources. The Bible certainly has a great deal to say, either directly or by implication, on the importance of a person's relationship with his surroundings. In the Book of Deuteronomy we find early laws for the protection of wildlife (22:6-7) and against the needless destruction of trees (20:19-20). In the Old Testament there are also repeated warnings to Israel of the danger of spiritual contamination through contact with paganism. That the nation fell victim to this environmental threat is startlingly evident in the Book of Judges. Not surprisingly, New Testament apostles used Israel's failure and fate to exhort Christians to avoid the contamination of evil. "Little children, keep yourselves from idols" (1 John 5:21); and, "Pure religion and undefiled before God and the Father is this, To . . . keep himself unspotted from the world" (Jas. 1:27).

**Study Aim:** *To recognize the contaminating power of evil and seek God's help in avoiding it*

## STUDYING THE BIBLE

This unit, entitled "The Rule of the Judges," consists of two lessons, the second focusing on one of these charismatic leaders, Gideon. There were twelve in all, one of them a woman, Deborah (chaps. 4—5). The length of the period in which they were active presents problems. Added together, their years of service as stated for each individual come to over 400, but there are indications that in several cases these periods overlapped as the judges functioned for different tribes, giving fewer than 200 years.

### I. An Incomplete Conquest (Judg. 2:1-10)

Disobedience was a main cause of the disasters that overtook Israel throughout its history. The covenant into which the people entered with their God took place at Sinai with the giving of the Ten Commandments. These laws would test their sincerity and, in their observance, would be for their good. God made no demands on His people that did not serve their highest interests, and when they transgressed the hurt was theirs as well as the Lord's. So it was in the instructions given for the conquest of Canaan. Through disobedience, Israel brought troubles upon themselves that lasted down the centuries.

**1. Divine interrogation (vv. 1-5).**—The opening verses of chapter 2 furnish a needed introduction to our lesson passage. The Lord reminded Israel of the covenant into which the nation had entered (v. 1). Though He had remained faithful, they had been disobedient by entering into compromising agreements with the inhabitants of Canaan, and sparing idol shrines that He had ordered to be destroyed. He asked, "Why have ye done this?" (v. 2). He had warned them of the consequences of this behavior (v. 3), a reminder that shocked the people into fearful lamentations (v. 4). They named the place where this happened "Weepers" (Bochim) to commemorate their tears, and there they worshiped the true God.

**2. Historic background (vv. 6-10).**—These verses bring to mind the words of Joshua 24:28-31 as they recall the death of Joshua. But whereas those verses conclude on a positive note, telling of the continuing influence of Joshua, the parallel passage in Judges records how "there arose another generation . . . which knew not the Lord, nor yet the works which he had done for Israel" (v. 10). The result of this forgetfulness is shown in the verses that follow.

## II. Lure of Idolatry (Judg. 2:11-13)

The Israelites were an easy prey to Canaanite religion which was sensual and degraded. Practices that the laws of God forbade were encouraged by the prevailing form of paganism. They appealed to fleshly lusts and offered opportunity for sexual indulgence in the name of worship. For this reason, the Lord had ordered the destruction of all the shrines, warning: "They shall be as thorns in your sides, and their gods shall be a snare unto you" (v. 3).

> 11 And the children of Israel did evil in the sight of the Lord, and served Baalim:
> 12 And they forsook the Lord God of their fathers, which brought them out of the land of Egypt, and followed other gods, of the gods of the people that were round about them, and bowed themselves unto them, and provoked the Lord to anger.
> 13 And they forsook the Lord, and served Baal and Ashtaroth.

**1. Baal.**—Chief among the Canaanite gods was Baal to whom was attributed the fertility of land, animals, and workers on the land. Different communities had their own shrines resulting in multiple deities, hence the plural, Baalim (v. 11). The relationship between these gods and localities is reflected in such place names as Baal-hazor (2 Sam. 13:23) and Baal-peor (Num. 25:3).

**2. Ashtaroth.**—The name appears variously as Astarte, Asherah, or

Ashtoreth (plural, Ashtaroth). In Canaan she appears as the wife of Baal. Her shrines were centers of sexual activity and pagan orgies that seduced Israelites away from their faith which called for personal discipline.

## III. Who Were the Judges? (Judg. 2:14-16)

The word *judge* is used to describe a variety of officials within our American judicial system. It is also used for those who make decisions in competitive sports, and other activities. Its appearance in our lesson passage should be interpreted to mean "deliverer," or "champion." Those who functioned under this title had less to do with legal procedures than they had with military leadership and daring exploits in behalf of their oppressed compatriots.

> **14 And the anger of the Lord was hot against Israel, and he delivered them into the hands of spoilers that spoiled them, and he sold them into the hands of their enemies round about, so that they could not any longer stand before their enemies.**
> **15 Whithersoever they went out, the hand of the Lord was against them for evil, as the Lord had said, and as the Lord had sworn unto them: and they were greatly distressed.**
> **16 Nevertheless the Lord raised up judges, which delivered them out of the hand of those that spoiled them.**

**1. Anger restrained.**—Attributing anger to God should not be understood in terms of the outbursts of anger of which we are sometimes guilty. A major emphasis of the Bible is on divine patience, exercised in full measure toward Israel. When anger was expressed it was the reaction of His absolute holiness to the evils committed by the people. It brought punishment in the form of oppression by neighboring tribes. But He was quick to respond to repentance and did so by raising up (3:9,15) deliverers, the first of whom was Othniel.

**2. A great woman (chaps. 4—5).**—Before focusing on Gideon, as we will next week, we could take time to look at some of the others. The most complex of these was Samson (chaps. 13—16) who allowed passion to dominate his life, and although credited with some deeds of courage, met with a tragic death. Although only a few verses are given to some of the male judges (Othniel, 3:8-11; Shamgar, 3:31, one verse; Tolar, 10:1-2), two chapters are devoted to a woman (chaps. 4—5). Deborah may have been more like a judge, as we understand the term, than others for it is said of her that "the children of Israel came up to her for judgment" (4:5). She inspired Barak to attack and defeat Sisera, a Canaanitish general.

## IV. A Repeated Cycle (Judg. 2:17-23)

The picture drawn in Judges is of a people in a state of anarchy, a word which means "without a leader." Two times the statement occurs, "In those days there was no king in Israel, but every man did that which was right in his own eyes" (17:6; 21:25). In the divine plan, Israel was to be a theocracy, that is, God was their ruler. But they rejected Him by turning to idols. Eventually they would seek a king from among themselves.

**17 And yet they would not hearken unto their judges, but they went whoring after other gods, and bowed themselves unto them: they turned quickly out of the way which their fathers walked in, obeying the commandments of the Lord; but they did not so.**

**18 And when the Lord raised them up judges, then the Lord was with the judge, and delivered them out of the hand of their enemies all the days of the judge: for it repented the Lord because of their groanings by reason of them that oppressed them and vexed them.**

**19 And it came to pass, when the judge was dead, that they returned, and corrupted themselves more than their fathers, in following other gods to serve them, and to bow down unto them; they ceased not from their own doings, nor from their stubborn way.**

**1. Spiritual infidelity (v. 17).**—Throughout the Scriptures, idolatry on the part of persons who knew the true God, is likened to adultery: "went a whoring after" is otherwise rendered, "lusted after" (NRSV). The generation of the judges were worse than their forefathers in the extent to which they yielded to pagan influences.

**2. God's "repentance" (v. 18).**—The application of the word *repentance* to the Lord, a frequent occurrence in Scripture, requires the explanation that He was not sorry, or repentant, for anything He had done. The statement here is elsewhere rendered that He was "moved to pity by their groaning" (NRSV). He set aside judgment in favor of mercy as He called judges into services to be deliverers of the oppressed people.

**3. Return to lawlessness (v. 19).**—The cycle continued to repeat itself: return to idolatry, penalty incurred, cries of distress and repentance, provision of a deliverer—and then back to idolatry again. The importance and influence of leadership is emphasized in each cycle. As long as the "judge" lived, the people toed the line. But with his/her death came renewed apostasy.

**4. Test of loyalty (vv.. 20-23).**—The concluding verses of our chapter make a surprising statement. The failure of the Israelites to complete the conquest of the land is attributed to the act of God. He allowed this to happen to provide a test of the nation's loyalty. In Eden He provided a tree with forbidden fruit. In such ways He challenges His people to faith and obedience, the very trials of life being opportunities to display trust in His wisdom or, on the other hand, to reveal weaknesses in our character.

## APPLYING THE BIBLE

**Multiple leaders.**—"The Rule of the Judges" is the title of this unit. There were twelve in all—eleven men and one woman. The period of the judges lasted approximately two hundred years and extended from the time of Joshua to Saul, Israel's first king. The period is known as "the dark ages of Hebrew history." But even in the darkest hours of Israel's history, there were some great leaders on the scene.

In 1809, when Napoleon was marching roughshod across Europe, the people thought all was lost. But in that very year some of the greatest people of history were born: Abraham Lincoln, William Gladstone, Charles Darwin, Alfred Tennyson, Oliver Wendell Holmes, Edward FitzGerald, Edgar Allan Poe, Fanny Kemble, Felix Mendelssohn, Frederic Chopin, and Cyrus McCormick—just to mention a few.

When evil runs rampant and hearts fail for fear, God is at work bringing about a new order of things.[1]

**Stonewall Jackson's testimony.**—Thomas J. "Stonewall" Jackson, referred to upon his death by General Robert E. Lee as "my right arm," was a Christian gentleman of sterling character. Once asked if he would go as a missionary should "the providence of God . . . direct you to drop every scheme of life and of personal advancement, and go on a mission to the heart of Africa for the rest of your days," Jackson replied, his eyes flashing, "I could go without my hat!"[2]

Obedience was the thing God most wanted from Israel—or wants from us—and it was the one thing Israel would not consistently give. Consequently, the nation was visited with tragedies and sorrows of every sort.

**The pagan generation is in the nursery.**—Judges 2:10 tells us that after Joshua's death, "There arose another generation . . . which knew not the Lord, nor yet the works which he had done for Israel." Thus, they forsook the Lord and served false gods and brought upon their generation the wrath of God.

It is sobering to realize that the generation that is in our church nurseries is, in fact, a pagan generation. It is "pagan" in the sense that they do not know God, and it is our responsibility to teach them and lead them to Christ. America is always just one generation away from being pagan!

**Idolatry.**—We all worship something. It is said of Benjamin Disraeli, the only Jew who ever served as prime minister of Great Britain, that he was "a self-made man who worshiped his `creator.'"

What is idolatry? Whatever you make most of is your god. Whatever you love more than God is your idol.

William Cowper summed it up like this:

*Help me to tear it from Thy throne*
*The dearest idol I have known,*
*Whate'er that idol be,*

*Help me to tear it from Thy throne*
*And worship only Thee."*[3]

Israel's idolatry was her undoing. Israel's greatest national tragedy is summed up in verse 12: "And they forsook the Lord God of their fathers . . . and bowed themselves unto them [other gods], and provoked the Lord to anger."

**Women who ran for president.**—Did you know several women have run for the presidency of the United States?

Among them were Victoria C. Woodhull, a thirty-four-year-old spiritualist and Wall Street broker, who ran for the presidency in 1872 and also in 1892; Belva Ann Lockwood, a fifty-four-year-old teacher and lawyer, who ran for the presidency in 1884 and 1888; Anna Milburn ran in 1940; Ellen L. Jensen ran in 1952; Yette Bronstein ran in 1964; and Charlene Mitchell ran on the Communist party in 1968 and received 1,075 votes; and Linda Jennes ran on the Socialist Workers party in 1972.

There were some great judges who led Israel during this period, and some were not so great. But one of the truly great ones was a woman named Deborah. Although only a few verses are given to some of the eleven male judges, two chapters are devoted to Deborah (chaps. 4—5).

## TEACHING THE BIBLE

▶ *Main Idea:* Israel's tragic pattern of life demonstrates that only with God's help can we avoid the contaminating power of evil.
▶ *Suggested Teaching Aim*: To lead adults to recognize the contaminating power of evil, and how they can use God's help to change their pattern of living.

### A TEACHING OUTLINE

1. *Read the case study to introduce the lesson.*
2. *Arrange the strip posters in order.*
3. *Examine the focal passage.*
4. *Identify how Israel's experience will help members overcome evil in their life.*

**Introduce the Bible Study**

Share the illustration "Idolatry" from *Applying the Bible.*

**Search for Biblical Truth**

In advance, enlist a member to use the *Holman Bible Dictionary* or other Bible dictionary to prepare a two- to three-minute report on Baal and Ashtaroth.

Make the following poster strips. Cut the strips in six pieces, separating the strips from each other and the Scripture from the strips. Tape these six pieces at random to the wall.

Lure of Idolatry (Judg. 2:11-13)

Leaders of Israel (Judg. 2:14-16)
Lasting Involvement (Judg. 2:17-19)

You can do this activity as a class or organize three groups and assign one heading to each group. Ask members to open their Bibles to Judges 2:11-19 and decide which Scripture reference goes with which heading.

Place the *Lure of Idolatry* poster on the focal wall. Set the passage in context by briefly summarizing "An Incomplete Conquest (Judg. 2:1-10)" *(Studying the Bible).* Call on the person enlisted to report on Baal and Ashtaroth. Point out why these gods were so dangerous.

Place the *Leaders of Israel* poster on the focal wall. Present a brief lecture describing how God provided judges to bring help to His people. Ask: What does the word *judge* mean when it is used in this manner? (deliverer or champion) How many judges can you name? Write these on a chalkboard or a large sheet of paper. Mention particularly Samson and Deborah. Point out that Deborah may have been more like a modern judge (Judg. 4:5) than the others.

Place the *Lasting Involvement* poster on the wall. Distribute paper and pencils. Ask members to paraphrase Judges 2:17-19. Call for several to read their paraphrases.

Ask: Why is the term *"adultery"* used to refer to spiritual idolatry? (Adultery is giving to another what belongs to your spouse; idolatry is giving our love that belongs to God to another.) How does even a little idolatry contaminate our spiritual lives? Why is God so opposed to idolatry?

**Give the Truth a Personal Focus**

Refer to William Cowper's poem under "Idolatry," in *Applying the Bible.* Ask members to suggest some ways of living that are hard to break that need to be torn away so they may worship only God. Point out an idol can be a habit, person, or even a belief. List these on a chalkboard or a large sheet of paper.

Ask: What in Israel's experience would offer help to someone struggling with a problem? (Members may offer many suggestions but consider this: Israel found that only with God's help could they break the cycle of being controlled by evil.) What steps can persons take to draw on God's help to change their pattern of living and avoid the contamination of evil? List these on a chalkboard or large sheet of paper.

Close with a time of silent prayer. Ask members to examine their life to identify areas they have allowed evil to contaminate. Then suggest they ask for God's help to deliver them from the power of evil. If your members are comfortable in doing so, ask them to join hands and pray silently for the persons on their right and left.

---

1. Adapted from Margarett Applegarth, *Men As Trees Walking* (New York, Evanston and London: Harper and Row, Publishers, 1952), 130.
2. Adapted from Walker B. Knight, *Knight's Master Book of New Illustrations* (Grand Rapids: Wm. B. Eerdman's Publishing Co., 1956), 446.
3. Ian MacPherson, *Live Sermon Outlines* (Grand Rapids: Baker Book House, 1974), 40.

# Deliverance by God's Hand

**Basic Passage:** Judges 6:1—8:21
**Focal Passages:** Judges 7:2-7,19-21

This is the story of a young man with a nickname. His birth name was Gideon, but the people of his community called him Jerubbaal, which meant, "Let Baal take care of him." The nickname is revealing because it belonged to a time when the people of Israel were so far given over to idolatry that they took sides with an idol against one of their own number. It also pays tribute to a man who was not naturally courageous, but who, trusting the promises of God, stood firm against two enemies, the seduction of paganism that was destroying the covenant relationship of His people to God, and the marauding tribes of Canaan that were destroying their food crops and reducing the people to hunger. Gideon progressed from hesitation to determination and won for himself a place in that New Testament roll of fame (Heb. 11:32) that extols the accomplishment of people who honored God, and helped others, by the exercise of faith. They are sometimes hailed as heroes, but the Bible's commendation of them is not for their physical feats or deeds of daring, but that they "obtained a good report through faith" (v. 39).

**Study Aim:** *To see Gideon as an example of the truth that "God hath chosen . . . weak things . . . to confound the . . . mighty" (1 Cor. 1:27)*

## STUDYING THE BIBLE

Camels are mentioned several times in Genesis, but the first mention of their use in warlike activities occurs in Judges 6:5. Fierce tribes from the east swept into Canaan and "they and their camels were without number." So terrifying and devastating were these attacks that "the children of Israel made them the dens which are in the mountains, and caves, and strongholds" (v. 2). After forty years of rest from enemy attacks (5:31), this new outbreak of terrorism reduced them to a state of abject fear. They had only themselves to blame for "they did evil in the sight of the Lord" (v. 1). The cycle was being repeated, and hope lay in divine intervention alone.

### I. Commissioning of Gideon (Judg. 6:1-6, 7-18)

The three chapters devoted to the Gideon story provide too much material for a single lesson. Yet we need to know something of this man's history prior to the victory over the Midianites, the subject of our printed passages. He is not presented at first as a heroic figure, but as a young man dominated by fear, as were the rest of his people.

**1. Threshing under difficulties (v. 11).**—Earlier in the chapter we are told that the Midianites waited until crops were planted and ready for the harvest, and then raided Israelitish territory and plundered it. As an attempt to outwit the enemy, Gideon was threshing wheat in a hollow place rather than on an exposed hilltop. But the lack of wind made the job nigh impossible. Midianites were descendants of Abraham (Gen. 25:1-2) and are an example of the animosities that can develop between people with a common origin.

**2. Called by God (vv. 12-18).**—As in many Old Testament revelations, what first appeared to be an angel proved to be the Lord Himself. Gideon doubtless echoed the thought of his people when he asked, "Why then is all this befallen us?" (v. 13), a question posed in spite of the prophetic message recorded in verses 7-10. Human nature is slow to accept the blame for its own tragedies. This hesitant and doubt-ridden young man, however, was God's choice to be the deliverer of His people. Once convinced of the divine call, Gideon proved himself worthy.

## II. How He Gained His Nickname (Judg. 6:25-32)

The extent to which God's people had given themselves over to paganism is disclosed by the fact that Gideon's own family had a private shrine dedicated to Baal and his female consort. The first test of Gideon's newfound courage and faith in God was the destruction of this shrine. He was also to offer a bull in sacrifice to the true God.

**1. A nighttime exploit (vv. 25-27).**—In the worst of times, God has His godly remnant. Gideon could count on ten men to help him. But he exercised caution by carrying out his plan at night. This should not be counted as cowardice, although Gideon had reason to fear, but rather as discretion since a daytime attempt could have aroused the whole community against him.

**2. The next morning (vv. 28-32).**—Joash's defense of his son showed great tact. "Since Baal is a god, he can take care of Gideon himself. Anyone who suggests otherwise should be put to death." The citizens of Ophrah accordingly gave Gideon the nickname already explained. The longer he lived, the more he could wear it with pride, for it declared the inability of Baal to avenge himself.

## III. Putting Out the Fleece (Judg. 6:33-40)

The phrase, "putting out the fleece," has entered into such general use that we should take note of its origin. Once again, Gideon is presented as a diffident person, needing constant proof of God's presence and promises. It would appear that his lack of confidence was in himself, not in the Lord. The menace to his people and their products grew more serious as Amalekites joined Midianites, with other "children of the east," by taking possession of the valley of Jezreel. Gideon first reacted with firm resolution. He sounded a call to arms that was answered by his own tribe, and then by others. But then a spirit of uncertainty came over him and once again he sought assurance from the Lord that He would save Israel through him (see v. 17). God bore with him in his predicament and by the fleece, first wet and then dry, encouraged His servant to enter into battle.

### IV. When Many Can Be Too Many (Judg. 7:1-7)

Honor in war is often sought and coveted. Soldiers wear their medals with pride and promotions are awarded for bravery in battle. Also, in modern times, it is not unusual for two warring countries both to claim that God is on their side. With Israel, the situation was very different. God was not only on their side but He was also in command. Victories were won, not by human effort but by divine enabling. Sometimes it was very necessary to make this clear to all combatants. It was in Gideon's day.

> 2 And the Lord said unto Gideon, The people that are with thee are too many for me to give the Midianites into their hands, lest Israel vaunt themselves against me, saying, Mine own hand hath saved me.
>
> 3 Now therefore go to, proclaim in the ears of the people, saying, Whosoever is fearful and afraid, let him return and depart early from mount Gilead. And there returned of the people twenty and two thousand; and there remained ten thousand.
>
> 4 And the Lord said unto Gideon, The people are yet too many; bring them down unto the water, and I will try them for thee there: and it shall be, that of whom I say unto thee, This shall go with thee, the same shall go with thee; and of whosoever I say unto thee, This shall not go with thee, the same shall not go.
>
> 5 So he brought down the people unto the water: and the Lord said unto Gideon, Everyone that lappeth of the water with his tongue, as a dog lappeth, him shalt thou set by himself; likewise everyone that boweth down upon his knees to drink.
>
> 6 And the number of them that lapped, putting their hand to their mouth, were three hundred men: but all the rest of the people bowed down upon their knees to drink water.
>
> 7 And the Lord said unto Gideon, By the three hundred men that lapped will I save you, and deliver the Midianites into thine hand: and let all the other people go every man unto his place.

**1. Thinning out the ranks (vv. 2-3).**—To reduce the size of Gideon's force, the "fearful and afraid" were told to leave the field of battle. The low morale of the Israelites has already been made clear in the early behavior of Gideon himself. Two thirds of the army took advantage of this release from military service, leaving only ten thousand men. Half-hearted servants of God are not always as honest as the 22,000 who went home.

**2. Test of alertness (vv. 4-7).**—But ten thousand were still too many to prove the point that the Lord wanted to make. So an interesting test was applied. On the banks of "the spring of Harod" (v. 1, NRSV), the thirsty soldiers were told to quench their thirst. Some of them kneeled down to drink; others cupped water in their hands and lapped it up like a dog. The latter, who only numbered 300, were retained while the larger number were dismissed. By kneeling down they exposed themselves to surprise attack for which they would be unprepared.

## V. Victory with Strange Weapons (Judg. 7:19-21)

The discrepancy between Gideon's 300 and the Midianites and their allies, who "lay along in the valley like grasshoppers for multitude, and their camels were without number" (v. 12), must have raised misgivings in Gideon's mind. He needed further assurance that God would give him the victory. So Gideon was told to take a servant with him and spy on the enemy camp. They overheard one Midianite tell another about a dream in which a loaf of bread hit a tent and leveled it to the ground. Enemy morale was also low for the dream was interpreted to mean defeat for the Midianites. "This is nothing else save the sword of Gideon . . . for into his hand hath God delivered Midian, and all the host" (v. 14).

> **19 So Gideon, and the hundred men that were with him, came unto the outside of the camp in the beginning of the middle watch; and they had but newly set the watch: and they blew the trumpets, and brake the pitchers that were in their hands.**
>
> **20 And the three companies blew the trumpets, and brake the pitchers, and held the lamps in their left hands, and the trumpets in their right hands to blow withal: and they cried, The sword of the Lord, and of Gideon.**
>
> **21 And they stood every man in his place round about the camp: and all the host ran, and cried, and fled.**

His confidence reinforced, Gideon first worshiped God, and then addressed his small force of men: "Arise; for the Lord hath delivered into your hand the host of Midian" (v. 15). His strategy was a night attack on three sides of the enemy camp. He divided his force into three, and furnished each man with a trumpet and an empty pitcher in which a lighted lamp was hidden. As in the attack on Jericho, the trumpets were curved rams' horns, used for their loud, strident noise.

At a signal from Gideon, the trumpets were blown, the pitchers smashed, and the lights from the lamp exposed. The enemy supposed that they were being assaulted by a large enemy force, took to their heels in terror and ran. The victorious Israelites acknowledged the help of God, as they cried, "The sword of the Lord, and of Gideon."

## APPLYING THE BIBLE

**When God turns weakness into strength.**—As the writer of our lesson today points out, there is little evidence that Gideon was naturally courageous. To the contrary, when the angel of the Lord appeared and told Gideon He would use him to deliver Israel from their enemies, Gideon's reply was: "But Lord, . . . how can I save Israel? My clan is the weakest in Manasseh, and I am the least in my family" (6:15, NIV).

But God joys in turning our weaknesses into strengths. For example, she was born on a farm outside Oxford, Massachusetts, on Christmas Day 1821. Her mother named her Clara and she was a terribly timid child. Fear so paralyzed Clara that she could hardly speak to her mother about her most personal needs.

At sixteen, Clara was a schoolteacher in a country schoolhouse, but some days she was so terrified she wouldn't even look her pupils in their eyes. But on the school grounds when Clara would see a small boy being bullied by a bigger boy, she would become fearless, defending the underdog like a lioness defending her cubs.

She overcame her timidity, finally, as a nurse in the Civil War. She was forty years old and she carried supplies to the wounded men on the battlefield and nursed them in their times of need. She was known as "the angel of the battlefield."

Her name was Clara Barton. When the Civil War ended, she volunteered to serve in the Franco-Prussian War as a battlefield nurse (1869). Out of all of this, she created and developed the American Red Cross which has helped more people in more crises than almost anything that one could name.

Indeed, God seems to glory and joy in turning our weaknesses into strengths.[1]

God took a lad who didn't think he had it in himself to do what needed to be done. But out of Gideon's fear and lack of self-confidence, God developed a great leader.

**A leader for the darkest days.**—After the fall of Dunkirk, during World War II, the invasion of England seemed to be imminent, and England was unprepared to defend herself: forty-seven warships had been sunk off Norway after Dunkirk; half of Great Britain's destroyers were in the shipyards for repairs; the Royal Air Force had lost 40 percent of its bombers; Britain was on the brink of famine; fifty thousand of her vehicles had been left in France; and the British Army was without adequate arms or equipment.

But Britain did have plenty of dogged determination. And she had

Winston Churchill.

Confessing that there was "hardly a weapon" in the whole British Empire, Churchill declared sternly to his people: "We shall fight on." When the French asked, "With what?" Churchill replied, "I do not know, but we shall fight on."[2]

In Israel's darkest days, God had an answer for them and that answer was Gideon, a divinely appointed deliverer.

**Selfish ambition defeats.**—Henry Wadsworth Longfellow wrote: "Most people would succeed in small things if they were not troubled with great ambitions."

Self-serving ambition was not Gideon's problem, and God used him mightily.

**The importance of little things.**—Little things can be mighty in the results they produce:

1. Amelia Earhart, flying around the world in 1937, missed tiny Howland Island, where she was to refuel, by perhaps as little as one degree. It is estimated the plane came within one hundred miles of Howland.
2. Andrew Johnson, the seventeenth president, was saved from being turned out of office by only one vote.
3. A Memphis, Tennessee, newspaper carried the story of a mole which burrowed into the base of a Red River levee in Arkansas, causing fifty feet of the levee to be washed away by the current.
4. Elisha Gray was two hours too late. He filed for a patent on the telephone two hours after Alexander Graham Bell did.
5. The building of the great Grace Baptist Church, and, consequently, Temple University—both in Philadelphia—began with a gift of fifty seven cents contributed by a little girl named Hattie Wyatt. The well-known preacher and author Russell Conwell was the pastor.
6. Dr. John Broadus worked out a series of lectures on preaching that he gave to one blind student at The Southern Baptist Theological Seminary, in Louisville, Kentucky. The lessons were later printed in a book titled *On the Preparation and Delivery of Sermons.* This book has been taught in seminary classrooms to tens of thousands of ministerial students.

Compared to the forces of the enemy, Gideon didn't have much—only three hundred men—but with these three hundred men he routed the Midianites with God's help.

## TEACHING THE BIBLE

▶ *Main Idea*: God's ability to use weak things to confound the mighty demonstrates that He can use any person or thing to achieve His purposes and accomplish His tasks.

▶ *Suggested Teaching Aim*: To lead adults to see how God used Gideon to defeat the Midianites, and to identify ways God can use them to accomplish some significant task.

## A TEACHING OUTLINE

*1. Write the Suggested Teaching Aim.*
*2. Enlist three participants.*
*3. Interview the participants.*
*4. Identify a class project God wants you to accomplish.*

**Introduce the Bible Study**

Use the illustration about Clara Barton, "When God turns weakness into strength" *(Applying the Bible),* to introduce the study. Point out that God can use anyone He chooses to accomplish His task.

**Search for Biblical Truth**

In advance, write the Suggested Teaching Aim on a large sheet of paper or a chalkboard and place it where members can see it. Ask members to share what they know about Gideon. Write these statements on a chalkboard or a large sheet of paper as members suggest them.

In advance, enlist a member to play the role of Gideon and one to play the role of a townsperson and a captured Midianite. Tell them that they will be interviewed by a television reporter from station WHEB, Hebron. Give a copy of the following questions to the participants. You may add additional questions but be certain the participants know what you will ask. Ask the three participants to study the material in the lesson well so they can elaborate on the questions and cover all of the lesson. They may use other resources such as the *Holman Bible Dictionary.* You will serve as the reporter.

**Gideon—**

I understand that you have a rather unusual nickname; would you explain how you received it? Isn't it rather presumptive to think that God would choose you to deliver His people? What proof do you have that He chose you?

**Townsperson—**

What do the people of Ophrah [AHF ruh] think about this Gideon and his destruction of the sacred grove of Baal? Why would people follow such a man as this? Tell me about the Midianites who oppressed you. Did many Israelites respond to Gideon's call to battle?

**Gideon—**

Tell our viewers about how you selected your army; I understand you did it in a very unusual manner. Why would your God even want you to go to battle with so few soldiers? I find it difficult to believe that you defeated the Midianite army with only 300 soldiers; how did you do it?

**Midianite Captive—**

What happened to the powerful Midianite army? Did your army get overconfident and careless? Did you have any indication that Gideon would attack you? What happened when the attack began? Who killed all of the Midianite soldiers if the Israelites stood in one place and blew trumpets and yelled? Why do you think this defeat occurred?

**Give the Truth a Personal Focus**

Call attention to the Suggested Teaching Aim. Explain that God can use any person or thing to achieve His purposes and accomplish His tasks. Ask, Why did God choose Gideon? (Be sure Gideon's willingness and God's choice are included in the answers.) What characteristics do people today need to possess for God to use them?

Ask members to think of some task God is calling the class to accomplish. Ask them to suggest what made Gideon so successful. Point out that God's strength is still as great today as in Gideon's time. If you need to arrange a meeting to follow up on the project, do so. Close in prayer that God will use your class as a group and individually to accomplish great things for Him.

---

1. Adapted from J. B. Fowler Jr., *Living Illustrations* (Nashville: Broadman Press, 1985), 58-59.

2. Adapted from Benjamin P. Browne, *Illustrations for Preaching* (Nashville: Broadman Press, 1977), 125.

October
16
1994

# Israel Demands a King

**Basic Passages:** 1 Samuel 7:15—8:22; 12:19-25
**Focal Passages:** 1 Samuel 8:4-9,19;12:19-25

We begin a new unit, "The Beginning of the Kingdom," with all three lessons taken from 1 Samuel. The following unit will have two lessons using passages from 2 Samuel. Who was this man to have two Old Testaments books named for him? Did he write these books? As a matter of fact, the two books of Samuel were originally one book, made into two at some point in their long transmission, presumably for the convenience of readers. The fact remains, a section of the Old Testament containing fifty-five chapters, carries the name of this man and covers the period between the rule of the judges and the beginning of the monarchy. He could not have been the author of all fifty-five chapters for much of their content happened after Samuel's death (1 Sam. 25:1). He may have left records that were embodied, by a later writer, into a history that begins with Samuel's birth and closes with the last days of David. So important was the role that Samuel played, however, that those who came after him honored him by giving his name to a major section of their nation's story.

**Study Aim:** *To recognize the purposes of God in giving freedom to the human will and allowing its consequences*

## STUDYING THE BIBLE

Was Samuel the last of the judges or the first of the prophets? He was both, and more, for he also performed the function of priest (1 Sam. 7:9). Our study passages begin with his latter years so there is need to remind ourselves of the earlier life of this great leader.

### I. The Epic of Samuel

Two tremendous summaries of Samuel's life and ministry compensate for a lack of detailed information. "All Israel from Dan even to Beer-sheba knew that Samuel was established to be a prophet of the Lord" (3:20); and "Samuel judged Israel all the days of his life. And he went from year to year in circuit to Bethel, and Gilgal, and Mizpeh, and judged Israel in all those places. And his return was to Ramah; for there was his house; and there he judged Israel; and there he built an altar unto the Lord" (7:15-17).

**1. Child of prayer (1 Sam. 1).**—Hannah, Samuel's mother, was childless, and suffered the taunts of her husband's second wife for her barrenness. She prayed for "a man child" who she promised to dedicate to God's service. The tabernacle was then located at Shiloh where Samuel was handed over to Eli, the high priest. "And the child did minister unto the Lord before Eli the priest" (2:11).

**2. God's messenger (1 Sam. 3:1-20).**—Eli had two sons who followed their father in the priesthood. They were evil men, however, misappropriating sacrificial meat for their own use, and practicing immorality with women who served the tabernacle. Through a night visitation, the Lord told Samuel of coming punishment on Eli and his family, and made him His messenger to the aging priest.

**3. Defeat of Philistines (7:3-17).**—At this period, the Philistines were Israel's chief enemy. They had captured the ark of the covenant in battle, but returned it when it brought suffering on them (chap. 6). Samuel called the people of Israel to repentance and summoned them to Mizpeh where he sacrificed to the Lord and prayed for the offenders. The Lord answered with a victory over the Philistines, whereupon Samuel erected a monument and called the place "Ebenezer, saying, Hitherto hath the Lord helped us" (7:12).

### II. "Give Us a King" (1 Sam. 8:4-9)

Two things were responsible for the call for a king: the demonstrated weakness of existing leadership in the decline of Samuel and the misconduct of his sons, and the continued harassment by the Philistines.

**4 Then all the elders of Israel gathered themselves together, and came to Samuel unto Ramah,**
**5 And said unto him, Behold, thou art old, and thy sons walk not in thy ways: now make us a king to judge us like all the nations.**
**6 But the thing displeased Samuel, when they said, Give us a king to judge us. And Samuel prayed unto the Lord.**
**7 And the Lord said unto Samuel, Hearken unto the voice of the people in all that they say unto thee: for they have not rejected thee, but they have rejected me, that I should not reign over them.**
**8 According to all the works which they have done since the day that I brought them up out of Egypt even unto this day, wherewith they have forsaken me, and served other gods, so do they also unto thee.**
**9 Now therefore hearken unto their voice: howbeit yet protest solemnly unto them, and show them the manner of the king that shall reign over them.**

**1. Samuel's displeasure (vv. 4-6).**—Reminding people that they are "old" needs to be done delicately (v. 5). There was nothing delicate about the people's request for a king. That Samuel should be hurt by their words was inevitable. After all the years of service he had rendered, he was being rejected. Nevertheless, he showed great wisdom in that he "prayed unto the Lord." He took his wounded spirit to God, sustaining his reputation as a man of prayer, as evidenced in other study verses (12:19-25).

**2. The Lord's response (vv. 7-9).**—Samuel's sensitivity was mildly rebuked when the Lord said, "They have not rejected thee, but they have rejected me" (v. 7). After long experience of divine goodness, they had turned from the true God and embraced idols. Now they were rejecting their distinction among other nations as a people ruled by God. Israel asked for uniformity with other nations by asking for a king. They would have their request. God does not retain the love and loyalty of people against their will. He also knew that only in experiencing monarchs and their ways would they learn how great was their mistake.

**3. The rule of God.**—The gospel of Jesus Christ is an invitation to enter "the kingdom of God," that is, to accept the rule of God in personal belief and behavior. What was long ago rejected by Samuel's generation is offered still to all who will accept God's terms. The gospel calls us to abandon self-will and submit to the authority of Jesus Christ as heaven's appointed King. This means the renunciation not only of self but also of Satan by repentance from sin and acceptance of forgiveness and salvation available at the cross.

### III. Samuel's Warning Unheeded (1 Sam. 8:10-22)

Samuel was determined that the people should understand all the implications of the choice they were making. They had asked for a king, "like all the nations" (v. 5). So he described for them the nature of those kings and what they might expect from kingship of the prevailing type. We should not assume, from the pattern he gave, that all monarchs fit this description of oppression. History, including Bible history, furnishes examples of good and bad rulers, the former winning the gratitude of their subjects, the later their hatred. Samuel's point was that they would be exchanging the authority of a merciful God for that of self-serving men, capable of becoming tyrants. In time of war, voluntary service would disappear as all available men would be recruited either for the line of battle or the production of instruments of war (vv. 11-12). The same condition exists, of course, in modern states that regard a total population as a legitimate resource of manpower for the furtherance of their plans. Samuel went on to describe the forceable use of women in the monarch's service, and the appropriation of lands and other property for the satisfaction of his greed. Israel was to have kings of this type. But Israel turned a deaf ear to Samuel's words.

> **19 Nevertheless the people refused to obey the voice of Samuel; and they said, Nay; but we will have a king over us;**

Verse 20 reads, "That we also may be like all the nations." A desire for uniformity with the world around besets the Christian church today, as it did Israel throughout history. The call of God to His people of old, and to His church today, is not to be conformed to the world, but to be different from it. "Do not be conformed to this world, but be transformed by the renewing of your minds, so that you may discern what is the will of God—what is good and acceptable and perfect" (Rom. 12:2, NRSV).

## IV. Divine Mercy and Judgment (1 Sam. 12:19-25)

Samuel did not give up easily. He knew that Israel was making a mistake in seeking to dethrone the Lord and replace Him with an earthly ruler. Yet he could not ignore the Lord's instruction, "Hearken unto their voice, and make them a king" (8:22). So Samuel anointed a young man named Saul (10:1), and presented him to the people (v. 24). They, in turn, doubtless responding to Samuel's words, expressed a sense of guilt for what they were doing.

> 19 And all the people said unto Samuel, Pray for thy servants unto the Lord thy God, that we die not: for we have added unto all our sins this evil, to ask us a king.
> 20 And Samuel said unto the people, Fear not: ye have done all this wickedness: yet turn not aside from following the Lord, but serve the Lord with all your heart;
> 21 And turn ye not aside: for then should ye go after vain things, which cannot profit nor deliver; for they are vain.
> 22 For the Lord will not forsake his people for his great name's sake: because it hath pleased the Lord to make you his people.
> 23 Moreover as for me, God forbid that I should sin against the Lord in ceasing to pray for you: but I will teach you the good and the right way:
> 24 Only fear the Lord, and serve him in truth with all your heart: for consider how great things he hath done for you.
> 25 But if ye shall still do wickedly, ye shall be consumed, both ye and your king.

In these verses Samuel (a) assured the people that, in spite of their rejection of God as their king, He would not abandon them; (b) but they must be careful not to add to their present error the worship of "vain things," that is, idols; (c) he would continue to pray for them and teach them "the good and the right way"; (4) they should not presume on God's continuing mercy for, if they turned to wickedness, they and their kings would come under judgment. This last warning was prophetic, for future kings would lead the nation in idolatrous practices, and bring on it the tragedies of invasion and destruction, followed by exile in foreign lands.

## APPLYING THE BIBLE

**Hannah's influence on Samuel.**—Samuel Taylor Coleridge, the noted English poet, told about talking to a man who said he didn't believe in giving children any religious instruction whatsoever. His theory was that the child's mind should develop without any prejudice in any direction.

In responding to the man's philosophy, Coleridge took the visitor outside. "Look," Coleridge said, "there is my garden!"

The man responded in surprise, "Why, this is not a garden at all! There is nothing growing here but weeds!"

"Well, you see, I did not wish to infringe upon the liberty of the garden in anyway. I was just giving the garden a chance to express itself and to choose its own production,"[1] Coleridge replied.

Providentially, Samuel grew up in a family where he was greatly influenced for good by his parent. The influence of Hannah, his mother, was especially powerful in molding his life.

**Israel gets what she wants.**—Israel wanted a king. She was willing to sacrifice the privilege of being a theocracy to become a monarchy. Israel was distinct, but she wanted to be like all her neighbors, and "keep up with the Joneses" and she set wheels in motion that ultimately brought her destruction.

Israel's foolish pride is well illustrated from an event in American history. Daniel Webster wanted to be president, but William Henry Harrison was nominated instead. When Webster was sought for vice president he was too proud to take the second position, and it went to John Tyler. Harrison had been in office only a month when he died and Tyler became president. Daniel Webster could have become president instead of Tyler, but Webster's pride cheated him out of his opportunity.

When Zachary Taylor was nominated as president, he asked Daniel Webster to be his running mate. Again, Webster's unbending ambition and selfish pride cheated him out of becoming president. Only sixteen months into his first term as president, Zachary Taylor died. Vice president Millard Fillmore became president—a position that could have gone to Daniel Webster if he had not been so proud. Driven by ambition and a selfish desire, Israel wanted a king, and God gave Israel what she wanted and she never recovered from it (v. 19).

**The language God understands.**—According to Benjamin P. Browne, an eighty-year-old woman applied for admittance to Princeton Seminary. When asked what course she wanted to study she replied, "Hebrew."

"Hebrew is such a difficult language, why do you wish to study it at your age" she was asked by the registrar.

Very properly, the octogenarian replied: "Well, I expect to go to heaven before very long, and I would very much like to be able to talk to God in his language!"

What is the language God understands? It is the language of

prayer, and the language in which the prayer is offered does not matter. From reading our lesson today, it is obvious that Israel was not talking to God at all—at least about the matter of a king. If they had been talking to God and listening to Him, they would have gotten the message that God alone wanted to reign over them.

**Genuine repentance?**—The former president could have been pardoned if only he had asked. But he refused.

The former president was Jefferson Davis, the Confederacy's only president.

At the end of the Civil War, when Davis delivered his farewell address as president of the Confederacy at the Mississippi Capitol in Jackson, he gave his reason: "Repentance must precede the right of pardon, and I have not repented!"

When Davis died in 1889 he still had not been pardoned. In the closing years of his life, he confessed: "If I were to do it over again, I would again do just as I did in 1861."

According to one writer, repentance or one of its derivatives appears 108 times in the Bible. It means "to turn back" or "a change of mind." Repentance expresses itself through a changed life-style. It is not a once-for-all experience, but a daily, ongoing thing. And this is where Israel's "repentance" fell short: It didn't last, as her history clearly reveals.

## TEACHING THE BIBLE

▶ *Main Idea*: God's granting Israel's demand for a king demonstrates that God can accomplish His purposes by giving freedom to the human will, and yet He holds us responsible for our decisions.

▶ *Suggested Teaching Aim*: To lead adults to describe how God gave Israel a king, and to identify how freedom and responsibility should be balanced in their life.

### Introduce the Bible Study

Use the illustration "Israel gets what she wants" *(Applying the Bible)*. Point out that Israel, like Webster, had the option to follow God. Instead, Israel chose to do its own thing. They wanted a king, and God gave them one—much to their ultimate tragedy.

### Search for Biblical Truth

Point out that this lesson begins a new unit entitled, "The Beginning of the Kingdom." Briefly set the context of this passage by describing Samuel's pattern of judging (1 Sam. 7:15-17). Locate Bethel, the possible location of Gilgal, and Ramah [RAY muh] on a map. (The location of Mizpah [MIZ pah] is unknown.)

Ask members to open their Bibles to 1 Samuel 8:4-9 and answer the following questions: Why did the Israelites demand a king? (decline of Samuel and the misconduct of his sons) What was Samuel's response? (felt rejected and prayed to God) What was the Lord's response? (said the people had not rejected Samuel but Him) What did God tell Samuel to do? (give them a king but warn them of the consequences).

Now ask members to turn to 8:19 to find the people's response.

---

### A TEACHING OUTLINE

1. *Introduce the new unit.*
2. *Guide members in a Scripture search.*
3. *Give a brief lecture.*
4. *Read life situations to apply the lesson.*

---

Use *Studying the Bible* to present a brief lecture over 1 Samuel 12:19-25 in which you cover the following points: (1) Israel's response when Samuel granted their wish; (2) Samuel's assurance that God would not abandon them; (3) Samuel's warning that they must avoid idolatry; (4) Samuel's covenant to pray for and support them; (5) and what would happen if they turned away from God.

**Give the Truth a Personal Focus**

Read the following life situations and let several members complete them: When she was a teenager, Carol committed her life to God at a church camp. She went to college where she met Brad. Brad had no interest in church, but he loved Carol and Carol loved him. She went to her pastor and asked, What's wrong with marrying Brad? The pastor replied . . .

Ed had always loved to farm. The day he graduated from high school, he made a promise that he would have a farm of his own in 10 years. He began working on a neighbor's farm and started trying to save money. He committed all his energies to making money to buy a farm. However, he soon realized he could never get enough money to buy his own farm. One day the man for whom he worked approached him with a "deal" by which they could get paid for not growing crops, but suggested that they could grow them on the side and pocket the profit. This would give Ed enough money for a down payment on his own farm. Ed said . . .

After members have discussed these two life situations, point out that we have the freedom to do many things but that God holds us responsible for what we do; we have to pay the consequences.

Ask members to suggest how God could work in each of the above situations to give both Carol and Ed what they wanted and yet not violate God's purposes. Close in prayer that members would have the courage to act responsibly in the decisions they make this week.

---

1. Adapted from *Windows, Ladders,* and *Bridges*, Dudley Dennison Jr., M.D. (Grand Rapids: Zondervan Publishing House, 1976), 163.

# Saul's Opportunity as King

**Basic Passages:** 1 Samuel 9:15—10:1,20-24
**Focal Passages:** 1 Samuel 9:15-17; 10:1,20-24

A somewhat obscure word that has gained a measure of familiarity in recent years is *serendipity*. It describes the experience of being engaged in a normal activity and, in the course of it, being confronted by something totally unexpected and very exciting. Saul, son of Kish, furnishes a good example of serendipity. He went looking for his father's lost donkeys, and found a throne. There was a day when two brothers, Peter and Andrew, arose to face, as they supposed, another day of family fishing in the Sea of Galilee. But before that day was through they were summoned to discipleship by the Lord Jesus Christ. That was serendipity. God has a wonderful way of encountering people in the course of daily life, opening up for them the prospect of significant service. For us, the important matter is how we respond. Saul, who began so well, allowed kingship to go to his head with consequent disappointment for all who knew him. Whatever opportunities come our way, they will be worthily used only as we honor the requirement "to do justly, and to love mercy, and to walk humbly with thy God" (Mic. 6:8).

**Study Aim:** *To be responsive to the leadership of God's Spirit as He opens doors of opportunity*

## STUDYING THE BIBLE

The printed passages for this lesson require familiarity with the total story as unfolded in chapters 9 and 10. Since the Lord Himself brought Saul and Samuel together with the introduction, "He it is who shall rule over my people" (9:17, NRSV), we may well wonder why the choice fell on a person who proved so disappointing. We cannot penetrate the divine mind, but it is reasonable to suppose that He was providing an early lesson in line with, "Put not your trust in princes, nor in the son of man, in whom there is no help" (Ps. 146:3).

### I. Search for Lost Donkeys

Saul is introduced as "a handsome young man. There was not a man among the people of Israel more handsome than he; he stood head and shoulders above everyone else" (9:2, NRSV). He belonged to the tribe of Benjamin, the smallest of the twelve, and his father Kish is described as a "man of wealth" (v. 1, NRSV). Some donkeys belonging to his father strayed and were lost. So Kish told his son to take a servant and go search for the animals. The search was thorough but unsuccessful (v. 4). Just as Saul decided to return home, the servants remembered that "a man of God" lived close by (v. 6). Doubtless he could help find the lost donkeys. As the two advanced toward the city, Samuel came out to conduct "a sacrifice . . . in the high place" (v. 12).

## II. Saul and Samuel Meet (1 Sam. 9:15-21)

This was no chance meeting for Saul and Samuel. The Lord had already told the prophet that the man chosen to be king would cross his path the next day "about this time." There was divinely ordered precision in the whole event.

> **15 Now the Lord had told Samuel in his ear a day before Saul came, saying,**
> **16 Tomorrow about this time I will send thee a man out of the land of Benjamin, and thou shalt anoint him to be captain over my people Israel, that he may save my people out of the hand of the Philistines: for I have looked upon my people, because their cry is come unto me.**
> **17 And when Samuel saw Saul, the Lord said unto him, Behold the man whom I spake to thee of! this same shall reign over my people.**

**1. A deliverer (v. 16).**—Like the judges before him, the new king was to save the people from a persistent enemy, in this case, the Philistines. These warlike people originated in the area of the Adriatic Sea, possibly in territory more recently known as Yugoslavia. They pursued their conquests southward, through Crete, in the direction of Egypt. In fact, Egypt may have been their intended destination, but their advance was stopped by Egyptian resistance and they accordingly settled along the Mediterranean coast and gave their name to the adjacent territory: Palestine. This happened approximately at the same time that the Israelites were entering Canaan from the east. They made no attempt to occupy Israel's God-given homeland, but were a longtime source of trouble by their raids into Israel's territory. Saul was expressly appointed to deal with this menace.

**2. Hospitality provided (vv. 19-20a).**—Samuel's acceptance of the divine will is indicated by the courtesy he showed to the future king. He made Saul and his servant his guests, and sat them in the place of honor at the table (v. 22). At the same time, he reassured Saul concerning the lost donkeys. The second half of verse 20 is variously translated, for example, "But what is it that all Israel is wanting? It is you and your ancestral house" (NEB); or, "And for whom is all that is desirable in Israel? Is it not for you and for all your father's household?" (NASB). However we read it, Samuel was telling Saul that he was the chosen leader.

**3. Modest response (vv. 20b-21).**—Clearly Saul was overcome by the announcement. He modestly understated the status of his family. The tribe of Benjamin was the smallest, it is true, but his father has already been described as "a mighty man of power," or, "a man of wealth" (v. 1, NRSV). It was part of Saul's tragedy that he did not maintain this humble spirit.

### III. Samuel Anoints Saul (1 Sam. 10:1-2)

Before Saul parted from Samuel and made his way back to his home, a solemn rite was observed. The concluding three verses of chapter 9 describe the setting. As the conclusion of the sacrifice to which Samuel had invited Saul (vv. 12,19), the two men returned to Samuel's home. There "a bed was spread for Saul on the roof, and he lay down to sleep" (v. 25, NRSV). The flat roof of a home was an ideal place to spend a cool night. Early the following morning, Saul was awakened and told to take his departure. Samuel accompanied him through the city, and, at the city limits, asked Saul to tell his servant to go ahead, thus leaving the two men alone. The purpose was stated, "That I may shew thee the word of God" (v. 27). So to the opening verse of chapter 10.

> **1 Then Samuel took a vial of oil, and poured it upon his head, and kissed him, and said**

Readers of other versions will find a longer statement than the above, as, for example, "You shall reign over the people of the Lord and you will save them from the hand of their enemies all around. Now this shall be the sign to you that the Lord has anointed you ruler over his heritage" (NRSV).

**1. The anointing (v. 1).**—Confirmation of certain persons to high office included a ceremony of anointing. The main ingredient was olive oil. In Exodus 30:22-25, Moses was instructed in the preparation of "an holy anointing oil" that contained several spices. This was used to anoint Aaron and his sons to the priesthood and, in addition, the furniture of the tabernacle. Severe restrictions were imposed on its use (vv. 32-33). We may assume that this was what Samuel used to anoint Saul, for God said of it, "This shall be an holy anointing oil unto me throughout your generations" (v. 31).

**2. The Lord's anointed.**—All kings of Israel were recognized as God's "anointed" (1 Sam. 24:6). As time passed, and a succession of monarchs failed to live up to expectations, the prophetic hope arose of a coming *Messiah*, the word meaning "anointed one." The Greek equivalent of Messiah is "Christ."

### IV. Saul Publicly Proclaimed (1 Sam. 10:17-27)

An interesting tidbit in verses 14-16 throws more light on Saul's early modesty. After his return from his search for the missing donkeys, an uncle asked him about his experience. Saul mentioned his meeting with Samuel, prompting the specific question, "Tell me, I pray thee, what Samuel said unto you" (v. 15). By way of reply, Saul told how Samuel provided news about the animals, "But of the matter of the kingdom, whereof Samuel spake, he told him not" (v. 16). Clearly, the younger man revealed that he not only had a humble nature, but also that he could keep a secret. News of his anointing as future king had to await a meeting of the tribes, convened by Samuel, at Mizpah, scene of a recent victory over the Philistines (chap. 7). There Samuel had erected a monument which he named, "Hitherto hath the Lord helped us" (7:12). There also, on this later occasion, he reminded the people of their deliverance from bondage in Egypt (10:18). They were rejecting God's leadership in asking for a king, but would have their desire.

> **20 And when Samuel had caused all the tribes of Israel to come near, the tribe of Benjamin was taken.**
>
> **21 When he had caused the tribe of Benjamin to come near by their families, the family of Matri was taken, and Saul the son of Kish was taken: and when they sought him, he could not be found.**
>
> **22 Therefore they inquired of the Lord further, if the man should yet come thither. And the Lord answered, Behold, he hath hid himself among the stuff.**
>
> **23 And they ran and fetched him thence: and when he stood among the people, he was higher than any of the people from his shoulders and upward.**
>
> **24 And Samuel said to all the people, See ye him whom the Lord hath chosen, that there is none like him among all the people? And all the people shouted, and said, God save the king.**

**1. Why did Saul hide? (vv. 20-22).**—We do not know for sure. It may have been another evidence of his modest nature at this early point in his life. On the other hand, a realization of the heavy responsibility of kingship may have overwhelmed him. He was found hiding "among the stuff," that is, the baggage of those who had traveled to Mizpah on behalf of the scattered tribes.

**2. Every inch a king (vv. 23-27).**—It has been said that while David was a man after God's own heart (13:14), Saul was a man after the peoples' heart. His physical attributes made an immediate appeal to those gathered at Mizpah (10:23), hence their cry, "Long live the king!" (v. 24, NRSV). Apparently Samuel authored a sort of constitution for the new kingdom (v. 25). When the assembly was dismissed, Saul immediately had his following. But there was also an opposition, indicative of troubles to come. At that time, Saul showed wisdom by ignoring his adversaries.

## APPLYING THE BIBLE

**Young adults have made significant contributions.**—Our lesson today declares that Saul was "a handsome young man" (9:2). He was young, handsome, strong, tall, and consequently had great appeal to the people. Unfortunately, although he had a lot of all those qualities, he had very little wisdom.

Young adults have been movers and shakers of history: Napoleon was only thirty-five when he became emperor of France. Thomas Jefferson was less than thirty when he was elected to the Senate. William Cullen Bryant was only sixteen when he wrote "Thanatopsis." Nathan Hale was only twenty-one when he spoke the words for which he is best remembered: "All I regret is that I have but one life to give to my country." The average age of the pilgrim fathers was twenty-six. Joan of Arc was only sixteen when she led France to victory. Mozart accomplished a great deal, but he died at thirty-five. The noted English poet John Keats died at twenty-six, but he left a marvelous legacy of literature. And Jesus, our precious Lord, lived only to be about thirty-three years of age. But He left behind a glorious kingdom that some day shall overcome all evil.

Saul was a young man when he came to the throne. He had the opportunity to make a significant difference in Israel's history; however, his self-centered ambition and lustful pride clipped his wings, and he never lived up to his potential. In addition, he brought a lot of grief upon Israel.

**How costly is pride!**—Joseph Parker, the well-known English preacher of the last century, told a fable about an ambitious, little watch. On a chain and around the neck of a beautiful lady, the watch was a striking thing. Often, as the watch looked up from the lovely lady's neck and saw Big Ben in its stately majesty high above London, the little watch thought to itself: *If I could ever get to be as important as Big Ben, and get as high as he is above the town, I would be something.*

The little watch's wish came true and one day, on a slender thread, it was hoisted to the tower by the side of Big Ben. But the watch that had been so beautiful on the lovely lady's neck could no longer be seen in its lofty tower by the passersby below. The watch got what its proud heart wanted, but the price it paid was too great.

**Never too little for God to use.**—Author Guy King says in his "Prayer Secrets": "You can easily become too big for God to use you, but you can never become too little." And that is true. Saul was not too little for God to use—just a rural boy out looking for his father's lost donkeys—but before long, as king, he became too big for God to use. His modesty gave way to pride and that was his ruination.

**Washington's humility.**—When George Washington was appointed commander-in-chief of the colonial army, he told every man in the room to remember that he did not believe himself equal to the honor thrust upon him. That attitude very definitely characterized Saul when Samuel told Saul he had been chosen to be king over Israel (vv. 20-22). But, unfortunately, he soon got over his gentle, humble attitude as his heart was filled with pride.

**William Carey's statement.**—William Carey, the Englishman who founded the Modern Mission Movement and who served so faithfully as a missionary in India, once said: "If God could use me, he can use anyone."

That seemed to be Saul's attitude when he "hid himself among the stuff" to keep from being found and made king (10:22). He, no doubt, felt most unworthy for that lofty position.

**Samuel's courtesy to Saul.**—Courtesy is a rare thing today. It is a rude, discourteous day in which we live. And that is a shame because courtesy is simply love in action.

The great English preacher F. B. Meyer told about a young soldier who was being transferred from India. A farewell dinner given in his honor by the officers of his regiment was the most important social function he had ever attended. Understandably, he was tense and shy as he was seated next to the presiding colonel.

After the soup was served a servant brought by a bowl filled with ice, but the young soldier who had never seen an ice cube had no idea what they were for. Taking a lump of ice and not knowing anything else to do with it, he put it in his soup. As half-smiles played upon the faces of the men around the table, his very proper and unflappable colonel took a piece of ice and put it in his soup. The other officers, in turn, put their ice in their soup when they were served.[1]

## TEACHING THE BIBLE

▶ *Main Idea*: God's choice of Saul as Israel's first king indicates that we should be responsive constantly to God's Spirit as He opens doors of opportunity.

▶ *Suggested Teaching Aim*: To lead adults to describe God's choice of Saul as Israel's first king, and to identify ways they can respond to God's leadership in their life.

### A TEACHING OUTLINE

1. *Make posters and organize members in four groups.*
2. *Guide members in discovering answers to the questions.*
3. *Apply the lesson by reading the case studies.*

### Introduce the Bible Study

Use the illustration "Never too little for God to use" *(Applying the Bible)*. Point out that our attitude keeps us from responding to God's leadership in our life.

### Search for Biblical Truth

Arrange the chairs in four groups. Prepare the following outline poster strips. On the back of the strips write the questions below the heading and place one strip in each group. As an alternative, you can use these to present a lecture or as a group discussion, if you have time.

THE LORD'S LEADERSHIP (9:15)

What is the background of this situation?
What indicates God was in the decision to choose Saul?
Why would God choose such a man as Saul?
How do you think Saul felt when told of God's choice?

THE LORD'S LEADER (9:16-17)
To what tribe did Saul belong?
What was significant about the tribe?
Who were the Philistines?
How do we know Saul was God's choice for king?

THE LORD'S ANOINTING (10:1)
With what did Samuel anoint Saul?
What was the purpose of the anointing?
To whom does anointing ultimately point?

THE PUBLIC DECLARATION (10:20-24)
What method of choosing did Samuel use?
How did Saul respond?
Why did Saul hide?
What was the people's response?

As members enter, ask them to go to one of the four groups and begin work on their questions. When members have finished their assignment, share the illustration in Introduce the Bible Study. Ask group 1 to place its poster on the focal wall and respond to the questions. Do this with the other three groups.

**Give the Truth a Personal Focus**

Read the following case studies: Charlotte had just finished medical school and her residency. She had accepted a job in a family clinic with an established physician who had built up a good practice over the years. Everything was going well with her life. Then a medical missionary spoke to her church, explaining the need for medical missionaries in so many parts of the developing world. Since then, she has felt unsettled about what she should do. How would you advise Charlotte?

Bruce, who is an automotive mechanic at a local garage, also heard the missionary speak. He is married and has two children, ages four and six. He, too, has felt that God wants him to do something in the area of missions. How would you advise Bruce?

Point out that God can use both Bruce and Charlotte for either long-term or short-term assignments. Ask members to consider areas to which God is leading them to respond and how they will respond. Close in prayer.

---

1. Adapted from Benjamin P. Browne, *Illustrations for Preaching* (Nashville: Broadman Press, 1977), 123.

October
30
1994

# King Saul Disobeys God

**Basic Passage:** 1 Samuel 13
**Focal Passage:** 1 Samuel 13:5-14

The test of love for and loyalty to God is in obedience to His wishes. This Old Testament message reappears in the New as we hear Jesus say, "If ye love me, keep my commandments," and, "If ye keep my commandments, ye shall abide in my love; even as I have kept my Father's commandments, and abide in his love" (John 14:15; 15:10). The tragedy of Saul can largely be accounted for by his willful behavior. Saul was determined to have his way regardless of what God said to him through Samuel, God's messenger. Our lesson passage contains one example of this. Chapter 15 records another. Few people had caused more trouble to Israel than the Amalekites, a loose-knit group of nomadic tribes that operated in southern Palestine. They had harassed the journeying Israelites during their wilderness wanderings (v. 2). Saul was ordered to destroy them and take no prisoners. But he "spared Agag the best of the sheep, and of the oxen . . . and all that was good" (v. 9). Saul pleaded that these animals were to be sacrificed to God (v. 21). To which Samuel gave the memorable reply, "Hath the Lord as great delight in burnt offerings and sacrifices, as in obeying the voice of the Lord? Behold, to obey is better than sacrifice, and to hearken than the fat of rams" (v. 22).

**Study Aim:** *To commit ourselves to unquestioning obedience to God in acknowledgment of His greatness and gratitude for His goodness*

## STUDYING THE BIBLE

To have a balanced view of Saul, we need to acquaint ourselves with passages outside our printed verses. His ultimate failure, rejection, and death are the more tragic because of early evidence that he gave effective leadership.

### I. Early Victories for Israel

After the ceremony at Mizpah (10:17-27), Saul returned to his father's home at Gibeah, four miles north of Jerusalem, then in enemy hands. Gibeah would become his headquarters. He resumed work in the family fields, and when "coming from the field behind the oxen" (11:5, NRSV) found the people of the town weeping. On inquiry, he learned that Ammonites were threatening the community. When asked for terms of peace, these invaders demanded the sacrifice of the right eye of every inhabitant. Enraged by this brutal requirement, Saul had an ox slain and cut up into pieces that were sent throughout Israel with the message that the same fate would befall the cattle of any who failed to rally to his side against the Ammonites. The response was immediate and adequate for a great victory against this cruel enemy (11:7-11).

**1. Saul's leadership confirmed.**—As a result, Saul's popularity was enhanced, and attempt was made to put to death those who opposed him (11:12). But Saul's response was, "There shall not a man be put to death this day: for to day the Lord hath wrought salvation in Israel" (v. 13). At the instigation of Samuel, a gathering was held at Gilgal and the kingship of Saul was reaffirmed (vv. 12-15).

**2. Jonathan and his thousand (13:1-4).**—Our study chapter begins by introducing a new character, Saul's son Jonathan (v. 16). At the head of 1,000 men, he attacked and defeated a Philistine garrison. This enraged the Philistines who assembled a large army for revenge. The record now returns to the subject of Saul.

## I. The Philistines Threaten (1 Sam. 13:5-7)

The disadvantage of the Israelites in their resistance of the Philistines is clearly indicated. The enemy's chariots were not matched in Israel. As conservative a scholar as Alfred Edersheim has expressed the opinion that 30,000 is obviously a copyist's mistake. He gave the opinion that the true number was 1,000 and explained how this number was multiplied to 30,000—"a number not only disproportionate to the horsemen but unheard of in history."[1] However, even the lower number presented an immense threat to the under-equipped men of Israel.

> **5 And the Philistines gathered themselves together to fight with Israel, thirty thousand chariots, and six thousand horsemen, and people as the sand which is on the sea shore in multitude: and they came up, and pitched in Michmash, eastward from Beth-aven.**
>
> **6 When the men of Israel saw that they were in a strait, (for the people were distressed,) then the people did hide themselves in caves, and in thickets, and in rocks, and in high places, and in pits.**
>
> **7 And some of the Hebrews went over Jordan to the land of Gad and Gilead. As for Saul, he was yet in Gilgal, and all the people followed him trembling.**

**1. Israel demoralized (vv. 6-7).**—The fear and desperation of the people is indicated in their search for any protection they could find. "When the Israelites saw that they were in distress (for the troops were hard pressed), the people hid themselves in caves and in holes and in rocks and in tombs and in cisterns" (v. 6, NRSV). Others left the country, crossing the Jordan and finding safety on its further banks.

Even those who remained with Saul are described as "trembling."

**2. Lack of weapons (vv. 15-23).**—This footnote to our chapter adds to the plight of the Israelites. Doing business with a potential enemy is always risky. Yet it would appear that the Israelites had become dependent on Philistines to sharpen their farming tools and were without spears and swords. Saul and Jonathan were the exception for they had swords. This must have been a temporary situation because, in 15:8, the Amalekites are said to have been destroyed "with the edge of the sword."

### III. Saul's Rash Behavior (1 Sam. 13:8-14)

The correct order of events is difficult to determine. To return to Saul's original encounter with Samuel, God's prophet told the chosen king to go to Gilgal where Samuel would join him for a sacrifice. This instruction was added, "Seven days you shall wait, until I come to you and show you what you shall do" (10:8, NRSV). We must assume that the situation described by Samuel was not immediate, but awaited the time of crisis recorded in chapter 13.

> 18 And he tarried seven days, according to the set time that
> Samuel had appointed: but Samuel came not to Gilgal; and the
> people were scattered from him.
> 19 And Saul said, Bring hither a burnt offering to me, and
> peace offerings. And he offered the burnt offering.
> 10 And it came to pass, that as soon as he had made an end
> of offering the burnt offering, behold, Samuel came; and Saul
> went out to meet him, that he might salute him.
> 11 And Samuel said, What hast thou done? And Saul said,
> Because I saw that the people were scattered from me, and that
> thou camest not within the days appointed, and that the
> Philistines gathered themselves together at Michmash;
> 12 Therefore said I, The Philistines will come down now
> upon me to Gilgal, and I have not made supplication unto the
> Lord: I forced myself therefore, and offered a burnt offering.
> 13 And Samuel said to Saul, Thou hast done foolishly: thou
> hast not kept the commandment of the Lord thy God, which he
> commanded thee: for now would the Lord have established thy
> kingdom upon Israel forever.
> 14 But now thy kingdom shall not continue: the Lord hath
> sought him a man after his own heart, and the Lord hath
> commanded him to be captain over his people, because thou
> hast not kept that which the Lord commanded thee.

**1. Refuge in religion (vv. 8-9).**—In the dire circumstances confronting him, his army was down to 600 men (v. 15), Saul's thoughts turned to God. We have no true insights into his thinking and therefore should reserve judgment. He apparently realized his need for divine help, and thought to obtain this by offering sacrifices. The tendency to resort to religion when the going gets hard is conspicuous in wartime situations and has produced the phrase "foxhole religion."

**2. Impatience prevails (v. 10).**—There was an understanding on Saul's part that, when a sacrifice was to be offered, he should delay action for seven days to allow Samuel to be present. This arrangement was an acknowledgment of Samuel's authority as God's priest and prophet. It amounted to a divine instruction, and should have been so regarded by Saul. But when the seventh day arrived, and Samuel was not present, Saul wasted no time. He went ahead and conducted the sacrifice himself, an act of presumption that was quickly followed by Samuel's appearance.

**3. A matter of authority.**—Our American concept of the separation of church and state does not fit into this biblical situation. As God's representative, Samuel's instruction had primacy over Saul's behavior, though Saul was king. At the political level, this is hard to reconcile with today's thinking. But the fact remains that all persons, VIPs and common folk alike, are answerable to God, whose commandments must be obeyed.

**4. Guilty before God (vv. 11-13).**—Saul felt he had good answers to Samuel's question, "What hast thou done?" His warriors were "slipping away" (v. 11, NRSV), perhaps because they were not willing to do battle without a ceremony of sacrifice; Samuel had not arrived on time; and the Philistines were threatening an attack. He claimed that, in these circumstances, he had "forced" himself to commit an act of disobedience. This was the test of his suitability to remain king, a test that he failed.

**5. Successor chosen (v. 14).**—Consequently, the Lord had chosen another to reign over Israel, "a man after his own heart," not named here, but soon to be revealed as David. From this point onward, Saul's story is one of deterioration, spiritually and mentally. He and David were to meet under dramatic circumstances (chap. 17). But the relationship between the two was sadly marred by Saul's uncontrollable jealousy and violent behavior.

## IV. Saul's Tragic End

This series of lessons is not intended to provide complete life histories of the characters studied. Its purpose is to forge major links in the chain of events in Israel's story "From the Conquest to the Kingdom" (this quarter's theme). Before proceeding to two lessons on David, we may want to check the tragic circumstances of Saul's death. Chapter 31 records the deaths of Jonathan, and two other sons of Saul, in battle with the Philistines. Sensing that he could not escape, Saul took his life with his own sword. The outlook for Israel was bad. However, God raised up another champion, David, part of whose story follows.

## APPLYING THE BIBLE

**Paralyzed by fear.**—During World War II, correspondent Edward R. Murrow wrote about Britain standing alone in the autumn of 1940. The German bombers came every night and the city of London was terribly damaged. Only with great difficulty did the people carry on during those days. Murrow said that on one of those occasions when devastation and tragedy were all about him, he saw a rudely lettered sign just off the East India Dock Road which carried a heavenly message: "If your knees knock, kneel on them."

Israel was terrified by her enemies. But God had His servant in Israel's darkest hour equipped and ready to lead them out of their fear to victory. His name was Saul. God always has his man or woman in life's dark days to show us the way and encourage us.

**The look of eagles in his eye.**—The late author and well-known Methodist minister William L. Stidger told about an old southern gentleman friends called Uncle Peter Goodwin. A lover of horses, Uncle Peter was given the opportunity to select the colt he wanted from a herd of what looked like ordinary two-year-olds. He chose the one everyone else had passed over because he looked like a second-rater that would never amount to much at the racetrack, "He will never run in the Kentucky Derby," they laughingly told Uncle Peter, but "Bluegrass" not only ran in the Kentucky Derby but won!

When Uncle Peter was asked why he chose that particular colt, he replied that it was because the colt had "the look of eagles in his eye."[2]

Stidger also told about an old man he once knew named Henry Rankin, who, as a boy, was Abraham Lincoln's office boy. Rankin told Dr. Stidger that generally Lincoln's face was listless, sad, and unanimated. But when the president was debating or comforting a brokenhearted mother or leading some great cause, his eyes would light up as though a great fire had been built behind them. "Then," said Rankin, "he looked like an eagle on a craig!"[3]

That's what Saul had—"the look of eagles in his eyes"—when he came to the throne knowing what the enemy had done to his beloved people, and what he must do to restore their courage and their land.

**The governor forgives the one who abused him.**—Missouri once had a governor named Stewart. Asked to pardon a certain convict, he had the man brought to him. Then he recognized him as a mate on a steamboat under whom Stewart once had served as a cabin boy.

Before handing the man his pardon, Stewart made him promise never again to take a stick of wood to a sick boy and force him out of his berth on a stormy night. "Promise me," Stewart said, "or someday that boy may be governor and you may want him to pardon you for another crime. I was that boy. Here is your pardon."[4]

After Saul had defeated the Ammonites who threatened Israel (11:1ff), his supporters were so enthusiastic that they wanted to slay all who had opposed Saul's becoming king. But Saul would have none of it (v:13). Forgiveness, pardon, and rejoicing were the things most important to Saul that day.

**"Pupil of John Philip Sousa."**—Sousa relates that on one occasion he was sitting in a hotel room when he heard an organ-grinder on the street below playing Sousa's "Stars and Stripes Forever."

Rushing out the door, Sousa took the organ away from the poor, bewildered man and began to turn the handle vigorously. As the music rushed out, spirited and snappy, Sousa said, "Don't drag it! This is the way it ought to be played!"

The next night Sousa heard the organ-grinder coming down the street again. This time, the march had good spirit and Sousa was proud. But when he looked out the window and saw a great crowd gathered around the player, Sousa was also shocked. For on a large card over the organ the man had printed his name and under his name was written the proud statement, "Pupil of John Philip Sousa."

The organ-grinder was quick to put into practice what he had learned. But such was not the case with Israel's first king. Lesson: The thing God demands and expects above everything else is obedience (1 Sam. 15:22).

## TEACHING THE BIBLE

▶ *Main Idea*: Saul's disobedience of God's commands illustrates that we are to give unquestioning obedience to God in acknowledgment of His greatness and gratitude for His goodness.

▶ *Suggested Teaching Aim*: To lead adults to examine Saul's disobedience of God's commands, and to commit themselves to unquestioning obedience to God in acknowledgment of God's greatness and gratitude for His goodness.

### Introduce the Bible Study

Use "Pupil of John Philip Sousa" *(Applying the Bible)*. Point out that God demands and expects obedience—which was what Saul refused to give Him.

### Search for Biblical Truth

Divide a chalkboard or a large sheet of paper in half vertically and make the following chart: Write *What Saul Did that Was Right* over one column and *What Saul Did that Was Wrong* over the other. Assign half of the class to listen for what Saul did that was right and the other half to listen for what he did that was wrong.

To explain the context, summarize the material under "Early Victories for Israel" (*Studying the* Bible). Call for groups to report. Members may suggest other right actions for Saul but these should be included: acted quickly, inspired people, refused to retaliate against opposition. Point out that Saul had many admirable characteristics.

Ask members to open their Bibles and read 13:5-7 silently and complete the chart. *Right: nothing. Wrong: refused to act.* Use *Studying the Bible* to explain the shortage of weapons.

## A TEACHING OUTLINE

*1. Discover how Saul's early leadership won him support.*
*2. Identify what Saul did that was right and what he did that was wrong.*
*3. Make a commitment to obey God because of God's greatness.*

Make five strip posters on which you write the five bold-faced headings under "Saul's Rash Behavior." Ask members to read silently 13:8-14. Present a brief lecture on these verses by using the information in *Studying the Bible.* As you lecture on each section, tape the strip poster to the wall.

When you are finished, ask the groups to fill in the chart. *Right: waited for seven days, recognized the need to sacrifice. Wrong: impatient, offered the sacrifice which was a priestly act, did not keep the commandments of God.*

Briefly summarize "Saul's Tragic End" and point out that next Sunday's lesson begins a new unit on "The Kingdom Under David and Solomon."

**Give the Truth a Personal Focus**

Ask members to look at the chart listing Saul's right and wrong actions. Let them list any other right or wrong decisions or actions. Ask: Did Saul have a choice in his behavior? (certainly) Why did Saul's life go down hill? What could he have done to prevent it? Be sure members understand that Saul had a choice in this matter.

Then ask, How is your life similar to Saul's—either good or bad? Point out that Saul's primary problem lay in a failure to obey God.

Distribute sheets of paper and pencils to all the members. Ask them to write a paragraph, a prayer, a poem, or a hymn that would affirm their commitment to obey God in acknowledgment of His greatness and gratitude for His goodness. Close in a prayer of commitment that each member will gain a victory this week.

---

1. Alfred Edersheim, *History, Vol 4* (Grand Rapids: William B. Eerdmans, Publisher, 1949), 59.
2. Adapted from William L. Stidger, *There Are Sermons in Stories* (Nashville: Abingdon- Cokesbury Press, 1962), 40.
3. Ibid., 41.
4. Adapted from G.B.F. Hallock, *Five-Thousand Best Modern Illustrations* (George H. Doran Co., 1927), 279.

# David Claims God's Promises

**Basic Passage:** 2 Samuel 7
**Focal Passage**: 2 Samuel 7:18-29

When Samuel announced to Saul that the Lord had rejected him as king, he described his successor, without naming him as David, as "a man after his own heart" (1 Sam. 13:14). The New Testament echoes this tribute in Acts 13:22 where the apostle Paul said of God's dealings with ancient Israel, "he raised up unto them David to be their king . . . a man after mine own heart." This did not mean that God's choice had fallen on a perfect person. In two lessons from David's life, we are given contrasted insights into this man's character: his devotion to God in intended deed (he wanted to build the temple) and verbal tribute (2 Sam. 7:18-29), and his transgression of God's moral law in his sin with Bathsheba. If God wanted perfect beings for the carrying out of His purposes, He would have used angels. In His wisdom and love He calls men and women, and little children, into His service. In spite of their frailty, His power and grace enable such to be effective in their assigned tasks. His unwavering requirement is found in our Lord's words: "Thou shalt love the Lord thy God . . . [and] thy neighbor as thyself" (Matt. 22:37-39).

▶ ▶ ▶ **Study Aim:** *To count our blessings and give thanks to God for them*

## STUDYING THE BIBLE

Important events for Israel are reported in chapter 5. Saul had not reigned over a united people, but over a loose confederacy of tribes. To begin with, David had been recognized as king of the tribe of Judah (2:4). Other tribes acknowledged a son of Saul as king, and the result was "long war between the house of Saul and the house of David" (3:1). But eventually, David prevailed, and representatives of all the tribes met at Hebron, "and they anointed David king over Israel" (5:3). Hebron was his capital for seven-and-a-half years until Jerusalem was taken from the Jebusites to become David's new capital (vv. 4-7).

### I. A Sanctuary Proposed (2 Sam. 7:1-3)

This lesson outline proposes to make use of all of chapter 7, assigned to us as the basic passage. But it will also be necessary to employ some flashbacks in order to add substance to our study material.

**1. The ark of the covenant (v. 2).**—See lesson for September 11 for information on this most sacred of the tabernacle's furnishings. It was the symbol of God's presence among His people. It fell into the hands of the Philistines (1 Sam. 4), but it brought them so much trouble that they were glad to return it to Israel. It was not housed at Shiloh, presumably because the sanctuary there had been destroyed, but in the house of Abinadab, where it remained for twenty years (1 Sam. 7:1-2). After he had taken Jerusalem to be his capital, David, accompanied by 30,000 men, brought the ark to that city in a triumphant parade (2 Sam. 6:1-5). There David provided a special tent for it until a permanent home was forthcoming (v. 17).

**2. David's plan (vv. 1-2).**—As David enjoyed his own home, and contemplated the victories he had gained, with consequent years of peace, he became uneasy in his mind. It was not appropriate that he should live in such comfort while the ark remained in a tent. He began to plan a sanctuary worthy of the God whom the ark represented.

**3. Nathan's support (v. 3).**—At this point we are introduced to Nathan the prophet, friend and counselor to David, a man who was to play an important part in future events (1 Kings 1:32-34). David confided his thoughts to Nathan, who promptly gave his support to the plan. But he was to have second thoughts on the matter.

## II. God's Universal Presence (2 Sam. 7:4-7)

Although the projected temple would have the approval of God, an important truth was safeguarded. The infinite God cannot be confined to a building, however splendid. In time to come, the temple itself would become an object of veneration, even of superstitious confidence (Jer. 7:4). The Scriptures reveal deep concern lest that which was provided to honor God became a cause for misunderstanding and misplaced trust. For Christians, our Lord's words in John 4:21-24 have deep relevance.

**1. Support withdrawn (vv. 4-5).**—In verse 3 Nathan spoke for himself. In verses 4 onward he spoke for God. Friendship with David caused him to endorse his proposal. Revelation from God changed Nathan's mind. We could believe that Nathan afterward wished he had taken the matter to the Lord before committing himself to the king's idea.

**2. The traveling tabernacle (vv. 6-7).**—Giving emphasis to God's constant presence, the nature of the original sanctuary was recalled. It was a tent that accompanied the Israelites wherever they went in their wilderness wanderings. At no time had the Lord asked for a "house of cedar," a building on a fixed location. He would permit a temple to be built for His worship, but not by David. Yet it must never be forgotten that God is omnipresent, available to those who love Him in all places and at all times.

## II. Blessings Received, Promises Made (2 Sam. 7:8-17)

We are dealing with one of the great messianic passages of the Old

Testament, containing promises that had their fulfillment in the coming of the Lord Jesus Christ. It begins with a reminder of David's own remarkable career.

**1. David's story (vv. 8-9).**—As a young shepherd, tending his father's sheep in the pastures of Bethlehem, David obtained entry into the court of King Saul. The occasion was the defiance of Israel by the Philistine giant, Goliath (1 Sam. 17). After killing the giant, David enjoyed Saul's favor for a time, but jealousy gradually turned Saul against David. After the death of Saul, a struggle for the throne continued between David and Saul's surviving son, Ishbosheth. Eventually, however, David was crowned king over all Israel (2 Sam. 5:1-3). There remained the Philistine problem, which was solved in the Valley of Rephaim where a double defeat was inflicted on the enemy (vv. 17-25). All this, and more, was summarized in God's words to David, "I took thee from the sheepcote . . . to be ruler over my people . . . and have cut off all thine enemies . . . and have made thee a great name" (7:8-9).

**2. God's gift of "an house" (vv. 10-11).**—There is a play on the word "house" in our larger passage. David desired to build what the Lord described as "an house for me to dwell in" (v. 6). This was because the king already had "an house of cedar" (v. 2) for himself. But, in withholding His permission for this project, the Lord said, through Nathan, that "he will make thee an house" (v. 11). In this case the word meant a dynasty, a royal family that would keep the throne from generation to generation. This second sense survives today in monarchies, for example, "the house of Windsor."

**3. An everlasting kingdom (vv. 12-17).**—David's son would build God's house, His temple, a promise fulfilled in Solomon. But this would not render David immune to punishment. He would suffer for his sins, but not lose his kingdom, as did Saul. For the Lord had in mind a throne to be "established for ever" (v. 16). When David's kingdom did come to an end with the Babylonian conquest, and the destruction of Jerusalem in 586 B.C., the Holy Spirit enabled people to realize that this promise would be fulfilled in a spiritual kingdom of which the Lord Jesus is head.

## IV. Praise Offered to God (2 Sam. 7:18-24)

When Nathan was through with his message, David "went in," presumably into the tent in which the ark was stored, and "sat before the Lord," a kneeling position in which the king sat back on his heels. Thus positioned before the ark, he addressed God in words that, while not comprising a psalm, remind us of this king's tremendous contribution in the Book of Psalms. He used his mastery of words to honor the Lord and provide believers of all ages with a treasury of devotional materials.

**18 Then went the king David in, and sat before the Lord, and**

he said, Who am I, O Lord God? and what is my house, that thou hast brought me hitherto?

19 And this was yet a small thing in thy sight, O Lord God; but thou hast spoken also of thy servant's house for a great while to come. And is this the manner of man, O Lord God?

20 And what can David say more unto thee? for thou, Lord God, knowest thy servant.

21 For thy word's sake, and according to thine own heart, hast thou done all these great things, to make thy servant know them.

22 Wherefore thou art great, O Lord God: for there is none like thee, neither is there any God beside thee, according to all that we have heard with our ears.

23 And what one nation in the earth is like thy people, even like Israel, whom God went to redeem for a people to himself, and to make him a name, and to do for you great things and terrible, for thy land, before thy people, which thou redeemedst to thee from Egypt, from the nations and their gods?

24 For thou hast confirmed to thyself thy people Israel to be a people unto thee forever: and thou, Lord, art become their God.

Notice the humility with which David spoke, "Who am I?" (v. 18). God had acted out of the goodness of His heart, thereby displaying His greatness. Unlike other nations that chose their gods, Israel had been chosen by God. He had done this by an act of redemption, taking Israel out of Egypt "to be a people unto thee for ever" (v. 24).

### V. Prayer Made to God (2 Sam. 7:25-29)

David concluded by asking the Lord to fulfill the great promises He had given. In doing so, He would magnify His name among the nations. There is no doubt expressed by David, but a sense of wonder at the things God had done and would yet do.

25 And now, O Lord God, the word that thou hast spoken concerning thy servant, and concerning his house, establish it forever, and do as thou hast said.

26 And let thy name be magnified forever, saying, The Lord of hosts is the God over Israel: and let the house of thy servant David be established before thee.

27 For thou, O Lord of hosts, God of Israel, hast revealed to thy servant, saying, I will build thee an house: therefore hath thy servant found in his heart to pray this prayer unto thee.

28 And now, O Lord God, thou art that God, and thy words be true, And thou hast promised this goodness unto thy servant:

29 Therefore now let it please thee to bless the house of thy servant, that it may continue forever before thee: for thou, O Lord God, hast spoken it: and with thy blessing let the house of thy servant be blessed forever.

## APPLYING THE BIBLE

**Failure need not be fatal.**—Failure need not be fatal, but sometimes it is. Babe Ruth hit seven hundred fourteen homeruns, but he struck out one thousand three hundred and thirty times. Edison experimented ten thousand times to perfect the storage battery, but still he could not get it to work. "I have just found ten thousand ways that will not work," he said. Napoleon was forty-second in his graduating class of forty-three, but this academic failure conquered Europe. Jean Francois Millet was a poverty-stricken failure of an artist at the outset of his career. But look at his marvelous *Angelus* or his simple *Man with the Hoe* and see what you think. So, failure need not be fatal.

But sometimes it is. Because of Saul's disobedience, God rejected him as king of Israel (1 Sam. 28:15). David has been anointed king of Judah and has also been made king over Israel (2 Sam. 5:5). A new day has dawned for Israel. Saul, who had a stubborn heart, has been replaced by David "A man after God's own heart" (1 Sam. 13:14; Acts 13:22). We must not fail to see in David the high cost of disobedience.

**Blessings in disguise.**—There are times when our blessings are disguised, and it is hard to see them as blessings. For example, if Winston Churchill had died before his sixtieth birthday and before his days of leadership as prime minister of Great Britain, he would have been a colossal failure. After a particularly bitter political defeat early in his career, a friend said: "Sir Winston, these are just blessings in disguise." Churchill, in his usual blunt way responded: "Well, if they are, then they are very well disguised."

**David's ambition.**—Ambition, in itself, is not a bad thing. Like anything else, it can be misdirected. Napoleon wrote an essay on the dangers of ambition when he was a boy, yet it was his own ambition that ultimately destroyed him. Michelangelo had the right idea when he prayed: "Lord, grant that I may always desire more than I can accomplish." Abraham Lincoln, who had the ambition to amount to something, often said to himself as a boy studying by the pine log fire at night: "I will study and get ready and perhaps my chance will come." And, indeed, it did come. George Washington Carver, born to a black slave mother, never knew his father. But he wanted to contribute worthily to life, and he did! Carver became the greatest black scientist in American history.

David's ambition was to build a house for God (2 Sam. 7:2). It was a big ambition, too. Here was a king with the dream of building a dwelling place for Him whose dwelling is the heavens! It was a worthy ambition, but David's sin kept him from carrying it out.

**A great prophecy about Christ.**—Predicting the future is a multi-billion dollar business today. Some of what is predicted comes to pass, a lot of it doesn't, and all of it is nothing more than guesswork.

One psychic named Criswell—a sometime teacher, mortician,

newspaperman, and newscaster—claims to have an 86 percent accuracy record about his predictions. But he was wrong when he predicted the Korean War would be revived by June 1969; wrong when he said that in October 1969 a major movie actor would be arrested for white slavery and would be charged with keeping thirty runaway girls in the basement of his Beverly Hills home; wrong when he predicted that on August 9, 1970, a woman would assassinate Fidel Castro; wrong when he predicted that in 1971 new islands would emerge in the Pacific after a volcano erupted; wrong when he predicted that by 1973 blacks would take over Mississippi and turn it into a model black state; and wrong in 1974 when he predicted that five thousand people in New Hampshire would die as a result of ice storms. But to be fair to Criswell, we must say that he guessed right on some things.

The Bible was not wrong and there was no guessing when it prophesied that through David a King would be given to Israel and the world whose kingdom would be established forever. That prophecy (7:16) was fulfilled in Jesus Christ.

## TEACHING THE BIBLE

▶ *Main Idea*: Examining how David claimed God's promises and expressed gratitude for them demonstrates that we should praise God for what He has done for us.

▶ *Suggested Teaching Aim*: To lead adults to describe how David claimed God's promises, and to identify ways they can praise God for what He has done for them.

### A TEACHING OUTLINE

*1. Summarize the background.*
*2. Identify what David praised God for.*
*3. Apply the lesson by writing a psalm or hymn.*

**Introduce the Bible Study**

Begin by sharing "Blessings in disguise"*(Applying the Bible)*. Point out that God has given us many blessings for which we need to be grateful.

**Search for Biblical Truth**

IN ADVANCE, enlist a member to read "Ark of the Covenant," in the *Holman Bible Dictionary* or some other Bible dictionary, and prepare a two- to three-minute report on the ark of the covenant.

Briefly summarize as much as you need of *Studying the Bible* to understand the context. Call for the report on the ark of the covenant. Point out: (1) David wanted to build a temple to house this ark but that God through Nathan refused to let him build it, (2) God promised instead that David's dynasty would extend forever (2 Sam. 7:16).

Write on a chalkboard or a large sheet of paper the following (do not write italicized references):

David Praised God for:

1. *What God had done in the past (7:18)*
2. *What God will do in the future (7:19-21)*
3. *God's Greatness (7:22-24)*

Cover points 2 and 3 with paper strips. Ask members to search 7:18-24 to find a verse or verses in which David praised God for what He had done in the past (v. 18 . . . although you may find others). Let members list some of the actions David may have had in mind.

Uncover point 2 and ask members to search 7:18-24 to find a verse or verses in which David praised God for what He will do in the future. (vv.19-21) Let members list what God would do in the future.

Uncover point 3 and ask members to search 7:18-24 to find a verse or verses in which David praised God for His greatness. (vv. 22-24) Let members list specific reasons David praised God for His greatness.

Ask a volunteer to read 7:25-29. As the volunteer reads, ask members to identify all of the names of God David used to describe Him: Lord God (vv. 25,29); Lord of Hosts (vv. 25,28-29); God of Israel (v. 27); God (v. 28).

Ask: What effect does the piling up of so many names of God have? What is David's attitude toward God? How has David's prayer that God's name be "magnified for ever" been answered?

**Give the Truth a Personal Focus**

Distribute paper and pencils to members and ask them to write a psalm or hymn that would praise God for what He has done, what He will do, and His greatness. Encourage several to read or sing what they have written as closing prayers. Conclude by singing the Doxology.

November
13
1994

# David Sins Against God

**Basic Passage:** 2 Samuel 11:1—12:19
**Focal Passages:** 2 Samuel 12:1-10,13

Memory can be used for self-serving purposes. With all the good the Bible records about David, we may choose to focus on his sin with Bathsheba. So it often is with Peter, for that which comes most readily to mind is his thrice-repeated denial of his Lord. Or Thomas, as we allow his lapse into doubting to predominate in our thinking about him. Such emphasis on others' failures may serve as excuse for our own. If men of this caliber, prominent in Scripture, had their weaknesses, we should not be blamed for ours. It was certainly not to serve this purpose that the Holy Spirit allowed inspired writers to record David's transgression. That a man of his standing before God, for we recall the description of him as "a man after God's own heart," could fall into the snare of Satan, is a strong warning to all to beware of his subtleties. The kind of trap Satan set for David has caused many a good person to stumble. "Wherefore let him that thinketh he standeth take heed lest he fall" (1 Cor. 10:12).

**Study Aim:** *To be made more aware of "the wiles of the devil" and so put on "the whole armor of God" (Eph. 6:11)*

## STUDYING THE BIBLE

To give balance to our opinion of David we could read 2 Samuel 9. In those days, victorious kings put to death the entire family of the monarch they had conquered, or succeeded. But when David became secure on his throne, he inquired whether there were any survivors of Saul's family. He discovered a grandson of the ex-king, named Mephibosheth, "lame on his feet" (v. 3). He took this handicapped prince into his palace and made provision for him "as one of the king's sons" (v. 11). All of this David did out of his love for Jonathan, Mephibosheth's father.

### I. Nathan's Difficult Task (2 Sam. 12:1-6)

The prophet Nathan, friend and counselor to David, reappears, this time with a sad task assigned by God Himself. David had grievously offended God's moral laws, first by committing adultery, and then conspiring for another's death. Nathan's approach showed understanding of David's true character since it appealed to the king's compassion and sense of justice.

**1 And the Lord sent Nathan unto David. And he came unto**

him, and said unto him, There were two men in one city; the
one rich, and the other poor.
2 The rich man had exceeding many flocks and herds:
3 But the poor man had nothing, save one little ewe lamb,
which he had bought and nourished up: and it grew up together
with him, and with his children; it did eat of his own meat, and
drank of his own cup, and lay in his bosom, and was unto him
as a daughter.
4 And there came a traveler unto the rich man, and he spared
to take of his own flock and of his own herd, to dress for the
wayfaring man that was come unto him; and took the poor
man's lamb, and dressed it for the man that was come to him.
5 And David's anger was greatly kindled against the man;
and he said to Nathan, As the Lord liveth, the man that hath
done this thing shall surely die:
6 And he shall restore the lamb fourfold, because he did this
thing, and because he had no pity.

**1. The story (vv. 1-4).**—As king, David would also function as judge. Nathan appeared before him as an attorney, pleading a case of injustice, but not revealing the identity of the plaintiff. He cleverly played on David's sympathy, describing in detail the relationship between a man and the family pet. We could safely assume that the owner of the lamb was in the employ of the rich man, a sort of tenant farmer perhaps. Hence the rich man knew of the existence of this favorite lamb and used his knowledge for an act of gross abuse of his authority. He served the pet lamb for dinner rather than kill one of his own large flock.

**2. David's reaction (vv. 5-6).**—The king's indignation was aroused by Nathan's well-told story. In his immediate anger, he said, "The man who has done this deserves to die" (NRSV). David was not passing sentence of death but emphasizing the seriousness of the offense. Then, in a more judicial mood, he fell back on the ancient law of his people, "If a man shall steal an ox or a sheep, and kill it, or sell it; he shall restore five oxen for an ox, and four sheep for a sheep" (Ex. 22:1).

## II. Indictment and Penalty (2 Sam. 12:7-14)

The laws of God do not admit preferential application. There is not a law for the rich, and another for the poor. The prophet's touching story was the basis for a face-to-face accusation of David who, though king, must answer to God for his misconduct.

7 And Nathan said to David, Thou art the man. Thus saith
the Lord God of Israel, I anointed thee king over Israel, and I
delivered thee out of the hand of Saul;
8 And I gave thee thy master's house, and thy master's wives
into thy bosom, and gave thee the house of Israel and of Judah;
and if that had been too little, I would moreover have given

unto thee such and such things.
9 Wherefore hast thou despised the commandment of the
Lord, to do evil in his sight? thou hast killed Uriah the Hittite
with the sword, and hast taken his wife to be thy wife, and hast
slain him with the sword of the children of Ammon.
10 Now therefore the sword shall never depart from thine
house; because thou hast despised me, and hast taken the wife
of Uriah the Hittite to be thy wife.
13 And David said unto Nathan, I have sinned against the
Lord. And Nathan said unto David, The Lord also hath put
away thy sin; thou shalt not die.

**1. Obligations incurred (vv. 7-8).**—Nathan did not mince his words. After David had expressed his wrath against a man who took and killed another's pet lamb, the prophet bluntly charged, "You are the man!" (NRSV). Then, speaking in behalf of God, he reminded David of the gratitude he owed to the Lord whose laws he had broken. Previously, speaking on the same theme, he said, "I took you from the pasture, from following the sheep to be prince over my people Israel" (7:8, NRSV). Picking up from that point, Nathan reminded David how he had been delivered from the hand of Saul and had become that king's successor, with rights to all his property. This included Saul's wives. Verse 8 is not a divine endorsement of polygamy but an acknowledgment of prevailing custom. David had also become king over a united nation, including both Israel and Judah; "and if that had been too little, I would have added as much more" (12:8, NRSV).

**2. David and Bathsheba (v. 9).**—David had been guilty of two serious offenses. The sordid story is recorded in chapter 11. He first committed adultery with a neighbor's wife. He was walking on the flat roof of his palace when he saw Bathsheba bathing herself, also on the flat roof of her home. He inquired who she was and, in full knowledge that she was married, sent for her and gratified his lust. As a result, Bathsheba became pregnant (11:1-5).

**3. David and Uriah (v. 9).**—Bathsheba's husband was a soldier, away from home fighting the Ammonites. In an effort to cover his sin, David ordered Uriah home. But Uriah was such a conscientious soldier that he would not resume relations with his wife while his comrades remained on the field of battle. As a consequence, David had to send Uriah back to his place of duty, but with him he sent a letter to the military commander telling him to put Uriah in the forefront of the battle where he would likely be killed. This evil plan worked, and with Uriah dead, David married Bathsheba (11:6-17,26-27). Such conduct would hardly have occasioned comment if committed by one of the despotic rulers of neighboring nations. But David was God's choice of king over His own covenant people, and better things were expected of him. His dual sins showed that he had "despised the commandment of the Lord" (see Ps. 51:4).

**4. Punishment pronounced (vv. 10-11).**—From this point forward in 2 Samuel we have the record of tragic events in David's family. His chief cause of grief was his son Absalom's intrigues. David was forced to leave his capital (15:14) and eventually take refuge across the Jordan (17:22). There he organized an army which engaged Absalom's men and routed them. Absalom died after being caught by his hair in a tree (18:9,14). David's grief was expressed in bitter weeping (v. 33).

**5. Confession made (vv. 12-14).**—"I have sinned against the Lord." The depth of David's repentance is expressed in Psalms 32 and 51, traditionally associated with this tragic period in David's life. Nathan was able to speak of divine forgiveness, "The Lord also hath put away thy sin." But pardon for wrongs committed does not carry with it escape from the consequences.

## III. Death of Bathsheba's Child (2 Sam. 12:15-23)

The first of many tragedies in David's life was the death of Bathsheba's child. Unhappily, the innocent get caught up in the chain of events that issues from immoral conduct. The emphasis in these verses is on the sorrow of David over the death of this little child. But we should also think of the effect on others, on Bathsheba, for example, who bore the helpless infant. She must have shared David's grief as she also shared in his sin. We might ask whether some blame is attributable to her. Her careless exposure of herself on her roof top started this course of events. The child's death had a message for her, as it did for David, that sinful conduct must bring its unhappy consequences. In the verses we are considering there is also mention of "the elders of his house" and "the servants of David" (vv. 17-18). To these, and to the people as a whole, the king's loss and consequent grief was a lesson not to be ignored. David's statement in verse 23, "I shall go to him, but he shall not return to me," may indicate a special revelation from God concerning a future life, as given also to Job (Job 19:25-27). But in Old Testament times, the prospect of future life was only vaguely perceived, awaiting the coming of Christ who "brought life and immortality to light" (2 Tim. 1:10).

## IV. Birth of Solomon (2 Sam. 12:24-25)

The God who gave the promise to David, "he will make thee an house" (7:11), kept His word. Bathsheba bore a second child who was named Solomon ("peace"). When Nathan learned of this he bestowed his own choice of name on the child, Jedidiah ("beloved of the Lord"). Thus a succession was assured to David and his kingdom was firmly established. For the God of justice is also the God of grace.

## APPLYING THE BIBLE

**Temptation common to all.**—In his book *But God Can*, Robert V.

Ozment wrote: "Temptation is the traveling companion of every person who walks down the corridor of life. It has no regard for custom, race, or heritage. It cuddled up to the rich and the poor. It stands beside the intellectual giant as well as the illiterate; it travels with those who ride in royal coaches and walks with the peasants." Ozment adds that temptation doesn't slight any race or skip any generation that it grabs both the saint and the sinner alike. Anyplace one finds human life, he finds temptation near, Ozment concludes.

How marvelously is this truth pointed out in the experience of David. Look at the sequence:

(1) Saw—2 Samuel 11:2
(2) Sent—2 Samuel 11:3
(3) Sought—2 Samuel 11:4
(4) Sex—2 Samuel 11:4
(5) Sorrow—2 Samuel 11:5,17 (see chap. 12).

**Where sin starts.**—Sin starts in the mind as a temptation. Marcus Aurelius (A.D. 121-180) was one of the five so-called "good emperors" of ancient Rome. He said, "The soul is dyed the color of its thoughts." And he was right. David's terrible sin began with a look and a thought (11:2). John said the same thing in 1 John 2:16 where he speaks about "the lust of the eyes." And Solomon, David's son, said in Proverbs 23:7: "For as he thinketh in his heart, so is he."

**To be or not to be.**—Shakespeare has Macbeth contemplating murder, but it is more than that: it is a vivid description of how temptation can plant a foothold in one's heart:

*Is this a dagger which I see before me,*
*The handle toward my hand? Come, let me clutch thee.*
*I have thee not, and yet I see thee still.*
*Art thou not, fatal vision, sensible*
*To feeling as to sight? or art thou but*
*A dagger of the mind, a false creation*
*Proceeding from the heat-oppressed brain?*
*I see thee yet, in form as palpable*
*As this which now I draw.*

David's "dagger of the mind," as Macbeth called it, was David's downfall. He clutched this dagger of temptation to his bosom and ultimately it was the ruin of Israel's great king.

**"A painful preacher of the truth."**—In an English cathedral there is a tomb in which a preacher of former times is buried. On the tomb is this epitaph: "He was a painful preacher of the truth."

Jean Baptiste Massillon was a preacher often heard by King Louis XIV. Called Louis the Great or the Grand Monarch (1638-1715), King Louis used to say that he enjoyed hearing other preachers but that he never enjoyed Massillon. When asked why, the king said that Massillon seemed to tear King Louis's soul wide open. Yet, the king said, that if he had to select one preacher and hear him only, he would wish that one preacher to be Massillon.

That's the kind of preacher Nathan was. Our lesson today focuses on Nathan the prophet's encounter with King David after the king had murdered Uriah and committed adultery with Uriah's wife, Bathsheba.

Like a gigantic thunderstorm in all of its fury, Nathan rained the divine wrath down on David and brought him to repentance and confession. And, more than anything else, that's what the sinner needs.

**The three hardest words to say.**—The late American evangelist Dwight L. Moody was fond of saying that the three hardest words in the English language to say are the words "I have sinned." But without saying these words from the heart, there is no cleansing from sin.

After Nathan had pointed the divine finger at David, David was overwhelmed by guilt and conviction. In 12:13 David cried out these three most-difficult words to say: "I have sinned." And quickly cleansing came: "The Lord also hath put away thy sin," Nathan replied.

**The divinest thing in man.**—One writer said that the divinest thing in man is repentance. The sin of David was great, but the repentance of David was also great. Some scholars believe that Psalm 51 is David's confession of the sins he had committed against God in having Uriah killed and in committing adultery with Bathsheba. Voltaire, the French infidel, tried to write a profane parody on Psalm 51 but he couldn't do it. He was so overcome by shame as he attempted to do it that he abandoned the foolish project.

## TEACHING THE BIBLE

▶ *Main Idea*: David's sin against God declares that we should always be on guard not to sin against God.

▶ *Suggested Teaching Aim*: To lead adults to describe David's sin against God, and to identify ways they can equip themselves to avoid falling prey to the devil's temptations.

### Introduce the Bible Study

Use "The three hardest words to say" *(Applying the Bible)* to introduce the lesson. Point out that acknowledging that we have sinned is one step we can take to keep from letting Satan destroy us.

Write the Teaching Aim on a chalkboard or a large sheet of paper and read it to the class.

### Search for Biblical Truth

Briefly summarize the introduction to *Studying the Bible*. IN ADVANCE, write the following Scripture references vertically down the left side of a chalkboard or a large sheet of paper: 12:1-4; 12:5-6; 12:7-8; 12:9; 12:10; 12:13. Ask members to open their Bibles to 12:1. If you have six or more people in your class, assign one Scripture reference to each person or group. Ask members to read the assigned passage and suggest a heading for it that summarizes the meaning. (For possible suggestions, see *Studying the Bible*; theirs will not be the same but should be similar.)

As members suggest each heading, ask members to tell what happened in their verses. After each heading use the following DISCUSSION QUESTIONS:

12:1-4: What are some modern examples of prophetic preaching?

12:5-6: What advantage does making restitution have when we commit a sin? How far can restitution go in removing the guilt of our sin?

12:7-8: How obligated are we to behave because of what God has done for us?

12:9: What role did Bathsheba have in the series of events? Who was more responsible, she or David? Why was David's sin wrong?

12:10: Does God always punish us for our sin? Explain.

12:13: What role does confession play in removing our sin?

How far does confession free us from the responsibility and consequences of our sin? How does God use our sin for His glory?

---

**A TEACHING OUTLINE**

*1. Summarize the introduction to Studying the Bible.*
*2. Ask members to suggest headings for Scriptures*
*3. Ask DISCUSSION QUESTIONS.*
*4. Identify ways to avoid temptation.*

---

**Give the Truth a Personal Focus**

Read the last part of the Teaching Aim. If you organized in groups, ask the same groups to identify ways they can equip themselves to avoid falling prey to the devil's temptations.

As members suggest answers, list these on a chalkboard or a large sheet of paper. Ask members to identify at least one suggestion they will practice this week.

IN ADVANCE, provide enough plain envelopes and a blank piece of paper inside the envelope. In the upper left hand corner of each envelope, number the envelopes in pencil. Write lightly so the number can be seen only by a person holding it. Distribute envelopes to members. Ask them (1) to note the small number on the outside, and (2) to write their name and phone number on the piece of paper and seal it in the envelope. Collect the envelopes, shuffle them, and then distribute the envelopes so each person has an envelope. (Be sure no person has his or her original envelope.)

Ask members to take the envelope home UNOPENED and place it in a prominent place where they will see it daily. Each time they see it, they are to pray for the person. Next Saturday, they are to open the envelope, call the person and tell him or her they have been praying for them this week and invite the person to Sunday School.

# Solomon's Glorious Reign

**Basic Passages:** 1 Kings 9:1-9; 10:1-24
**Focal Passages:** 1 Kings 9:1-3; 10:1-7,23-24

Studies in such characters as Saul, David, and Solomon impress us with the fact of human frailty. The best human beings turn out to have feet of clay. Thus our present lesson on "Solomon's Glorious Reign" has to be followed by another with the title, "Solomon Turns from God." The disappointment that comes from the second part of this king's life is the more intense because of the success of his earlier years. The fame of his wisdom and wealth spread throughout the world of his day, bringing Israel to a point of power and prestige that was never exceeded and, unfortunately, soon forfeited. But we can pause in this study to consider the splendor of Solomon's reign and wonder at the transformation of the nation Israel's fortunes in the space of some 400 years. From the mixed multitude that left Egypt after centuries of slavery they became a leading force in the ancient world. It appeared as though the purpose of God for His people were moving toward an early consummation. But disloyalty and apostasy brought progress to a sudden halt, so that God had to follow other plans, which had their realization in Jesus Christ and His eternal kingdom.

**Study Aim:** *To learn that true success does not come from material possessions but from a right attitude toward God*

## STUDYING THE BIBLE

There will be need, as there was last week, to review other passages of Scripture in order to give depth to the assigned verses. For example, in 9:2 there is reference to an appearance of the Lord to Solomon at Gibeon, and we need to know what happened there. It had been the site of a victory by David over the Philistines, mentioned in 2 Samuel 5:25, where Gibeon is called "Geba." The location was some five miles northwest of Jerusalem.

### I. Solomon's Good Beginning (1 Kings 9:2)

The preceding chapter records the dedication of the temple and Solomon's dedicatory prayer. Verses worthy of special note are 8:27-30. Here Solomon appeared at his best, honoring the Lord and interceding for the nation, while "kneeling on his knees with his hands spread up to heaven" (v. 54). This exceptional encounter with God had an earlier counterpart, as 9:2 indicates.

2 That the Lord appeared to Solomon the second time, as he had appeared unto him at Gibeon.

**1. A king's humility (3:7-8).**—Solomon had built an altar to the Lord at Gibeon (v. 4) and had gone there for sacrifice and worship. The Lord appeared to him in a dream, and said, "Ask what I shall give thee" (v. 5). In response, Solomon gave thanks for the mercies shown to David his father, including his own birth. He expressed his inadequacy as king over "a great people," describing himself as "a little child" (v. 7).

**2. Request for wisdom (3:9).**—Solomon was apparently exercised over the responsibility of acting as judge, maybe, even at this stage, feeling his unworthiness to judge others. An example of the kind of case he would have to adjudicate is given in verses 16-28.

**3. Promise of fame (vv. 10-13).**—The Lord was pleased with Solomon's request, for he could have asked for riches and the lives of his enemies. So God granted Solomon the riches for which he had not asked and a worldwide reputation for wisdom.

### II. Building the Temple (1 Kings 9:1,3)

The Lord had promised David that a son born to him would "build an house for my name" (2 Sam. 7:13). The magnificent structure that Solomon produced became known as Solomon's temple and lasted over four hundred years until it was destroyed by the Babylonians.

1 And it came to pass, when Solomon had finished the building of the house of the Lord, and the king's house, and all Solomon's desire which he was pleased to do.

3 And the Lord said unto him, I have heard thy prayer and thy supplication, that thou hast made before me: I have hallowed this house, which thou hast built, to put my name there forever; and mine eyes and mine heart shall be there perpetually.

**1. Construction in progress (6:1; 7:51).**—These two verses mark the beginning and end of temple construction. Something of the magnificence of the temple may be gathered by reading 6:21-22. There is a break in this account in 7:1-13 for a description of Solomon's palace and a house for his Egyptian queen; also "the house of the forest of Lebanon" (v. 2), which was his armory (see 10:16-17), and two other structures, "the Hall of Pillars" and "the Hall of the Throne" (7:6-7, NRSV), an impressive complex of buildings adjacent to the temple.

**2. Temple dedication (8:1-66).**—The early verses of this chapter describe the bringing of the ark of the covenant into its new home on which occasion "the glory of the Lord . . . filled the house of the Lord" (v. 11). Solomon's prayer of dedication is a memorable statement in which the king acknowledged that no building could contain God (v. 27). It was to this prayer that the Lord referred in 9:3, giving His approval to the work by saying, "I have hallowed this house which thou hast built."

### III. Visit of Sheba's Queen (1 Kings 10:1-9)

Indicative of the widespread influence of Solomon and his kingdom was his association with foreign women. Early in his reign he married a daughter of the ruler of Egypt (3:1), a political union that is highly significant since it demonstrated the rise in importance of people who had once been slaves in Egypt. No breach of law was involved since the only prohibition of marriage was concerned with Canaanites. Legends have been woven around the visit of the queen of Sheba that have no basis in recorded fact. The claim that the ruling house of Abyssinia is descended from the union of Solomon and this woman is equally unproven. The probability is that the visit had strictly commercial purposes, specially in view of the costly items mentioned in verses 2 and 10.

> 1 And when the queen of Sheba heard of the fame of Solomon concerning the name of the Lord, she came to prove him with hard questions.
>
> 2 And she came to Jerusalem with a very great train, with camels that bare spices, and very much gold, and precious stones: and when she was come to Solomon, she communed with him of all that was in her heart.
>
> 3 And Solomon told her all her questions: there was not anything hid from the king, which he told her not.
>
> 4 And when the queen of Sheba had seen all Solomon's wisdom, and the house that he had built,
>
> 5 And the meat of his table, and the sitting of his servants, and the attendance of his ministers, and their apparel, and his cupbearers, and his ascent by which he went up unto the house of the Lord; there was no more spirit in her.
>
> 6 And she said to the king, It was a true report that I heard in mine own land of thy acts and of thy wisdom.
>
> 7 Howbeit I believed not the words, until I came, and mine eyes had seen it: and, behold, the half was not told me: thy wisdom and prosperity exceedeth the fame which I heard.

**1. Royal encounter (vv. 1-5).**—Sheba, or "Saba," was located in southwestern Arabia, where a cluster of oil-rich countries are now. The trip to Jerusalem covered some fifteen hundred miles, with camels as the means of transportation. After the custom of the Orient, the queen came to ply Solomon with "hard questions," literally, "riddles." She was accompanied by "a very great train" (v. 2), a royal entourage of great splendor. She also brought with her precious gifts (v. 10), perhaps to form a basis for future trade. Solomon responded by opening up his treasures to the queen and engaging in conversation with her that impressed her with his wisdom. The record states that, as a result, "there was no more spirit in her" (v. 5), literally, the experience took away her breath.

**2. Impressed but not persuaded (vv. 6-9).**—When the fame of

Solomon first reached the ears of the queen of Sheba it was "fame due to the name of the Lord" (v. 1, NRSV). The achievements of the king were associated with the God he worshiped. Probably the splendor of the temple he had built was responsible for much of his worldwide fame. It was a testimony to the relationship between the king and his God. Having satisfied herself that all she had heard was true, the queen said, "Blessed be the Lord your God, who has delighted in you and set you on the throne of Israel! Because the Lord loved Israel forever, he has made you king to execute justice and righteousness" (v. 9, NRSV). She recognized the part that the Lord had played in Solomon's life, but that knowledge did not persuade her that she should worship this mighty God. She returned to Sheba as she had come, a pagan queen, and an example of the tragedy of those who make contact with the truth but fail to respond to it.

### IV. The Royal Splendor (1 Kings 10:14-24)

We do not know when the books of Kings were composed (they were originally a single book), but certainly some hundreds of years after the events described. By then, Israel's glory had considerably dimmed, and there was a natural interest, and pride, in the days gone by. Hence, the detailed description of Solomon's wealth. The "weight of gold" (NRSV) mentioned in verse 14 was estimated to be worth $16 million forty years ago, so its value today would be considerably greater. After further statements on Solomon's splendor (vv. 15-22), we read . . .

> **23 So king Solomon exceeded all the kings of the earth for riches and for wisdom.**
> **24 And all the earth sought to Solomon, to hear his wisdom, which God had put in his heart.**

For the Christian, Old Testament studies should lead our thoughts into the New. Our Lord Jesus Christ made two references to Solomon that merit attention. (1) *Matthew 6:29*. Talking to His disciples, in the Sermon on the Mount, Jesus warned against undue worry over the necessities of life. He pointed to the wild flowers, probably anenomes, prolific in Palestine and rich in color. Of these he said, "That even Solomon in all his glory was not arrayed like one of these." They grow and thrive without any effort on their part because they are the creation of God and He cares for them. (2) *Matthew 12:42*. Reacting to the unresponsiveness of people to Him and His message, Jesus said that such indifference is rebuked by "the queen of the south," who "came from the uttermost parts of the earth to hear the wisdom of Solomon." Then He added concerning Himself, "a greater than Solomon is here." A pagan queen condemns those who, though hearing about Jesus and His gospel, pay no attention to it.

## APPLYING THE BIBLE

**"Ashes, Old Boy—just ashes!"**—"Ian Fleming was the writer of the James Bond stories. Shortly before his death, someone asked Fleming what it was like to be famous. The author replied: 'Well . . . I suppose it was alright for a bit; nice being known in restaurants and having people take notice of you. But now, . . . ashes, Old Boy—just ashes!'"[1]

Solomon's fame has traveled to the ends of the earth and the Queen of Sheba has come to see if all she has heard about this magnificent king is true (1 Kings 10:1). But before his life is over, all Solomon's fame turns to ashes and emptiness. Look at how he sums life up in Ecclesiastes 2:17.

**Reverence and humility.**—In his book *Wellsprings of Wisdom*, Ralph Woods tells about a young piano student who visited the home of Beethoven one summer while vacationing in Europe. She asked the guard for permission to play Beethoven's piano, and was granted permission. After playing only a few bars, she turned to the guard and said, "Do all the great pianists play Beethoven's piano when they visit here?"

The guard replied: "No indeed. All the great pianists have visited here and have viewed Beethoven's piano, but none of them has touched it. They did not feel worthy to do so." Continuing, the guard added: "I have found that all the truly great people are truly humble. Perhaps that is the secret to their greatness."

The humility of King Solomon needs to be understood as a background for this lesson today. (Look at 3:7-8.) But nothing shows it more than verse 9 and Solomon's prayer request. God had told Solomon (v. 5) that He (God) would give Solomon whatever he would ask. Solomon's humility is beautifully pictured in verse 9, where he asks for neither riches nor fame for himself but for "an understanding heart to judge thy people."

At least at the beginning of his reign Solomon had a true humility based on a reverence for God and God's people.

**Solomon builds a temple for God.**—Solomon was the third king of Israel and reigned forty years (*ca.* 1000 B.C.). His greatest accomplishment was the building of Solomon's temple. David, Solomon's father, planned the temple and accumulated great wealth and gifts for the temple, but Solomon was the one who built it. There were three historical temples in succession: Solomon's, Zerubbabel's, and Herod's. Herod's temple was really a rebuilding of Zerubbabel's temple and both are called the"second temple" Solomon's temple was the first temple. David had acquired the temple hill during his reign (2 Sam. 24:18-25). The hill on which the temples were built is identified as Mount Moriah, where Abraham had offered up Isaac (2 Chron. 3:1; Gen. 22:1-14). Today on the place where these three temples stood, is the Moslem Dome of the Rock. A brief glimpse at Solomon's temple reveals it was shaped as a "long house" with three successive rooms from east to west. It had a vestibule fifteen feet deep, the holy place which was sixty feet long and the most holy place which was thirty feet long (1 Kings 6:2-3,16-17). It was about thirty-feet wide and forty five-feet high on the inside. This does not count the porch and entryway. The inside was paneled with cedar, floored with cypress, and inlaid with gold throughout. Inside the most holy place, which was a windowless fifteen-foot cube, was the ark of the covenant dominated by two guardian cherubim. They were fifteen feet tall with outstretched wings spanning fifteen feet and touching each side wall (1 Kings 6:15-28). Solomon's temple was destroyed by the Babylonians in 586 B.C.[2]

**Longest prayer in the Bible.**—Solomon's prayer on the occasion of the dedication of the temple (8:12-61) is, so far as I know, the longest prayer in the Bible. It is a magnificent expression of humility, faith, and gratitude and humbly asks God for His blessings to be upon His people. Solomon's prayer to God was heard and answered.

## TEACHING THE BIBLE

▶ *Main Idea:* Solomon's glorious reign demonstrates that true success does not come from material possessions but from a right attitude toward God.

▶ *Suggested Teaching Aim:* To lead adults to examine Solomon's glorious reign and to list reasons why true success comes from a right attitude toward God, not from material possessions.

---

### A TEACHING OUTLINE

1. *Organize the class in groups of three to four people.*
2. *To examine the focal passage, make creative writing assignments.*
3. *To apply the lesson, read and react to a case study.*

---

**Introduce the Bible Study**

IN ADVANCE arrange the chairs in groups of three to four. Write the following assignments on a piece of paper and place them on the floor in the center of each group of chairs: *Material wealth is (not) a blessing from God.* Make half of the assignments positive and the other half negative. Instruct the groups to list why they agree or disagree with their assignment.

As members arrive, ask them to sit in one of the groups. They should begin discussion as soon as the group is complete. After a brief time, ask groups to report.

Point out that today's lesson examines "Solomon's Glorious Reign." On a map of Solomon's time locate Gibeon [GIB ih uhn] and Sheba [SHEE bah]. Using *Studying the Bible,* explain the significance of these two places.

**Search for Biblical Truth**

Distribute paper and pencils for members to use in a creative writing assignment based on 1 Kings 9:1-3; 10:1-7,23-24. Write the following assignment on a chalkboard or a large sheet of paper.

1. Imagine you are Solomon and the Lord has just appeared to you and told you that He has accepted the temple you have built. What are your feelings at this point?

2. Imagine you are the queen of Sheba. What are your feelings about Solomon's situation and especially his worship of Yahweh?

3. Imagine you are a resident of Jerusalem during the height of Solomon's reign. What are your feelings about why all this has happened?

Instruct members to select an assignment from the list. Their report should reflect the biblical text but encourage them to imagine what the people were *feeling* in this situation.

Call for volunteers to read their reports. Ask: What evidence indicates that Solomon believed his success came from God?

**Give the Truth a Personal Focus**

Ask: What would you have done if you had been Solomon? What have you done with what and who you are?

Read the following case study: Carole had determined as a little girl that she was not going to be poor when she grew up. She became an overachiever. Everything she did, she did well. She became ruthless in the pursuit of her goals. By the time she was thirty, she had become a successful businesswoman and moved in the best circles with the right people. One day she met Judy, who was just as successful as Carole, but she seemed kind and appeared to care genuinely about Carole. Finally Carole asked Judy what made her the way she was. Judy replied that long ago she had learned that true success came from a right attitude toward God, not from an attempt to gain material possessions. Carole's response was that God had nothing to do with her life; she had gained her success all on her own. If you were Judy, how would you respond to Carole?

Allow opportunity for members to discuss what Judy could say. Then ask if they would agree with this statement: *No person is successful if that person leaves God out of his or her life.*

---

1. Robert J. Dean, *God's Big Little Words* (Nashville: Broadman Press, 1975), 18-19.
2. *Holman's Bible Dictionary* (Nashville: Holman Bible Publishers, 1991), 1325-30.

# Solomon Turns from God

**Basic Passage:** 1 Kings 11
**Focal Passage:** 1 Kings 11:1-13

There are no cover-ups in Bible biographies. Under the guidance of the Holy Spirit, biblical writers told the truth about their characters, even the best of them, though the truth was often embarrassing. This honest reporting begins with the first two humans, Adam and Eve, and continues through their descendants. Of course, God could have made us immune to the pressures of evil, robot-like beings with no power of choice and no susceptibility to sin. But He chose to make us like Himself in that we can determine what we will do and not do, and He did this at great risk to Himself. When the human race took the downward path, it became necessary for Him to send His Son to rescue us and forfeit His life in so doing. Solomon was a great man who honored the Lord in much of his activity. The temple he built caused the name of Yahweh to be known the world around. The proverbs he collected provided moral and spiritual guidance for millions of people. But he succumbed to "the lust of the flesh, and the lust of the eyes, and the pride of life" (1 John 2:16). Once again, a floodlight is focused on a danger sign that we ignore at our peril.

**Study Aim:** *To beware of the potential for disaster in ungodly associations*

## STUDYING THE BIBLE

The regal splendor that Solomon cultivated (see previous lesson) was to be a source of trouble for him and his kingdom. He took as his model the rulers of pagan nations and exceeded them in extravagance and lifestyle. After chapters that record his better qualities, chapter 11 begins to unfold the darker side of his character.

### I. Tolerance Leads to Apostasy (1 Kings 11:1-8)

As previously noted, Solomon's marriage to an Egyptian princess violated no Hebrew law. But as the years passed, he built up a huge harem of "many foreign women (v. 1, NRSV), some of whom came under the designation of Canaanites, and he made these unions in disregard of the prohibition and warning of such passages as Deuteronomy 7:1-4.

**1 But King Solomon loved many strange women, together with the daughter of Pharaoh, women of the Moabites,**

Ammonites, Edomites, Sidonians, and Hittites;
2 Of the nations concerning which the Lord said unto the
children of Israel, Ye shall not go in to them, neither shall they
come in unto you: for surely they will turn away your heart after
their gods: Solomon clave unto these in love.
3 And he had seven hundred wives, princesses, and three
hundred concubines: and his wives turned away his heart.
4 For it came to pass, when Solomon was old, that his wives
turned away his heart after other gods: and his heart was not
perfect with the Lord his God, as was the heart of David his
father.
5 For Solomon went after Ashtoreth the goddess of the
Sidonians, and after Milcom the abomination of the
Ammonites.
6 And Solomon did evil in the sight of the Lord, and went not
fully after the Lord, as did David his father.
7 Then did Solomon build an high place for Chemosh, the
abomination of Moab, in the hill that is before Jerusalem, and
for Molech, the abomination of the children of Ammon.
8 And likewise did he for all his strange wives, which burnt
incense and sacrificed unto their gods.

**1. Forbidden marriages (vv. 1-3).**—Some commentators see these multiple marriages as evidence of Solomon's diplomatic skills, whereby he established good relationship with other countries. Doubtless they were this, but they are also evidence of his insatiable lust. The statements that he "loved many foreign women" and "clung to these in love" (vv. 1,2, NRSV) indicate fleshly indulgence on a large scale. In addition to these wives he is stated to have had "three hundred concubines," enslaved women retained largely for sexual gratification. The devil uses basic human urges to lead the unwary into sin, with its varied penalties. Wealth and power too often produce undisciplined living, as history has repeatedly shown.

**2. Idolatrous influences (vv. 4-8).**—To please his pagan wives, Solomon provided them with shrines to the deities they worshiped. The repeated word "abomination" describes anything that is loathsome and repugnant to God. Here it is applied to objects associated with idolatry and heathen deities. *Ashtoreth* (or Astarte) was a goddess of fertility, consort of Baal. *Milcom* (or Molech) was a god of war in whose worship children were sacrificed. *Chemosh* was a similar deity worshiped by the Moabites. Solomon first displayed tolerance toward these false and evil deities, but tolerance led him to accompany his wives in their pagan worship. That he erected shrines near Jerusalem (v. 7) was an open affront to the Lord God of the temple there.

## II. Judgment and Mercy (1 Kings 11:9-13)

Solomon had enjoyed special revelations from God and these

added to the guilt of his apostasy. Special privilege brings special responsibility, and this applies not only to kings but to all who have enjoyed fellowship with the Lord. There is a solemn statement in the New Testament, "For the time is come that judgment must begin at the house of God" (1 Pet. 4:17), a reminder to us as Christians that divine justice cannot ignore the disloyalties of those who profess God's name.

**9 And the Lord was angry with Solomon, because his heart was turned from the Lord God of Israel, which had appeared unto him twice.**

**10 And he commanded him concerning this thing, that he should not go after other gods: but he kept not that which the Lord commanded.**

**11 Wherefore the Lord said unto Solomon, Forasmuch as this is done of thee, and thou hast not kept my covenant and my statutes, which I have commanded thee, I will surely rend the kingdom from thee, and will give it to thy servant.**

**12 Notwithstanding in thy days I will not do it for David thy father's sake; but I will rend it out of the hand of thy son.**

**13 Howbeit I will not rend away all the kingdom; but will give one tribe to thy son for David my servant's sake, and for Jerusalem's sake which I have chosen.**

**1. Revelation disregarded (vv. 9-10).**—In these studies we have noted two special appearances of the Lord to Solomon (3:5 and 9:2). Normally the communication would be through prophets, as with David and Nathan. But these occasions in Solomon's life indicate a direct communication, and in both cases Solomon's response was to his credit. But such high spiritual experiences imposed a heavy responsibility that the king failed to meet, particularly in that he committed the very evils concerning which he had been warned (9:3-4).

**2. Prophesied penalties (vv. 11-13).**—The warning given in 9:7 was that if Solomon should turn from God to idols, "Then will I cut off Israel out of the land which I have given them." This drastic penalty was mercifully suspended, but Solomon was told, "I will surely rend the kingdom from thee" (11:11). However, "for David my servant's sake, and for Jerusalem's sake" (v. 13) one tribe would remain loyal to Solomon when, during his son's reign, revolt would split the kingdom. So it happened when Rehoboam succeeded his father on the throne (chap. 12).

## III. Rise of Jeroboam (1 Kings 11:26-30)

With the whole of chapter 11 assigned as basic study material, we should acquaint ourselves with facts concerning the breakup of Solomon's kingdom. It began with rebellions in two neighboring territories that had been conquered by David and brought under his rule. The first of these was Edom, southeast of the Dead Sea (vv. 14-22), whose king had taken refuge in Egypt, from which he returned to Edom at the news of David's death. The second disturbance took place to the north, in Syria, led by a man named Rezon (vv. 23-25). The most serious threat, however, came from within Israel. Jeroboam was an aspiring young man who Solomon put in "charge over all the forced labor of the house of Joseph" (v. 28, NRSV). For plotting against Solomon, he was caused to flee the country and seek refuge in Egypt. On the king's death, he returned and led the revolt of ten tribes which became the Northern Kingdom of Israel (12:16-20).

**1. Cause for grievance (vv. 26-28).**—The revised translation of verse 28 (see above) introduces one of the grievances of the people against Solomon, namely, forced labor. Although in 9:22 we find the statement that "of the children of Israel did Solomon make no bondmen," this must have been limited to the occasion described. The complaint of Jeroboam was against "the grievous service" and "heavy yoke" imposed on the people by Solomon, a situation that Rehoboam, Solomon's son, threatened to intensify (12:11). We may be reminded of the warning, given by Samuel when the people first asked for a king, concerning the unreasonable demands that he would impose (1 Sam. 8:10-18).

**2. Events foretold (vv. 29-40).**—A prophet named Ahijah met Jeroboam and dramatized coming events. He was wearing a new garment which he tore into twelve pieces, giving ten of these to Jeroboam, and saying, "Behold, I will rend the kingdom out of the hand of Solomon, and will give ten tribes to thee" (v. 31). This is a striking example of prophetic method that combined both word and action. The departure of the ten tribes to form the new Northern Kingdom left two with Rehoboam, Judah and Benjamin. The latter's territory adjoined Judah on the north, and was small in area. The tribe of Benjamin waffled in its allegiance to Judah, for which reason, perhaps, it is infrequently mentioned, although ultimately it remained loyal to the Southern Kingdom. In Ahijah's prophecy only one tribe is mentioned as left to Rehoboam, Solomon's son and heir (vv. 32,36). To Jeroboam, who was to become ruler of the new Kingdom of Israel was given the same promise, conditional on his obedience, as was given to David: "I will be with thee, and build thee a sure house, as I built for David, and will give Israel unto thee" (v. 38). Unhappily, Jeroboam and his successors failed to meet the conditions so that the Northern Kingdom was first to go into captivity.

## IV. Death of Solomon (1 Kings 11:41-43)

This death notice is interesting for its reference to"the book of the acts of Solomon," reminding us that the biblical writers had sources of information available to them that are lost to us. The forty-years reign of David's son began with great promise, and achieved unparalleled heights of prosperity. But it was quickly followed by the tragedy of a divided kingdom, the penalty for disloyalty to God, spelled out by Ahijah, "Because . . . they have forsaken me . . . and have not walked in my ways, to do that which is right in mine eyes, and to keep my statutes and my judgments" (v. 33).

## APPLYING THE BIBLE

**Two laws that govern marriage.**—William M. Taylor, in his book *Ruth the Gleaner and Esther the Queen*, says there are two laws that ought to govern marriage: the first is the law of nature—don't marry one you do not love; and the second is the law of grace—do not marry one who does not love Jesus.

If Solomon had obeyed the laws of nature and of grace, he would not have brought so much suffering upon himself and his nation. But King Solomon ignored these laws and "loved many strange women . . . and he had seven hundred wives, princesses, and three hundred concubines: and his wives turned away his heart" (1 Kings 11:1,3).

Young people today ought to be guided in considering marriage by the laws of nature and grace. And especially they ought to heed Paul's admonition in 2 Corinthians 6:14: "Be ye not unequally yoked together with unbelievers: for what fellowship hath righteousness with unrighteousness? and what communion hath light with darkness?" To ignore that warning is to invite tragedy and unbelievable heartache.

**Mark Twain's attitude affects his wife.**—Olivia Langdon was a believer. Her faith was simple and she was a devout Christian. When she married Mark Twain they read a chapter from the Bible every day and had grace at meals, but soon this was abandoned. Twain, it seems, was not much of a believer, if at all. Olivia gave up some of her religious convictions, she said, as time went along. She traveled across Europe with her husband and listened to his friends who had forsaken what faith they had in God. When sorrow struck their home—three of their children died—he said to his wife, "Livy, if it comforts you to lean on the Christian faith do so." Her pet name for Twain was "Youth," and she replied,"I can't, Youth; I haven't any."

It was Solomon's lust for and association with these hundreds of wives and concubines—many of whom were pagan—that turned Solomon's heart away from God (11:3-4) as Twain turned his wife away from God.

**Ears that could not hear.**—Heinrich Heine (1797-1856), one of Germany's greatest poets, tells about being in Paris during the revolution. Weary, unbelieving, almost helpless in his endeavors to escape the rampant horror, he entered a room filled with art treasures and fell down before the small *Venus de Milo*. Heine said he looked up imploring at its symmetrical beauty but saw that its ears were marble and could not hear his supplication, and its arms were broken off and could not reach down to his aid. Its heart was stone and could not feel, and its eyes were empty and could not see.[1] She was adored and praised as a goddess, but Venus de Milo was a goddess that could not respond to Heine's needs.

Not so with Solomon and his relationship with God! First Kings 11:9 says, "The Lord was angry with Solomon, because his heart was turned from the Lord God of Israel." Solomon's sins had caused God to turn His face away so that He would not hear.

**Sin will find us out.**—Gill Laine, writing in *Proclaim* magazine, told about a salesman who was waiting in the office of a prospective customer to submit his company's bid on a job. He was the only one in the room, and as he looked at the secretary's desk he noticed a competitor's bid for the job. But he couldn't see the amount of the bid because a can of juice on the table covered the figures. What did he do? You guessed it. He picked up the can in order to see the bid, and perhaps refigure his bid, and when he did thousands of B.B's poured from the bottomless can and spilled across the floor.[2]

The Bible minces no words about our sins finding us out, as the salesman quickly discovered: "Be sure your sin will find you out" (Num. 32:23).

Solomon's sins found him out, and he and the nation paid a terrible price. We're told about this in 1 Kings 11:11: "Wherefore the Lord said unto Solomon, Forasmuch as this is done of thee, and thou hast not kept my covenant and my statutes, which I commanded thee, I will surely rend the kingdom from thee, and will give it to thy servant."

**The greatness of God's mercy.**—Charles Haddon Spurgeon, said, "The greatness of one's sins demands the greatness of God's mercy." And English preacher Richard Baxter declared, "O Lord, it must be great mercy or no mercy, for little mercy is of no use to me."

Mercy—great and abundant—was extended Solomon (11:11-13) but his sin still exacted an awful price, as it always does.

## TEACHING THE BIBLE

▶ *Main Idea*: Solomon's turning from God demonstrates the potential for disaster in ungodly associations.

▶ *Suggested Teaching Aim*: To lead adults to examine what caused Solomon to turn from God, and to identify practices and relationships in their life that have the potential for leading them astray.

### A TEACHING OUTLINE

1. *Examine the potential in relationships.*
2. *Present a panel to examine the focal passage.*
3. *To apply the lesson, each member will examine five significant relationships.*

**Introduce the Bible Study**

IN ADVANCE write at the top of a large sheet of paper: *Every human relationship has the potential for disaster*. Leave most of the paper blank but write across the bottom: *Every human relationship has the potential for blessing*. Place this sheet on a wall and ask members to suggest kinds of relationships that could end in disaster. Write their responses in the center of the paper. Read the first statement and ask why they would agree or disagree. Call attention to the second statement. Ask, Why do you agree or disagree with this statement?

Point out that Solomon could have influenced his wives for good; instead, he let them lead him away from God.

**Search for Biblical Truth**

IN ADVANCE enlist four panelists to lead the Bible study by making a two- to three-minute report to the class.

**Panelist 1**: Review how Solomon was led into apostasy by entering into marriages prohibited by the law. Base your report on 1 Kings 11:1-3 and other sources.

**Panelist 2**: Review the idolatrous influences that helped to lead Solomon into apostasy. Base your report on 1 Kings 11:4-8. Explain *abomination* and briefly describe each of the pagan deities mentioned in these verses.

**Panelist 3**: Review why Solomon's turning from God was so open. Base your report on 1 Kings 11:9-10. Explore why Solomon disregarded the two special revelations from God.

**Panelist 4**: Review God's judgment and mercy for Solomon based on 1 Kings 11:11-13 and other sources. Explain why God granted this reprieve; explain also how Solomon's actions would affect his son.

Seat the panelists at the front of the room facing the members. Call on the panelists to present their reports.

After panelists have finished, allow volunteers to tell panelists what they heard in the reports. Suggest each person mention only one idea until all have had an opportunity to respond. Add any points not mentioned.

**Give the Truth a Personal Focus**

Distribute paper and pencils. Ask them to list the five most important human relationships in their life.

On a chalkboard or a large sheet of paper write: *Parents, Children, Spouse, Friends.* Ask: How can these relationships bring disaster? What can we do to keep the relationships from creating disaster in our lives?

Asks members to look at the five most important relationships they listed. Based on these relationships, ask them to respond silently to these questions: Is any one of these relationships coming between you and God? Do you love any one of these five people more than you love God? Does any one of these relationships need to be changed so it does not bring disaster in your life? What steps can you take to control the relationship rather than letting it control you?

Provide some time for meditation and contemplation. Then close by singing or reading the words to "Have Thine Own Way, Lord" (No. 294, *The Baptist Hymnal,* 1991).

---

1. Adapted from R. C. Campbell, *Keeping the Foundation* (Nashville: Broadman Press, 1948), 19.

2. Adapted from Gill Laine, *Proclaim* magazine (which appeared in "All in a Day's Work" *Readers Digest*: Jan. 1983), 150.

# Jesus the Fulfillment

**Books from BROADMAN & HOLMAN for Study and Teaching**

*Holman Bible Dictionary,* Trent C. Butler, ed.
*The Broadman Bible Commentary,* Volume 8
*Layman's Bible Book Commentary,* Volume 15
*The New American Commentary,* Volume 22
*The Teacher's Bible Commentary,* Paschall and Hobbs, eds.
*Holman Bible Handbook,* David S. Dockery, ed.
*Atlas of the Bible Lands,* Harry Thomas Frank, ed.

## INTRODUCTION

For the next three months, we will study the Gospel of Matthew under the title, "Jesus the Fulfillment." Our study focuses on Jesus Christ as the fulfillment of the Old Testament promises. How Jesus lived the Old Testament message and how different people responded to Him will be highlighted throughout the study.

**Unit I** is about "Jesus and John: Setting the Scene." John the Baptist is featured as the herald of Jesus and the kingdom.

**Unit II** is about the birth of Jesus and how He was received by different people under the title, "Emmanuel: God with Us."

**Unit III** studies the main part of Jesus' earthly life under "Jesus: The Son of David."

**Unit IV**, "Jesus Christ: Victor over Sin and Death," brings the study of the life and ministry of Jesus to its climax. Our study closes with Jesus' commission to make disciples of all people.

December
4
1994

# John Heralds Jesus' Coming

**Basic Passage:** Matthew 3
**Focal Passage:** Matthew 3:1-15

Matthew's Gospel is often referred to as "The Gospel of the Kingdom." It was primarily (though not exclusively) addressed to Jews of the first century, descendants of people who had suffered disappointment, even disaster, as the result of misrule by earthly rulers. Our previous quarter's studies have been preparation for the announcement of a new beginning and the proclamation of a new kingdom under the rule of God whose new King is a suffering Savior, the Lord Jesus Christ. He came of David's line (1:1) to fulfill the ancient promise of a kingdom that would know no end (2 Sam. 7:16). As local merchants have been reminding us, Christmas is only so many days away. For this reason, we will postpone the story of Christ's birth as recorded in the opening chapters of Matthew's Gospel. But it is appropriate to remind ourselves now that He was born in Bethlehem, as was David, establishing another link with the promises of the Old Testament and their fulfillment in the New.

**Study Aim:** *To invite Jew and Gentile alike into the kingdom of our Lord and Savior Jesus Christ*

## STUDYING THE BIBLE

Though first in order in the New Testament, Matthew's Gospel probably was not first to be written. It was preceded by Mark's Gospel, but was given first place because it begins with a genealogy of Jesus that traces His descent from Abraham and through David. It is a distinctively Jewish piece of writing, with the purpose of presenting Jesus as the Messiah-King.

### I. Kingdom Messenger (Matt. 3:1-5)

In chapter 3, John the Baptist bursts upon the Palestine scene like a resurrected Elijah, after 400 years of prophetic silence. Actually, he had been set apart for his ministry from his conception as the child of Zacharias, an aged priest, and his wife Elisabeth (Luke 1:5-17).

**1 In those days came John the Baptist, preaching in the wilderness of Judea,**

**2 And saying, Repent ye: for the kingdom of heaven is at hand.**

**3 For this is he that was spoken of by the prophet Isaiah, saying, The voice of one crying in the wilderness, Prepare ye the way of the Lord, make his paths straight.**

4 And the same John had his raiment of camel's hair, and a
leathern girdle about his loins; and his meat was locusts and
wild honey.
5 Then went out to him Jerusalem, and all Judea, and all the
region round about Jordan,
6 And were baptized of him in Jordan, confessing their sins.

**1. John's preaching (vv. 1-6).**—In lifestyle and message, John fulfilled the role of an Old Testament prophet. His home was the wilderness; and he dressed accordingly, obtaining his food from his natural surroundings, insects and honey. Moreover, he laid claim to Old Testament authority, citing Isaiah 40:3 for his credentials. The figure used was common in the East where heralds would proclaim the coming of an important person, and gangs would repair the road he was taking. Both Isaiah's and John's reference, of course, was to the Messiah of Israel, who came in the person of Jesus Christ.

**2. Popular response (vv. 5-6).**—Prevailing conditions among the Jews assured attention to John's message. National fortunes were at a very low ebb, for a proud people was subject to the authority of Rome. Everywhere were signs of their subjection, from the presence of foreign soldiers to the circulation of Roman currency (22:16-22). John's message, therefore, was good news for he talked of "the kingdom of heaven," the sovereign rule of God. This was "at hand" (v. 2), a promise of early deliverance from foreign bondage and a restoration (as was supposed) of lost national prestige. He called for personal readiness for this great event in the confession of sin. Many Jews responded, and submitted to the rite of baptism, then recognized as the sign of a change of life and a new beginning.

## II. Stern Reproof (Matt. 3:7-9)

The motivation of some people who came to John for baptism was seen by him to be entirely wrong. He accused some religious leaders of being like a "brood of vipers" (v. 7, NRSV). When a grass fire occurred, snakes nesting in the grass would make a hurried escape. This was the figure John used, implying that these Pharisees and Sadducees were not committing themselves to his message but merely seeking to avoid the coming judgment.

7 But when he saw many of the Pharisees and Sadducees
come to his baptism, he said unto them, O generation of vipers,
who hath warned you to flee from the wrath to come?
8 Bring forth therefore fruits meet for repentance:
9 And think not to say within yourselves, We have Abraham
to our father: for I say unto you, that God is able of these stones
to raise up children unto Abraham.

**1. Proof of repentance (vv. 7-8).**—It is not enough to say, "I am sorry for my sins." Repentance must be accompanied by a change of heart and transformed behavior. Those who came to John for baptism could do this in a spirit of self-righteousness, using the rite to make public display of their goodness. Pharisees particularly were known for their religious performances at public places, in order to impress others (6:1-5). Baptism, as a symbol of repentance, must be followed by "fruits," that is, conduct that proves a change of direction in life. Christian baptism (see below) requires that "we also should walk in the newness of life" (Rom. 6:4).

**2. False confidence (v. 9).**—Matthew, who wrote this Gospel, had Jewish readers in mind when he recorded this false confidence based on racial descent. To be descended from Abraham, many believed, was to be included in the blessings promised to Abraham, to possess an insurance policy for life and the hereafter. Not so, said John, for God could, and would, break down this exclusiveness by creating children of Abraham from most unlikely material, Gentiles, for example, who, by faith, could become part of the covenant of grace (Rom. 4:16). The apostle Paul, who was Christ's messenger to the Gentile world, developed this theme.

### III. Another Baptism (Matt. 3:10-12)

Two subjects are in these verses, with the idea of judgment running through them. In presenting them, John made a comparison between himself and the Lord Jesus that is particularly impressive when we remember that the two were related through their mothers, and that John was first to be born (Luke 1:36). In another place, the Baptist bore testimony to the preexistence of Christ when he said of Him, "he was before me" (John 1:15).

> **10 And now also the ax is laid unto the root of the trees: therefore every tree which bringeth not forth good fruit is hewn down, and cast into the fire.**
>
> **11 I indeed baptize you with water unto repentance: but he that cometh after me is mightier than I, whose shoes I am not worthy to bear: he shall baptize you with the Holy Ghost, and with fire:**
>
> **12 Whose fan is in his hand, and he will thoroughly purge his floor, and gather his wheat into the garner; but he will burn up the chaff with unquenchable fire.**

**1. The Holy Spirit (v. 11).**—Fire is often a symbol of Deity in Scripture and, on the day of Pentecost, was associated with the descent of the Holy Spirit (Acts 2:3). Here the context requires that we associate it with divine judgment. The promised Messiah would not only bring deliverance but also judgment. In stating this, John magnified Christ in the superior nature of the baptism he would introduce. Instead of a baptism that only signified repentance from sin, Christian baptism would bring a new beginning made possible by the power of the Holy Spirit. The believer in Christ would receive the Holy

Spirit to be an inward, continuous source of enabling. "But ye shall receive power, after that the Holy Ghost is come upon you" (Acts 1:8).

**2. Coming judgment (vv. 10, 12).**—The two figures of felled trees and winnowed grain would be familiar to John's listeners. He was still addressing Pharisees and Sadducees, who as religious leaders can be considered as representatives of the nation. The long-anticipated Messiah would execute judgment between good and bad fruit (v. 10) and wheat and chaff (v. 12). This would be a discriminating judgment, for that which was wholesome would survive: He "will gather his wheat into the granary" (v. 12, NRSV). The preaching of the gospel would be the great divider, separating believer and unbeliever.

## IV. Affirmation from heaven (Matt. 3:13-17)

Jesus' request for baptism puzzled John, and needs explanation for us. All four Gospels record Jesus' baptism, but Matthew shows concern to make clear that it took place over John's protest, and the acknowledgment of his inferiority to Jesus. This may have been to correct a later movement that magnified the importance of John.

> 13 Then cometh Jesus from Galilee to Jordan unto John, to be baptized of him.
> 14 But John forbade him, saying, I have need to be baptized of thee, and comest thou to me?
> 15 And Jesus answering said unto him, Suffer it to be so now: for thus it becometh us to fulfill all righteousness. Then he suffered him.

**1. Jesus' baptism (vv. 13-15).**—"Let it be so now; for it is proper for us in this way to fulfill all righteousness" (v. 15, NRSV). By accepting baptism at John's hands, our Lord did two things: He affirmed the ministry of John the Baptist and explained His own ministry by identifying with sinners. Though sinless, He would later take upon Himself the sins of the world as He died for us on the cross.

**2. Voice of the Father (vv. 16-17).**—The empowerment of Jesus was illustrated by the descent of the dove and the authority of Jesus was established by the voice from heaven. The Father expressed pleasure in Him and in what He was doing. At the outset of His public ministry, He humbled Himself in baptism and committed Himself to the task given Him by the Father to fulfill the role of the Suffering Servant, who is also Messiah-King, a dual role that has confused some but brings joy and confidence to those who believe in Him.

## APPLYING THE BIBLE

**"In those days came John the Baptist preaching."**—Richard Baxter, the noted seventeenth century English preacher, wrote: "I have preached as never sure to preach again, and as a dying man to dying men."

Robert Murray McCheyne, the young Scottish preacher who died at thirty, said a preacher should never preach on everlasting punishment without tears.

In an English cathedral there is a tomb in which reposes the body of a preacher of earlier times. On the tomb is his epitaph: "He was a painful preacher of the truth."

John the Baptist was a painful preacher of the truth, and for that Herod beheaded John. This cousin of Jesus was a magnificent example of what preachers and preaching ought to be.

**"Cheap preaching."**—The late Vance Havner once said: "There is a lot of cheap preaching going around over the country. I heard of a preacher some years ago when haircuts were selling for 50 cents who had a barber in the crowd who said, 'I'll cut your hair for nothing. I'll take it out in preaching.' The preacher said, 'Well, I'll have you know that I don't preach any 50-cent sermons!' And the barber said, 'That's all right. I'll come several times.'"

John the Baptist did no "cheap" preaching. His message was "Repent! Repent! Repent!" And that's the costliest kind of preaching there is!

**The hardships that make us.**—Beethoven, deaf at forty-two, listened to melodies in his quiet mind and wrote deathless music. Blind John Milton dictated to one of his daughters and wrote literature that will never die. Pasteur, the father of modern medicine, had a stroke at forty-six and was handicapped for life. But we owe a great debt to this French chemist who was made by hardship.

The hardship of prison produced: Daniel Defoe's, *Robinson Crusoe;* John Bunyan's, *The Pilgrims Progress;* Sir Walter Raleigh's, *History of the World;* and Martin Luther's translation of the Bible.

John the Baptist too, was prepared for his preaching by hardships and a strenuous life. Descriptive of his hardships is the sentence, he was clothed with "camel's hair, and [had] a leathern girdle about his loins; and his meat was locusts and wild honey" (3:4). But these tough times and divine disciplines prepared John for his work!

God had only one Son without sin, but He has no sons and daughters without sorrows and hardships. They are the stuff out of which character is made.

**God wants fruit.**—Harry Emerson Fosdick once told about a friend who visited an apple grower in Maine. The visitor observed that the trees were heavily loaded with fruit and all the lower branches were propped up with sticks to keep the apples off the ground. When he looked at the trunk of the tree, he was astounded to discover that the tree had been badly cut and wounded with deep gashes.

"That is something we have learned about apple trees," the owner of the orchard said. "When the trees tend to run to wood and leaves and not to fruit, we gash it and cut it and all of its energies are then turned to fruit. We don't know why it happens, but it does," he said.

According to verse 8, John told the Pharisees and Sadducees to "bring forth therefore fruits meet for repentance." To say that one has repented is not sufficient. God says, "Give me the proof." And the proof is in the fruit we bear.

**Getting rid of the blemishes.**—Before his death, Dr. J. Earl Mead was the "dean" of Southern Baptist ministers of education. In his book *With God in the Heights,* Mead tells about having heard Dr. T. W. Ayres, the first Southern Baptist medical missionary.

Dr. Ayres told about an old Chinese woman who came to see him about a large growth on her head. When Dr. Ayres asked, "Does it hurt?" she replied, "No." "Is it growing?" Ayres asked. "No," the lady replied. Then, Ayres asked, "Why then do you want to have it removed?" And the elderly saint replied: "I'm getting old, and I'm going to meet Jesus soon. I don't want Him to see me with this blemish."

Sin is a blemish on the soul and life of the sinner, and the only way to get rid of that blemish is to deal with it. And the only way to deal with it is to confess it and forsake it (v. 6). Of course, this confession also involves repentance from the sin and faith in the Savior.

## TEACHING THE BIBLE

▶ *Main Idea:* John's heralding of Jesus' coming demonstrates that Jesus invites Jews and Gentiles alike into His kingdom.
▶ *Suggested Teaching Aim:* To lead adults to examine how John heralded Jesus' coming, and to accept Jesus' invitation into His kingdom.

### Introduce the Bible Study

Use the illustration "Cheap preaching" (*Applying the Bible*) to introduce the lesson.

### Search for Biblical Truth

IN ADVANCE, enlist a reader who will read Matthew 3:1-15 aloud. You may want to use a modern translation. Prepare and distribute the following study guide to each member (without italicized answers):

1. What Old Testament authority did John the Baptist claim? *(See Isa. 40:3.)*
2. Why did a "kingdom of heaven" sound like such good news to the Jews of the first century A.D.? *(Many thought it would be deliverance from Roman oppression.)*
3. What symbol did John demand and why was it appropriate? *(The people saw baptism as a sign of a changed life.)*
4. With what did John link baptism to prove that repentance was real? *(Conduct that proved a changed life.)*
5. Why was descent from Abraham not sufficient to enter the kingdom? *(God could raise children from stone.)*
6. In addition to deliverance, what would the promised Messiah bring? *(Fire of judgment.)*

7. How does Christian baptism differ from John's baptism? *(Christian baptism would bring a beginning made possible by the power of the Holy Spirit.)*

8. What two figures of speech did John use to describe the judgment? *(Felled trees and winnowed grain)*

9. What did Jesus declare by being baptized by John? *(He affirmed John's ministry and explained His own ministry by identifying with sinners.)*

10. How did Jesus' baptism point to His death on the cross? *(Though sinless, He would later take on Himself the sins of the world as He died on the cross.)*

---

## A TEACHING OUTLINE

*1. Introduce the unit.*
*2. Use a study guide to guide readers through the Focal Passages.*
*3. Use a creative writing assignment to apply the lesson to members' lives.*

---

Ask members to answer questions 1, 2, and 3.

Call for the reader to read Matthew 3:7-9. Ask members to answer questions 4 and 5.

Call for the reader to read Matthew 3:10-12. Ask members to answer questions 6, 7, and 8.

Call for the reader to read Matthew 3:13-15. Ask members to answer questions 9 and 10.

**Give the Truth a Personal Focus**

Distribute sheets of paper and pencils to all members. Ask them to participate in a creative writing activity. Organize members in four groups. (Groups may have as few as one person.) Assign each group one of the four segments of Scripture read by the reader. Ask the groups to find from their passage of Scripture two principles that would apply to life today and share these with the class.

Allow four to five minutes for study and then call for reports.

Challenge members to examine their lives to be certain they are not counting on something other than genuine repentance and faith in Jesus for their salvation. Close in prayer that all would accept Jesus' invitation into the kingdom.

# Jesus Affirms John's Message

**Basic Passage:** Matthew 11:2-15
**Focal Passage:** Matthew 11:2-15

Appreciation is of great positive value. Appreciation expressed has even greater value. For persons who toil, year in and year out, without a word of praise, even important work can become drudgery. This can be true in Christian service, a fact that needs recognition within the church. Our Lord spoke gracious words of praise for John the Baptist at a time when He was also answering questions that revealed doubts in the mind of His forerunner. He expressed no criticism of John's doubts but sought to resolve them. Then He proceeded to compliment the Baptist. In the Christian life few people escape periods of doubt. Young persons are particularly prone to doubt. Reasons may vary, but the condition should always be met with sympathetic understanding and positive efforts to deal with their doubts, with an absence of condemnation. Doubts sincerely faced and dealt with may lead to a stronger faith. They can be indicative of an inquiring mind that will readily respond to friendly persuasion.

**Study Aim:** *To explore the causes of doubt and seek its remedy for both ourselves and others*

## STUDYING THE BIBLE

Chapter 11 begins with a statement of the growing ministry of our Lord. Some scholars feel the verse belongs to the previous chapter, but where it is the verse contrasts the freedom enjoyed by Jesus with the prison confinement of John the Baptist. Although the forerunner had said of Him, "He must increase, but I must decrease" (John 3:30), the cruel restraints of Herod's Dead Sea jail ate into John's spirit and disturbed his confidence.

### I. John in Prison (Matt. 11:2)

The circumstances of the imprisonment of John are delayed until 14:1-12. Here there is only passing reference to that imprisonment as introduction to our Lord's high tribute to the Baptist.

**2 Now when John had heard in the prison the works of Christ, he sent two of his disciples.**

According to Matthew 14, Herod the tetrarch was criticized by John for marrying one of his brother's wives. Herod divorced his first wife to marry her. Herod was angry enough to want John killed, but public opinion persuaded him to imprison the Baptist at Machaerus, on the Dead Sea. On the king's birthday, the daughter of Herodias, the woman to whom he was adulterously married, danced in a way that so pleased Herod that he offered to reward her with whatever she might ask. The girl referred the matter to her mother who sought her own revenge on John by asking for his head on a platter. Herod, who hated John no less but feared the consequences, acceded to his wife's cruel wish and had the Baptist beheaded. A sense of guilt remained with the aging king so that, when he heard of Jesus, he concluded that He was John the Baptist risen from the dead (14:2).

### II. Question and Answer (Matt. 11:3-6)

During his imprisonment, John learned about the ministry of our Lord. In his lonely isolation, we can imagine his eagerness for news. But when it reached him it was not of the sort he expected. Reference to "two of his disciples" is an indication of the Baptist's continuing influence. There is clear evidence in the Gospels that the early church denied that John was the Messiah. A small sect exists to this day, in Mesopotamia, that majors on the person of John and his place in Christian tradition. Our lesson passage honors him but ranks him only as a messenger (v. 10).

> 3 And said unto him, Art thou he that should come, or do we look for another?
> 4 Jesus answered and said unto them, Go and show John again those things which ye do hear and see:
> 5 The blind receive their sight, and the lame walk, the lepers are cleansed, and the deaf hear, the dead are raised up, and the poor have the gospel preached to them.
> 6 And blessed is he, whosoever shall not be offended in me.

**1. John's perplexity (v. 3).**—When we look at terms used by John in proclaiming Christ, we can understand his perplexity, particularly in the depressing conditions of life in a dungeon. He had seen himself as the herald of a coming conqueror (3:3), and had spoken of Him wielding an ax (v. 10) and separating wheat from chaff (v. 12). But the ministry of Jesus did not conform to this expectation. Moreover, He had done nothing to free His forerunner from Herod's prison.

**2. The witness of works (vv. 4-6).**—John was entertaining the same mistaken thinking about the Messiah that was held by most Jews of his day, even by the disciples (Acts 1:6). They focused on those Old Testament prophecies that portrayed Him as a mighty deliverer and overlooked others that presented Him as a Suffering Servant (Isa. 53). So in answering the two disciples of John our Lord called attention to His activities of compassion and grace that were foreshadowed in such passages as Isaiah 35:5-6; 42:6-7; and 61:1-3. He then pronounced a blessing on those who did not stumble over the nature of His activities. The time would come when He would die on a cross, thus creating for some "a stumbling block," but for others the good news of salvation (1 Cor. 1:22-24).

### III. Jesus' Tribute to John (Matt. 11:7-15)

Our Lord watched the two disciples from John as they turned away and began to retrace their steps. He was clearly anxious that nothing He had said to them reflected on the character of John, for whom He had both admiration and gratitude. Could He have secured John's release from prison? As God's Son, He undoubtedly commanded the power to do so. But this would have been inconsistent with His mission which involved suffering for Him and His people.

> 7 And as they departed, Jesus began to say unto the
> multitudes concerning John, What went ye out into the
> wilderness to see? A reed shaken with the wind?
> 8 But what went ye out for to see? A man clothed in soft
> raiment? Behold, they that wear soft clothing are in kings' houses.
> 9 But what went ye out for to see? A prophet? yea, I say
> unto you, and more than a prophet.
> 10 For this is he, of whom it is written, Behold, I send
> my messenger before thy face, which shall prepare thy way
> before thee.
> 11 Verily I say unto you, Among them that are born of
> women there hath not risen a greater than John the Baptist:
> notwithstanding he that is least in the kingdom of heaven is
> greater than he.
> 12 And from the days of John the Baptist until now the
> kingdom of heaven suffereth violence, and the violent take it
> by force.
> 13 For all the prophets and the law prophesied until John.
> 14 And if ye will receive it, this is Elijah, which was for
> to come.
> 15 He that hath ears to hear, let him hear.

**1. Portrait of strength (vv. 7-8).**—Concern for the reputation of the Baptist led Jesus to ask a number of questions. At the height of his popularity, the Baptist drew crowds from all over Palestine. What did they go to see? A weakling? The obvious answer was no. John's recent experience with doubt must not change opinions about him. Jesus said that people went to the wrong place, the wilderness, if they wanted to see a man elegantly dressed. John's physical appearance witnessed to his moral and spiritual strength. John was in the tradition of the ancient prophets.

**2. More than a prophet (vv. 9-10).**—But he was more than a prophet. John bridged the gap between God's spokesman of old and the future messengers of the gospel. By quoting Malachi 3:1, the Lord confirmed the description of the Baptist given in Matthew 3:3. He was the fulfillment of prophetic utterance, the first of the two messengers mentioned by Malachi (whose name, by the way, means "messenger"), John and then Jesus. John came in fulfillment of prophecy and by his message prepared the way for Christ and His gospel.

**3. Greater than John (v. 11).**—According to Jesus, there was none greater than John, that is, up to that time. John was compared to Elijah (v. 14), considered greatest of the prophets. Elijah appeared with Moses at our Lord's transfiguration (17:1-3). Jesus testified to John's prominence. But John's message preceded the preaching of the gospel based on Christ's ministry, death, and resurrection, events that were still in the future. Those who responded to that gospel, and engaged in spreading it, would belong to a higher level of ministry even than John.

**4. Difficult verses (vv. 12-15).**—The meaning of verse 12 is obscure and most conservative commentators hesitate to give a firm interpretation. The equating of John with Elijah clearly is based on Malachi 4:5, a prophetic statement that occasioned expectation that the prophet would reappear in a role preparatory to the coming of God's kingdom. But our Lord's words cannot be taken as an endorsement of reincarnation, a concept that is foreign to Scripture. "John the Baptist and Elijah are two different men . . . but John the Baptist fulfilled the role associated with the name Elijah."[1] The phrases used by our Lord, "if ye will receive it" and, "He that hath ears to hear, let him hear" (vv. 14-15), indicate that His listeners needed to exercise powers of perception to rightly understand what He was saying. We are promised the help of the Holy Spirit in our quest for revealed truth.

## IV. Shallow Criticism Condemned (Matt. 11:16-19)

Matthew's passage on Jesus and John includes these additional verses that merit our attention. Did our Lord hear murmurs of disagreement among His listeners as He spoke approvingly of John? His reaction would suggest this. He compared the critics (including those who criticized Him) to small children fussing at one another over the games they would play. Nothing could satisfy them, for what one suggested the other side objected. Since both Jesus and John dealt with important spiritual matters, such trifling was serious and inexcusable.

**1. John's critics (v. 18).**—He was rejected for being too much of an acetic, a wilderness hermit who ate strange food and wore strange clothes. This was only an excuse for spurning his call to repentance. We may suppose that people known as Herodians, because of their support of the Herods, resented John's criticism of the reigning Herod for his irregular marriage.

**2. Jesus' critics (v. 19).**—Indicative of the fickleness of such people, our Lord said that they accused Him of being a glutton and a drunkard (NRSV). They had no ground for this, except that He associated with sinners, seeking their salvation (9:10-13).

## APPLYING THE BIBLE

**The gift of suffering.**—It may sound strange, but to some God gives "the gift of suffering" (see Phil. 1:29). It was so with Jesus and John the Baptist and sometimes it is so with us. Discussing this, the great New Testament scholar A. T. Robertson spoke about Jesus, "A man of sorrows, and acquainted with grief" (Isa. 53:3); the "captain" of our salvation was made perfect through sufferings (Heb. 2:10); Paul spoke about "filling up in his turn" the sufferings left over by Christ (Col. 1:24); Paul compared the Christian life to an "athletic" contest—which gives us our words agony, and agonize (Col. 2:1; 1 Tim. 6:2; Heb. 12:1); and then there are the frequent biblical admonitions to rejoice in our afflictions. John had his share of sufferings, both in his formative years and when he was cast into prison by Herod. The character of God's children is fashioned both in the cradle and on the cross.

**About doubt.**—Great Christians have wrestled with doubt, and it was a contributing factor to their making: William Lyon Phelps, who taught at Yale, said about his doubts: "My religious faith remains in possession of the field only after prolonged civil war with my naturally skeptical mind." Puritan preacher Increase Mather was a man of great faith, but in his diary one will read entries such as this: "Greatly molested with temptations to atheism." When one sings Martin Luther's mighty hymn, "A Mighty Fortress Is Our God," one would suppose Luther never questioned God. But on one occasion he wrote: "For more than a week Christ was totally lost. I was shaken by desperation and blasphemy against God." And Robert Louis Stevenson, not a preacher but a renowned Scottish poet and novelist, said in his younger days that the religion in which he was reared was "the deadliest gag and wet-blanket that can be laid on man." He even called himself "a youthful atheist." Later, he wrote, "But there is a manifest God for those who care to look for him." Then, in later life, he began talking about his "cast-iron faith."

John the Baptist, while in prison, was so overwhelmed by doubt that he sent two of his disciples to ask Jesus to give proof that He, indeed, was the Messiah (11:3-7).

Thanks be to God, He doesn't blush over our doubts or resign His sovereignty because of it!

**"The Black Dog" of depression.**—John's doubt likely resulted from his depression. Unfortunately, depression is common to all of us.

William Cowper was plagued by it all his life and even tried to commit suicide on several occasions. But it was he who wrote the magnificent hymn, "There Is a Fountain Filled with Blood."

Winston Churchill, the savior of Europe during World War II, often spoke about his frequent battles with what he called, "The Black Dog" of depression.

Painter Vincent Willem van Gogh, whose paintings have brought some of the highest prices ever paid for art, once cut off his ear in a time of despair.

Abraham Lincoln, the immortal sixteenth president, had a running, lifelong battle with melancholy.

Out of Edgar Allen Poe's depression came such works as "The Pit and the Pendulum." The English poet Thomas Gray, author of "Elegy Written in a Country Churchyard," confessed he never liked himself. To a friend he once confided, "low spirits are my true and faithful companions." And what about the strong characters we read about in the Bible? Moses wanted to die. Job saw no reason to continue living. Elijah, overwhelmed by depression, fled from Jezebel. Jonah saw no need to go on and wanted to die.

"The Black Dog" of depression even laid its hands on John the Baptist about whom Jesus said: "Among them that are born of women there hath not risen a greater than John the Baptist" (11:11).

**My roof is too low for you!**—Those of us who have heard Marian Anderson sing, understand Arturo Toscanini's summation of her ability: "A voice like hers comes once in a century."

Miss Anderson once sang for Jean Sibelius (1865-1957), one of Finland's best-known composers and musicians. He listened to Miss Anderson spellbound and then with tears in his eyes he said, "My roof is too low for you!" He was not referring to her physical size but to her spiritual stature. It was so of John the Baptist.

## TEACHING THE BIBLE

▶ *Main Idea:* Jesus' affirmation of John's message indicates that He cares when we face doubt and despair.

▶ *Suggested Teaching Aim:* To lead adults to examine how Jesus affirmed John, and to identify how they can encourage themselves and others when they face doubt.

### A TEACHING OUTLINE

*1. Make a study outline.*
*2. Use the study outline to guide a group discussion.*
*3. Participate in a role play.*
*4. Identify ways to encourage themselves and others when they doubt.*

**Introduce the Bible Study**

Ask members to share times in their lives when they seriously questioned God's goodness or existence. Point out that John the Baptist questioned Jesus' identity and sought to find out who Jesus was.

**Search for Biblical Truth**

IN ADVANCE, write the following study outline on a chalkboard or a large sheet of paper:

1. Accepted John's Question Without Criticism (11:2-3)
2. Appealed to Lessons of History (11:4-6)
3. Affirmed John's Ministry (11:7-15)

Cover points 2 and 3 until you are ready to use them. Ask members briefly to describe John's relationship with Jesus. Be sure they include the following: had baptized Jesus, had heard God's affirmation of Jesus, had declared Jesus was the Messiah, had preached that Jesus was coming to bring judgment.

Point out the first statement on the study outline: "Accepted John's Question Without Criticism (11:2-3)." Use the material in *Studying the Bible* to explain why John was in prison. Ask: Why do you think John doubted that Jesus was the Messiah when he had preached that fact? What did John do when he doubted? Point out that what John did when he doubted is what we must do as well. Ask: What was Jesus' response to John's questioning?

Uncover the second point on the outline: "Appealed to Lessons of History (11:4-6)." Ask: How did Jesus seek to answer John's question? Why do you think Jesus responded in this way? Point out that Jesus gave John a history lesson. Ask members briefly to suggest examples of each of the ministries Jesus suggested He had done. (Some of the examples members suggest may be after John's death, but we do not have a complete record of all Jesus' miracles.)

Uncover the third point on the study outline: "Affirmed John's Ministry (11:7-15)." Ask members to turn to someone sitting near them and spend a couple of minutes looking at 11:7-15 to identify how Jesus affirmed John's ministry. Then let members share. List these on a chalkboard or a large sheet of paper. Members may list others but be sure these are included: John was stable, more than a prophet, no greater person ever born on this earth than he, equated John with Elijah. Ask members to turn to Malachi 4:5 and ask a volunteer to read this Old Testament prophecy about Elijah. Use the material in *Studying the Bible* to explain the relationship between John the Baptist and Elijah.

**Give the Truth a Personal Focus**

Ask two people to role-play how John may have responded when his disciples reported to him what Jesus had said.

Ask members to turn to the same person they had grouped with earlier and answer this question:

> How can you encourage yourself and others when you face doubt? Allow three minutes for discussion and then ask members to share their suggestions. List these on a chalkboard.

Suggest members identify at least one specific step they can and will take to help either themselves or someone who is questioning God. Ask members to covenant to pray for each other this week. Close in prayer that Jesus' reaction to John's questions will help them be more open with their questions so they, too, may find affirmation.

---

1. Frank Stagg, *The Broadman Bible Commentary,* Vol. 8 (Nashville: Broadman Press, 1969), 142.

December 18 1994

# Jesus Is Born

**Basic Passage:** Matthew 1
**Focal Passage:** Matthew 1:18-25

Christmas took a long time to shake itself free from the charge of association with pagan observances. The closing days of the year were dedicated by the Romans to a festival that honored their god of agriculture, Saturn. The observance was known as Saturnalia, a time of great happiness that culminated in the exchange of gifts. The emperor Constantine, who made Christianity the official religion of Rome in the fourth century, took over the pagan festival and dedicated it to the celebration of the birth of Christ. Objection to the observance on account of its pagan background survived in this country until the eighteenth century. In Puritan New England the keeping of Christmas Day was declared illegal and penalties were imposed on people who engaged in special feasting on December 25. But the day was finally claimed as marking the Savior's birth, and so we observe it today. But the paganizing of Christmas continues in commercial exploitation and partying that bears no religious significance. Christians need to take back Christmas, certainly for themselves, and make December 25 a day that honors the Son of God.

**Study Aim:** *To make Christmas Day 1994 a time of remembering the coming into this world of Emmanuel, God with us*

## STUDYING THE BIBLE

Matthew began his Gospel with the words, "The book of the generation of Jesus Christ, the son of David, the son of Abraham." Thus he made the New Testament begin, like the Old, with a *genesis* (genealogy), not the only parallel between his Gospel and the Old Testament. He was writing for his own people, the Jews, though not exclusively. Thus he traced the descent of our Lord through Abraham and David, his purpose being to present Jesus as the Messiah-King.

### I. Table of Descent (Matt. 1:1-17)

There is another genealogy of our Lord in Luke 3:23-38 that traces His descent back to Adam. This followed Luke's purpose in presenting Jesus as the Savior of all people. Many think that the major difference between the two genealogies is that Luke traces the descent through Mary, and Matthew through Joseph, who while not our Lord's biological father, was Jesus' legal father. However, this is a matter for disagreement.

**1. Three divisions.**—Matthew states that his genealogy is divided into three parts of fourteen generations each: Abraham to David,

David to the Babylonian captivity, and the captivity to Christ (v. 17). But the names do not add up to fourteen in each case, suggesting that the numeral 14 was more important to Matthew than the listing. Numbers played an important part in Jewish interpretation of Scripture so we must conclude that fourteen was of symbolic value to Matthew, though the reason is not clear to us. Since seven is the number for completeness, twice that number may stand for absolute perfection in the outworking of the purpose of God. But this is speculation.

**2. Surprising names.**—Normally, genealogies of the time only included the names of males. It is, therefore, both interesting and significant that Matthew listed four women: Tamar (v. 3), widow of one of Judah's sons who tricked her father-in-law into fathering her twin sons (Gen. 38:12-30); Rahab (v. 5), the harlot of Jericho who sheltered Israel's two spies (Josh. 2:1-22); Ruth (v. 5), the Moabitish woman who married Boaz; and Bathsheba (v. 6), referred to only as the "wife of Uriah," with whom David had an illicit relationship (2 Sam. 11:2-5). "The long line of ancestors is not a line of moral saints but of forgiven sinners, through whom the faithfulness of God is ever and again manifested anew. Matthew intentionally mentioned Rahab the prostitute, and Ruth the Moabitess. In opening the Kingdom to prostitutes and pagans, Jesus could declare Himself the bearer of the divine initiative to which the Old Testament testifies."[1]

## II. Mary and Joseph (Matt. 1:18-19)

After a series of "begats," as Matthew traced the birth of Jesus from Abraham and through David, the Gospel writer began the story of a different kind of begetting. He stated that "Jacob begat Joseph," but not that "Joseph begat Jesus," although Joseph is named as "Mary's husband." Matthew went on to describe precisely what he meant, affirming the virgin birth of our Lord. Luke, in his narrative of the nativity, affirmed the virgin birth when Mary exclaimed, "How shall this be, seeing I know not a man?" (Luke 1:34). The verb "know" is used here, as it is in Matthew 1:25, for sexual union.

**18 Now the birth of Jesus Christ was on this wise: When as his mother Mary was espoused to Joseph, before they came together, she was found with child of the Holy Ghost.**

**19 Then Joseph her husband, being a just man, and not willing to make her a public example, was minded to put her away privately.**

**1. Engaged couple (v. 18).**—The word "espoused" can be compared to our word *engaged,* except that the contract between man and woman was considered binding. An act of divorcement was required to end the "espoused" relationship, and, if the man should die, his partner was considered a widow. "This preliminary state therefore had a very close resemblance to definitive marriage."[2] For the woman to become pregnant exposed her to the charge of adultery. This was the problem confronted by Joseph before he was made aware that Mary was "with child of the Holy Ghost."

**2. Contemplated divorce (v. 19).**—Joseph is described as "a just man," which means "righteous." Indicative of his righteousness was his compassionate behavior toward Mary whom he could have publicly divorced, exposing her to the shame of having been unfaithful. Instead of this, he decided to take the necessary legal action in private. Though we know little about Joseph, this presents him as a man of a compassionate and loving spirit, with a devotion to Mary that is borne out by his future actions.

### III. Angel Messenger (Matt. 1:20-21)

God speaks to people in a variety of ways, sometimes by an intermediary (that is, prophets), sometimes through visions, and in Joseph's case by a dream. We may be sure that his mind was greatly exercised over the condition of Mary, probably causing him sleeplessness. But during a period of sleep, the Lord made plain to him the truth about his loved one. An important thing is that he was open to receive what God had to say, and to act on it.

> **20 But while he thought on these things, behold, the angel of the Lord appeared unto him in a dream, saying, Joseph, thou son of David, fear not to take unto thee Mary thy wife: for that which is conceived in her is of the Holy Ghost.**
> **21 And she shall bring forth a son, and thou shalt call his name JESUS: for he shall save his people from their sins.**

**1. Joseph reassured (v. 20).**—The message brought by the angel was startling in its uniqueness. Joseph was called on to believe something that had never happened before, conception by a virgin through divine action. By addressing Joseph as "thou son of David," the angel reminded him of God's covenant promises to that king, which were to have fulfillment in the birth of the Messiah. The decline in the fortunes of the royal line is shown by the fact that Joseph was a village carpenter. There are reasons to believe that Mary was also a member of the royal line, in which case she and Joseph were probably cousins.

**2. Unborn child named (v. 21).**—The name *Jesus* was common in New Testament times, as it is today in some Catholic countries. It was popular because it was borne by one of the heroes of Israel, Joshua, the Hebrew form of "Jesus." In either language, the meaning is "God [Yahweh] is salvation," appropriate to the man who led the Israelites into Canaan and settled them in the land. But a new significance to the name was given by the angel, who said, "he shall save his people from their sins." This Joshua-Jesus would be more than a national deliverer, as was the Old Testament Joshua when he overthrew Jericho. He would be the Savior, bringing deliverance from the power and penalty of sin.

## IV. Prophecy Fulfilled (Matt. 1:22-23)

In his purpose to prove that Jesus was the promised Messiah, Matthew used over sixty quotations from the Old Testament. To establish this in connection with the Savior's birth was obviously important, so it is not surprising to find several of these in his first two chapters (see 2:5-6, 15, 17-18, 23).

> 22 Now all this was done, that it might be fulfilled which was spoken of the Lord by the prophet, saying,
> 23 Behold, a virgin shall be with child, and shall bring forth a son, and they shall call his name Emmanuel, which being interpreted is, God with us.

This quotation is from Isaiah 7:14 and records words spoken to Ahaz, king of Judah, by God through the prophet. This king was facing the combined forces of Israel and Syria and was guilty of a pious pose that he would not bother God to give him assurance of victory. So Ahaz was told that, wanting it or not, "the Lord himself shall give you a sign . . . a virgin shall conceive, and bear a son, and shall call his name Immanuel." Whatever immediate meaning this may have had, Matthew, under the inspiration of the Holy Spirit, accepted this as referring to the coming Messiah, who was Jesus Christ. He was Emmanuel (either spelling is permissible), "God is with us," a much more profound concept of messiahship than that commonly entertained. As John the apostle wrote, "the Word was God . . . and the Word was made flesh and dwelt among us" (John 1:1,14).

## V. Birth of the Savior (Matt. 1:24-25)

Joseph was a man of great faith. In spite of the strangeness of the circumstances, he believed the angel's message, and affirmed Mary as his wife. Others might continue to be judgmental toward Mary and her pregnancy, and they were, for all kinds of false allegations were circulated, but Joseph remained at her side to defend and protect her.

> 24 Then Joseph being raised from sleep did as the angel of the Lord had bidden him, and took unto him his wife:
> 25 And knew her not till she had brought forth her firstborn son: and he called his name Jesus.

Though now wedded to Mary, Joseph continued to respect the sanctity of her body and the Child she carried. Their relationship was loving, but not intimate, "till she had brought forth her firstborn son." These are important words for they correct the erroneous teaching of the perpetual virginity of Mary. She bore other children, some of whom are named in 13:55-56.

## APPLYING THE BIBLE

**Remembering Jesus.**—Anatole France (1844-1924) was a French novelist and critic who won the Nobel prize for literature in 1921. France once told a story about Pontius Pilate and a friend who had served together for a time in Judea. They talked about the dancing girls, the good times they had had, and the tumultuous history of which they had been a part. Casually, his friend asked Pilate if he remembered Jesus of Nazareth who had been crucified during Pilate's reign. Knitting his brow in serious contemplation, Pilate answered: "Jesus, Jesus of Nazareth? I cannot call him to mind."

At this Christmas season all the world—and we Christians especially— call Jesus to mind with joy and great thanksgiving.

**Brought down to eye level.**—Some of us have been to Trafalgar Square in London to admire the statue of Lord Horatio Nelson lifted high above the busy park on a colossal column. He was given an exalted position by the ambitious sculptor, but Nelson is too far above the busy square for people to see him clearly and know what he was like. But in 1948, for a special exhibition, an exact plastic replica of Nelson on top of the colossal column was placed at eye level where all could examine it. He was brought down to eye level where those who had long admired him could see him clearly. This is similar to the meaning of Bethlehem where the Creator and Sustainer of the universe came down, dwelt among us, "And the word was made flesh, and dwelt among us, and we beheld his glory" (John 1:14). "God with us" is the true meaning of Christmas.

**Are angels for real?**—According to a recent Gallup Poll (1992) American teenagers, apparently, believe more in angels today than at any time in the past fifteen years. Seventy-six percent of American teens surveyed said they believe in angels. In 1978 that figure was 64 percent of teens who thought angels were real. Since that time, the number has been increasing.

Unfortunately, more teenagers believe in ghosts than before. But among teens, belief in astrology, ESP, clairvoyance, witchcraft, Bigfoot and the Loch Ness Monster is declining.

The angels play a very vital part in the birth of Jesus, and in the Bible as well. Read, again, the Christmas story and see what a prominent place the angels played in the birth and ministry of the Lord Jesus.

**The virgin birth of Jesus.**—Many of the world's great leaders have claimed a supernatural birth. Among them are Buddha, Zoroaster, Pythagoras, and Plato. The Greeks had a fable that Perseus, the mythological son of Zeus (Jupiter) and Danaë, was born of a virgin and that Jupiter had come down from above in a shower of gold. The Hindu myth claims that Krishna, one of the Hindu names for God, was born of the virgin Davaki. All these meaningless myths and foolish folklore cannot compare with the verity of Scripture that states: "Behold, a virgin shall be with child, and shall bring forth a son, and they shall call his name Emmanuel, which being interpreted is, God with us" (1:23).

**To see God walk down the street.**—Since the time of Adam and

Eve, mankind has wanted to know and see God. Why else have so many statues of gods and goddesses been created? Plato, the Greek philosopher, expressed the sentiments of all people of all time when he said that one day he hoped to see God walk down the streets of Athens. The desire of that great thinker, and the desire of multitudes from all races and times, was realized when Jesus Christ walked down the staircase of heaven and out on to the dusty roads of Judea.

## TEACHING THE BIBLE

▶ *Main Idea:* The birth of Jesus reminds us that God is with us.
▶ *Suggested Teaching Aim:* To lead adults to examine the birth of Jesus, and to list reasons why they believe God is still with them.

### A TEACHING OUTLINE

1. *Introduce the Christmas lesson.*
2. *Summarize the background material.*
3. *Lead a group discussion.*
4. *Lead class members to identify why they believe God is still with them.*

**Introduce the Bible Study**

Use the illustration "To see God walk down the street" (*Applying the Bible*) to introduce the Bible study.

**Search for Biblical Truth**

Today we will use the headings in *Studying the Bible* for our guide in the Bible search.

**I. Table of Descent (Matt. 1:1-17)**

Briefly summarize the material under this heading. Do not devote a lot of time to this. Take most of your time with the questions to guide group discussion under the following headings.

**II. Mary and Joseph (Matt. 1:18-19)**

1. What was different about the way Matthew described Joseph's relationship to Jesus and the way he described the other people's relationship to their descendants? *(They begat; Joseph was the husband of Mary to whom Jesus was born—Matt. 1:16)*

2. What does the word *espoused* mean? *(engaged but more binding than modern engagements)*

3. What was Joseph's reaction to Mary's pregnancy? *(to divorce her privately)*

**III. Angel Messenger (Matt. 1:20-21)**

1. Who appeared to Joseph and how? *(Angel of the Lord in a dream)*

2. What Old Testament name means the same as Jesus? *(Joshua)*

3. What does Joshua-Jesus mean? *(God is salvation)*

**IV. Prophecy Fulfilled (Matt. 1:22-23)**

1. What Old Testament prophet did Matthew quote to prove Jesus' virgin birth? *(Isaiah)*

2. What was the setting of the quotation in Isaiah? *(Isaiah's words to King Ahaz)*

3. What does the word *Emmanuel* mean? *(God is with us.)*

**V. Birth of the Savior (Matt. 1:24-25)**

1. What was Joseph's response to the angel's message? *(took Mary to be his wife)*

2. What does the phrase "knew her not till she had brought forth her firstborn son" mean? *(did not have sexual relations with her until after Jesus was born, but did have sexual relations then)*

3. What name did Joseph give to the baby? *(Jesus)*

**Give the Truth a Personal Focus**

Write the words *So What?* on a chalkboard or a large sheet of paper. Organize the class in groups of two to three. Assign the groups the following question:

> What difference does it make *to you* that Jesus was named "God with us"?

Allow about three minutes for groups to discuss this question and then call for reports. As groups report, list their responses on a chalkboard or a large sheet of paper.

After all the groups have responded, ask members to evaluate the list on the board. Ask them as a class to rank these in the order of their importance.

Since this is the final week before Christmas, suggest that members discuss in their groups how the top three responses will help them this week. Ask each group to share one way each of the top three responses will encourage them this week.

Close by reminding them that Jesus is God and that He is indeed with us.

---

1. Suzanne de Dietrich, *The Gospel According to Matthew* (Richmond: John Knox Press, 1961), 16

2. Daniel-Rops, *Daily Life in the Time of Jesus* (New York: Hawthorn Books, 1962), 124.

# The Wise Men Worship Jesus

**Basic Passage:** Matthew 2
**Focal Passage:** Matthew 2:1-12

Christmas is a season of beauty. For many people the earth is carpeted with snow. City streets are decked with colored lights. Store windows are dressed to perfection. Homes are decorated outside and inside. Holly, mistletoe, and Christmas trees enliven many living rooms. And so it should be, provided all this effort is put forth in gratitude for the true meaning of the season, and as a salute of love and adoration to Emmanuel, God with us. But the celebration and joy of Christmas need to be kept in balance by the realization that not everybody was glad to learn of His birth. True, wise men traveled hundreds of miles to do Him honor; but in Jerusalem reigned a king who trembled with fear and rage. While the magi presented their gifts, Herod was plotting His death. There we have the paradox of the Christ. Some accepted Him; others rejected Him. "He came unto his own, and his own received him not. But as many as received him . . . " (John 1:11-12). To which category do we belong?

**Study Aim:** *To challenge us to take our stand boldly with those who honor Christ at this commemoration of His birthday*

## STUDYING THE BIBLE

We may wonder that Matthew, with his strong Jewish emphasis, gave so much space to a visit of foreign astrologers to Bethlehem in order to pay homage to Mary's child. With his deep knowledge of the Old Testament, evidenced by his many quotations, Matthew would be aware of prophetic references to Christ's universal mission, beginning with the Abrahamic promise, "in thee shall all families of the earth be blessed" (Gen. 12:3). He would want his readers to recognize that Jesus fulfilled every Old Testament expectation.

### I. The Herods

The Herods were a line of princes who ruled Palestine, in whole or part, for around one hundred fifty years. They were Idumeans (Edomites) who gained favor with Rome so that one of their number, Herod the Great, was appointed king in 40 B.C. It was during his reign that Jesus was born in Bethlehem. After his death, his kingdom was divided between his three sons. One of these, known as Herod Antipas, is frequently referred to in the New Testament. It was he who ordered the beheading of John the Baptist. In the Book of Acts, Herod

Agrippa II appears, great-grandson of Herod the Great, whom the apostle Paul called an "expert in all customs and questions which are among the Jews" (Acts 26:3). He was the last of the Herodian kings.

## II. Visiting Magi (Matt. 2:1-6)

It was natural that the wise men should seek direction in Jerusalem, for not only was Herod's palace there, but he had also gained fame for his reconstruction of the temple, a structure that had suffered serious damage and loss through various military campaigns. Herod completed the inner sanctuary before his death, but the remainder of the work took the next fifty years, and, likely was not finished when the temple was destroyed by the Romans in A.D. 70. This was the temple that Jesus knew.

> **1 Now when Jesus was born in Bethlehem of Judea in the days of Herod the king, behold, there came wise men from the east to Jerusalem,**
>
> **2 Saying, Where is he that is born King of the Jews? for we have seen his star in the east, and are come to worship him.**
>
> **3 When Herod the king had heard these things, he was troubled, and all Jerusalem with him.**
>
> **4 And when he had gathered all the chief priests and scribes of the people together, he demanded of them where Christ should be born.**
>
> **5 And they said unto him, In Bethlehem of Judea: for thus it is written by the prophet,**
>
> **6 And thou Bethlehem, in the land of Judah, art not the least among the princes of Judah: for out of thee shall come a Governor, that shall rule my people Israel.**

**1. The wise men (vv. 1-2).**—Most Eastern cultures in biblical times had their wise men: students of life and the universe whose pronouncements were treated with high respect. The Bible has its Wisdom Literature, of which Proverbs and Ecclesiastes are examples. The wise men, or *Magi* (meaning,"diviner"), of the nativity story, are described as "from the east," which leaves open their place of origin. They could have come from Persia (modern Iran) or from some place further east. Legend has unfortunately played a large part in our presentday concept of these men, expressed in a carol that begins, "We three kings of Orient are." The Bible does not say how many there were and does not describe them as kings. They were more likely a type of priest. They studied the heavens for answers to their questions and light on coming events, after the manner of astrologers. A new star in the sky was understood by these men to betoken the birth of a king. Throughout the world at that time was expectation of a great deliverer. It was the motion of the star that brought them to Jerusalem. They were doubtless aware of the Jewish hope of a Messiah, and associated the star with that hope.

**2. Herod's agitation (vv. 3-4).**—The aging Herod had reasons for feeling insecure and apprehensive. He had maintained his throne with great brutality, having sent one of his wives and two of his sons to the executioner. The wise men had asked about "born King of the Jews," and Herod had certainly not been born king but had obtained that rank through political intrigue. He knew that he was facing a serious competitor. His agitation soon became known and the people of Jerusalem were themselves troubled for fear of what Herod might do. His first action was to summon the Jewish religious leaders and ask them where the expected Messiah was to be born.

**3. Answer from Scripture (vv. 5-6).**—God spoke to the wise men first through nature, but it took the revelation of Scripture to take them to their destination. The quotation is from Micah 5:2, slightly paraphrased by Matthew to support his theme of Jesus as Shepherd-King of His people. The word translated "Governor" can also mean "Shepherd," a concept of kingship found in the Old Testament and fulfilled in Jesus Christ, "the good shepherd" (John 10:11). The ancient prophet was precise in naming "Bethlehem, in the land of Judah," for there was another Bethlehem north of Nazareth. The Judean Bethlehem had been the birthplace of David.

## III. Guiding Star (Matt. 2:7-10)

Astronomers have studied records of heavenly bodies in hope of solving the mystery of the Christmas star. Their various suggestions are interesting. But the Bible story indicates that the Creator of the universe put that star in the sky as His messenger to people outside the borders of Israel, and as their guide to the "born King," His Son and our Savior.

> **7 Then Herod, when he had privily called the wise men, inquired of them diligently what time the star appeared.**
> **8 And he sent them to Bethlehem, and said, Go and search diligently for the young child; and when ye have found him, bring me word again, that I may come and worship him also.**
> **9 When they had heard the king, they departed; and, lo, the star, which they saw in the east, went before them, till it came and stood over where the young child was.**
> **10 When they saw the star, they rejoiced with exceeding great joy.**

**1. Herod's hypocrisy (vv. 7-8).**—This king's careful inquiry is not to be explained by a desire to follow the wise men to Bethlehem for the purpose of worship, but by his later revealed intention of putting the child Jesus to death. If he could learn when the star first appeared he would know the age of the child, and who therefore to target in his murderous scheme.

**2. Reward of search (vv. 9-10).**—Since we believe that the star was a special manifestation, provided by God Himself, to announce the incarnation beyond Jewry, the star could not complete the purpose of its revelation until it had led the wise men to Mary's firstborn son. The star's reappearance and course in the sky brought them to Bethlehem, not more than five miles south of Jerusalem.

### IV. Gifts for Mary's Child (Matt. 2:11-12)

The slaughter, under Herod's cruel edict, of children two years old and under, indicates the approximate age of Jesus at the time. He and Mary His mother are now described as being in "the house," having moved from the temporary shelter of the stable into a home of some kind, humble in style we may be sure.

> **11 And when they were come into the house, they saw the young child with Mary his mother, and fell down, and worshiped him: and when they had opened their treasures, they presented unto him gifts; gold, and frankincense, and myrrh.**
>
> **12 And being warned of God in a dream that they should not return to Herod, they departed into their own country another way.**

The three kinds of gifts suggest three donors, but this is not necessarily so. There may have been more than three, though religious art has maintained the supposition of three. The gifts themselves were normal for those times, especially for royal recipients. The gold was appropriate for royalty, the frankincense suggested worship due to divinity, and the myrrh, used in embalming, was a provision against death. Each has its own special significance in the case of the Lord Jesus.

### V. The Continuing Story (Matt. 2:13-23)

Notwithstanding the failure of the wise men, under divine instruction, to report back to Herod, the danger was not over. The concluding verses of Matthew 2, all contained in the basic passage, merit our attention.

**1. Flight to Egypt (vv. 13-15).**—There had been a strong Jewish colony in Egypt since before Jeremiah's time (Jer. 44:1). Though under Roman rule, that country was outside the jurisdiction of Herod. In obedience to God, Joseph took Mary and the child Jesus to safety there.

**2. Herod's crime (vv. 16-18).**—Frustrated in his original plan by the action of the wise men, the brutal Herod resorted to a hideous crime in his attempt to destroy the "born King" Jesus. Having estimated our Lord's birth as having taken place some two years before, Herod ordered the slaughter of all Bethlehem children who were two years old and under. Following his pattern, Matthew quoted an Old Testament passage appropriate to this tragic situation (Jer. 31:15).

**3. Home in Nazareth (vv. 19-23).**—The death of Herod made possible the return of Joseph, Mary, and Jesus to their native land. They settled in Nazareth of Galilee, where the child Jesus grew to manhood before beginning His public ministry.

## APPLYING THE BIBLE

**What kind of world was it into which Jesus was born?**—Politically, Caesar Augustus ruled in Rome and Herod governed Palestine. Sociologically, the world was morally corrupt and philosophically had failed to satisfy; religiously, the ritualism of the Jewish temple was vain and hollow and the pagan gods were powerless and their oracles were dumb. And prophetically, Jesus came, as Paul said, "In the fullness of time": the Greek language had provided a means to communicate the gospel; the Roman peace had made access to lands available; and the Roman roads made transportation possible. He came at the best possible time for it was a time ordained and prepared by God.[1]

**How Mary and Joseph got to Bethlehem.**—It was a census that got Mary and Joseph from Nazareth in Galilee to Bethlehem. It was the means by which God the Father moved them to the place where Jesus, of the lineage of David, could be born in the city of David. God often uses strange means to accomplish His purposes and to fulfill His Word.

The "census," as the Romans called it, took place in the Roman empire every fourteenth year. It involved not only Roman citizens but also reached out to the areas of Roman conquest: Spain, Gaul, Egypt, Syria, and Palestine. The purpose of the census was twofold: it provided relevant information that could be used for such things as calling men up for military service and for taxation purposes. In countries conquered by Rome, taxation was the chief reason.

Only by having this census and thus taxing the people could Rome maintain her strength and her luxury: magnificent buildings, sporting arenas, extravagant living, and "bread and circuses" which the emperors loved to give on a grand scale.

Two censuses need to concern us here: The first one was taken in A.D. 6 by Cyrenius, when Coponius was the first procurator of Judea. But this cannot be the one referred to in Scripture because by this time Jesus would have been at least ten years old. But a Roman fragment found some time ago at Antioch indicated that Cyrenius took an earlier census between 10 and 7 B.C. And that's the one around which the Christmas story rotates.[2]

**Is today really Christmas?**—Of course, it's Christmas! But when was Jesus really born?

A Scythian monk, Dionysius Exiguus, made some miscalculations in the sixth century. He was instructed in A.D. 533 to date the beginning of the new era (Christian era) by working back. But the monk forgot to insert the year 0 between 1 B.C. and A.D. 1. To complicate matters further, he overlooked the four years when Caesar Augustus, the emperor, had ruled under his original name Octavian.

We know Jesus was born when Herod was the king (2:1). We also know from secular documents that Herod was named king of Judea in 40 B.C. and that he died in 4 B.C. Since Herod wanted to kill all the boy babies two years of age and under (2:16), this gives us some idea about the approximate year Jesus was born. It had to be before 4 B.C., perhaps around 6 to 7 B.C.

Christmas Day has been celebrated on December 25 since A.D. 336. It was the beginning of the winter solstice, a week of loose living and carnival, and the Christians felt safe from persecution on that day. Thus, they adopted it for their holy celebration.[3]

**What does Jesus look like?**—All of us have seen the familiar paintings of Jesus, but what does He really look like? Many years ago, Dewitt Talmage wrote a sermon titled, "The Red Word." In the sermon, he gave this description of Jesus: "Twenty centuries ago there lived one Jesus. Publius Lentulus, in a letter to the Roman Senate, describes Him as 'A man of stature somewhat tall; His hair the color of chestnut fully ripe, plain to the ears, whence downward it is more orient, curling and waving about the shoulders; in the midst of His forehead is a stream or partition of His hair; forehead plain and very delicate; His face without a spot or wrinkle, a lovely red; His nose and mouth so forked as nothing can be represented; His beard thick, in color like His hair—not very long; His eyes gray, quick and clear.'"

The French army in Italy found a brass plate on which was a copy of Jesus' death warrant, signed by John Zorobabel, Raphael Ronani, Daniel Robani, and Capet.

Now "whether these descriptions and this warrant are authentic we have no way of knowing," as Talmage put it. But it is interesting to say the least.

## TEACHING THE BIBLE

▶ *Main Idea:* The wise men's worship of Jesus demonstrates that we should take our stand boldly to honor Christ at this commemoration of His birth.

▶ *Suggested Teaching Aim:* To lead adults to describe events surrounding the wise men's worship of Jesus, and to identify ways they will stand boldly for Christ.

### A TEACHING OUTLINE

*1. Prepare assignments for three groups.*
*2. Organize the class in three groups for Bible study and give them their assignments.*
*3. Lead members to accomplish their assignments.*
*4. Lead a discussion on how members can stand boldly for Christ.*

**Introduce the Bible Study**

Bring figures of the wise men from a manger scene. Point out that although the Bible does not even say there were three magi, tradition suggests several things about them: There were three men whose names were Gaspar (or Caspar), Balthazar, and Melchoir [Kauffman, *Dictionary of Religious Terms,* p. 298]. They came from the three continents of Asia, Europe, and Africa. While this is strictly legend, it does show us that they were humans like us looking for the Christ.

### Search for Biblical Truth

IN ADVANCE, write the words *Herod, Magi,* and *Star* on three large sheets of paper. Place these around the room on the wall with a felt-tip pen. Collect various Bible dictionaries, handbooks, and commentaries for each group. Place the following DIRECTIONS by each poster:

**Group 1—Herod**

DIRECTIONS: Your assignment is to present information to the group about the Herods and particularly Herod the Great as he related to Jesus' birth. Read Matthew 2 and share information with the rest of the class. Use your quarterly and available commentaries, dictionaries, and other resources. You will have ten minutes for your study and five minutes for your presentation to the rest of the class.

**Group 2—The Magi**

DIRECTIONS: Your assignment is to present information to the group about the magi as they related to Jesus' birth. Read Matthew 2 and prepare information to share with the rest of the class. Use your quarterly and available commentaries, dictionaries, and other resources. You will have ten minutes for your study and five minutes for your presentation to the rest of the class.

**Group 3—The Star**

DIRECTIONS: Your assignment is to present information to the group about the star of Bethlehem as it related to Jesus' birth. Read Matthew 2 and prepare information to share with the rest of the class. Use your quarterly and available commentaries, dictionaries, and other resources. You will have ten minutes for your study and five minutes for your presentation to the rest of the class.

As members enter, ask every third person to go to one of the sheets of paper and instruct them to begin their study. Call for reports when they have finished.

### Give the Truth a Personal Focus

Ask members to list ways the wise men demonstrated courage. Then ask them to suggest ways they can stand boldly for Christ in today's world. List these ways on a chalkboard or a large sheet of paper.

Call attention to the figures of the wise men and suggest that as they stood boldly when Herod threatened them, we should dare to stand for Christ today.

---

1. Adapted from J. Ralph Grant, *The Word of the Lord for Special Days* (Grand Rapids: Baker Book House, 1964), 161-62.
2. For more information see Werner Keller, *The Bible As History* (New York: William Morrow and Co., 1956) 343-44.
3. Ibid, 353.

January
1
1995

# Deliverance and Forgiveness

**Basic Passage:** Matthew 8:1—9:8
**Focal Passage:** Matthew 8:28—9:8

The apostle Peter, speaking of the Lord Jesus to a Roman centurion and his household, said of Him that He "went about doing good" (Acts 10:38). This simple tribute is so gloriously true that it may well introduce us to our continuing studies in the ministry and redemptive death of the Son of God. Peter's statement is prefaced by a claim for divine authority bestowed on Jesus whom "God anointed . . . with the Holy Ghost and with power." The good that He did had the approval of His Heavenly Father, in whose power it was performed, and whose compassionate nature it reflected. For Jesus sought no credit for Himself, but both in word and deed bore witness to the love of God, which sent Him into the world, and to whom, after the completion of His task, He returned. We can therefore balance what Peter said about the Son with the words of John the apostle concerning the Father, "God is love" (1 John 4:8). In Christ, He demonstrated that love in the miracles of healing that He performed, miracles that showed concern for the total person: body, soul, and spirit. Yet the supreme evidence of the Father's love must be found in the vicarious death of Jesus on the cross.

**Study Aim:** *To show the concern of God the Father and God the Son in both the spiritual and physical well-being of people*

## STUDYING THE BIBLE

There is design in Matthew's Gospel. He grouped the teachings of Jesus in chapters 5–7, what we know as the Sermon on the Mount. This important section of the Gospel has had previous attention in this series of lessons, and will be returned to again. For now we shall focus on chapters 8 and 9 in which are recorded ten miracles, with emphasis on the authority of our Lord over nature, disease, and even death.

### I. A Varied Ministry (Matt. 8:1-27)

Early in this Gospel Matthew wrote, "And Jesus went about all Galilee, teaching in their synagogues, and preaching the gospel of the kingdom, and healing all manner of sickness and all manner of disease among the people" (4:23). Teaching, preaching, healing: these three activities consumed His time, brief as it was. Each was important to Him, each had a place in the task He was to perform.

**1. Great Teacher (v. 1).**—Our chapter begins by forging a link with what had previously happened as it states, "When he was come down from the mountain, great multitudes followed him." He had been teaching, first His disciples, and then the crowd that assembled to listen. Of that crowd we are told, "The people were astonished at his doctrine: for he taught them as one having authority, and not as the scribes" (7:28-29). The kind of teaching they were accustomed to depended on the authority of others, rabbis and scholars versed in the Jewish faith. But Jesus spoke with the personal authority of the Son of God.

**2. Great Physician (vv. 2-17).**—The authority of His deeds confirmed the authority of His words. He did what none other could do, none other, that is, but God. And all Jesus did showed His compassion for humanity. The first half of Matthew 8 records the healing of a leper (vv. 2-4), the paralyzed servant of a Roman centurion (vv. 5-13), Peter's mother-in-law (vv. 14-15), and concludes with this wide-embracing statement, "When the even was come, they brought unto him many that were possessed with devils: and he cast out the spirits with his word, and healed all that were sick" (v. 16). Characteristically, Matthew found an Old Testament Scripture appropriate to this healing ministry (v. 17).

## II. In Gentile Territory (Matt. 8:23-34)

All this teaching and healing had gone on to the west of the Sea of Galilee, perhaps near Capernaum. Jesus then decided to cross the lake into Gentile territory on the east side. The crossing was notable in that it provided opportunity for display of a different kind of authority, namely, over nature. Caught by a storm, Jesus and His disciples were threatened with drowning, but He stilled the boisterous elements with a word, causing the amazement expressed in verse 27.

> 28 And when he was come to the other side into the country of the Gergesenes, there met him two possessed with devils, coming out of the tombs, exceeding fierce, so that no man might pass by that way.
>
> 29 And, behold, they cried out, saying, What have we to do with thee, Jesus, thou Son of God? art though come hither to torment us before the time?
>
> 30 And there was a good way off from them an herd of many swine feeding.
>
> 31 So the devils besought him, saying, If thou cast us out, suffer us to go away into the herd of swine.
>
> 32 And he said unto them, Go. And when they were come out, they went into the herd of swine: and, behold, the whole herd of swine ran violently down a steep place into the sea, and perished in the waters.
>
> 33 And they that kept them fled, and went their ways into the city, and told everything, and what was befallen to the possessed of the devils.

34 And, behold, the whole city came out to meet Jesus: and when they saw him, they besought him that he would depart out of their coasts.

**1. Two demoniacs (vv. 28-32).**—Because most of us are not familiar with the phenomenon of demon possession, the concept is hard for us to understand. Missionaries in pagan lands, however, witness to seeing this condition in modern times. Many Bible references compel our acceptance of it as a reality, which Luke, a physician, distinguished from ordinary diseases (Luke 4:40-41). The question asked of Jesus by the afflicted men meant, "What have we in common with you?" They recognized the unique personality of Jesus and addressed Him as Son of God. The demons knew judgment awaited them and feared that it might be imposed right away. There are unanswered questions about the swine and their owners. If they were Jews, they were breaking the law, and the loss of them was a judgment against them.

**2. Crowd reaction (vv. 33-34).**—We are not told the reason for the action of the townspeople in asking Jesus to leave. Was it anger at the loss of the swine? Or fear over all that had happened? Perhaps both. In either case, they dismissed Jesus and the message He carried, more concerned over the loss of their property than the salvation of their souls. The Gospel of Mark, which records only one demoniac, tells of his request to remain in the company of Jesus. But he was sent back to his home and told, "Tell them how great things the Lord hath done for thee" (5:19). So the people of the city were not left without witness.

### III. Sickness and Sin (Matt. 9:1-8)

The opening words of this chapter are, "And after getting into a boat he crossed the sea and came to his own town" (NRSV). This is confirmed as Capernaum in Mark 2:1. After beginning His public ministry, Jesus made this town His center. Peter lived there (Matt. 8:5,14), as also did Andrew, and possibly James and John (Mark 1:29). Capernaum was a small but busy fishing center on the northwest shore of the Sea of Galilee.

1 And he entered into a ship, and passed over, and came into his own city.
2 And, behold, they brought to him a man sick of the palsy, lying on a bed: and Jesus seeing their faith said unto the sick of the palsy; Son, be of good cheer: thy sins be forgiven thee.
3 And, behold, certain of the scribes said within themselves, This man blasphemeth.
4 And Jesus knowing their thoughts said, Wherefore think ye evil in your hearts?
5 For whether is easier, to say, Thy sins be forgiven thee; or to say, Arise, and walk?
6 But that ye may know that the Son of man hath power on

earth to forgive sins, (then saith he to the sick of the palsy,) Arise, take up thy bed, and go unto thine house.
7 And he arose, and departed to his house.
8 But when the multitudes saw it, they marveled, and glorified God, which had given such power unto men.

**Recrossing the lake (v. 1).**—We have noticed the change from "ship"(KJV) to "boat"(NRSV), which corrects possible misunderstanding. We reserve "ship" for larger vessels, whereas those used in the fishing business around the shores of Galilee were comparatively small, but sturdy, to withstand the fierce storms that frequently arose. Our Lord had ready access to boats for transportation because several of His disciples were Galilean fishermen.

**2. Response to faith (v. 2).**—Many of our Lord's healing miracles were performed in response to the faith of the afflicted person. Some were not. Consider the case of Jairus's daughter (9:18-19, 23-26) and the centurion's servant (Luke 7:1-10). In the present case, it was the faith of those who brought the paralytic to Jesus that induced His response. We are encouraged to intercede for others believing that the Lord's response is not limited by rigid rules. However, personal faith is a requirement for salvation (Acts 16:31).

**3. Critical comment (v. 3).**—Our Lord's response to the paralytic was to pronounce forgiveness of his sins. This must not be interpreted to mean that all physical ailments are the consequence of sins committed, although ailments in general may be regarded as the result of the fall. Capernaum was our Lord's base, and He may have known this man and the cause of his sickness. The impression made is that the sufferer was depressed over the memory of some wrongdoing, for Jesus said to him, "Son, be of good cheer." In such case, the healing of his emotions preceded the healing of his body. Some religious leaders who were present criticized Jesus for usurping the authority of God by pronouncing forgiveness.

**4. Healing completed (vv. 4-8).**—Jesus read the thoughts of His critics and asked them a question they hesitated to answer. Obviously, to say, "Arise, and walk" was more difficult because it required visible results. Were Jesus to speak these words, and the man remain unhealed, He would stand revealed as an impostor. But, since He could speak words of healing that proved effective, He could also claim the authority to forgive. He sent the man away, walking on his two feet, both healed and forgiven.

**5. Calling of Matthew.**—Before we leave this chapter we should note that verse 9 records the call of Matthew to discipleship. He was a tax collector for the Romans, and in this account belonged to a despised class, also suspected of extortion. He was also known as Levi (Mark 2:14). Up to this point, therefore, he must have depended on other sources for his Gospel narrative, possibly in part on Mark's Gospel.

## APPLYING THE BIBLE

**Abraham Lincoln's kindness.**—General George E. Pickett led the valiant but futile charge of the Confederate Army at Gettysburg on July 3, 1863. It, along with the battle at Vicksburg the same month, shattered Lee's army.

After the Battle of Five Forks, Richmond surrendered and word came to Mrs. Pickett that her husband had been killed in battle. But she never believed the report which later proved to be false.

One day shortly after Richmond had fallen, someone knocked at the Pickett's front door and she opened the door to find a tall, sad-faced, gaunt man standing there.

"Is this George Pickett's place?" he asked. "Yes," Mrs. Pickett replied, "but he is not here."

The tall man in ill-fitting clothes replied he was aware of that but just wanted to stop by and see his home. He then introduced himself as Abraham Lincoln.

"The President!" she gasped. But Lincoln shook his head and replied, "No ma'am, it's just Abraham Lincoln, George's old friend."

Although General George Pickett and Abraham Lincoln were on opposite sides in the great conflict, a gentle, tenderhearted president had time to remember an old friend.

Our lesson writer today quotes the words of Luke about Jesus where it is written, "He went about doing good" (Acts 10:38). It is a simple tribute to the gracious and kind Savior who was never too busy to be good and kind to hurting people.

**The ministry of Jesus.**—In Exodus 15:26 the Lord said: "For I am the Lord that healeth thee." In the Hebrew it is "Jehova Ropheca." He is the healer of all diseases, both physical and emotional problems, regardless of the medicines, procedures, or therapy used.

About Jesus it is said in our lesson background for today that He "went about all Galilee, teaching in their synagogues, and preaching the gospel of the kingdom and healing all manner of sickness and all manner of disease among the people" (Matt. 4:23). The three activities that consumed His time were teaching, preaching, and healing. And we Christians are involved in the same triune ministry: we teach the Word of God; we preach the gospel; and our Christian hospitals minister to the sick. But all have but one purpose: to point men and women to Jesus Christ who takes away the sin of the world. He is the Great Physician, the Great Savior, and the Great Teacher.

**Satan is still alive and active.**—Few passages in the New Testament show the awful power of Satan more than the scene in 8:28-34. According to Matthew, two men were possessed with devils and Jesus cast out the devils and sent them into a herd of swine feeding nearby, and they all plunged "down a steep place into the sea, and perished in the waters" (v. 32). Although sophisticated people today scoff at the idea of a personal devil, all one has to do to believe in

Satan and his power is look at our world. And surely none of us doubts that demon possession, such as our lesson refers to today, is still a reality in the twentieth century.

Satan is active (Job 1:7; 1 Pet. 5:8); his power is limited (Job 2:6; Rev. 20:10); he resists God and His people (Zech. 3:1); the Lord rebukes him (v. 2); Satan wants us to worship him (Matt. 4:10); he even tempted Jesus (Matt. 4); he uses people (16:22-23); he steals the word of God out of the hearts of people (Mark 4:15); but he can be resisted (Eph. 6:10-19).

**The sweetest word in the Bible.**—The late Clarence E. Macartney told about a cemetery not too far from New York City in which a headstone has one word inscribed on it. It is the word, *Forgiven*. On the headstone there is no name, date of birth, or date of death. It is a plain, simple, unembellished headstone with a one-word tribute. But it's the sweetest word in the Bible.

To the man sick with the palsy (Matt. 9:2) Jesus said, "Son, be of good cheer; thy sins be forgiven thee."

Search the Scriptures through. Read carefully. And you will conclude that *Forgiven* is the sweetest word in the Bible.

## TEACHING THE BIBLE

▶ *Main Idea:* Jesus' deliverance and forgiveness demonstrate the concern of God the Father and God the Son in both the spiritual and physical well-being of people.

▶ *Suggested Teaching Aim:* To examine Jesus' healing of the demoniacs and the paralytic, and to list ways they have experienced God's concern for their spiritual and physical well-being.

### Introduce the Bible Study

Use the illustration "Abraham Lincoln's kindness" (*Applying the Bible*) to introduce the Bible study.

### Search for Biblical Truth

To set the context of this lesson, read or summarize the first two paragraphs under *Studying the Bible.* Organize the class in two groups or use the alternate procedure that follows. Assign group 1 Matthew 8:28-34; assign group 2 Matthew 9:1-8.

---

**A TEACHING OUTLINE**

*1. Set the context by reading from Studying the Bible.*
*2. Choose either the question/answer method or the biblical simulation method and make the proper preparations.*
*3. Encourage members to list ways God has shown His concern for their spiritual and physical well-being.*
*4. Lead members to write how they feel about God's provisions for them.*

---

Instruct the groups that they are to study both passages of Scriptures. For their assigned passage, they are to write questions they will ask the other group. They are to study the alternate passage so they can answer the questions the other group will ask them. Allow ten minutes for the study and ten minutes for each group to question the other.

— OR —

Conduct a biblical simulation (or use these questions to guide a group discussion). You or someone you enlist could serve as a television reporter to interview the two demoniacs and the paralytic after Jesus healed the men. You also could interview persons who saw what happened. Use the following questions and add to them any you wish.

> **The Demoniacs—**
>
> Tell me about your life before you met Jesus. What was it like to be demon possessed? When did you first know Jesus was coming to the country of the Gergesenes? What was your reaction to Jesus' presence? Why do you think the demons requested Jesus to let them go into the swine? Why did the townspeople react the way they did? Why didn't they want Jesus to stay in their area? What was Jesus' reaction to their request? How did you feel about Jesus leaving? What did you do after He left?
>
> **The Paralytic —**
>
> Tell me about your life before you met Jesus. How did you know Jesus? How did you get to Jesus? What did Jesus say to you? What was the reaction of the scribes to your healing? What was Jesus' response to the scribes? What was the crowd's reaction? What did you do after you left?

**Give the Truth a Personal Focus**

After using either of the suggestions above, write the words *Spiritual* and *Physical* on a chalkboard or a large sheet of paper. Ask members to suggest ways that God has shown His concern for their spiritual and physical welfare. List these as members suggest them.

Distribute paper and pencils. Ask members to choose one of their experiences and to write how they felt when they realized how God had provided for them. Ask several volunteers to share what they wrote with the class.

# Jesus, the Son of David

**Basic Passage:** Matthew 12
**Focal Passage:** Matthew 12:9-23

Two titles are given to our Lord in our lesson passage: "son of David" (v. 23) and "Son of man" (v. 32). The former was used by admirers who confessed amazement over His healing powers. The second by Jesus Himself, a title that He borrowed from Daniel 7:13. When the crowds questioned whether He might be "the son of David," they were recalling Old Testament promises of a coming deliverer, born into the line of their celebrated king, who they supposed would be their champion against the Roman aggressors. When Jesus used the term, "Son of man," He was deliberately avoiding a messianic claim because of the misunderstanding associated with it. To have done otherwise would have led to conflict with the Roman authorities who were quick to react to any suggestion of rebellion against their rule. More importantly, it would have misrepresented His mission, for although a crown eventually awaited Him (a universal, not a national crown), it would be attained by way of a cross. His immediate purpose was the provision of salvation, "for he shall save his people from their sins" (1:21).

**Study Aim:** *To personally take to heart the words of the Lord Jesus, "He that is not with me is against me" (Matt. 12:30)*

## STUDYING THE BIBLE

Matthew again shows design in his Gospel by concentrating in chapter 12 on several examples of opposition to the Lord Jesus. Though writing primarily to Jewish readers, he did not conceal the animosity against Jesus on the part of religious leaders. He thus countered rumors that Jesus was a revolutionary who provoked opposition from the Romans. The controversies in which He was involved were caused by the rigid legalism of Pharisees and others which Jesus set aside in order to carry out His ministry of compassion for the handicapped.

### I. The Sabbath Conflict (Matt. 12:1-8)

On their return from Babylonian exile, the Jews developed a strong identity consciousness in which they sought means to distinguish themselves from other races and religions. The rite of circumcision and the observance of the Sabbath became badges of Jewishness that separated them from others. They defended these with excessive zeal.

**1. The disciples' offense (vv. 1-2).**—The Mosaic law allowed persons using footpaths through farmed property to help themselves to whatever was growing. The disciples plucked ears of corn (small grain), which they shucked by rubbing the grains between their hands. This was condemned by the Pharisees as Sabbath labor, a breach of the law, as interpreted by them. They had listed a number of trifling activities as prohibited, including tying or untying a knot and writing two letters of the alphabet. The disciples' action, in their eyes, was the equivalent of reaping and winnowing crops.

**2. Our Lord's defense (vv. 3-8).**—In light of what follows, these are important verses. Jesus argued that, from the action of David (1 Sam. 21:1-6) and the practice of temple priests (1 Chron. 9:32), ritual laws must give place to human need. He made two tremendous claims for Himself: one, that He was "greater than the temple," and, two, that He was "Lord even of the sabbath day." These claims were sufficient, in the opinion of the Pharisees, to condemn Him for blasphemy.

## II. Incident in Synagogue (Matt. 12:9-13)

The local synagogue furnished opportunity for the Pharisees to expose publicly our Lord's attitude toward the sabbath. The origin of synagogues is debated, but their purpose is clear. They did not duplicate the worship of the temple, having no altars or priests, but were centers of biblical instruction and prayer. Any community could introduce a synagogue, governed by "rulers" selected from the local population.

> 9 And when he was departed thence, he went into their synagogue:
> 10 And, behold, there was a man which had his hand withered. And they asked him, saying, Is it lawful to heal on the sabbath days? that they might accuse him.
> 11 And he said unto them, What man shall there be among you, that shall have one sheep, and if it fall into a pit on the sabbath day, will he not lay hold on it, and lift it out?
> 12 How much then is a man better than a sheep? Wherefore it is lawful to do well on the sabbath days.
> 13 Then saith he to the man, Stretch forth thine hand. And he stretched it forth; and it was restored whole, like as the other.

**1. Loaded question (vv. 9-10).**—One of the Sabbath laws sponsored by the Pharisees was that healing should only be attempted in life-and-death situations. Obviously, a man with a withered hand did not fit into that category, though his need was great, and Jesus had the power to relieve that need. The Pharisees sensed what His response would be, and so addressed a question to Him which required an answer which challenged their rigid ruling.

**2. Man or sheep? (vv. 11-13).**—Our Lord surprised His critics with a question that exposed their inconsistency. Many of them kept sheep and if one of these fell into a pit on the Sabbath, they would get it out. Then the pointed question, "How much then is a man better than a sheep?" Jesus laid down the important principle that "it is lawful to do well on the sabbath days," that is, a good deed is appropriate any day of the week. Where the observance of the Sabbath interfered with the performance of kind actions, the observance must yield to human need. Having thus silenced His critics, Jesus healed the man's withered hand.

## III. Violence Versus Gentleness (Matt. 12:14-21)

We should not think of Pharisees as basically evil people. They were extremely religious, with deep-seated loyalties to what they believed to be essential rituals for the preservation of their race. Among them were some who would go to any lengths to defend these rituals, and these were the people who became the enemies of our Lord. There were other reasons for their bitter hostility, including the thought that the teaching and practice of Jesus constituted a challenge to their authority.

14 Then the Pharisees went out, and held a council against him, how they might destroy him.
15 But when Jesus knew it, he withdrew himself from thence: and great multitudes followed him, and he healed them all;
16 And charged them that they should not make him known:
17 That it might be fulfilled which was spoken by Isaiah the prophet, saying,
18 Behold my servant, whom I have chosen; my beloved, in whom my soul is well-pleased: I will put my spirit upon him, and he shall show judgment to the Gentiles.
19 He shall not strive, nor cry; neither shall any man hear his voice in the streets.
20 A bruised reed shall he not break, and smoking flax shall he not quench, till he send forth judgment unto victory.
21 And in his name shall the Gentiles trust.

**1. Hostile action (vv. 14-15).**—The incident of the man with the withered hand precipitated extreme action on the part of the Pharisees. Jesus had embarrassed them publicly by His question, "How much then is a man better than a sheep?" and they decided that the only remedy was to do away with Him. Made aware of their intention, our Lord left the area, for He still had work to do. That the common people did not share the attitude of the Pharisees is evident from the "great multitudes" that followed Him. He continued His ministry of healing for the afflicted among them.

**2. Old Testament portrait (vv. 16-21).**—Our Lord's request of the people not to spread the news of His healing work prompted Matthew to show how this avoidance of publicity fitted into Isaiah's portrait of the Suffering Servant (Isa. 42:1-4). He also showed how the conduct of Jesus contrasted with that of His enemies. They drew attention to themselves by practicing their piety and good works on street corners (Matt. 6:1-5). Gentiles are mentioned twice in Isaiah's passage, making this other contrast that while He was rejected among His own people, "in his name shall the Gentiles trust." From the Book of Acts onward, the New Testament records belief in the Lord Jesus on the part of innumerable Gentiles. An immediate reason for Jesus to discourage the spreading of news about His healing ministry was that this was subordinate to His chief mission as the Savior from sin.

### IV. The Sin Without Forgiveness (Matt. 12:22-32)

Throughout His ministry, even beyond His resurrection (Acts 1:6), Jesus had to contend with the mistaken notion that His messiahship would be expressed in political action to end the Roman domination and restore Jewish power and prestige. The Isaiah passage already quoted was intended to change the idea of a militant messiahship by depicting a Suffering Servant engaged in a redemptive mission. This portrait is made even clearer in Isaiah 53. Too much talk about His miracles could encourage a false image of the Messiah, divert attention from His spiritual mission, and even provoke action on the part of Rome. But these dangers did not deter Jesus from continuing to heal.

> **22 Then was brought unto him one possessed with a devil, blind, and dumb: and he healed him, insomuch that the blind and dumb both spake and saw.**
>
> **23 And all the people were amazed, and said, Is not this the son of David?**

**1. Messianic title (vv. 22-23).**—Another line of prophecy that stirred Jewish hopes of national restoration concerned promises made to David that "thy throne shall be established for ever" (2 Sam. 7:16). The Messiah was expected to be a descendant of that famous king, hence the crowd's reaction, "Is not this the son of David?" As the genealogy with which Matthew's Gospel begins indicates, Jesus was indeed born into the royal line.

**2. Bitter allegation (vv. 24-30).**—This popular acclaim only provoked our Lord's enemies to deeper hostility. They accused Him of performing miracles with Satan's help. He countered by asking two questions: Some of their followers claimed to be able to cast out demons. Were they doing this by satanic power? And, if Satan casts out Satan, how can his dominion last?

**3. Unpardonable sin (vv. 31-32).**—Because of misunderstanding concerning "the unpardonable sin," not itself a Bible phrase, these verses merit careful consideration. Interpretation depends on context. The sin that "hath never forgiveness" (Mark 3:29) is rejection of Christ, to whom the Holy Spirit bears witness that He is the Son of God and Savior.

## APPLYING THE BIBLE

**The names of Jesus.**—Jesus said "I am Alpha and Omega, the first and the last" (Rev. 1:11). "Alpha" is the first letter in the Greek alphabet, and "Omega" is the last letter. Jesus is saying that to us He will be everything we need from "A to Z."

I do not know by how many names Jesus is called in Holy Scripture, but look at these:

Advocate (1 John 2:1)
Beloved (Matt. 3:17)
Christ (John 1:41)
Deliverer (Rom. 11:26)
Eternal Life (1 John 5:20)
Friend of Sinners (Matt. 11:19)
God (John 1:1)
I Am (John 8:58)
Immortal (1 Tim. 1:17)
Jesus (Matt. 1:21)
King of Kings (Rev. 17:14)
Life (John 14:6)
Man of Sorrows (Isa. 53:3)
Nazarene (Matt. 2:23)
Offspring of David (Rev. 22:16)
Only Begotten (John 1:14)
Pearl of Great Price (Matt. 13:46)
Prince of Peace (Isa. 9:6)
Quickening Spirit (1 Cor. 15:45)
Redeemer (Isa. 59:20)
Savior (Luke 2:11)
Truth (John 14:6)
Unspeakable Gift (2 Cor. 9:15)
Vine (John 15:1)
Word of Life (1 John 1:1)

**The Jewish sabbath.**—Today's lesson touches on the importance of the Jewish Sabbath in Jesus' day. The Jews reckoned time from sunset to sunset. This is based on the account of creation where "the evening and the morning" constituted a day. Notice that it does not say from "morning to evening." Thus, the Jewish Sabbath begins at sunset on Friday and ends with sunset on Saturday.

"Sabbath" means "to cease" or "to desist." It's primary meaning is that of cessation from all work. In both accounts of the giving of the Ten Commandments, it is stated that the Sabbath belonged to the Lord. Six days the Israelites could work, but the seventh, which belonged to the Lord, was to be a day of rest and worship. It was a holy day because God rested on the seventh day after creation (Ex. 20:8-11). It also was a reminder of their redemption from Egyptian slavery (Deut. 5:12-15).

During the interbiblical period (between Malachi and Matthew, a span of four hundred years), the Sabbath became the heart of the law, and prohibitions governing the Sabbath were expanded to where thirty-nine tasks were banned even to the tying or untying of a knot. These tasks or activities were expanded until the day lost its spirit and original intention and became only a legalistic requirement.

Jesus observed the Sabbath as a day of worship, but He refused to comply with the legalistic, minute restrictions that had developed after the law was given. Consequently, Christ's unorthodox observance of the Sabbath was a constant irritation to the Jewish religious leaders.

It needs to be pointed out, however, that we Christians observe Sunday as the "Christian sabbath" because of Christ's resurrection on the first day of the week and His postresurrection appearances to His disciples, at least eleven of which took place on the first day of the week.

**The synagogue.**—The word *synagogue*, with reference to Jesus and His ministry, appears about forty times in the Gospels. Since it was such an important place in the life and ministry of Jesus, perhaps we should look at it.

*Young's Analytical Concordance* defines *synagogue* as a "place where people are led together." The synagogues were the local meeting places of Jews during New Testament times, and synagogues existed both in and outside Israel where Jews lived. The temple was destroyed in A.D. 70, and until that time it was the center for sacrificial worship, but the Jews also participated in their local synagogues. A synagogue could be established in any community in which as many as ten Jewish men lived. That, no doubt, was the reason ancient Philippi had none (Acts 16:13). Local elders had the general oversight of the synagogue.

In the Gospels, Jesus is often found in the synagogue. When He was home in Nazareth, He attended the Nazareth synagogue (Luke 4:16). Frequently, He taught and preached in the synagogues. He even healed in the synagogue (Matt. 12:9-13).

## TEACHING THE BIBLE

▶ *Main Idea:* Jesus' response to the title "the son of David" shows His understanding of His messiahship.

▶ *Suggested Teaching Aim:* To lead adults to examine Jesus' understanding of His messiahship, and to list ways His messiahship affects their lives.

### A TEACHING OUTLINE

*1. Introduce the Bible study by using a case study.*
*2. Guide a group discussion.*
*3. Develop and examine principles that relate to our helping others and worshiping Jesus.*

**Introduce the Bible Study**

Read the following case study and let members complete it. John and Brenda were sitting at the breakfast table Sunday morning. Both taught Sunday School, and they were putting the finishing touches to their lessons when Charlotte, their next-door neighbor knocked on their door. She was quite upset because her husband had not come home the night before. She had suspected for some time that he had been having an affair. She was talking, crying, and making threats about what she might do. Both John and Brenda realized the need to talk to Charlotte, but they also had commitments at church. They could sense each other's feelings about what they should do, so John . . .

**Search for Biblical Truth**

Point out that knowing how to respond to our commitments can be difficult at times. However, Jesus laid down some important guidelines.

Ask members to open their Bibles to Matthew 12 and have a volunteer to read verses 9-13. IN ADVANCE, enlist a member to read

"Synagogue" in the *Holman Bible Dictionary* or other Bible dictionary and share a two- to three-minute report.

Use the following questions to guide a group discussion: Why did the Jews consider it unlawful to heal on the Sabbath? What was the significance of Jesus' response to their question? What principle did Jesus set up about the importance of people compared to the importance of religious institutions?

DISCUSSION QUESTION: What guidelines can you set up to determine whether helping someone or obeying a religious rule is more important?

Ask a volunteer to read verses 14-21. Ask: Why did Jesus' response upset the Pharisees so much? Why did Jesus withdraw at this point instead of confronting the Pharisees? Why did Jesus urge those He healed not to tell people? What was Matthew's purpose in referring to Isaiah 42:1-4 at this point?

DISCUSSION QUESTION: What guidelines for reaching people can you draw from Matthew's reference to Gentiles?

Ask a volunteer to read 12:22-23. Ask: How did Jesus' healing of the man who could not see nor hear support Jesus' claim to be the Messiah? What did the term "son of David" mean?

DISCUSSION QUESTION: How did Jesus' understanding of His messiahship affect how He responded to people?

**Give the Truth a Personal Focus**

Ask: How does the principle Jesus established in 12:12 apply to you? How does Jesus' concern for the Gentiles affect you? How does Jesus' messiahship affect your day-to-day activities? How should it affect you?

As members suggest answers to the last question, list these on a chalkboard or a large sheet of paper. Read verse 30 and ask, What is the relationship between accepting Jesus' messiahship and verse 30?

Ask members to suggest areas similar to the opening case study where they could see tension between helping persons and worshiping Jesus. Point out that if conflict exists, the conflict comes because we have misunderstood what Jesus wants us to do.

> If you prefer a "Sanctity of Life" lesson, it can be found in the back of this book.

January
15
1995

# A Foreigner's Faith

**Basic Passage:** Matthew 15:1-31
**Focal Passage:** Matthew 15:21-31

There are increasing reports of racial strife, not only in this country, but also throughout the world. Some of the most extreme racists among us claim biblical grounds for their position. It is therefore important for us to know the mind of Christ on such matters. Our study passage focuses on Jesus' dealings with a Gentile woman, a foreigner. On the surface, some of His words may seem to support a policy of racial discrimination. But by His actions He disproved any such assumption. It will be our task to explain and reconcile the two. For the moment, we might take the writer of the first Gospel, Matthew, as a guide to right understanding of this subject. Himself a Jew, Matthew wrote with Jewish readers in mind. He began by presenting Jesus as "the son of David, the son of Abraham" (1:1), and quoted extensively from the Old Testament to establish his claim that Jesus was the promised Messiah-King. But he alone of the evangelists preserved the story of the wise men (chap. 2), and he concluded his Gospel with the announcement of a worldwide mission for the disciples when Jesus said, "Go ye therefore, and teach all nations, baptizing them in the name of the Father, and of the Son, and of the Holy Ghost" (28:19). Such a command tore down all barriers.

**Study Aim:** *To reflect Christ's love for all persons, regardless of social or racial differences*

## STUDYING THE BIBLE

The varied ministry of the Lord Jesus is well marked in the Gospel of Matthew. For example, chapter 13 is composed of parables, those wonderful illustrations from life that He used to teach spiritual truths. Chapter 14 records the death of John the Baptist and continues the account of Jesus' miracles, including the feeding of the five thousand (14:15-21), of particular interest since our lesson chapter contains another story of feeding, this time of four thousand (15:32-38). Unhappily, this chapter also returns to the controversy between our Lord and Jewish leaders.

### I. Human Traditions (Matt. 15:1-9)

Our Lord repeatedly affirmed His loyalty to the laws of God. His protest was against the rules and regulations added by the religious leaders, referred to as "the tradition of the elders" (v. 2). The problem was that the Pharisees gave to these the same authority as to the Old Testament laws. The washing of hands was the point at issue. Washing was required, not for hygienic purposes, but as a matter of religious ritual. The Pharisees complained that the disciples did not carry out this ritual, a criticism that was probably directed also at Jesus Himself.

**1. Hypocrisy exposed (vv. 3-6).**—Our Lord's response was to accuse His critics of ignoring the divine law of responsibility for parents (Ex. 20:12). They avoided this responsibility by a practice called "Corban," in Mark 7:11, an Aramaic word for "given to God." Property thus dedicated could not be given to others, though retained by the owner. Jesus said that the practice "made the commandment of God of none effect" (v. 6).

**2. Old Testament reproof (vv. 7-9).**—This kind of behavior was rebuked in Isaiah 29:13, which our Lord quoted against His critics. They were guilty of the worst kind of pretense, professing to honor God while "their heart is far from me." Their guilt was the deeper because of the enmity they were showing toward God's Son.

## II. Causes of Defilement (Matt. 15:10-20)

The implication of the failure of the disciples to wash their hands was that they were therefore eating defiled food. This led our Lord to discuss the subject of defilement, significant for this chapter which goes on to report His dealings with Gentiles, considered unclean by Jews, who avoided contact with them for fear of defilement.

**1. Source of defilement (vv. 10-11).**—The rigid food laws of the Old Testament encouraged the idea that what a person eats can cause defilement. Not so, said our Lord; what issues from a person in words, thought, and attitudes are defiling. He elaborated on this in verses 18-19.

**2. Peter's questions (vv. 12-20).**—This disciple listened with concern as his Master repudiated some of the basic teaching of the Pharisees. But He replied by restating what He had already said and by comparing the Pharisees to "blind leaders of the blind." Peter himself remained blind to this matter until the incident recorded in Acts 10:9-18.

## III. A Gentile's Plea (Matt. 15:21-28)

In the incident concerning Peter mentioned above, God used dietary laws about clean and unclean foods to teach that apostle a lesson about another assumed source of ritual defilement, contact with Gentiles. Jews went to extraordinary lengths to avoid association with non-Jews. The woman at Sychar's well was right when she said that "the Jews have no dealings with the Samaritans" (John 4:9). Matthew recorded that, to avoid further conflict with the Pharisees, Jesus went into Gentile territory, "the district of Tyre and Sidon" (Matt. 15:21, NRSV). There, in an incident that requires careful study, He responded to a Gentile's cry for help.

> **21 Then Jesus went thence, and departed into the coasts of Tyre and Sidon.**
>
> **22 And, behold, a woman of Canaan came out of the same coasts, and cried unto him, saying, Have mercy on me, O Lord,**

thou son of David; my daughter is grievously vexed with a devil.
23 But he answered her not a word. And his disciples came
and besought him, saying, Send her away; for she crieth after us.
24 But he answered and said, I am not sent but unto the lost
sheep of the house of Israel.
25 Then came she and worshiped him, saying, Lord, help me.
26 But he answered and said, It is not meet to take the
children's bread, and to cast it to dogs.
27 And she said, Truth, Lord: yet the dogs eat of the crumbs
which fall from their masters' table.
28 Then Jesus answered and said unto her, O woman, great
is thy faith: be it unto thee even as thou wilt. And her daughter
was made whole from that very hour.

**1. Apparent rejection (vv. 21-24).**—The woman exhibited strong faith in addressing Jesus as "son of David" for this was a messianic title. She may have heard others speak of Him this way (9:27). That our Lord made no response creates a problem that we must try to resolve, for it was so contrary to His nature. The disciples' reaction is understandable. To them, this Gentile woman was bothering Jesus and them, for apparently she was keeping up with the group as she repeated her plea. In tune with the feeling of the disciples, our Lord seemed to conclude the matter by declaring His mission to be exclusively to "the lost sheep of the house of Israel." Had the incident ended there, we would have great difficulty explaining it.

**2. Successful appeal (vv. 25-28).**—But the woman was persistent, and, in her earnestness, fell at Jesus' feet with the cry, "Lord, help me." He still seemed unmoved as He spoke of not giving the children's bread to dogs. The word He used was "little dogs," puppies, or family pets. Could we have seen the expression on His face as He said this we might better understand the hopeful reply of the suppliant. She rose to the occasion, was commended for her faith, and the daughter was healed in "that very hour."

**3. Possible explanations.**—The most valid are these. (1) He was testing and encouraging the woman's faith. She would not be surprised at His first reaction, which was that of a typical Jew toward a Gentile. But she did not give up, for she had a higher opinion of Him whom she addressed as "son of David." She took His reference to dogs and turned this into an evidence of her faith for which she had the Master's praise. (2) Jesus was teaching His disciples by first assuming their prejudiced attitude and then turning everything around by granting the woman her request.

**4. Later developments.**—This incident can be seen as a foreshadowing of the ministry of the church, exemplified in the evangelistic work of the apostle Paul. The message of the gospel was to the Jew first, for it was God's purpose from the call of Abraham to raise up a people for Himself through which "all families of the earth [might] be blessed"

(Gen. 12:3). When Jesus commissioned His disciples, on the day of His ascension, He charged them to be witnesses "both in Jerusalem, and in all Judaea," and then, "in Samaria, and unto the uttermost part of the earth" (Acts 1:8). The apostle Paul and his associates followed these instructions, and only when entry into synagogues was barred for them did they say, "Lo, we turn to the Gentiles" (13:46). Witness to Jews is a continuing responsibility to Christians.

## IV. Compassion for All (Matt. 15:29-31)

In his parallel account, Mark told that, after leaving the area of Tyre and Sidon, Jesus came into "the region of the Decapolis" (Mark 7:31, NRSV). This was Gentile territory, east of the Sea of Galilee, though we need also remember that Galilee itself was known as "Galilee of the Gentiles" because of its heavy non-Jewish population. It is a fair assumption that these closing verses of Matthew 15 describe a ministry to these people. The statement that, after our Lord had healed many, "they glorified the God of Israel," strengthens this supposition for this was a phrase Gentiles would use.

> **29 And Jesus departed from thence, and came nigh unto the sea of Galilee; and went up into a mountain, and sat down there.**
> **30 And great multitudes came unto him, having with them those that were lame, blind, dumb, maimed, and many others, and cast them down at Jesus' feet; and he healed them:**
> **31 Insomuch that the multitude wondered, when they saw the dumb to speak, the maimed to be whole, the lame to walk, and the blind to see: and they glorified the God of Israel.**

**1. Many healed (vv. 29-31).**—Matthew gives us some insight into the prevalence of sickness and disease in gospel times. No attempt is made to catalog all the ailments with which people were afflicted. The important point is that Jesus had power, and willingness to heal them all. When they brought these poor sufferers and "cast them down at Jesus' feet" they had reached a point of despair. All else had failed and only God, working through His Son, could help.

**2. Many fed (vv. 32-39).**—Matthew had already recorded the feeding of the five thousand in 14:15-21. This second similar miracle seems to have been performed for the benefit of Gentiles and is not a repeated account of the previous miracle. What our Lord did for Jews He now did for Gentiles, for He is the universal Savior.

## APPLYING THE BIBLE

**Christ's compassion contrasted with Napoleon's ambition.**—In 1812 Napoleon and his army advanced into Russia. He had been warned about the Russian winters, but Napoleon scoffed at the warning. By September 14 his French army had reached Moscow.

But the Russians counterattacked and the cold winter did the rest.

Forced to retreat, Napoleon and his once-proud army crept back to France after a bitter two-month march. He had led more than five hundred thousand French soldiers into Russia, but fewer than twenty thousand made it back to France. And most of them were sick from typhus, frostbite, and starvation.

But Napoleon did not seem the least bothered that he had left no fewer than four hundred eighty thousand husbands, fathers, and sons dead in the Russian snow. To Austrian statesman and diplomat Prince von Metternich, Napoleon commented: "A man such as I is not much concerned over the lives of a million men."

Our lesson today vividly contrasts Napoleon's attitude toward humanity with Christ's attitude toward those who were hurting.

**Jesus and the hypocrites.**—Check a Bible concordance and you will discover that Jesus used the word *hypocrite* something like twenty times in the Gospels. And He used it in our lesson today. A hypocrite is a pretender, an actor, a deceiver.

In *The Madman: His Parable and Poems,* writer Kahlil Gibran tells about a mother and her daughter both of whom walked in their sleep. One night, Gibran writes, "walking, yet asleep, [they] met in the mist-veiled garden." The mother exclaimed, "At last, at last, my enemy! You by whom my youth was destroyed, have built up your life upon the ruins of mine! Would I could kill you!" And the daughter's judgment of her mother was just as harsh: "O hateful woman, selfish and old! Who stands between my freer self and me! Who would have my life an echo of your own faded life! Would you were dead!"

The crowing of a rooster suddenly awakened both women, and, very gently, the mother asked, "Is that you, darling?" And just as gently the daughter answered, "Yes, dear!" (See vv. 7-9.)

Jesus scathingly rebuked hypocrisy: acting one way but feeling another way; saying one thing, but meaning something else. Nothing stirred His ire as did hypocrisy! The "sinners and publicans" gathered about Him and He blessed them all. But He had no patience with the pretenders.

**Spurgeon's books banned.**—Surely God despises few things more than He despises racial prejudice. Our Lord Jesus is color-blind!

Our lesson today deals with the Jew's prejudice toward the Gentiles. But one of the most beautiful stories in the New Testament is in today's lesson. It shows Christ's contact with and blessings on a Gentile woman.

The greatest preacher in Christendom, after Paul, many think, was Charles Haddon Spurgeon. The great English Baptist preacher of the last century was called mad when he built the five-thousand seat Metropolitan Baptist Tabernacle in London. "He will never fill it," his critics exclaimed! But for thirty-seven years Spurgeon filled it, his fame spread around the world, and his weekly sermons in a forty-year period sold one hundred and fifty million copies.

A brave and courageous preacher, Spurgeon preached against

slavery and racial prejudice. Although his sermons had been very popular in America's Southland, Spurgeon's strong preaching for the freedom of the black man caused his books and sermons to be boycotted and banned in the South for a ten-year period. And in some cases, they were burned. But God used him mightily. Spurgeon wrote one hundred and thirty five books that were read worldwide.

Christ loved even the Gentile woman, respected and honored her faith, and blessed her because of it. There is no place for prejudice in the Christian church.

## TEACHING THE BIBLE

▶ *Main Idea:* An examination of Christ's relationship with a foreign woman portrays Christ's love for all persons regardless of social or racial differences.

▶ *Suggested Teaching Aim:* To examine Christ's relationship with the foreign woman, and to identify guidelines for relating to all persons regardless of social or racial differences.

### A TEACHING OUTLINE

1. *Introduce the Bible study.*
2. *Prepare a lecture using strip posters.*
3. *Lead the class in identifying guidelines for relating to all persons regardless of social or racial differences.*

**Introduce the Bible Study**

Use the illustration "Spurgeon's books banned" (*Applying the Bible*) to introduce the Bible study.

**Search for Biblical Truth**

IN ADVANCE, place a map on the wall showing Tyre and Sidon and the Sea of Galilee. Prepare strip posters of the following study outline:

I. Apparent Rejection (Matt. 15:21-24)
II. Successful Appeal (Matt. 15:25-28)
III. Compassion for All (Matt. 15:29-31)

Place the first study outline strip on the wall. Call on a volunteer to read Matthew 15:21-24. Point out Tyre and Sidon on the map and explain that this is not Jewish territory. Using *Studying the Bible*, present a brief lecture in which you cover the following points:

(1) the woman's use of the term "son of David";
(2) why Jesus first refused to respond to the woman;
(3) the disciples' reaction to the woman.

Place the second study outline strip on the wall. Call on a volunteer to read Matthew 15:25-28. Present a brief lecture in which you cover the following points:

(1) the woman's persistence;

(2) what Jesus meant by His play on words ("dogs");
(3) the woman's response to Jesus' comment;
(4) possible explanations;
(5) the significance of this event for Jesus' ministry and for the disciples.

Place the third study outline strip on the wall. Call on a volunteer to read Matthew 15:29-31. Locate Decapolis on the map and point out that this is also Gentile territory. Present a brief lecture in which you cover the following points:

(1) the incidence of sickness and disease in Gospel times;
(2) Jesus' compassion and power to heal;
(3) the people's reaction to Jesus' healing.

**Give the Truth a Personal Focus**

Organize the class in three groups. Assign each group one of the strips from the study outline. Ask them to do the following:

(1) examine their passage of Scripture to identify guidelines for relating to all persons regardless of social or racial differences;

(2) develop a case study, modern role-play, or skit that would present the guideline(s) to the class.

Allow the groups about five to six minutes to work, and then call for reports. Each group will have three minutes for its report.

As the groups report, write their guidelines on a chalkboard or a large sheet of paper. After the groups have listed all the guidelines, ask members if they can think of others they would want to add.

Ask: Considering these guidelines, how well does our class measure up in reaching all persons regardless of social or racial differences? What changes, if any, do we need to make? Let the class determine their response to these questions and make any changes necessary.

Close in prayer.

# Jesus Is Transfigured

**Basic Passage:** Matthew 17:1-23
**Focal Passage:** Matthew 17:1-13

Some events in life make an indelible impression that becomes a benchmark in the development and confirmation of Christian belief. For the apostle Peter, the transfiguration of our Lord was such an event. He, with fellow disciples James and John, was privileged to witness what happened that day on an unnamed mountain in northern Palestine. Peter wanted to give permanence to this glorious experience (v. 4), and though this was denied, the memory was prolonged in his heart and mind as an affirmation of the glory that will be Christ's at His second coming. In the second of his epistles, Peter spoke of being "eyewitnesses of his majesty" as an answer to those who accused him and others of promoting "cunningly devised fables" when they referred to Christ's return (2 Pet. 1:16). The apostle had no doubts about the reality of events on that remarkable day, and no doubts about that coming day when the Lord Jesus will receive universal honor and praise. May we catch a glimpse of that future glory as we study together the record of Matthew 17.

**Study Aim:** *To crown Jesus Lord here and now as we eagerly await the day when He assumes the throne of an everlasting kingdom*

## STUDYING THE BIBLE

Bible books were not written with chapter divisions. These were introduced for the convenience of readers, and we are grateful for them. But when studying the Bible it is often helpful to ignore these divisions and realize that we are reading what was written as a continuous narrative. This way, context will often play an important part in our understanding of a particular passage.

### I. Previous Events (Matt. 16:13-28)

This way, the transfiguration narrative is seen to relate to what had gone before. Our Lord had been facing the future in full knowledge of the pain and suffering He would have to endure. The disciples had been acquainted with the coming tragedy and the ongoing price they would pay for loyal discipleship. Both Jesus and His men, therefore, were ready for the manifestation of divine glory that took place when He took them up "into an high mountain apart" (v. 28).

**1. Peter's confession (vv. 13-20).**—Whether Peter spoke for himself or for all the disciples we do not know, but at Caesarea Philippi he made a great confession of faith when he said, "Thou are the Christ, the Son of the living God" (v. 16). The Master replied by saying that on the "rock" of this confession He would build His church.

**2. Peter's confusion (vv. 21-23).**—But when Jesus spoke of rejection and death, this same disciple responded in a way that gained him stern rebuke. He missed the reference to Christ's resurrection as he drew back in horror from the prospect of His cross.

**3. Our Lord's prediction (vv. 24-28).**—Jesus spoke of His sacrifice and that which His followers must be willing to make before speaking of His coming glory. We can only imagine the confusion in the minds of His disciples at seemingly conflicting statements.

## II. Mountaintop Experience (Matt. 17:1-8)

Against this background of mingled hope and fear, confidence and bewilderment, suffering and rejoicing, something happened that ministered to the needs of both our Lord and His followers. Jesus was "transfigured," or, "transformed," that is, His appearance was changed from that of "the likeness of men" (Phil. 2:7) to that of the glorified Son of God.

> **1 And after six days Jesus taketh Peter, James, and John his brother, and bringeth them up into an high mountain apart,**
> **2 And was transfigured before them: and his face did shine as the sun, and his raiment was white as the light.**
> **3 And, behold, there appeared unto them Moses and Elias talking with him.**
> **4 Then answered Peter, and said unto Jesus, Lord, it is good for us to be here: if thou wilt, let us make here three tabernacles; one for thee, and one for Moses, and one for Elias.**
> **5 While he yet spake, behold, a bright cloud overshadowed them: and behold a voice out of the cloud, which said, This is my beloved Son, in whom I am well pleased; hear ye him.**
> **6 And when the disciples heard it, they fell on their face, and were sore afraid.**
> **7 And Jesus came and touched them, and said, Arise, and be not afraid.**
> **8 And when they lifted up their eyes, they saw no man, save Jesus only.**

**1. Jesus glorified (vv. 1-3).**—The trio who accompanied our Lord were His chosen companions on other significant occasions (26:37). They were clearly being prepared for special ministry in the future. Both Peter and James were eventually martyred, but John outlived most of his companions and fellow witnesses and became the author of the Fourth Gospel. That figures recognized as Moses and Elijah were in the company of Jesus was significant, Moses representing the law and Elijah the prophets. Thus the Old Testament was made to bear witness to Jesus in two people whose lives ended uniquely, Moses being buried by God (Deut. 34:5-6) and Elijah ascending to heaven in a whirlwind (2 Kings 2:1). In his account of the transfiguration, Luke told us that the subject of discussion was "his decease which he should accomplish at Jerusalem" (Luke 9:31), a subject that had greatly troubled Peter previously (Matt. 16:21-23).

**2. Peter's request (v. 4).**—For the moment Peter was happy, so happy, in fact, that he wanted to make the experience permanent. He could not ignore the conversation about our Lord's coming death, but he thought to prevent, or at least postpone, that dreaded event. Whatever else we read into his behavior, we should not overlook his love for the Master, for whom he wished nothing but good. On this occasion he spoke, as Luke explained, "not knowing what he said" (Luke 9:33), that is, not understanding the impossibility of that for which he asked.

**3. Voice from heaven (vv. 5-8).**—The descent of a cloud symbolized the presence of God, who spoke acknowledging Jesus as His "beloved Son." The added words were, "hear ye him." It was important that all who heard Him speak should pay heed to His words, but particularly so for the three men there on the mount with Jesus. Words He had said (16:21), and would again say (17:12), were hard for them to accept. But they were of the very essence of the gospel which Peter and others would be given the responsibility to proclaim. The plan of redemption required the death of Jesus, "In whom we have redemption through his blood, the forgiveness of sins, according to the riches of his grace" (Eph. 1:7).

## III. On the Way Down (Matt. 17:9-13)

So long as they basked in the glory of the transfigured Christ, the three disciples were content. But the voice from heaven, accompanied by the dense cloud, reduced them to fear. They were released from their trembling by the quiet voice of Jesus Himself as He said, "Arise, and be not afraid." Opening their eyes "they saw no man, save Jesus only," and at His bidding they began the descent of the mountain.

> 9 And as they came down from the mountain, Jesus charged them, saying, Tell the vision to no man, until the Son of man be risen again from the dead.
>
> 10 And his disciples asked him, saying, Why then say the scribes that Elias must first come?
>
> 11 And Jesus answered and said unto them, Elias truly shall first come, and restore all things.
>
> 12 But I say unto you, That Elias is come already, and they knew him not, but have done unto him whatsoever they listed. Likewise shall also the Son of man suffer of them.
>
> 13 Then the disciples understood that he spake unto them of John the Baptist.

**1. Silence imposed (v. 9).**—The ban of silencc was complete. "Tell . . . no man," Jesus said, and that included the other disciples. In looking for a reason, we remember how our Lord told persons He had healed not to tell others (8:4; 9:30). He was not seeking a reputation as a worker of miracles, and saw possible mischief in reports of this kind. The transfiguration was so mysterious an event that those who witnessed it were not qualified at that point to discuss it with others. Attempted descriptions would doubtless lead to exaggerations that would prove obstacles to the carrying out of our Lord's true mission.

**2. Question about Elijah (vv. 10-13).**—For the three disciples to raise this question about Elijah suggests that they were at a loss as to what to say. But the presence of that prophet with the transfigured Christ had stirred their imaginations since it was widely believed that Elijah would come to prepare the way for the Messiah. This belief was based on Malachi 4:5-6. Setting aside a literal approach to this prophecy, Jesus said that Elijah had come in the person of John the Baptist. (See lesson for December 11.) The sad comment of our Lord was that John's role had not been recognized, leading to his death (Matt. 14:1-12), and the same fate awaited Him. Thus, in the context of the transfiguration, Jesus made clear reference to the cross which He must endure to enter into His ultimate glory (Rev. 5:12).

## V. Frustration in the Valley (Matt. 17:14-21)

While Simon Peter was expressing a wish to pitch his tent on the mountaintop, a human tragedy was taking place in the valley below. These verses are included in our basic study material and are worthy of our attention. Matthew clearly intended them to be part of his transfiguration narrative.

**1. Need not met (vv. 14-17).**—Nine disciples were left at the foot of the mountain. There they were confronted by a distressed father seeking healing for his acutely afflicted son. They attempted to respond, but failed. We can only assume that they supposed that, through their association with Jesus, they shared His power to heal. Therefore, in confidence falsely placed, self-confidence, they attempted the impossible.

**2. Lack of faith (vv. 18-21).**—Our Lord diagnosed this failure as due to lack of faith, not "unbelief" (KJV). "Why could not we cast it out? . . . Because of your little faith" (NRSV). What faith they had was wrongly exercised, for Jesus acknowledged that mustard-seed-size faith can remove mountains, that is, mountainous problems or obstacles. Verse 21 is not considered part of Matthew's record, but a later addition, since it is not found in some reliable manuscripts (see NRSV note).

## APPLYING THE BIBLE

**Peter's great confession.**—Peter's great confession of faith, "Thou are the Christ, the Son of the living God," is a high-water mark in the New Testament. Since that time when Peter enthusiastically blurted out his heartfelt confession of faith in Jesus, millions upon millions of believers have followed his example.

Several prominent literary figures were visiting in London years ago discussing the great men of the past.

One of the men raised the question, "Gentlemen, what would you do if John Milton entered the room?" One of the men quickly replied, "We would give him such an ovation as might compensate for the tardy recognition accorded him by the men of his day."

Another asked, "And what would you do if Shakespeare were to enter?" And someone else replied, "We would arise and crown him master of song."

Another asked, "And what if Jesus Christ were to enter the room?" And Charles Lamb, noted for his literary brilliance, said, as silence settled over the room, "We would all fall on our faces."[1]

This was Peter's attitude. He fell on his face, as it were, and confessed that Jesus is "the Christ, the Son of the living God." For a Jew to confess that Jesus, the man, was the fulfillment of the messianic prophecies, was the noblest confession a Jew could make—or any of us can make, for that matter.

**Centered around the cross.**—Matthew gives us the background for our lesson today which follows in chapter 17: "From that time forth began Jesus to shew unto his disciples how that he must go unto Jerusalem, and suffer many things . . . and be killed, and be raised again the third day"(16:21).

It was too much for Peter. He understood only that Jesus had spoken about His death. He failed to understand Jesus' promise that He would rise again the third day. Peter's misunderstanding is suddenly evident, as verse 22 says: "Then Peter took him, and began to rebuke him."

The late R. G. Lee reminded us that Christ's crucifixion is mentioned in every book of the New Testament except Philemon, 2 John, and 3 John. It is a statement about the centrality of the cross in New Testament teachings.

Matthew mentions the crucifixion in 141 verses; Mark in 116 verses; Luke gives two long chapters to Christ's arrest and crucifixion; one-half of John's Gospel deals with the events immediately preceding and including the crucifixion as well as His resurrection; everything in Acts centers around the cross: at Pentecost, Peter tells the Jews they have "killed the Prince of Life" (Acts 3:15); the apostles are arrested and brought before the authorities and speak about "Jesus, whom ye slew and hanged on a tree" (5:30); and Cornelius was told about Jesus whom "God raised up the third day" (10:40). All through the New Testament the cross is central. Writing about the cross, Lee declared: "Take the cross out of our preaching— whether that preaching be in tent or crude tabernacle or the isolated church up the creek or the country church or the big church in the city—is like taking heat out fire, melody out of music, numbers out of mathematics, fact out of history, mind out of metaphysics, words out of vocabulary."[2]

**Christ preeminent.**—One of the greatest artists of the Italian Renaissance was Leonardo da Vinci (1452-1519). *The Last Supper,* a mural painted by da Vinci in the dining hall of the monastery of Santa Maria delle Grazie, in Milan, is considered to be one of the greatest paintings in the world.

It is related that after da Vinci had finished T*he Last Supper,* he invited one of his artist friends to look at the painting and give his views.

After the painting was thoroughly examined by the artist, he said to da Vinci: "You have painted the chalice on the table with exquisite beauty. It is the most beautiful thing in the whole picture and captivates the eyes of the beholder."

Benjamin P. Browne, in his book *Illustrations for Preaching,* wrote that da Vinci picked up his palette and brush and with a few, masterful strokes removed the magnificent beautiful chalice from the painting.

When asked why he had done such a thing, da Vinci replied that he wanted nothing to take the viewer's attention away from Jesus. "It is the Christ who must be preeminently seen as the center of my painting," da Vinci replied.[3]

On the mountain, Christ was the preeminent personality and His death was the preeminent subject discussed.

## TEACHING THE BIBLE

▶ *Main Idea:* The transfiguration of Jesus assures us that He is worthy of our highest praise and worship.

▶ *Suggested Teaching Aim:* To lead adults to examine the significance of Jesus' transfiguration, and to identify ways they can crown Jesus Lord here and now.

### Introduce the Bible Study

Ask members briefly to share with you what they consider mountaintop experiences. After two or three have shared, ask: What purpose did these serve in your life? (Their answers will vary but point out that great religious experiences will encourage and strengthen our faith.)

---

### A TEACHING OUTLINE

*1. To introduce the Bible study, let members share mountaintop experiences.*
*2. Let members ask questions from strip posters.*
*3. Use a brainstorming activity to apply the lesson.*

---

### Search for Biblical Truth

IN ADVANCE, write the following headings on large strips of paper; write the questions on the back of each strip. Tape the strips to the backs of five chairs. You will find the answers to these questions in *Studying the Bible.*

**1. Jesus Glorified (Matt. 17:1-3)**

(1) Who were the three disciples who accompanied Jesus to the mount of transfiguration and why do you think Jesus chose

these three?

(2) What happened to these three disciples after Jesus' death?

(3) What two Old Testament figures were present at the transfiguration and what did they symbolize?

(4) What was unique about the deaths of these two Old Testament figures?

(5) What did Jesus and Moses and Elijah talk about?

**2. Peter's Request (Matt. 17:4)**

(6) What was Peter's reaction to the transfiguration experience?

(7) Why do you think Peter reacted this way?

**3. Voice from Heaven (Matt. 17:5-8)**

(8) What did God say to Peter and the other disciples on the mount of transfiguration?

(9) On what other occasions did God make a similar statement?

(10) What was the significance of these words at this time?

**4. Silence Imposed (Matt. 17:9)**

(11) What was Jesus' instruction to the three disciples about what they saw on the mount and why?

(12) Why do you think Jesus included the other disciples?

**5. Question About Elijah (Matt. 17:10-13)**

(13) Why did Peter, James, and John raise the question about Elijah?

(14) What was the relationship between Elijah and Jesus?

(15) What was the relationship between the transfiguration and the cross?

To understand the setting of the transfiguration, briefly summarize the information in "Previous Events (Matt. 16:13-28)."

Ask the person who has questions 1-5 to read the Scripture and ask the class to answer the questions. Call on the person with questions 6-7, 8-10, 11-12, and 13-15. After the persons have asked each set of questions, tape the large strip to the wall.

Summarize "Frustration in the Valley (Matt. 17:14-21)."

**Give the Truth a Personal Focus**

Ask, What is the meaning of the transfiguration for us today? List responses on a chalkboard or a large sheet of paper as members suggest them. Ask them to list meanings without commenting on them at this point. Read the last part of the suggested teaching aim. Ask members to rank the five reasons that would help them crown Jesus Lord here and now.

---

1. Adapted from Hugh R. Horne, *Light on Great Bible Themes* (Grand Rapids: William B. Eerdmans Publishing Company, 1964), 29-30.

2. Robert G. Lee, *The Must of the Second Birth* (Westwood, N.J.: Fleming H. Revell, 1959), 10-12.

3. Benjamin R. Browne, *Illustrations for Preaching* (Nashville: Broadman Press, 1977), 54.

# The People Proclaim Jesus the Son of David

**Basic Passage:** Matthew 20:17—21:17
**Focal Passage:** Matthew 21:1-11, 14-16

One of the most remarkable descriptions of our Lord in the whole Scripture is that He was "the Lamb slain from the foundation of the world" (Rev. 13:8). This affirms that the plan of redemption was in the mind and heart of God before creation. It also carries the tremendous implication that, when He made the first man, He knew that He would have to redeem the human race at great personal cost, the sacrifice of His Son. Thus "God so loved the world" is given a new perspective. Also it enables us to see the purposes of the Father being worked out in the conduct of the Son. One Gospel says of Him that "he steadfastly set his face to go to Jerusalem" (Luke 9:51), and in our passage from Matthew we see how He controlled the situation that was to lead to His death on the cross. There was no hesitation on His part, but evidence of a definite plan that He followed in order to present Himself as Messiah to His own people, and, in rejection, become the Savior of the world.

**Study Aim:** *To know the difference between superficial patronage and loyalty to high purposes and convictions*

## STUDYING THE BIBLE

Our larger lesson passage helpfully begins at Matthew 20:17. There Jesus and His disciples are described as "going up to Jerusalem." The apparent purpose was to attend the Passover celebration, in which they were accompanied by a large number of pilgrims from Galilee and elsewhere. These constituted "a great multitude" (v. 29). But for Jesus there was another overriding purpose which He plainly stated in verses 18-19. With extraordinary detail He described the treatment that awaited Him, first at the hands of "the chief priests and . . . scribes," and then of "the Gentiles" represented by Pilate and his soldiers. He added, "and the third day he shall rise again," but this, and similar previous statements, seemed to escape His disciples' attention. Perhaps the idea was too wonderful for them to grasp.

### I. The Road to Jerusalem (Matt. 20:17-34)

Passing over the narrative in these verses, the request of Zebedee's children, James and John, and the healing of two blind men, we can helpfully focus on the two titles of our Lord that appear here. They emphasize two distinct functions, that of Savior and that of Messiah.

**1. Son of man (20:28).**—Jesus consistently used this title when speaking of Himself (see Dan. 7:13). It avoided mistaken notions of His mission and emphasized His identification with the human race, in line with "made in the likeness of men" (Phil. 2:7) and other Scriptures. It also speaks to the redemptive nature of His coming as the Philippian passage says, "he humbled himself, and became obedient unto death, even the death of the cross" (v. 8).

**2. Son of David (20:30-31).**—This title others used about Him. It summarized their messianic hope that a descendant of David would become His people's deliverer from earthly domination. In truth, it anticipated His coming role when He assumes an eternal kingship at His return.

## II. A Prearranged Plan? (Matt. 21:1-5)

With full knowledge of what awaited Him, our Lord left Galilee and started toward Jerusalem. We read that "he left Galilee and went to the region of Judea beyond the Jordan" (19:1, NRSV). The territory He entered, on the east side of the river, was known as Perea. He then travelled south as far as Jericho, where He recrossed the Jordan and proceeded toward Jerusalem. Matthew told of Him reaching Bethphage (21:1), but both Mark and Luke, in their parallel narratives, link Bethphage with Bethany (Mark 11:1; Luke 19:29). Bethany was the home of Lazarus, brother to Mary and Martha, friends of our Lord (John 11).

> 1 And when they drew nigh unto Jerusalem, and were come to Bethphage, unto the mount of Olives, then sent Jesus two disciples.
>
> 2 Saying unto them, Go into the village over against you, and straightway ye shall find an ass tied, and a colt with her: loose them, and bring them unto me.
>
> 3 And if any man say aught unto you, ye shall say, The Lord hath need of them; and straightway he will send them.
>
> 4 All this was done, that it might be fulfilled which was spoken by the prophet, saying,
>
> 5 Tell ye the daughter of Zion, Behold, thy King cometh unto thee, meek, and sitting upon an ass, and a colt the foal of an ass.

**1. Disciples instructed (vv. 1-3).**—The preciseness of these instructions encourages the belief that prior arrangements had been made for the use of the animals. The record of the raising of Lazarus (John 11) contains several statements that suggest that he and his sisters were well-known and respected in Bethany and beyond (see vv. 31, 33, 36, 45). They would have the contacts necessary to provide the two animals and make them available to Jesus. "The Lord hath need of them" could have been a prearranged password.

**2. Prophet quoted (vv. 4-5).**—In a prophetic context about the overthrow of Israel's enemies, Zechariah 9:9 tells Jerusalem to rejoice because "thy King cometh unto thee: he is just, and having salvation; lowly, and riding upon an ass, and upon a colt the foal of an ass." Matthew saw a clear fulfillment of this Scripture that day when our Lord rode into the holy city. The ultimate blessing of God's people would not be victory over their enemies but the establishment of a reign of righteousness under heaven's King.

### III. A Royal Ride (Matt. 21:6-11)

The events of this day, a week before Passover and the crucifixion, reversed our Lord's policy of refraining from use of the title Messiah. He spoke of Himself instead as "Son of man." Now He deliberately presents Himself in what A. T. Robertson called, "A Day of Messianic Demonstration."[1] His years of teaching and healing had been accompanied by growing opposition from the religious leaders, who were actually plotting His death. Putting aside His past reticence, Jesus embarked on a final appeal, addressed to the people on the occasion of their greatest festival, in which He would present Himself in the role of Messiah.

> **6 And the disciples went, and did as Jesus commanded them,**
> **7 And brought the ass, and the colt, and put on them their clothes, and they set him thereon.**
> **8 And a very great multitude spread their garments in the way; others cut down branches from the trees, and strewed them in the way.**
> **9 And the multitudes that went before, and that followed, cried, saying, Hosanna to the son of David: Blessed is he that cometh in the name of the Lord; Hosanna in the highest.**
> **10 And when he was come into Jerusalem, all the city was moved, saying, Who is this?**
> **11 And the multitude said, This is Jesus the prophet of Nazareth of Galilee.**

**1. Cheering crowds (vv 6-9).**—There was a strange mixture of self-promotion and humility in that day's procession. Jesus was obviously playing the role of a royal visitor, and the people made appropriate response along the route that He took. But there was a noticeable difference in that He did not ride on a stately steed but a humble donkey. He thus avoided the comparison with a military victor and appeared in line with His character as meek and mild. The crowds who greeted Him were not discouraged by the apparent contradiction. They saluted Him in royal terms, combining Old Testament Scripture with their words of praise. "Save now, I beseech thee, O Lord . . . Blessed is he that cometh in the name of the Lord" (Ps. 118:25-26).

**2. Cries of Hosanna (v. 9).**—The Hebrew word originally meant,

"Save, we pray," But in New Testament use, prayer became praise. The very branches the crowd waved and strewed on the streets were called hosannas. And they used the word to express their joy over Him who was making so dramatic an entrance into the city of David. They also hailed Jesus as that king's "son," a term that meant descendant, and was filled with messianic significance.

**3. "Who is this?" (vv. 10-11).**—The question seems to have come from different persons from those who cheered our Lord. Perhaps the questioners were citizens of Jerusalem while the cheering crowds were pilgrims from far and near, many from Galilee. These truthfully answered, "This is Jesus the prophet of Nazareth of Galilee." His humble background was thus linked with the expectations of Israel for a coming Messiah.

## IV. Christ in the Temple (Matt. 21:12-16)

Two sides of the mission of our Lord are strikingly evident in the following verses. The contrasted aspects of His personality, both Messiah-King and peaceful prophet, were illustrated in His conduct. When Jesus entered the house of worship, God Himself came to His temple, and He came in a spirit of judgment against its abuse. But in the same sacred precincts He showed His loving mercy toward the afflicted.

**1. Act of judgment (vv. 12-13).**—The high priest Annas, who served under the authority of the Romans, had allowed the outer court of the temple, the court of the Gentiles, to become the scene of commercial graft. Pilgrims coming from outside Jerusalem needed sacrifices to offer, and temple coinage for which their own currency had to be exchanged. The merchants took advantage of them by high prices and tricky transactions, and it was these that aroused the indignation of our Lord. Matthew's quote was from Jeremiah 7:11, another example of the writer's ability to find Old Testament support for New Testament events.

> 14 And the blind and the lame came to him in the temple; and he healed them.
>
> 15 And when the chief priests and scribes saw the wonderful things that he did, and the children crying in the temple, and saying, Hosanna to the son of David; they were sore displeased,
>
> 16 And said unto him, Hearest thou what these say? And Jesus saith unto them, Yea; have ye never read, Out of the mouth of babes and sucklings thou hast perfected praise?

**2. Deeds of mercy (vv. 14-16).**—Another Old Testament passage (Ps. 8:2) provided our Lord with an answer to His critics. That He performed miracles in the temple itself constituted part of His final appeal to believe Him as God's appointed response to the cries of the people for a deliverer. He would leave Jerusalem and its leaders without excuse for their rejection of His person and message.

## APPLYING THE BIBLE

**The importance of little things.**—One should not underestimate the importance of little things. Some anonymous "researcher" said it takes seventy thousand two hundred and seventy-six drops of water to fill a gallon bucket. The late Texas Methodist minister Gaston Foote said about all this: "When the container was full he had a bucketful of water instead of a bucketful of drops." To be short one drop is not to have a gallon!

There are only twenty-six letters in the alphabet, but these twenty-six letters can be organized into as many as eight hundred thousand English words. Every book, poem, legal document, or piece of literature written in English consists of only twenty-six letters. A piano has only seven basic notes, but by using these seven basic notes Beethoven composed his *Fifth Symphony*, his immortal *Moonlight Sonata* and Handel composed his *Messiah*.

There are only ten numbers. Count them—one to ten. Our entire mathematical system consists of only ten numbers. Even J. Paul Getty and Howard Hughes counted their billions one dollar at a time.

The importance of little things is underscored in our lesson today when Jesus chose a donkey, rather than a stallion on which to ride into Jerusalem on His triumphal entry (21:2, 7).

**The unknown, unnamed believers.**—Have you ever noticed how many unknown and unnamed people appear in the Scriptures helping move forward the kingdom of God? And isn't it the same today? It isn't the one who sits on the platform and is the most visible who is necessarily doing the most for Jesus. Sometimes it's someone in the back of the room whose name is unknown and whose work is never praised.

An example of this appears in our lesson today. The cross was drawing near, and Jesus was on His way to Jerusalem for what we call the triumphal entry. He instructed His disciples to go to a village, find a donkey with her colt, and bring them to Him. If the owner asked any questions, Jesus said to simply say: "The Lord hath need of them; and straightway he will send them" (21:3). The man is unknown and unnamed, but here is a tribute in the Scriptures to a man who though unheralded, was faithful to what he could do. It might be looked at another way: he was just a common, ordinary person, but Jesus used him. And is not the kingdom of God built out of common, ordinary people such as you and me?

Robert Moffatt was one of those common, ordinary little boys who asked his pastor about the possibility of becoming a missionary some day. The pastor encouraged the lad, and Robert Moffatt, the father-in-law of Dr. David Livingstone, opened Africa to the gospel. When Moffat was only a boy, his pastor's superiors visited the church one day and rebuked the pastor because the church wasn't growing. The pastor confessed they had had only one addition that year, and he was only an ordinary boy. But that boy was Robert Moffatt.

Jesus specializes in using little things and common, ordinary folks to build His kingdom.

**"Praze."**—Ian MacPherson tells about traveling one time by train across England. The train stopped at a small station, and through the open window of the car, MacPherson heard someone calling out, "Praise! Praise! Praise!"

MacPherson almost expected to see a Hebrew psalmist going through a ritual of worship, but looking out the window he saw only the porter and learned later that the porter was simply calling out the name of the small town, "Praze!" MacPherson said he concluded: "It must be wonderful always to live in praise!"

Praise greeted Jesus when He arrived in Jerusalem (21:8-9). Although it was an enthusiastic praise, it was mostly misunderstood because the Jews were looking for a military Messiah and conqueror. Jesus did not rebuke the people who accepted Him as best they understood.

## TEACHING THE BIBLE

▶ *Main Idea:* The people's proclamation of Jesus as the son of David challenges us to know the difference between superficial patronage and loyalty to high purposes and convictions.

▶ *Suggested Teaching Aim:* To lead adults to examine the significance of the people's proclamation of Jesus as the son of David, and to identify ways to distinguish in their life between superficial patronage and genuine loyalty and praise to Jesus.

---

### A TEACHING OUTLINE

*1. Introduce the Bible study by sharing the illustration.*
*2. Copy and distribute DISCUSSION QUESTIONS.*
*3. Summarize the material in Studying the Bible.*
*4. Apply the Scripture by reading a biblical skit.*

---

**Introduce the Bible Study**

Use the illustration "Praze" in *Applying the Bible* to introduce the Bible study.

**Search for Biblical Truth**

IN ADVANCE, write the following DISCUSSION QUESTIONS on slips of paper to hand to class members. Or, if you prefer, raise the questions with the whole class.

1. Did Jesus use supernatural knowledge or a prearranged signal to set up the use of the animal (Matt. 21:1-5)?
2. What difference does it make that Zechariah's prophecy foretold Jesus' actions (Matt. 21:5)?
3. What does Jesus' entry in the city on a donkey say to us

about the way we should serve Jesus (Matt. 21:6-11)?

4. How can you give total, joyous praise to Jesus (Matt. 21:8-9)?

5. How can we distinguish in our worship and service to Jesus between superficial patronage and genuine loyalty and praise (Matt. 21:15)?

Using the material in *Studying the Bible*, summarize the material in "A Prearranged Plan? (Matt. 21:1-5)." Then ask discussion question 1 followed by discussion question 2.

Using the material in *Studying the Bible*, summarize the material in "A Royal Ride (Matt. 21:6-11)." Then ask discussion question 3 followed by discussion question 4.

Using the material in *Studying the Bible*, summarize the material in "Christ in the Temple (Matt. 21:12-16)." Then ask discussion question 5.

**Give the Truth a Personal Focus**

IN ADVANCE, enlist three readers to read the following:

**1:** Fraud!

**2:** Imposter!

**1:** He's no religious man.

**2:** How could a religious man go against the Bible?

**1:** How could a religious man go against the government?

**3:** Are you sure He is going against both of these?

**2:** I sure am. Our religious leaders said so.

**3:** What makes them right?

**1:** Well . . . they're our religious leaders. They wouldn't lead us astray . . . would they?

**3:** What about the praise and worship from the people? That seems sincere enough. They really believe He is the Messiah.

**2:** Well, it is possible that they are sincerely wrong.

**1:** Yes, they're just caught up in the excitement of the moment—like people at the games.

**3:** Yes, that is possible, but how do you really know? Is it possible that even if what you say is true that Jesus is who they say?

**2:** No! He can't be. That would destroy everything our religion is built on.

**1:** Why, if that were true, that would mean Jesus . . . really . . . is . . .

**3:** God!

Ask members to identify one superficial action in their worship of Jesus and pray for strength to eliminate it.

---

1. A. T. Robertson, *A Harmony of the Gospels* (New York: Harper, 1922), 152.

# Jesus Institutes the Lord's Supper

**Basic Passage:** Matthew 26:17-35
**Focal Passage:** Matthew 26:20-30

It is a sad reflection that an observance instituted by our Lord, immediately before His death, and intended to emphasize Christian unity, has become a cause of division. The very terms used to describe this simple ritual are often made the occasion for deep disagreement. Some Christians object to the word *communion,* feeling that it puts too much emphasis on human fellowship. Yet Paul used this word (Gr., *koinonia,* fellowship) when he wrote of "the communion of the blood of Christ" and "the communion of the body of Christ," in clear references to the Lord's Supper (1 Cor. 10:16). Another avoided word is *eucharist,* meaning "thanksgiving," but associated by some with high church. However, it has had long acceptance in many Christian circles. Another word, *mass,* is so closely associated with Roman Catholicism as to be avoided by Protestants. The preferred term,"The Lord's Supper," signifies the observance without providing, however, any definition of its nature. This lesson gives opportunity, not only to study the inauguration of the Lord's Supper, but also to make its meaning and purpose clear.

**Study Aim:** *To better understand the Lord's Supper and so enter upon its observance with greater comprehension of its meaning*

## STUDYING THE BIBLE

What is known as the Passion Week was drawing to an end. Matthew 26 begins with events in Bethany on Tuesday evening, which was the start of the Jewish Wednesday and the crucifixion was only two days away. The hours that stood between our Lord and a brutal death were full of contrasts.

### I. Contrasts in Behavior (Matt. 26:1-16)

As He had done repeatedly before, Jesus sought to prepare His disciples for what lay ahead. Only now He associated His death with the celebration of Passover. As He spoke, His enemies were meeting to determine how they might bring about His death. They decided to wait until after the Passover had been celebrated so as not to create a disturbance among the crowds assembled for the feast.

**1. Honored in Bethany (vv. 6-13).**—While some plotted His death, an incident occurred in Bethany that was a gesture of love. An unnamed woman anointed His head with a precious perfume. Amid the criticism of some present, our Lord accepted the act as a preparation for His burial, and said that the loving action would become known throughout the world.

**2. Betrayed by Judas (vv 14-16).**—In sharp contrast, Judas offered to help our Lord's enemies in their murderous intentions. He asked for money to betray Him, and was given "thirty pieces of silver," approximately three months pay for a laboring man. The traitor then began to look for an opportunity to carry out his treacherous deed.

## II. Preparing for the Passover (Matt. 26:17-19)

Originally, the Passover and the Feast of Unleavened Bread were separate observances, one following the other. But in the passage of time the two had become one, and together lasted eight days. The overall celebration was then known by either name, hence, "the first day of the feast of unleavened bread" (v. 17).

**1. Historic observance (v. 17).**—The Passover commemorated the day of deliverance from Egyptian bondage recorded in Exodus 12. The meal centered around the slain lamb whose sprinkled blood gave protection to Hebrew households. The following seven days memorialized the unleavened bread that the emancipated people took with them on their journey to Canaan (v. 34).

**2. Disciples' task (vv. 18-19).**—Once again the possibility of advanced preparation is suggested in verse 18. Someone had already reserved a room for Jesus and the twelve and it was only necessary to take possession. The disciples would follow procedure in having the lamb for their meal slaughtered in the temple and then carried to the place of meeting.

## III. In the Upper Room (Matt. 26:20-25)

Wednesday of Passion Week, according to Jewish reckoning, began "when the even was come" (v. 20), at which time our Lord sat down with His disciples for the Passover meal. We would more correctly envision the situation by recognizing they reclined on couches to partake of a meal.

> 20 No when the even was come, he sat down with the twelve.
>
> 21 And as they did eat, he said, Verily I say unto you, that one of you shall betray me.
>
> 22 And they were exceeding sorrowful, and began everyone of them to say unto him, Lord is it I?
>
> 23 And he answered and said, He that dippeth his hand with me in the dish, the same shall betray me.
>
> 24 The Son of man goeth as it is written of him: but woe unto that man by whom the Son of man is betrayed! it had been good for that man if he had not been born.
>
> 25 Then Judas, which betrayed him, answered and said, Master, is it I? He said unto him, Thou hast said.

**1. Announcement of betrayal (vv. 20-24).**—The Passover meal was in progress when Jesus made the startling announcement that there was a traitor among the twelve. The reaction of those present is well expressed in this translation, "And they became greatly distressed and began to say to him one after another, 'Surely not I, Lord?'" (v. 22, NRSV). They were amazed at our Lord's statement, and momentarily questioned their own loyalty, each being unwilling to attribute such treachery to the others. It was customary to use a common dish for sauce into which food was dipped before being eaten (v. 23). Whether Judas alone, or several disciples, were using the dip is not clear from verse 23. But the traitor well knew that the solemn words of the next verse were spoken of him. Better that he had not been born than his name should go down the centuries in infamy as the betrayer of the Son of God. It would seem that our Lord was giving Judas repeated opportunities to back away from his evil plan. But Judas was too deeply committed to his treachery. He had already taken money from Jesus' foes.

**2. Reaction of Judas (v. 25).**—Most Christian communities exercise some measure of control over who partakes of the Lord's Supper. The apostle Paul made this matter a personal responsibility when he wrote, "Let a man examine himself" (1 Cor. 11:28). The question certainly arises as to whether Judas left the table, and the room where the Passover meal was being eaten, after the exchange of verse 25. The statement in John 13:25-30 would indicate that he did, though for some unstated reason John made no reference to the institution of the Supper. However, the total inappropriateness of Judas's presence at the continuing meal persuades most scholars that he made his exit after asking, "Master is it I?" (Matt. 26:25), and being answered in the affirmative, "You have said so" (NRSV).

## IV. Christ Our Passover (Matt. 26:26-30)

Links between the Jewish Passover and the Lord's Supper are obvious. Both are celebrations of deliverance, the former from Egyptian bondage, the latter from sin's power and penalty. Both are occasions of remembrance, ministering to the human tendency to forget even the most important things. For the Jews this was a matter of history; for Christians, of salvation. In the apostle Paul's detailed account of how the Lord's Supper was instituted, our Lord twice speaks of keeping the observance "in memory of me" (1 Cor. 11: 23-26). There is one basic difference. Whereas the Passover looks back, the Lord's Supper also looks forward "till he come" (v. 26).

> 26 And as they were eating, Jesus took bread, and blessed it, and brake it, and gave it to the disciples, and said, Take, eat; this is my body.
> 27 And he took the cup, and gave thanks, and gave it to them, saying, Drink ye all of it;

**28 For this is my blood of the new testament, which is shed for many for the remission of sins.**

**29 But I say unto you, I will not drink henceforth of this fruit of the vine, until that day when I drink it new with you in my Father's kingdom.**

**30 And when they had sung an hymn, they went out into the mount of Olives.**

**1. Bread and wine (vv. 26-27).**—As He replaced the old memorial meal of Passover, Jesus used no complicated ceremonial for the Lord's Supper. Food from the table served His sublime purpose. First He took a flat round loaf of bread, cooked without leaven for Passover use. He broke this in pieces and distributed it among the disciples, and bade them eat it. In saying "this is my body" He clearly meant, "This symbolizes my body," for He was present in His body, not yet subjected to the agonies of the cross. A cup of wine was then passed around, symbolic of His blood, then pulsing in His veins but soon to be "shed for many for the remission of sins." One writer warns against regarding the Lord's Supper as *mere* symbol. He writes, "The Supper employs symbols, bread and cup; but if genuine, it is more than symbolism. . . . It is a grateful act of worship, memory, hope, fellowship, and proclamation, employing symbolism."[1]

**2. A new covenant (v. 28).**—Reading the word *testament* as *covenant*, we get nearer to its meaning. God's relationship with His people, whether in the old dispensation or the new, is in the form of a covenant. Biblical covenants consist of commitments on God's part and corresponding obligations on the part of people. In the Old Testament it was customary for covenants to be ratified by the shedding of an animal's blood. The entirely new God-man relationship initiated by our Lord was sealed in His blood, shed at Calvary. By partaking of the bread and the cup Christians acknowledge their oneness with one another and with their Lord, a unity expressed in loyalty and service.

**3. A forward look (vv. 29-30).**—While the Lord's Supper has its major emphasis on the redemptive death of our Lord, He struck a note of glorious hope before He left the upper room with His disciples. He would not again partake of wine on this earth, but the time would come when he would drink it "new" (fresh) in His Father's kingdom. The next few hours would be determined by human authority, first the ecclesiastical leaders, then the procurator of Rome. But that authority, though present throughout the centuries of Christian history, would give place to the rule of God, a time of celebration both for Jesus and His people. Then He would provide a banquet for all His people, in which He would share the joys of the divine victory. The meal being ended, He led His disciples in the customary singing of part of the Hallel (Ps. 115—118), which concludes, "O give thanks unto the Lord; for he is good: for his mercy endureth for ever."

## APPLYING THE BIBLE

**Office upstairs.**—The late Presbyterian minister Clarence E. Macartney tells the familiar story of an old Southern doctor who had his office upstairs over a drugstore in the small town where he lived. In front of the drugstore there was a sign reading, "Dr. Riley is upstairs."

After many years of sacrificial service to his community, traveling day and night to tend the sick and often without any payment for his services, the old doctor died. Before he died he wrote, "Paid Off," in his journal across each account owed him.

He had collected little money, and there was nothing left even to provide for his funeral services. But the people who loved their doctor buried him, gathered stones from the nearby hill and placed them over his grave. Then someone went into town, retrieved the sign and nailed it on the cross at the head of his grave. His epitaph read, "Doctor Riley is upstairs."[2]

In verses 6-13 we encounter another one of those unnamed disciples of Jesus who did for Him what she could. And about her Jesus said to the critics, "She has wrought a good work upon me" (v. 10). Then Jesus added: "Wheresoever this gospel shall be preached in the whole world, there shall also this, that this woman hath done, be told for a memorial of her" (v. 13).

As Doctor Riley was lovingly remembered by his townspeople, so the woman who anointed Jesus has been lovingly remembered by believers for these two thousand years.

**The greed of Judas.**—Doctor Edwin St. John Ward, an American physician, was in charge of an American hospital in Beirut a number of years ago. A Syrian man came in who had been waylaid by bandits. To keep bandits from stealing his money, he had swallowed twenty-six pieces of gold. When Dr. Ward operated on the man and returned the gold to him, the man's eyes gleamed with joy.[3]

Doctor A. J. Gordon once told about a wealthy miser who had cataracts on both eyes. He consulted a well-known surgeon and was told what it would cost to remove the cataracts. The man's reply was, "Just fix one of them. I will be able to see well enough then to count my money."[4]

Was Judas much different? The Gospels tell us he was the treasurer of the apostolic band and carried the money. John tells us in his Gospel that Judas was the one who rebuked the woman for her "waste." And it was Judas, remember, who sold out the Lord out for thirty pieces of silver (v. 15). What was his problem? The same problem a lot of Christians have today: he loved his money more than he loved Jesus.

**A beautiful memorial.**—Many of us believe General Robert E. Lee was one of the greatest Americans who ever lived. He was a man of such Christian character that his great enemy, General Ulysses S. Grant, never questioned Lee's integrity.

On Monument Avenue in Richmond, Virginia, which was the final capital of the Confederacy, one can see displayed the monuments to the great Confederate leaders. The most striking and largest is the memorial to General Robert E. Lee who sits astride his faithful horse Traveller.

An old Confederate veteran, who served in the terrible war with Lee, was standing by the statue admiring it one day. To a passerby who stopped nearby, the old veteran said barely audibly: "I have seen it silhouetted against the setting sun and it was beautiful. I have seen it at noontime with all the glory of the sun radiating from it, and it was beautiful. I have seen it, against the background of the James River and it was beautiful."

The statue was beautiful because the old veteran loved the man to whose memory it had been erected. And those of us who are followers of Jesus would have to say about the Lord's Supper, "It is beautiful." It is beautiful because of the One it memorializes, even Jesus Christ our Savior and Lord.

## TEACHING THE BIBLE

▶ *Main Idea:* Jesus' institution of the Lord's Supper shows that we should observe it with meaning and dignity.

▶ *Suggested Teaching Aim:* To lead adults to describe the events surrounding the institution of the Lord's Supper, and to identify ways they can observe the Supper with meaning and dignity.

### Introduce the Bible Study

IN ADVANCE, write on sheets of paper: *Communion, Eucharist, Lord's Supper, Mass.* Place these around the room. Ask: What do these terms have in common? Which term do you like the least for the last supper? Which term do you like best?

### Search for Biblical Truth

Write the following on a chalkboard or large sheet of paper:

BETRAYAL
- A. Of Jesus
- B. Of the Disciples
- C. Of Self

Ask members to open their Bibles to Matthew 26 and read verses 20-25. As they read, ask a third of the class each to look for ways Judas betrayed Jesus, the disciples, and himself.

---

### A TEACHING OUTLINE

*1. Examine different words used to refer to the Lord's Supper.*
*2. Use a chalkboard activity to examine Judas's betrayal and the fellowship of the last supper.*
*3. Read case studies to apply the lesson.*

---

Call for reports and then write the following on the chalkboard or large sheet of paper:

FELLOWSHIP

A. With God

B. With Others

Ask members to read Matthew 26: 26-30. Ask half of the class to look for ways the Lord's Supper is fellowship with God. Ask the other half to look for ways the Supper is fellowship with others. Call for reports.

Ask members to describe the relationship between Judas' betrayal and the Last Supper by writing a summary sentence that would combine the meaning of the two for believers today. The following is only an example; let members put together their own: *We can betray Jesus when we come to the Lord's Table if we have unconfessed sin in our hearts and lives.* Write the sentence members suggest on a chalkboard or a large sheet of paper. Let members suggest changes until all would agree that they have captured the meaning of the passage for today.

**Give the Truth a Personal Focus**

Read the following case study: Bryan was a deacon at First Downtown-Suburban Church. Recently in one of the pastor's sermons, the pastor had made a statement about giving that had angered Bryan. As a result, Bryan had been talking to some other deacons about what they needed to do to get rid of the pastor. When it came time for the quarterly observance of the Lord's Supper, someone suggested that since Bryan was out of fellowship with the pastor, he should not serve or partake of the Supper. What do you think?

Ask members to suggest other situations under which observance of the Lord's Supper might be questionable. List these on a chalkboard or large sheet of paper.

Now ask them to suggest positive actions or steps they can take to make the observance more meaningful. List these as well. Ask members to rank these either personally or as a group to determine steps they will take for the next observance of the Lord's Supper. Read or sing "Blest Be the Tie" as a closing prayer.

---

1. Frank Stagg, *The Broadman Bible Commentary,* Vol. 8 (Nashville: Broadman Press, 1969), 233.
2. Adapted from Clarence Edward Macartney, *Macartney's Illustration* (New York, Nashville: Abingdon-Cokesbury Press, 1965), 101.
3. Adapted from A Dudely Dennison, Jr., M.D., *Windows, Ladders, and Bridges* (Grand Rapids: Zondervan Publishing House, 1976), 95.
4. Ibid., 96.

February
12
1995

# Jesus Is Rejected

**Basic Passage:** Matthew 26:36-68
**Focal Passage:** Matthew 26:57-68

Some names are irrevocably associated with treachery. One is the name of a Norwegian who betrayed his country to the Nazis in World War II. Vidkun Quisling was tried and executed at the end of the war, but his infamy lives on in the word *quisling* that stands for any kind of traitor. There is another name more infamous, the name *Judas* that belonged to the man who sold the Lord Jesus into the hands of His enemies. When his dastardly scheme was made known to the disciples, without disclosing his identity, the question went around the table, "Is it I?" That question should give every Christian cause to ponder. We recoil from the conduct of Judas but we need to realize, and acknowledge, that the possibility of betrayal exists with every one of us. It is, of course, impossible to minimize the gravity of the Judas deed. Christians can engage in minor acts of betrayal and either ignore them or deny their seriousness. When Jesus said, "He that is not with me is against me" (Matt. 12:30), He covered every area and aspect of life—including yours and mine.

**Study Aim:** *To seek divine help in living in loyalty to Jesus Christ and the mission He has given us*

## STUDYING THE BIBLE

We follow our Lord as, after instituting the Lord's Supper, He and His disciples left the upper room and "went out into the mount of Olives" (26:30). This meant crossing the Kidron Valley, to the northeast of Jerusalem, and entering the tree-covered slopes that led to Bethany, not more than two miles away. There the small group stopped.

### I. The Garden of Gethsemane (Matt. 26:36-46)

Gethsemane was probably a piece of private property to which Jesus had access, and to which He frequently retreated when in Jerusalem. Judas knew it to be a likely place for him to find Jesus. The word *Gethsemane* is Aramaic and means "oil press," so olives may have been processed there at one time.

**1. The prayer of Jesus (vv. 36-39).**—The distress of Jesus as He faced the death of the cross evidences His true humanity. He shrunk from pain as we do; yet He mastered His emotions and submitted to the will of His Father.

**2. Failure of disciples (vv. 40-41).**—The conduct of the disciples is in sharp contrast. They allowed their humanness to control them, failing to stay awake during this crucial period. Throughout the rest of their lives they would need the exhortation of Jesus, as we do, "Watch and pray."

**3. Jesus resolute (vv. 45-46).**—Aware that His enemies were closing in on Him, our Lord made no attempt at escape. Rather, He summoned His disciples to arouse themselves and go with Him to meet His enemies. Though the supposed victim, He was in charge of the situation. See verse 53.

## II. Jesus Betrayed by Judas (Matt. 26:47-56)

Events were moving fast. Judas had informed the religious leaders where they could find Jesus. Members of the temple guard joined forces with others to enter the garden of Gethsemane, sufficient in number to suggest that they expected resistance.

**1. False friendship (vv. 47-52).**—Judas had agreed to identify our Lord by kissing Him, a normal greeting when friend met friend. But this was a case of gross betrayal. That Jesus should respond by addressing the traitor as "Friend" (v. 30) suggests a last attempt to redeem Judas so that he would abandon his chosen course. John's Gospel tells us it was Peter who drew the sword (18:10) and earned the Master's rebuke.

**2. Fleeing disciples (vv. 55-56).**—Our Lord also had a rebuke for those who were accosting Him. Had He not openly taught in the temple? Why had they not arrested Him then, and not resorted to a show of violence as now? Matthew saw what happened as fulfillment of prophecy. He was also among those of whom he wrote, "all the disciples forsook him, and fled" (v. 56). Peter, too!

## III. In the High Priest's House (Matt. 26:57-60a)

Caiaphas was son-in-law and successor to Annas, both appointees of the Romans. Annas continued to wield authority after the appointment of Caiaphas. Both were unscrupulous men who used their high-priestly office for personal gain.

> **57 And they that had laid hold on Jesus led him away to Caiaphas the high priest, where the scribes and the elders were assembled.**
> **58 But Peter followed him afar off unto the high priest's palace, and went in, and sat with the servants, to see the end.**
> **59 Now the chief priests, and elders, and all the council, sought false witness against Jesus, to put him to death;**
> **60 But found none: yea, though many false witnesses came, yet found they none.**

**1. Assembled Sanhedrin (v. 57).**—The groups named, and the use of the word "council" (v. 59), indicate the supreme court of the Jews, assembled hurriedly during the night. Known as the Sanhedrin, this court's powers had been limited by the Romans. It could pass sentence of death, but not carry it out. This is why our Lord was referred to the Roman procurator, Pilate.

**2. Peter's recovery (v. 58).**—This disciple's volatile nature is again in evidence. Though he had fled from Gethsemane, his love for his Lord caused him to follow at a distance and to summon the courage to enter the high priest's residence and sit in its open courtyard with the servants. There he waited to see how matters would conclude. According to John 18:15, Peter was accompanied by another disciple, presumably the writer of that Gospel.

**3. Search for accusers (vv. 59-60a).**—One of the aims of the writers of the Gospels was to establish our Lord's innocence of any true crime. The report had been widely circulated, and believed, that He was a revolutionary who merited the punishment of death. Matthew told of the difficulty the Sanhedrin had in finding witnesses against Him. Though "many false witnesses" were found, their stories were evidently too wild for anybody to believe, even enemies looking for reasons to charge Jesus.

### IV. Jesus Accused and Condemned (Matt. 26:60*b*-68)

Finally, the Sanhedrin scraped up two people willing to testify against Jesus, and apparently sufficiently well coached to be believed. As we shall see, however, their testimony was based on misunderstanding of Jesus' words and carried little weight.

> 60 . . . At the last came two false witnesses,
> 61 And said, This fellow said, I am able to destroy the temple of God, and to build it in three days.
> 62 And the high priest arose, and said unto him, Answerest thou nothing? what is it which these witness against thee?
> 63 But Jesus held his peace. And the high priest answered and said unto him, I adjure thee by the living God, that thou tell us whether thou be the Christ, the Son of God.
> 64 Jesus saith unto him, Thou hast said: nevertheless I say unto you, Hereafter shall ye see the Son of man sitting on the right hand of power, and coming in the clouds of heaven.
> 65 Then the high priest rent his clothes, saying, He hath spoken blasphemy; what further need have we of witnesses? behold, now ye have heard his blasphemy.
> 66 What think ye? They answered and said, He is guilty of death.
> 67 Then did they spit in his face, and buffeted him; and others smote him with the palms of their hands,
> 68 Saying, Prophesy unto us, thou Christ, Who is he that smote thee?

**1. Misunderstood words (vv. 60b-61).**—The words Jesus was accused of saying are recorded in John 2:19, "Destroy this temple, and in three days I will raise it up." The writer of the Fourth Gospel felt it necessary to add this comment, "But he spake of the temple of his body" (v. 21). In another place Jesus spoke of the destruction of the Jerusalem temple, "There shall not be left here one stone upon another" (Matt. 24:2). In this case He was referring to the sacking of Jerusalem by the Romans in the year A.D. 70. The temple, intended as a place of worship, became almost an object of worship as time passed. Jeremiah warned against a superstitious attitude toward the sacred buildings (Jer. 7:4). Any threat against the temple came to be regarded as a threat against God Himself, hence the seriousness of the charge made against Jesus, which, as we have seen, was a distortion of His meaning since He was referring to His death and resurrection, three days later.

**2. Charge of blasphemy (vv. 62-66).**—Jesus made no attempt to respond to this false accusation, probably because He knew that the minds of His ecclesiastical enemies were fully made up and nothing He might say to defend Himself would change the course of events. Determined to have more substantial evidence against our Lord, the high priest questioned Him directly as to whether "thou be the Christ, the Son of God" (v. 63). This was a double-edged question. A claim to be the Messiah (Christ) would likely endanger Jesus with the Romans by whom such a deliverer would be regarded as a threat to their authority. On the other hand, to claim to be the Son of God would have serious theological implications, amounting to blasphemy. By saying, "I adjure thee by the living God," the high priest was putting Jesus under oath to tell the truth. His answer, "Thou hast said" (v. 64), was the equivalent of, "You have said so" (NRSV), that is, an affirmative. Then, to men then planning to put Him to death, Jesus, calling Himself "the Son of man," told of His return in power, "coming in the clouds of heaven." He whom they were about to crucify would be vindicated in future glory.

**3. Jesus abused (vv. 67-68).**—For the moment, He was in the hands of evil men who showed their rejection of Him by their abuse. They held Him up to ridicule, to which He submitted although He had power to strike His tormentors dead. And He did this for us. Every sordid detail of His treatment at the hands of His enemies calls us to affirm our love and loyalty toward Him. In our present world that abuses Him by indifference rather than hostility, we His people must proudly bear His name. We are *Christ*ians.

## APPLYING THE BIBLE

**Leonardo da Vinci paints Judas.**—There is an old story—whether true I cannot tell—about Leonardo da Vinci who was painting his grand masterpiece *The Last Supper.* He was searching for the perfect model for Christ. Someone suggested to da Vinci that he contact a young man who sang in the choir of one of the old churches for Rome. "Ask for Pietro Bandinelli," da Vinci was told. "He is a young man of such pure life and noble countenance that he will make a fine model for Jesus."

Leonardo da Vinci found the young man. He not only possessed a beautiful countenance, but his life was as beautiful and pure as his face. At last da Vinci could complete the painting for he had found the perfect model to sit for Jesus.

After da Vinci had finished painting Jesus, he painted the eleven disciples and considerable time was required for him to finish the painting. When finally he came to paint Judas, da Vinci began to search the city over for someone to sit as a model for Judas. Da Vinci wanted someone whose face was hardened and upon whose features sin had drawn heavy lines.

At last he found his man. He was the perfect model for Judas for he had the marks of a hard and wicked life written across his countenance. When da Vinci asked the man his name, the man replied: "I am Pietro Bandinelli. I also sat some years ago as your Christ."

Da Vinci could not believe it, but there before him was the evidence of what sin does in one's life.[1]

**The humanity of Jesus.**—Our lesson writer today points out that "the distress of Jesus as He faced the death of the cross evidences His true humanity. He shrunk from pain as we do; yet He mastered His emotions and submitted to the will of His Father" (*Studying the Bible*).

The late and great preacher R. G. Lee, well-known for his sermon *Payday Someday*, is well-known for saying: "Jesus was as much God as God is God but as much man as man is man." As Augustine put it: "He is the God man."

**"And He went a little farther."**—Six places in the Gospels we are told that Jesus went "apart to pray."[2] And, certainly, each of those times was an important time of prayer. But in the life of Jesus, when He "went a little farther" to pray in Gethsemane, He faced the greatest crisis of His life. And the intensity of His prayer revealed the depth of the crisis.

**Jesus at prayer.**—The Gospels reveal Jesus at prayer on numerous occasions: at His baptism (Luke 3:21-22); after a day of healing the hurting at Capernaum (Mark 1:35-38); after healing the leper (Luke 5:12-16); prior to selecting His disciples (Luke 6:12-16); when feeding the five thousand (Mark 6:45-46); on the mount of transfiguration (Luke 9: 28-29); in giving the Model Prayer where He taught His disciples how to pray (Luke 11:1-4); in the garden of Gethsemane (Matt. 27:36-46); and when hanging on the cross (Matt. 27:46).

**Failure need not be fatal.**—The disciples, including Peter who had been so boastful, miserably failed Jesus in His hour of greatest need (vv. 56, 69-75). But the failure of the disciples was not fatal! The exception to this, of course, was Judas and his failure. From it he never recovered.

Our original failure, whatever sort it be, may not be as important as what we do about it. In twenty-one years, Babe Ruth struck out one thousand three hundred and thirty times. But he recovered from his failure and hit seven hundred and fourteen home runs. Thomas Edison failed ten thousand times to perfect his electrical storage battery. But he recovered from his failure and patented more than one thousand one hundred inventions many of which we still use today. "Curly" Whistler failed so miserably at being a soldier that he was dismissed from the United States Military Academy at West Point. Look at his immortal painting, *Whistler's Mother,* and you will agree that he recovered from his initial failure. Noted evangelist Billy Sunday was a professional baseball player and a wretched drunk, but Jesus saved him and he recovered from his failure to become an outstanding evangelist who preached to more than a million people in his lifetime.

The disciples failed Jesus when He most needed them. But their failure was no worse than the failure of multitudes of us who fail to count for Jesus when and as we should.

## TEACHING THE BIBLE

▶ *Main Idea:* Jesus' rejection by Judas and the Sanhedrin shows that we need divine help in living in loyalty to Jesus and the mission He has given His people.

▶ *Suggested Teaching Aim:* To lead adults to explain the significance of Jesus' rejection, and to suggest steps they can take to live in loyalty to Jesus and the mission He has given them.

### A TEACHING OUTLINE

1. *Enlist two people for a report and a monologue.*
2. *Use a map to identify significant places.*
3. *Use a poster to guide the search for biblical truth.*
4. *Apply the Bible study by identifying ways members can show their loyalty to Jesus and His mission*

**Introduce the Bible Study**

Use the illustration "Leonardo da Vinci paints Judas" (*Applying the Bible*) to introduce the Bible study.

**Search for Biblical Truth**

IN ADVANCE, enlist one person to prepare a two- to three-minute report on the Sanhedrin. Suggest this person consult *Holman Bible Dictionary* or other Bible dictionaries for information. Enlist another to prepare a two- to three-minute monologue on Judas, describing why he rejected Jesus. If you choose not to use the report and the monologue, present the material yourself. Place a map of Jerusalem on the focal wall.

On the map, locate Jerusalem, Kidron Valley, Mount of Olives, and Gethsemane. Call on the two persons enlisted to share the monologue on Judas and the report on the Sanhedrin.

On a chalkboard or a large sheet of paper, prepare the following poster. The italicized answers are suggestions only; yours may differ and still be correct.

JESUS IS REJECTED BY:
**Judas:** (*took money from Sanhedrin; informed religious leaders where they could find Jesus; refused Jesus' offer of friendship at the last supper; led the soldiers to Gethsemane; kissed Jesus; we do not know exactly why he did this, but it may have been to try to force Jesus to free Israel from Roman rule)*
**The Sanhedrin:** (*conspired with Judas; enlisted false witnesses; refused to hear Jesus' defense; demanded Pilate execute Him; the reason apparently was to save their positions)*
**You:**

Organize the class in two groups. Ask group 1 to use the focal passage to explain why and how Judas rejected Jesus. Ask group 2 to use the focal passage to explain why and how the Sanhedrin rejected Jesus. Allow time for groups to work, and then call for reports. As the groups report, write their responses on the poster.

**Give the Truth a Personal Focus**

Ask members to continue in their groups to list all the ways they have rejected Jesus. Allow two minutes for them to list the ways. Alternately, ask one person from each group to suggest a way members betray Jesus. List these on the poster.

When members have listed all the ways, ask the class what they can do to live in loyalty to Jesus and the mission He has given them. List these suggestions on the poster.

Ask members to covenant to pray for class members this week that they will be successful in their loyalty to Jesus and His mission.

---

1. J. B. Fowler, Jr., *Illustrating Great Words of the New Testament* (Nashville: Broadman Press, 1991), 167.
2. C. Roy Angell, *Shields of Brass* (Nashville: Broadman Press, 1965), 37.

# Jesus Mocked and Crucified

**Basic Passage:** Matthew 27:1-61
**Focal Passage:** Matthew 27:27-44

The restraint shown by all four Gospel writers, in describing the agonizing death of our Lord, was obviously intentional. Their purpose may have been to direct attention away from physical pain and focus on the spiritual suffering of the sinless Son of God as He bore the sins of guilty humankind. The cry from the cross, "My God, my God, why hast thou forsaken me?" (v. 46), expressed an agony of soul that defies full exploration. It has been left to commentators and hymn writers to describe the suffering Jesus endured in order to become the world's Savior. Crucifixion was probably taken over from the Persians by the Romans when they sought a shameful and painful means of death for those whom they considered serious offenders. This extreme penalty was reserved for non-Romans and used freely as a means of suppressing insurrection in conquered lands. The victims were stripped naked, made to straddle a peg protruding from the upright beam, their hands and feet either nailed or bound to the cross. Slow torture was the result, often lasting several days until the victim expired. As we recoil from the spectacle, we need to remember our Lord's words to the women of Jerusalem, "Weep not for me, but weep for yourselves, and for your children" (Luke 23:28).

**Study Aim:** *To join with Paul in exclaiming, "the Son of God, who loved me, and gave himself for me" (Gal. 2:20)*

## STUDYING THE BIBLE

The tragic end of Judas is recorded in verses 1-7. The usual word for "repented" is not used here, for what Judas experienced may have been remorse rather than repentance. As so often, Matthew found an Old Testament reference to suit this occasion (vv. 9-10).

### I. Jesus Before Pilate (Matt. 27:11-26)

In order to avoid the religious charges brought against Jesus, the chief priests had represented these as a matter of breach of civil law, thus bringing it within Pilate's jurisdiction. Hence the question, "Art thou the King of the Jews?" (v. 11), a claim which, if true, could make Jesus guilty of insurrection.

**1. Barabbas or Jesus? (vv. 15-23).**—Pilate, on the lookout for a reason to release Jesus, recalled a custom intended to curry favor with an oppressed country, by releasing a prisoner during the Passover season. He offered to release Barabbas or Jesus, the former having been charged with rebellion and even murder (Mark 15:7). By now, the governor had been made aware of the true reason the priests were clamoring for Jesus' death (vv. 18-19). But his effort was of no avail for the ecclesiastics had persuaded the people to be satisfied with nothing else than the sentencing of our Lord.

**3. Pilate surrenders (vv. 24-26).**—Pilate was already out of favor in Rome and could not risk any further complaints, even if without justification. He surrendered to the demands of the priests after a meaningless gesture of denied responsibility. He spoke of Jesus as "this just person" yet abandoned Him to His fate. The response of the crowd, "his blood be on us and on our children" (v. 25), was prophetic of future tragedy. The statement, "when he had scourged Jesus," added to Pilate's guilt and passes lightly over a cruel practice that involved beating with leather thongs, loaded with pieces of bone and metal. The result was serious lacerations of the flesh.

## II. Mocked by Pilate's Men (Matt. 27:27-31)

The fate of our Lord was now sealed. Roman soldiers would carry out the sentence imposed on Him. But first they must make cruel sport of one whom they naturally assumed to be guilty of the charges made.

> 27 Then the soldiers of the governor took Jesus into the common hall, and gathered unto him the whole band of soldiers.
>
> 28 And they stripped him, and put on him a scarlet robe.
>
> 29 And when they had platted a crown of thorns, they put it upon his head, and a reed in his right hand: and they bowed the knee before him, and mocked him, saying, Hail, King of the Jews!
>
> 30 And they spit upon him, and took the reed, and smote him on the head.
>
> 31 And after that they had mocked him, they took the robe off from him, and put his own raiment on him, and led him away to crucify him.

These were men trained in the art of brutality and were free to do what they liked with a prisoner. For these Jesus would pray, "Father, forgive them; for they know not what they do" (Luke 23:34). Gentiles shared the guilt of others for what happened to Jesus. For all they knew, He had claimed to be King of the Jews, so they held Him up to ridicule on these grounds, dressing Him in a purple robe and forcing a crown of thorns on His head. A reed for a scepter completed this cruel caricature.

## III. The Road to Calvary (Matt. 27:32-44)

The Roman cross consisted of an upright beam which was implanted in the ground and a traverse beam that the accused was required to carry. On reaching the place of execution, the victim was nailed, or tied, to the cross beam that was then raised into position.

32 And as they came out, they found a man of Cyrene, Simon
by name: him they compelled to bear his cross.
33 And when they were come unto a place called Golgotha,
that is to say, a place of the skull,
34 They gave him vinegar to drink mingled with gall: and
when he had tasted thereof, he would not drink.
35 And they crucified him, and parted his garments, casting
lots: that it might be fulfilled which was spoken by the prophet.
They parted my garments among them, and upon my vesture
did they cast lots.
36 And sitting down they watched him there;
37 And set up over his head his accusations written, THIS IS
JESUS THE KING OF THE JEWS.
38 Then were there two thieves crucified with him, one on
the right hand, and another on the left.
39 And they that passed by reviled him, wagging their heads,
40 And saying, Thou that destroyest the temple, and buildest
it in three days, save thyself. If thou be the Son of God, come
down from the cross.
41 Likewise also the chief priests mocking him, with the
scribes and elders, said,
42 He saved others; himself he cannot save. If he be the King
of Israel, let him now come down from the cross, and we will
believe him.
43 He trusted in God; let him deliver him now, if he will
have him: for he said, I am the Son of God.
44 The thieves also, which were crucified with him, cast the
same in his teeth.

**1. Simon's task (v. 32).**—In Mark 15:21 Simon is identified as "the father of Alexander and Rufus," apparently well-known Christians at the time this Gospel was written. When our Lord staggered under the burden of the cross beam, Simon was recruited by the Romans to carry it. Whether Simon himself became a Christian is not known, but it seems likely.

**2. The place of a skull (vv. 33-38).**—All we know about this location is that it was "outside the gate" (Heb. 13:2), that is, of Jerusalem, and probably the regular place for executions. It may have been a hill shaped like a skull, or so named because of the skulls of previous victims left exposed there. It was likely close to a highway for public viewing. The vinegar "mingled with gall" was intended to numb the senses, a gesture of mercy in an otherwise cruel activity, but declined by our Lord apparently because He wished to retain full consciousness. Dividing garments among the soldiers was the common practice for which Matthew characteristically found an Old Testament reference in Psalm 22:18. The charge lodged against our Lord was inscribed on a notice above His head. Pilate may have intended to deride the Jews in this way. The two thieves, probably guilty of insurrection, associated Jesus with their crime, though falsely.

**3. Jesus derided (vv. 39-44).**—The false charge that He had threatened to destroy the temple was taken up by passersby. The chief priests, however, spoke more truly than they imagined when they said, "He saved others; himself he cannot save." Love bound Jesus to the cross where He gave Himself "a ransom for many" (20:28). By the willing sacrifice of Himself he atoned for the sins of the world, the purpose for which He was born, and the real reason why He died.

### IV. Redemption's Work Completed (Matt. 27:45-56)

Our basic passage invites us to linger at the cross until our Savior breathed His last. It would seem that the world of nature reacted to the tragic drama of the cross, humanity's rejection of its only hope of salvation. The sun was obscured for three hours as Jesus died.

**1. Jesus embraces death (vv. 46-50).**—Our Lord spoke in Aramaic, which caused the confusion shown in verse 47. The offer of vinegar ("sour wine," NRSV) was this time accepted (compare v. 34), its only purpose being to assuage thirst. The statement that"he cried again with a loud voice" (v. 50) indicates that Jesus did not die from exhaustion, but in deliberate fashion yielded Himself to death. His mission was accomplished.

**2. Accompanying phenomena (vv. 51-56).**—The rent veil in the temple, separating the holy of holies, gave evidence that a way had been opened up into the presence of God Himself (Heb. 10:19-20). Three days later, following our Lord's resurrection, people were also raised from the dead. The centurion, presumably in charge of the crucifixion confessed that "this was the Son of God" (v. 54), an acknowledgement from a surprising source that Matthew doubtless hoped others would make after reading his account of Jesus' story.

## APPLYING THE BIBLE

**Cost of the cross.**—A fourteen-foot bronze crucifix was stolen from Calvary Cemetery in Little Rock, Arkansas, in 1988. For more than fifty years it had stood at the entrance to the cemetery. Thieves, apparently, cut it off at its base and hauled it away in a pickup.

The cross was donated to the cemetery in 1930 by the late Catholic Bishop John B. Morris and was valued at ten thousand dollars. Although today it would be worth perhaps as much as fifty thousand dollars, the cemetery offered only a one thousand dollar reward for the return of the cross.

After it was stolen probably it was cut into small pieces and sold as scrap metal for fifty cents a pound. Police said the nine hundred-pound cross probably brought only about four hundred and fifty dollars.

What is the cost of the cross? What did it cost God the Father and

Jesus, His only begotten Son? What is the cross worth to you?

**"Into their hearts forever."**—In one of his plays, George Bernard Shaw tells about Joan of Arc being told she is to be burned at the stake. Foreseeing the effect it will have upon the people, she says: "If I go through the fire, I shall go through it to their hearts forever and ever!" Only the cross reveals the depth of God's love for a sinful world (Rom. 5:8). God says to us at the cross, "I would rather die than live without you!" That is exactly what happened when God in Christ offered Himself for our sins.

**The crucifixion of Jesus.**—In a "Baptists Beliefs" article written twenty- five years ago, Herschel H. Hobbs, a former president of the Southern Baptist Convention, discussed the crucifixion of Jesus.

"We have become so familiar with the crucifixion that it has largely lost to us its horror. It was the most painful of deaths ever devised by man, especially in hot climates. Among the Romans it was reserved only for Roman subjects, not citizens, and then only for insurrectionists and/or other gross criminals. Jesus, a Roman subject, was accused by the Jews of insurrection. Thus He was first scourged and then crucified.

"The upright pole of the cross was placed in a hole in the ground. The cross piece was laid flat on the ground. Jesus, stripped naked, was made to lie on the ground, His arms outstretched on the cross piece. To render Him helpless, his arms and legs were jerked out of joint. After His hands were nailed to the cross piece, He was lifted into position. The cross piece was fastened to the upright pole.

"To prevent the nails from tearing, Jesus' feet perhaps rested on a little shelf about two feet above the ground. They were crossed and nailed to the wood. Usually victims cursed and screamed. But Jesus only prayed for the crucifiers—then and now.

"Jesus was on the cross from 9 a.m. until his death about 3 p.m. His dead body was removed before sunset. But during those six hours He suffered excruciating agony. His body was so stretched that you could count His rib bones. Every nerve and tendon in His body became a throbbing agony. Blood slowly dripped from His wounds. The wounds became inflamed, producing fever throughout His body.

"The heart and stomach arteries became surcharged with blood, producing a terrific throbbing headache. Both from bleeding and dehydration He suffered intense thirst. His naked body exposed to the sun, every sunbeam became a leech sucking life-giving fluid from every pore of His skin. His lips were parched and cracked. His mouth and throat were dry as a desert. His tongue became swollen, and his vocal cords were inflamed. The victim of crucifixion died a thousand deaths.

"Added to Jesus' physical suffering was mental and spiritual agony. The crowds mocked and cursed. Darkness reigned from noon until 3 o'clock. During this time evidently the mob sat about in terrified silence. Out of the darkness came only the sighs and groans of the dying. Then out of the gloom came the cry, 'My God, my God, why hast thou forsaken me?' (Matt. 27:46).

"Here we are in the Holy of Holies of Christ's redemptive work. We cannot understand it. But somehow the Father turned His face from the Son now become sin. A holy God cannot look with favor on sin. But never was He more pleased with His Son, who was doing His will fully to die for man's sin.

"The beginning of sin is to forsake God. The end of sin is to be God-forsaken which is hell itself. So Jesus endured the agonies of hell for us. It was for only a moment. But it was the infinite suffering of the infinite God for the infinite guilt of finite man." (Read Ps. 22; Isa. 53.)[1]

## TEACHING THE BIBLE

▶ *Main Idea:* Jesus' humiliation and crucifixion demand that we recognize Him as God's Son.

▶ *Suggested Teaching Aim:* To lead adults to evaluate Jesus' humiliation and crucifixion, and to identify ways they can recognize and serve Him as God's Son.

### A TEACHING OUTLINE

*1. Introduce the Bible study by sharing the illustration.*
*2. Examine some people present at the trial and crucifixion.*
*3. Apply the lesson by examining how we are like these people and what we can do to recognize and serve Jesus as God's Son.*

**Introduce the Bible Study**

Use the illustration "Into their hearts forever" (*Applying the Bible*) to introduce the Bible study.

**Search for Biblical Truth**

IN ADVANCE, on a chalkboard or a large sheet of paper write the following:

THE CRUCIFIXION: Persons in the Drama

1. Member of the Sanhedrin
2. An observer at the trial
3. Barabbas
4. Pilate
5. Centurion
6. Apostle
7. Thief on the cross
8. Jewish citizen who saw the crucifixion

Ask members to look at the list and choose one person and describe the crucifixion from that person's perspective. They may choose to present their character any way they choose. They may do a monologue, dialogue, drama, creative writing, or any other method they think is proper. They may work alone or work with others. Ask them to answer the following questions about their character:

(1) What role did this person serve in the trial?

(2) How did the events affect this person?
(3) What made this person's action so bad?
(4) What other course of action could this person have taken?

Encourage members to use the background Scripture, Matthew 27:1-61, and their sanctified imaginations to share what the people may have thought. Let members choose and write their names beside the person chosen. More than one member can choose the same biblical character, but try to encourage members to choose a variety of characters. Allow ten minutes for study and then call for reports in the order of the names on the poster.

If you choose not to make individual assignments, use the above list of characters and ask the four questions about several of the characters. Let class members respond. The following poster will help. Do this for each name on the above list. Write the answers to the four questions in the space opposite the parenthetical numbers.

1. Member of the Sanhedrin
   (1)
   (2)
   (3)
   (4)

**Give the Truth a Personal Focus**

Ask members who selected a character to answer these questions: How are you like this person? How are you different? Based on your past actions, if you had been present at the crucifixion, how would you have responded? What can you do to recognize and serve Jesus as God's Son?

---

1. From the Texas *Baptist Standard,* March 15, 1967.

# The Risen Christ Commissions Disciples

**Basic Passage:** Matthew 27:62—28:20
**Focal Passage:** Matthew 28:1-10, 16-20

A crucifix is not the emblem of Christianity. A crucifix leaves Christ still hanging on the cross. An empty cross is a more appropriate emblem, but even that is inadequate for it tells nothing of His resurrection, a major feature in the preaching of His apostles. False reports, spread by Christ's enemies, needed the testimony of eyewitnesses to affirm that He indeed rose from the dead. But the messengers of Christ also kept a commendable balance of emphasis. Paul wrote, "When the fullness of time was come, God sent forth his Son, made of a woman, made under the law" (Gal. 4:4). Peter spoke about Him going "about doing good" (Acts 10:38) and wrote of His transfiguration (2 Pet. 1:16-18). Paul again gloried "in the cross of our Lord Jesus Christ" (Gal. 6:14) and proclaimed that "Christ died for our sins . . . was buried, and . . . rose again the third day" (1 Cor. 15:3-4). In addition, he preached the second coming when "the Lord himself shall descend from heaven . . . and so shall we ever be with the Lord"
(1 Thess. 4: 16-17). All this, and more, is included in the gospel which we are commanded to share with "all nations" (Matt. 28:19).

**Study Aim:** *To embrace the gospel story in all its fullness from the incarnation to Christ's return and eternal reign*

## STUDYING THE BIBLE

Matthew tells us how the body of our Lord was placed "in his own new tomb" by Joseph of Arimathaea but omits reference to Nicodemus (Matt. 27:57-60; John 19:38-40). Our Lord's death apparently persuaded these two men to make their discipleship known.

### I. Vain Efforts (Matt. 27:62-66)

As a precaution Christ's enemies persuaded Pilate for permission to seal the tomb. They recalled how He had said, "After three days I will rise again" (v. 63). They feared that His disciples might steal His body by night, "so the last error shall be worse than the first" (v. 64). The first error, in their estimation, was belief in Jesus as the Messiah, an error that would be compounded if claim could be made to His resurrection. They also set guards over the tomb, but all in vain because the grave could not hold the Lord of life. Even Christ's enemies could not deny that the sepulcher was empty.

## II. Resurrection Morning (Matt. 28:1-8)

Early on Sunday morning the event that changed the world took place. Jesus was raised from the dead and was thus "declared to be the Son of God with power" (Rom. 1:4). Every Lord's Day commemorates that glorious event (Rev. 1:10).

1 In the end of the sabbath, as it began to dawn toward the first day of the week, came Mary Magdalene and the other Mary to see the sepulcher.

2 And, behold, there was a great earthquake: for the angel of the Lord descended from heaven, and came and rolled back the stone from the door, and sat upon it.

3 His countenance was like lightning, and his raiment white as snow:

4 And for fear of him the keepers did shake, and become as dead men.

5 And the angel answered and said unto the women, Fear not ye: for I know that ye seek Jesus, which was crucified.

6 He is not here: for he is risen, as he said. Come, see the place where the Lord lay.

7 And go quickly, and tell his disciples that he is risen from the dead; and, behold, he goeth before you into Galilee; there shall ye see him: lo, I have told you.

8 And they departed quickly from the sepulcher with fear and great joy; and did run to bring his disciples word.

9 And as they went to tell his disciples, behold, Jesus met them, saying, All hail. And they came and held him by the feet, and worshiped him.

10 Then said Jesus unto them, Be not afraid: go tell my brethren that they go into Galilee, and there shall they see me.

**1. The empty tomb (vv. 1-4).**—The women, "Mary Magdalene and the other Mary," appear not to have been aware of the anointing of our Lord's body by Joseph of Arimathaea. Either that, or they wanted to bring their token of love for their beloved Lord. Unbeknown to them, an earthquake had rolled back the stone from the mouth of the tomb, a task assigned to "the angel of the Lord." That the angel "sat upon it" suggests supreme contempt for any attempt to confine the Son of God. The guard set to watch the tomb was rendered totally ineffective. We might note that the women had expressed doubt about their ability to roll back the stone (Mark 16:3). Every obstacle, however, had been removed. What remained was for faith to triumph over fear.

**2. Women bear the news (vv. 5-8).**—The angel sought to calm the women's fear. Knowing they were looking for Jesus (identified as "crucified"), the angel said, "He is not here: for he is risen, as he said."

The Greek in verse 6 is better translated "he has been raised" (NRSV). This indicates that God raised Jesus. The women were invited to enter the tomb and see for themselves that the body of Jesus was not there. Jesus had been resurrected from the dead!

Once the women were eyewitnesses of the empty tomb, they were sent to tell the good news. The women were to "go quickly" and "tell the disciples" of Jesus' resurrection and desire to meet them in Galilee. The women responded quickly to carry out the angel's instructions. Women were entrusted by God as the first bearers of the good news of Jesus' resurrection. Today every Christian has the privilege and responsibility to tell this good news. Could God still be saying, "Go quickly"?

### III. Bribed Soldiers (Matt. 28:11-15)

Matthew is the only Gospel that tells of the Jewish religious authorities bribing the soldiers to say, "His disciples came by night, and stole him away while we slept" (v. 13). When Matthew wrote his Gospel, this lie was still being told (v. 15).

### IV. The Great Commission (Matt. 28:16-20)

The eleven disciples (Judas was now dead) met Jesus in Galilee on "a mountain where Jesus had appointed them" (v. 16). Matthew often refers to mountains as a place where God reveals Himself and has fellowship with His people.

> 16 Then the eleven disciples went away into Galilee, into a mountain where Jesus had appointed them.
>
> 17 And when they saw him, they worshiped him: but some doubted.
>
> 18 And Jesus came and spake unto them, saying, All power is given unto me in heaven and in earth.
>
> 19 Go ye therefore, and teach all nations, baptizing them in the name of the Father, and of the Son, and of the Holy Ghost:
>
> 20 Teaching them to observe all things whatsoever I have commanded you: and, lo, I am with you always, even unto the end of the world. Amen.

**1. Worship and doubt (vv. 16-17).**—Arriving at the appointed mountain, the resurrected Jesus appeared. We are not sure if only the eleven are present. Verse 16 says, "the eleven disciples." The question is who are "they" and "some"(v. 17)? It appears to be the same group. Some of the eleven immediately worshiped Jesus. Some of the eleven "doubted." It is to the credit of the Bible that it speaks the truth about the heroes of faith: "some doubted." Belief in Jesus' resurrection was not easy. To worship someone other than Yahweh was difficult for these men. However, the truth that the crucified (dead) Jesus was alive was manifested before their eyes: "they saw him." Faith overcame their doubt and confusion.

**2. All power (v. 18).**—Jesus claimed to have the power of God ("in heaven and in earth") to carry out the mission of the church. Jesus' power is God's power. As believers tackle the church's mission (vv. 19-20), they go with the power of Almighty God. Notice the "therefore" in verse 19. Because Jesus has "all power," we can expect victory as we carry out God's program of making disciples.

**3. Making disciples (vv. 19-20).**—Every Christian needs to be able to "make disciples of all nations" (NIV). Making disciples should be a very natural thing for believers. It should take place in the ordinary happenings of life. It should be inclusive rather than exclusive. God is interested in every person on earth. Can God's people be concerned with less than every person on earth?

The word "go" is a participle like "baptizing" and "teaching." The controlling verb is "make disciples" (NIV). The three participles tell believers how to do their task of making disciples.

As Christians are *going* about daily tasks, make disciples. We may be *going* to work. The lost are at work. We may be *going* to play. The lost also play. We may be *going* to see family members. They are often lost also. As we are *going*, we are urged by Jesus to watch for opportunities to win people to faith in Christ.

Once people are disciples, we should be "baptizing them in the name of the Father, and of the Son, and of the Holy Ghost." In other words, we should take the new believers into our church. Baptism makes new Christians members of the New Testament church. Notice the trinitarian formula connected with baptism.

We have not discipled the believers until we have begun"teaching them to obey everything I have commanded you" (NIV). Believers are considered discipled when they live lives obedient to God's will. The true Christian is a follower of the resurrected Lord. Obedience to God characterized Jesus' life. Obedience must also be the Christian's way of life. Teaching new converts is our job. God's will as found in the Bible is what we teach.

**4. The abiding Presence (v. 20b).**—Not only does Jesus have "all power," but also He promised to be with us "unto the end of the world." How can the church fail when God's power and presence is available for the task of making disciples of every person on earth?

## APPLYING THE BIBLE

**God makes use of what we have.**—Sometimes what we have to offer Jesus seems very insignificant, but He uses it and the kingdom of God moves forward. Consider: Moses had a rod, but God used it. Noah had wood, and God used it to save the race. David had a sling, and God used it to deliver His people. Joseph had influence, and God used him to save the lineage from which the Savior would be born. Samson had strong arms, and God used them. Peter had a boat, and Jesus preached from it. The lad had a lunch of cold biscuits and fishes, and Jesus fed a multitude with it. Martha and Mary had a home, and to it Jesus retreated again and again. Peter and John had a fishing net, and

God used it and them to perform a great miracle. The unnamed woman about whom we studied a few weeks ago had a vial of perfume, and Jesus blessed her when she anointed His body. And Joseph of Arimathaea had a tomb and in it Jesus was laid, and Joseph has been forever loved and memorialized (27:57-60). God does not necessarily reward us for the big things we do, rather He rewards us because we do what we can.

**News too good to keep.**—Alfred, Lord Tennyson, England's noblest poet, was a believer. One weekend, as Tennyson put it, he decided to go down to the coast and spend the weekend "with some perfectly good Methodists!" When he neared the home where he was to stay, he saw his hostess out in the yard. "What's the good news?" he called out. And she called back in the words of Paul, "Christ died for our sins according to the Scriptures." And Tennyson called back to her, "That's not only good news but it's old news and always new news." And I would add, it's news too good to keep. When the angel appeared to the two Marys (v. 1) he told them what to do next: "go quickly, and tell." That's news too good to keep.

**The postresurrection appearances of Jesus.**—The late New Testament scholar Dr. Ray Summers notes that Jesus made at least eleven postresurrection appearances to His disciples: Mary Magdalene (v. 1); a group of women who had gone to the tomb to complete the anointing of His body (28:9-10); late on the first Easter two disciples on the road to Emmaus (Luke 24:13-32); in Jerusalem that same evening He appeared to Simon Peter alone (Luke 24:34; 1 Cor. 15:5); His fifth appearance was also on Easter evening to the disciples in the upper room, excluding Thomas (John 20:19-25); a week later on Sunday He appeared to the disciples again, with Thomas present (20:26-31); His seventh appearance was to a group of seven disciples by Galilee (21:1-23); His eighth appearance was to more than five hundred people on a mountain in Galilee (Matt. 28:16-20); He appeared to Paul (1 Cor. 15:7; Acts 9:1-22; 22:3-16; 26:1-20); an appearance to James, the Lord's half-brother (1 Cor. 15:7); to all the apostles (v. 7). This may be the same mentioned by Luke (Acts 1:3-8); and the last was at His ascension (Luke 24:50-53). But these must also be added: His appearance to Stephen as he was being martyred (Acts 7:55-56); and Paul (Acts 9:10)[1]

**The most frequently asked question**—Have you ever visited the British Museum in London? Founded in 1753, it holds thousands of precious treasures.

In the Egyptological section of the museum, there is an ancient stone coffin in which a man who died more than three thousand years ago lies buried. Although the body was crudely embalmed, it was marvelously preserved by the dry sand in which it was originally buried. And the body is still intact. The thin skin, like old, worn-out parchment, covers the frail, brittle skeletal remains.

The man was buried in a crouching position so that his body looks much like a large question mark. As one stands by the side of that coffin peering down on the ancient form, it seems to be asking the ancient question of Job, "If a man die, shall he live again?" (Job 14:14).

This is history's most-frequently asked question. Each of us has asked. Our parents before us, their parents before them, and the generations back to Adam and Eve have all asked it. Many have asked it but have been disappointed that heaven seemed to be silent in the face of their challenge. Others have asked it and have gone to their eternal rest confident that God has given to them an affirmative answer and has pointed out to them the way home.

But it is Easter that really answers our question for if there had been no Easter morning there would still be no answer. Easter morning changed our question about the eternal tomorrow into a period.

## TEACHING THE BIBLE

*Main Idea:* The risen Christ's commissioning of His disciples demands that believers share the gospel throughout the world.

*Suggested Teaching Aim:* To lead adults to examine Jesus' resurrection and commission, and to identify ways they can share the gospel in their world.

### A TEACHING OUTLINE

*1. Determine how the resurrection affects members.*

*2. Use a biblical simulation to examine the text.*

*3. Use brainstorming to determine mission projects members can do as a class and personally.*

**Introduce the Bible Study**

Ask, How does the resurrection affect you? Without comment, list member's responses on a chalkboard or a large sheet of paper. You will use these again in Give the Truth a Personal Focus.

**Search for Biblical Truth**

IN ADVANCE, plan to use a biblical simulation. You will need an old microphone or something to resemble one. You are to be an eyewitness reporter from WJER in Jerusalem. You will interview four persons who saw the resurrection. Give the four persons the following questions for them to answer during your interview.

**Guard–**

DIRECTIONS: Please study Matthew 27:62—28:20 and be prepared to answer the following questions: (1) I understand you were a guard at the tomb. Why were you there? (2) Would you explain what happened? (3) What about the rumor that Jesus' disciples stole His body. Is it true? (4) If Jesus did come back to life, how would this affect you?

**Mary Magdalene–**

DIRECTIONS: Please study Matthew 27:62—28:20 and be prepared to answer the following questions: (1) I understand you are one of Jesus' followers. What is your relationship with Him? (2) How did you discover that His body was missing? (3) Why had you come to the tomb so early in the morning? (4) Were you by yourself? (5) There have been reports of an earthquake; can you tell us anything about it? (6) What about the reported sighting of angels? (7) What did you do after you saw the angel? (8) If Jesus did come back to life, how would this affect you?

**Religious Leader–**

DIRECTIONS: Please study Matthew 27:62—28:20 and be prepared to answer the following questions: (1) What do you make of these reports that Jesus has risen from the dead? (2) Didn't Jesus promise He would rise from the dead? (3) How can you ignore this type of evidence? (4) How will you explain what happened? (5) If Jesus did come back to life, how would this affect you?

**One of the Eleven Apostles–**

DIRECTIONS: Please study Matthew 27:62—28:20 and be prepared to answer the following questions: (1) Several days ago, reports circulated that Jesus had risen from the dead. Now I understand that you and the other disciples have actually seen Him. Is that so? (2) How did you know where to meet Him? (3)What was the reaction of these eleven men? (4) What did Jesus do or say when you saw Him? (5) Exactly what did Jesus mean by going into all the world? If you'll pardon me, that is a little humorous. You are a fisherman. You've never even been outside of Palestine. How can you do that? (6) If Jesus did come back to life, how would this affect you?

Introduce the simulation by stating that reports have come that Jesus's body has disappeared and that you are going to interview some people who have been directly involved. Conclude by saying that you will try to get an interview with Jesus, and when you do, you will return to them with the live interview.

### Give the Truth a Personal Focus

Refer to members' statements at the beginning of class. Ask members to brainstorm ways they can share the gospel in the worlds in which they move. List these without evaluating them. Ask members to select one group activity they can do from the list. You may need to enlist some members to help plan this outside of class. Also, ask them to choose one personal activity they can accomplish this week.

---

1. Adapted from Ray Summers, *The Life Beyond* (Nashville: Broadman Press, 1959), 37-43.

# Christians Living in Community

**Books from BROADMAN & HOLMAN for Studying and Teaching**

*Holman Bible Dictionary,* Trent C. Butler, editor
*Holman Bible Handbook,* David S. Dockery, editor
*The Bible Atlas,* Charles F. Pfeiffer, editor
*Layman's Bible Book Commentary,* Volumes 20, 21
*The Broadman Bible Commentary,* Volumes 10, 11
*Disciple's Study Bible* (NIV text)
*The Heart New Testament,* H. I. Hester
*Introducing the New Testament,* Joe Blair
*Learning to Teach/Teaching to Learn,* C. Doug Bryan
*Learning to Study the Bible,* Earl P. McQuay
*Spiritual Gifts: Empowering the New Testament Church,* Ken Hemphill

## INTRODUCTION

Paul's dealings with the Corinthian church are recorded in Acts 18:1-18 and in 1 and 2 Corinthians. As a result of these two long letters, we know more about the church at Corinth than any of Paul's other churches. His letters deal with a variety of issues and challenges that face Christians and churches in every generation.

**Unit I,** "Responding to Challenges of Life in Community," focuses on four concerns of contemporary Christians—sharing the truth of the gospel clearly, being faithful in the face of difficulties, resisting temptation, and resolving conflict.

**Unit II,** "Nurturing the Life of the Community," deals with Christian growth within the body of Christ. The first two lessons consider the nature of the Christian community as a growing body and its growth through worship. The Easter lesson focuses on believers as a "resurrection people." The two concluding lessons consider the voluntary restriction on one's freedom in Christ and sharing one another's burdens.

**Unit III,** "Ministering as a Christian Community," invites the church to live and proclaim the gospel at all times and all places. Lesson subjects include self-denial as a means of outreach, active efforts toward reconciliation, sharing life's riches with others, and expressing love for all.

March
5
1995

# Speaking the Truth Plainly

**Basic Passage:** 1 Corinthians 1:18—2:16
**Focal Passage:** 1 Corinthians 2:1-13

Paul encountered a greater variety of problems in dealing with the Corinthian church than with any other one church. The church was confused and divided over many issues: leaders, sexual immorality, marriage, Christian freedom, the Lord's Supper, spiritual gifts, and the future resurrection. In addition, a group in the church strongly attacked Paul and his leadership. Back of these many problems lay the central problem of selfish pride. Paul's description of their divisive disruption over leaders, for example, repeats the word *I* over and over (1 Cor. 1:10-13). Against this basic human problem of sin, Paul set the way of the cross expressed in self-giving love. Early in the letter he emphasized that he had clearly made known the heart of God's saving grace by bearing witness to Christ crucified.

**Study Aim:** *To make known clearly and plainly the saying and transforming message of the cross*

## STUDYING THE BIBLE

Following Paul's description of the selfish pride and divisive disruption in the Corinthian church, Paul began his description of the cure. He made prominent use of the word *wisdom.* The Greeks placed strong emphasis on wisdom. Likely, Paul's critics in the church had accused him and his message of a lack of what they thought of as wisdom. Paul insisted that the message of the cross is revealed by the Spirit of God to be the only true wisdom (1:18-31). Paul then showed how the way of the cross was exemplified by the manner of his ministry at Corinth (2:1-5). Paul proceeded to show that divine wisdom is revealed truth under the ministry of the Holy Spirit (vv.6-16).

### I. God's Wisdom and the Cross (1 Cor. 1:18-31)

From Paul's point of view, the epitome of true wisdom is the message of the cross. From the world's point of view, the message of the cross is the exact opposite of wisdom. The world considers both the content and method of the message to be foolishness.

**1. Preaching Christ crucified (vv. 18-21).**—The "preaching of the cross" refers to the content of the cross as well as to the method of preaching it. This message seems foolish to those who are perishing in sin; but to those who have been saved through the crucified, risen,

Lord, the cross is the power of God. God has turned the tables on the worldly wise. With all their wisdom, they cannot find God, because God cannot be found by human works or wisdom. God's wisdom provides a way of salvation for all who will lay aside their pretensions to wisdom and goodness, and receive the grace of God with humility and trust.

**2. Foolishness or wisdom? (vv. 22-25).**—Many proud unbelievers are offended by the cross. The idea of a crucified Messiah was abhorrent to many Jews, who were looking for a king who would restore their national fortunes. How could God bring in His kingdom by a Messiah who died the death of a common criminal? Jesus had professed to save others, but He couldn't save Himself from the humiliation and suffering of crucifixion. The Greeks, who were of a philosophical mind-set, considered the cross to be a foolish basis for a religion. Believers, however, from both Jews and Greeks, found through experience that the way of the cross is the way of life and true wisdom. We know that what seems weak and foolish to the world is actually the power and wisdom of God.

**3. Glorying in the cross (vv. 26-31).**—Paul challenged the Corinthian believers to take a good look at the kind of people they were. Not many were rich and famous; instead they were from the poor of society. Paul saw in this a sign and testimony of God's grace. Those who were slaves and poor people knew that they did not have anything in which to boast. The fact that God chose them and saved them is testimony to His grace. All glory, therefore, belongs to Him.

## II. Paul's Preaching in Corinth (1 Cor. 2:1-5)

**1. Preaching Christ crucified (vv. 1-2)**

> 1 And I, brethren, when I came to you, came not with excellency of speech or of wisdom, declaring unto you the testimony of God.
>
> 2 For I determined not to know any thing among you, save Jesus, and him crucified.

Paul enlarged on his earlier theme of the preaching of the cross by describing his ministry in Corinth. His method of presenting the gospel was consistent with the gospel he preached. He did not rely on human ability but on the clear proclamation of the message of Christ crucified. Paul reminded the Corinthians of his own preaching style when he came to their city. Paul did not depend on eloquence of style or carefully planned arguments. Instead he simply delivered the testimony of what God had done in the life, death, and resurrection of Jesus Christ. Paul had determined that this was his task—to bear witness to what God had done. He was a witness, not a wise philosopher nor an eloquent orator.

**2. Fear and trembling (v. 3)**

3 And I was with you in weakness, and in fear, and in much trembling.

Paul delivered the message of the cross with fear and trembling. The message he delivered was awesome. The responses of the people to the message would determine their eternal destiny. No wonder Paul was afraid. He wanted to be sure that he faithfully made known the way of salvation. He knew some would reject. He knew some would attack the messenger, but what he feared was the possibility of failing to deliver the message. Like Ezekiel, Paul saw himself as the watchman who had the responsibility of making known a message that would determine life or death for the hearers (Ezek. 3:17-22).

**3. Power of the Spirit (vv. 4-5)**

4 And my speech and my preaching was not with enticing words of man's wisdom, but in demonstration of the Spirit and of power.

5 That your faith should not stand in the wisdom of men, but in the power of God.

Fortunately Paul was not doing this in his own strength. That would be the world's way. Paul relied not on human ability but on the power of God's Spirit. Thus believers of Paul's message became much more than Paul's converts; they became children of God who were saved by God's powerful Spirit. When we rely on our own strength, we get what our own strength is capable of doing. When we rely on the Spirit of God, the results are what only God is able to do. "Not by might, nor by power, but by my spirit, saith the Lord of hosts" (Zech. 4:6).

## III. God's Revealed Truth (1 Cor. 2:6-16)

**1. A revealed mystery (vv. 6-9)**

6 Howbeit we speak wisdom among them that are perfect: yet not the wisdom of this world, nor of the princes of this world, that come to nought:

7 But we speak the wisdom of God in a mystery, even the hidden wisdom, which God ordained before the world unto our glory:

8 Which one of the princes of this world knew: for had they known it, they would not have crucified the Lord of glory.

9 But as it is written, Eye hath not seen, nor ear heard, neither have entered into the heart of man, the things which God hath prepared for them that love him.

Paul wanted to emphasize that the Lord's message and way represent true wisdom. There is a vast gulf between divine and human wisdom. Human wisdom is a product of human endeavor and achievement. People sometimes assume that their wisdom can bring them to God Himself. Divine Wisdom is what God reveals and makes possible by His grace and power. The wisdom of God is revealed and made effective at the cross. The wisdom of God is made known and effected in the human heart by His Spirit.

We think of a "mystery" as something secret that we have to solve. By contrast, God's mystery is not something that God has tried to keep secret. His goal has been to reveal Himself to people, but many have refused to receive God's mystery. Various "mystery religions" of the first century promised special insight and experiences to a small group who had been initiated into the secrets of the religion. By contrast, God's mystery is not something He tries to keep secret for a select group. His purpose is to reveal the mystery of His saving grace to all people.

However, the hearts of many are closed to God's revelation; thus only the "perfect" (spiritually mature) are open to receive God's revelation. The world and the powerful people of the world are blind to this message of grace that God has been planning since before the foundation of the world. Nothing we have yet experienced prepares us for the full glory that the Lord has prepared for His people.

**2. Revealed by the Spirit (vv. 10-13)**

10 But God hath revealed them unto us by his Spirit: for the Spirit searcheth all things, yea, the deep things of God.
11 For what man knoweth the things of a man, save the spirit of man which is in him? even so the things of God knoweth no man, but the Spirit of God.
12 Now we have received, not the spirit of the world, but the spirit which is of God; that we might know the things that are freely given to us of God.
13 Which things also we speak, not in the words which man's wisdom teacheth, but which the Holy Ghost teacheth; comparing spiritual things with spiritual.

None of this is something that people have discovered on their own; it is something that God has and will reveal. He reveals His grace and power through His Spirit. The Holy Spirit is the presence of God at work in and among us. He Himself is the One who makes known the mystery of His wisdom and grace. Just as my own human spirit understands things that are personal to me, so does the Spirit of God have full knowledge of the things of God. God's Holy Spirit makes these things known to people of faith.

**3. Spiritual and unspiritual people (vv. 14-16).**—The "natural man" describes those who do not allow the Spirit of God to work in their lives. They value only what they can see, feel, and count. No wonder the cross and the other things of God seem foolish to them. Their minds are totally controlled by purely worldly thoughts and possibilities. By contrast, spiritual people are those who allow God to work in their lives. The Spirit gives them insight and wisdom into the mind of Christ and the will of God.

## APPLYING THE BIBLE

**The sin of pride.**—Among the seven things that are an abomination unto God, "a proud look" is the first thing listed (Prov. 6:16-18). And we are also told in Proverbs: "A man's pride shall bring him low" (29:23).

Clovis Chappell was a great Methodist preacher of an earlier generation. In his book *Faces About the Cross,* Chappell tells about the frog that wanted to go south for the winter. He struck up a deal with two wild geese and they agreed to take him south. They would hold the end of a string in each of their beaks and the frog would hold on to the middle of the string with his mouth. And all went well until a farmer, looking up, saw the strange sight and called out: "Who invented that?" And the frog replied, "I did!" As Chappell puts it: "And a moment later the farmer had a bit of minced frog at his feet."[1]

As our lesson today points out, the church at Corinth was divided over a multitude of problems but selfish pride lay at the bottom of them all.

**The main thing.**—Artist William Hunt once took his students out into the country to paint the sunset. As he walked from student to student looking over their shoulders to see how they were doing, he came to a young man who was very meticulously painting the picture of an old barn that stood on the hillside. Tapping the young fellow on the shoulder, Hunt said: "Son, if you waste so much time on that old barn, you won't get around to the sunset until it's too late."

Hunt was emphasizing the importance of staying with the main thing. The sunset, not the barn, was the main thing. At Corinth, Paul told his readers that he came to them determined to stay with the "main thing" which was the preaching of the cross. Although the worldlings called the cross foolishness, Paul said the cross reveals both the wisdom and power of God (1:18-21). As the preaching of the cross was the main thing with Paul, so it must be the main thing with us today.

**The preacher who met Jesus on the way to the pulpit.**—Arthur John Gossip (1873-1954) was one of Scotland's most noted preachers. His most famous sermon, preached immediately after the death of his wife, is one of the best-known sermons ever printed. Appropriately, it is titled, "But When Life Tumbles In, What Then?"

William Barclay, another noted English preacher, said that "Gossip lived closer to God than any man I have ever known." Barclay added that when Gossip was minister of St. Matthew's Church in Glasgow, he related how the week had been one of intense pressure and difficulty and that he had not had time to make the preparations to preach that he needed to make. Gossip then added: "You know the stair up to the pulpit in St. Matthew's? You know the bend on the stair? Jesus Christ met me there. I saw Him as clearly as I see you." Gossip then said that Jesus asked, "Is this the best you could do for Me this week?" And Gossip replied: "Yes, Lord, it is the best I can do this week." Then Gossip added: "Jesus Christ took that poor thing that Sunday morning and in His hands it became a trumpet."[2]

The best Paul could ever do in his preaching was to "hone in" on the cross. And that's exactly what he did for he declared, "For I determined not to know anything among you, save Jesus Christ, and him crucified" (2:2).

**God honors humility.**—One of the greatest Christian men ever to live was Dr. Albert Schweitzer. A missionary doctor to Africa, Schweitzer was also an organist and an authority on Bach. He gave up a promising career to serve in his hospital at Lambarene in Africa. On one occasion, Schweitzer was up on the roof of his hospital at Lambarene doing some repair work. Schweitzer called down to a young black man to hand up some tools and the young man replied with considerable pomp: "Sir, I am a scholar! I do not do day labor!" Looking down gently and speaking compassionately, Schweitzer replied: "Yes, I had a try at that, too. But it did not take!"[3]

Once Paul had possessed an abundance of the pride exemplified by the young black man. In his early years, Paul was a proud Pharisee leaving no stone unturned to keep his religion pure. Then he met Jesus and, as he said to the Philippians, he counted all things loss that he might know Christ. Here he demonstrates that attitude of humility when he tells the Philippians: "I was with you in weakness, and in fear, and in much trembling" (2:3). Paul's humility was one of the key reasons he was so mightily used by God.

## TEACHING THE BIBLE

▶ *Main Idea:* Paul's emphasis on speaking the truth plainly demonstrates that believers should make known clearly and plainly the saving and transforming message of the cross.

▶ *Suggested Teaching Aim:* To lead adults to examine Paul's emphasis on speaking the truth plainly, and to outline some ways they can make known the message of the cross.

### A TEACHING OUTLINE

*1. Introduce the quarter's study.*
*2. Share an illustration.*
*3. Identify ways Paul spoke the truth plainly.*
*4. Outline ways members can speak the truth plainly.*

### Introduce the Bible Study

Share the illustration "The Sin of Pride" *(Applying the Bible)* to introduce the Bible study.

### Search for Biblical Truth

Prepare a quarter poster on which you list the lesson titles, Scriptures to be studied, and the dates of the study. In advance enlist a member to use the *Holman Bible Dictionary* to prepare a two- to three-minute report on the city of Corinth. Provide a map of the New

Testament world that locates Corinth. Write the words *Christ Crucified* on a banner or chalkboard.

Point out the lesson on the quarter poster. Call on the enlisted member to share the report on Corinth. Locate Corinth on the map. Call attention to the banner and explain to the class that this is the theme of Paul's message to the Corinthians.

Ask members to open their Bibles to 1 Corinthians 2:1 and find the verse that supports this. Then ask: What characterized Paul's preaching to the Corinthians? (weakness, fear, trembling, not with wise words but in the Spirit's power)

DISCUSSION QUESTION: What are some evidences of human strength and wisdom in the proclamation of the gospel today?

Use the material in *Studying the Bible* to prepare a two- to three-minute lecture to explain Paul's use of *wisdom* and *mystery* in 2:6-9.

Ask members to look at verse 9 in the context and paraphrase this verse.

Ask half the class to read verses10-13 and look for what the Spirit's role is. (searches, reveals God) Ask the other half of the class to find how the Spirit helps us. (teaches us the mind of God)

DISCUSSION QUESTION: How can we know the Holy Spirit and not the spirit of the world is leading us or someone else?

**Give the Truth a Personal Focus**

To apply the lesson, read the last portion of the Suggested Teaching Aim: to outline some ways they can make known the message of the cross.

Ask, How has the church as a whole confused the message of the cross and made it unintelligible? List these on a chalkboard or a large sheet of paper.

Ask members to turn to someone near them and outline some ways they can clearly make known the message of the cross. Ask them to consider this from two perspectives: (1) What do I need to do personally to make known clearly the message of the cross, and (2) What do we as a Sunday School class/church need to do? Suggest that they might want to reverse some of the statements that cause confusion listed earlier.

After members have had a few minutes to list their responses, call for reports. As they share their ideas, list these on the chalkboard or sheet of paper. After all of the ideas are listed, urge members to choose one action they will take to clearly proclaim the message of the cross. Close in prayer that the Holy Spirit will lead them to keep their commitments.

---

1. Clovis G. Chappell, *Faces About the Cross* (Nashville, New York: Abingdon Press, 1961), 159.
2. Adapted from William Barclay, *A Spiritual Autobiography* (Grand Rapids: William B. Eerdmans Publishing Co., 1975), 13.
3. Adapted from Margaret T. Applegarth, *Men As Trees Walking* (New York: Harper and Row Publishers, 1952), 143.

# Being Faithful Under Stress

**Basic Passage:** 1 Corinthians 4
**Focal Passage:** 1 Corinthians 4:1-2, 6-16

As we noted in the first lesson, the basic problem in Corinth was selfish pride, which expressed itself in many ways. The specific problem in 1 Corinthians 1—4 was divisiveness that arose among the Corinthians about leaders. Each group championed a different leader: Paul, Apollos, Cephas (1:12). In various ways Paul tried to show them the folly of such divisive pride. In chapter 3, he showed the folly of arguing about the relative merits of Paul and Apollos. Paul and Apollos were only servants whom the Lord used, each in his own way. The Corinthians should have been concentrating on the Lord Himself rather than arguing about leaders.

**Study Aim:** *To recognize that following Christ requires faithfulness and self-sacrifice*

## STUDYING THE BIBLE

Paul completed his discussion about leaders in chapter 4. He showed that the Lord expects faithfulness of His servants and that only He can judge any of us (vv. 1-7). Paul used the apostles as examples to show that following Christ means following Him in the way of the cross (vv. 8-13). The apostle appealed to the Corinthians to follow his fatherly teachings and personal example of self-sacrifice (vv. 14-21).

### I. Faithful Servants of the Lord (1 Cor. 4:1-7)

**1. Faithful servants and stewards (vv. 1-2)**

1 Let a man so account of us, as of the ministers of Christ, and stewards of the mysteries of God.
2 Moreover, it is required in stewards, that a man be found faithful.

Some of the Corinthians almost idolized Paul; others were critical of Paul and idolized Apollos. Paul did his best to focus the Corinthians' worship on the only One worthy to it. In verse 1, Paul used two words to describe himself and Apollos: "servants" and "stewards." He had used another word for *servant* in making the same point in 1 Corinthians 3:5. The word he used in verse 1 emphasized lowly service. It originally was used of those who pulled the lowest row of oars on a large ship.

A steward was an administrator of another's possessions. With very little supervision, he was entrusted with using the master's goods in the best way possible. Paul and Apollos were stewards of everything the Lord had entrusted to them, especially the good news itself. They had received the good news of Christ, and the Lord had entrusted them with the task of making known the revealed mystery of God's grace in Jesus Christ.

What does the Lord expect of stewards? Verse 2 states this clearly, used in a good form to commit to memory. The Lord requires stewards to be faithful. All our accomplishments are nothing if we are not faithful.

**2. Accountable only to the Lord (vv. 3-5).**—Paul refused to be swayed by the judgments of others. He did not even put trust in his own judgment about himself. He was not his own judge, nor were others his true judges. Only the Lord was Paul's Judge. When we presume to pass judgment on others or even on ourselves, we are presuming to do what only the Lord will do on the day when He brings all things to light and judges our innermost thoughts.

**3. Questions for servants and stewards (vv. 6-7)**

> **6 And these things, brethren, I have in a figure transferred to myself and to Apollos for your sakes; that ye might learn in us not to think of men above that which is written, that no one of you be puffed up for one against another.**
>
> **7 For who maketh thee to differ from another? and what hast thou that thou didst not receive? now if thou didst receive it, why dost thou glory, as if thou hadst not received it?**

In verse 6, Paul explained to the Corinthians that he had been using himself and Apollos to try to illustrate an important lesson. Believers ought not to be puffed up against one another. Such selfish, divisive pride is contrary to what is written in the Holy Scriptures.

Verse 7 contains several probing questions designed to reinforce the lesson stated in verse 6. The first question could be stated like this: "Who is responsible for the different gifts of believers?" Keep in mind that the Corinthians were depreciating the gifts of other leaders than their favorite, and they were acting as if they had developed their own gifts. Later in 1 Corinthians, Paul dealt more in depth with the issue of spiritual gifts (see 1 Cor. 12—14). Here, early in the letter, Paul reminded them that spiritual gifts are just that—gifts! And they are from the Lord. If God gave you a different gift and opportunity from me, that is no reason for you to be proud or for me either to envy or disparage you.

The second question could be put like this: "What do you have that you did not receive?" James 1:17 states it well: "Every good gift and every perfect gift is from above, and cometh down from the Father of lights, with whom is no variableness, neither shadow of turning." What a humbling recognition! What a dose of reality! Everything that we call our own really belongs to the Lord. He has merely loaned it to us. This realization instills both a deep sense of gratitude and strong sense of accountability.

The third question could be put like this: "If everything you have has been received as a gift from God, why do you boast as if what you have received was your own doing?"

## II. Sacrificial Service for the Lord (1 Cor. 4:8-13)

**1. Pride of the Corinthians (v. 8)**

8 Now ye are full, now ye are rich, ye have reigned as kings without us: and I would to God ye did reign, that we also might reign with you.

The Corinthians were acting as if they had already received all the promised blessings of the coming kingdom. In a later letter, Paul condemned some who taught that the future resurrection is already past (2 Tim. 2:18). In light of what Paul wrote in 1 Corinthians 15:12, some of the Corinthians may also have believed that. Whatever their actual beliefs, verse 8 shows that they were acting as if they already had the full blessings of reigning with Christ. They were like the risen Lord's description of the proud self-sufficiency of the Laodicean church in Revelation 3:17.

Paul himself believed that Christians already experience the blessings of the kingdom in foretaste through faith. Our true citizenship is in heaven, but meanwhile we live in a world that acts contrary to the King and His righteousness. Thus most Bible students think that if Paul had been *speaking* the words of verse 3 to the Corinthians, he would have had a note of sarcasm in his voice. It was if he said, "So you Corinthians have already arrived at the full blessings of the kingdom; would that all of us had truly arrived!"

**2. Sacrifices of the apostles (vv. 9-13)**

9 For I think that God hath set forth us the apostles last, as it were appointed to death: for we are made a spectacle unto the world, and to angels, and to men.

10 We are fools for Christ's sake, but ye are wise in Christ; we are weak, but ye are strong; ye are honorable, but we are despised.

11 Even unto this present hour we both hunger, and thirst, and are naked, and are buffeted, and have no certain dwelling place;

12 And labor, working with our own hands: being reviled, we bless; being persecuted, we suffer it:

13 Being defamed, we entreat: we are made as the filth of the world, and are the offscouring of all things unto this day.

Paul presented the vivid contrast between the Corinthians'

perception of their own condition and the actual condition of the apostles. The apostles were publicly displayed for all to see like condemned criminals led into the arena for execution. The Corinthians thought of themselves as wise, strong, and honorable; the apostles were fools for Christ's sake, weak, and despised. The Corinthians thought of themselves as full and rich; but the apostles were hungry, thirsty, poorly clothed, beaten, and homeless. The apostles worked with their hands—something the Greeks considered degrading for well-to-do people. The apostles were reviled and persecuted, but they practiced the Lord's command to bless their persecutors and to endure hardship. When they were ridiculed and slandered, they gave back good for evil by entreating their enemies. In the eyes of polite society, the apostles appeared to be nothing but filthy waste.

Paul's point in all of this was to remind the Corinthians that those who follow Jesus Christ are called not to a bed of roses, but to the way of the cross (Luke 9:12). The apostles were faithful under stress. The Corinthians, by contrast, had so compromised with the world that they endured none of what comes to true followers of Christ.

### III. A Fatherly Appeal (1 Cor. 4:14-21)

**1. An example to follow (vv. 14-16)**

14 I write not these things to shame you, but as my beloved sons I warn you.

15 For though ye have ten thousand instructors in Christ, yet have ye not many fathers: for in Christ Jesus I have begotten you through the gospel.

16 Wherefore I beseech you, be ye followers of me.

Paul's tone became gentler in verse 14. He did not want them to misunderstand the emotional harshness of what he had just written. He reminded them that he thought of them as his children in the faith. He had brought the good news to Corinth and had been the human instrument in beginning the church. Thus he explained his harsh words as fatherly warnings, not as attempts to shame them.

Then Paul appealed for them to follow his example. Modern readers may think that this was an arrogant thing to say until we remember the situation in first-century Corinth. It was a wicked city. Most of the converts had come out of paganism. They knew little about the Scriptures or about the Christian life. Paul tried to teach them with words, but he knew that the best way to teach was by personal example. Just as children learn from the examples of their parents, so Paul wanted the immature believers to learn by his example. If they watched Paul, they would see someone who walked the way of the cross and was faithful in hard times.

**2. Travel plans (vv. 17-21).**—Paul could not come immediately to Corinth. At the time he was trying to enter the open door at Ephesus (1 Cor. 16:9). Because he could not come, he had sent Timothy, a faithful servant of Christ, who could represent Paul's point of view. Paul knew that some of his harshest critics were puffed up and were claiming that Paul himself did not dare show his face again in Corinth. Paul said that if they wanted a showdown, he would give it to them; and then power, not empty words would determine the outcome. After all, God's kingdom is power, not words. Paul said that it was up to them whether he came to Corinth for fatherly discipline or in fatherly love.

## APPLYING THE BIBLE

**"Let us have harmony."**—More than thirty years ago a brief story appeared in *Reader's Digest* about a town in Minnesota that got its name in a strange way. When the community was first settled, it had no name. People began to move to the area and soon the townspeople called a meeting to choose a name for their town. Many suggestions were made, but they couldn't agree on the name. The discussion soon became heated and quarrelsome.

One man in attendance that night became so disgusted by the way things were going that he jumped up, pounded on the table with his fist, and shouted, "Let us have harmony!"

Someone present suddenly seized the idea and shouted back, "Yes! Let's have harmony!" And the town got its name: Harmony, Minnesota.

Harmony was one thing the church at Corinth did not have as one readily discovers in reading chapters 1—4. The church was divided about leaders. Some chose Paul, others chose Apollos, and others Cephas (1:12). Paul showed them in chapter 3 the foolishness of quarreling over leaders. Paul shows that the Lord Jesus was the One on whom the church should have been concentrating, not Peter, Paul, or Apollos.

**Our last day on earth.**—An ancient saint was approached one day by one of his disciples who found the saint hoeing beans in his garden. The disciple asked, "What would you do, my brother, if you knew that this would be your last day on earth?" Quickly, but quietly, the aged saint replied, "I would finish hoeing this row of beans."

A number of years ago, Dean Christian Gauss, of Princeton University, asked the faculty what they thought the most important word was in the English language. The word that headed the list was *loyalty*. Perhaps we would not do injustice to the Princeton professors if we used the synonym, "faithfulness."

To the quarreling, divisive Corinthian church, Paul underscored the preeminence of faithfulness when he wrote: "Moreover, it is required in stewards, that a man be found faithful" (4:2). No talent, however brilliant, surpasses the gift of faithfulness in importance.

**We need to be careful about the example we set.**—Amos Kendall was postmaster general of the United States under presidents Andrew Jackson and Martin Van Buren. Kendall wasn't a professing Christian, but he contributed a rather large sum of money to build the Calvary

Baptist Church of Washington, D.C. He gave the money on the condition that the church would maintain two kinds of membership in the church: by profession of faith and baptism, and membership on the basis one would contribute regularly to the work of the church. He himself joined as a member of the congregation. One day a woman went to see Kendall and said to him: "My son died without accepting Christ as his personal Savior. If that means he is eternally lost, it is your fault, because every time we talked to him about surrendering his life to Christ he gave as his excuse for not doing so, Amos Kendall is a good man. He doesn't need to be a professing Christian. Why should I?" Kendall was so moved by the mother's statement that, as an old man, he professed his faith in Christ and was baptized into the old East Street Baptist Church.[1]

It is commendable that Kendall at last became concerned about setting a good example, but he neglected to do so for too many years. Paul, more concerned about his example, wrote to the Corinthians: "Wherefore I beseech you, be followers of me" (v. 16).

Dare we say the same thing to others?

**The beautiful life is the sacrificial life.**—Two plowshares were made from the same chunk of pig iron. The farmer bought one of the plowshares and used it regularly in plowing his fields. The other plowshare remained unsold on the hardwood shelf. At first it was bright and shiny as was the farmer's plowshare. Pretty soon, however, it began to rust and its bright beauty soon faded. An occasion presented itself where the two plowshares met again. The one the farmer had bought and used regularly was bright and shining as a silver mirror. The other one was rusty and old looking.

The rusty plowshare asked the shining one, "How is it that you are still so bright and beautiful? Look at me!"

"I was kept busy," replied the shining plowshare. "The beautiful life is the sacrificial life."[2]

## TEACHING THE BIBLE

▶ *Main Idea:* Paul's description of being faithful under stress indicates that Christ requires faithfulness and self-sacrifice.

▶ *Suggested Teaching Aim:* To lead adults to examine Paul's description of being faithful under stress, and to identify ways they can demonstrate faithfulness and self-sacrifice.

### A TEACHING OUTLINE

*1. Define faithful stewards and servants.*
*2. Establish a principle of relating to other Christians.*
*3. Examine the pride of the Corinthians.*
*4. Identify some of the hardships of the apostles.*
*5. Discover how Paul held himself up as an example and what members can do to be faithful examples.*

**Introduce the Bible Study**

Use "We need to be careful about the example we set" from *Applying the Bible* to introduce the Bible study.

**Search for Biblical Truth**

IN ADVANCE, prepare a teaching outline poster by listing the following on strips of paper:

1. Faithful Servants and Stewards (4:1-2)
2. Questions for Servants and Stewards (4:6-7)
3. Pride of the Corinthians (4:8)
4. Sacrifices of the Apostles (4:9-13)
5. An Example to Follow (4:14-16)

As you teach each segment, place the proper strip on the focal wall. Place the first teaching outline strip on the wall. Ask, What two terms did Paul use to describe himself and Apollos? (ministers, stewards) Explain the background of the word *steward.*

Place the second teaching outline strip on the wall. Point out that in 4:6 Paul established a principle: believers should not be puffed up against one another.

Ask members to look at verse 7 and identify the three questions Paul raised and explain how these questions fit Paul's argument. Suggest that members paraphrase the three questions. (See *Studying the Bible* for possible examples.)

Place the third teaching outline strip on the focal wall. Ask several members to read verse 8 in other translations. Ask them to explain if they think Paul was using sarcasm and why?

Place the fourth teaching outline strip on the focal wall. Ask members to read verses 9-13 silently and determine the spirit in which Paul wrote these words. (Paul sought to show how far the apostles were from reigning—v. 8.)

On a chalkboard or a large sheet of paper, write *We* and *Ye.* Ask members to look at verse 10 and list the contrast Paul made between himself and Apollos and the Corinthians.

Ask members to skim verses11-13 and suggest specific examples that Paul may have in mind. (Possible responses: Paul made tents as he worked "with our own hands"; he was "persecuted" when he was whipped and placed in a Philippian jail.)

Place the fifth teaching outline strip on the wall. Ask, in verse 14, to what does "these things" refer (vv. 14-16) Ask: How do you think the Corinthians heard these questions from Paul? (possibly as a criticism) How did Paul mean them? (as a warning or instruction) What term did Paul use to address the Corinthians and why? ("beloved sons" or children to show a fatherly attitude toward them)

Write *Follow Me!* on a chalkboard or a large sheet of paper. Ask half the class to suggest why this statement could be interpreted as an arrogant thing to say. Ask the other half to explain why it was not arrogant. (See *Studying the Bible.*)

**Give the Truth a Personal Focus**

Read aloud verse 2, and ask members how that verse applies to them. On the chalkboard or large sheet of paper, list ways they can demonstrate their faithfulness and self-sacrificing.

Close in prayer that they will be able to live such lives for Christ that they, too, will be able to encourage others to follow their example.

---

1. Clarence Cranford, *His Life Our Pattern* (Nashville: Broadman Press, 1950), 111-12.

2. Adapted from G.B.F. Hallock, *Five-thousand Best Moderate Illustrations* (New York: The Homolitic Review, George H. Doran Co., 1927), 623.

# Resisting Temptation



**Basic Passage:** 1 Corinthians 10:1-17
**Focal Passage:** 1 Corinthians 10:1-17

Beginning in 1 Corinthians 8:1, Paul dealt with the issue of meat sacrificed to idols. Chapters 8—10 contain Paul's answer. Some awareness of all three chapters is necessary in order to understand 1 Corinthians 10:1-17. Since we will focus on chapters 8 and 9 in later lessons, only a summary of Paul's overall position will be given here.

In chapter 8, Paul argued that eating meat sacrificed to idols is not a moral issue within itself, since idols are not real. A Christian might eat such meat with a clear conscience somewhere other than at a pagan feast, so long as another Christian was not offended by such an action. Insofar as possible, Christians should avoid actions that place stumbling blocks in the way of others. In chapter 10, Paul dealt with another possible danger of eating meat sacrificed to idols. Christians should beware doing this as part of pagan worship.

**Study Aim:** *To beware of the dangers of flirting with temptation and to take the way of escape that God provides*

## STUDYING THE BIBLE

Paul warned the Corinthians of presumption by reminding them of the fate of the Israelites who presumed on their privileges after deliverance from Egypt (vv. 1-5). The apostle used specific Old Testament examples as warnings of sins to avoid (vv. 6-11). Then Paul made three applications: beware overconfidence (v. 12), take the way of escape provided by God (v. 13), and flee from idolatry (vv. 14-17).

### I. Warnings from the Scriptions (1 Cor. 10:1-11)

**1. Dangers of presumption (vv. 1-5)**

1 Moreover, brethren, I would not that ye should be ignorant, how that all our fathers were under the cloud, and all passed through the sea;

2 And were all baptized unto Moses in the cloud and in the sea;

3 And did all eat the same spiritual meat;

4 And did all drink the same spiritual drink: for they drank of that spiritual Rock that followed them: and that Rock was Christ.

5 But with many of them God was not well-pleased: for they were overthrown in the wilderness.

Paul began by reminding the Corinthians of what happened to the presumptuous Israelites who came out of Egypt. Paul occasionally used a form of Old Testament study that sees certain Old Testament events as types or foreshadowings of New Testament realities. For example, in verses 1-2, he compared the Israelites passing safely through the Red Sea to Christian baptism. Paul did not intend to teach that their experience baptized them "unto Moses" in exactly the same way that Christians are baptized into Christ (see Rom. 6:3). He only meant that some parallels exist.

In verses 3-4, "spiritual food" refers to the manna (Ex. 16:4, 14-18); and "spiritual drink" refers to the water that the Lord provided when they were thirsty (Ex. 17:6; Num. 20:7-11). Since the water often came from a rock, Paul spoke of that as a type of the Rock, Christ Himself. The abiding presence of the Lord with His people and His constant provision for their needs is what Paul meant by the "spiritual Rock that followed them." Most Bible students think that Paul was comparing these Old Testament experiences to the Lord's Supper, which he dealt with in 1 Corinthians 10:16-17; 11:20-34.

In spite of these spiritual privileges, the first generation out of Egypt rebelled against God and was condemned to die in the wilderness (Num. 14:16). Only Joshua and Caleb remained of that first generation.

**2. Examples of sins to avoid (vv. 6-11)**

> **6 Now these things were our examples, to the intent we should not lust after evil things, as they also lusted.**
> **7 Neither be ye idolaters, as were some of them; as it is written, The people sat down to eat and drink, and rose up to play.**
> **8 Neither let us commit fornication, as some of them committed, and fell in one day three and twenty thousand.**
> **9 Neither let us tempt Christ, as some of them also tempted, and were destroyed of serpents.**
> **10 Neither murmur ye, as some of them also murmured, and were destroyed of the destroyer.**
> **11 Now all these things happened unto them for examples: and they are written for our admonition, upon whom the ends of the world are come.**

The Old Testament Scriptures were inspired by God and constitute God's Word to His people (2 Tim. 3:16-17). The people and events of the Old Testament contain examples for how Christians are to live. Many of the examples are warnings of sins to avoid. Paul listed some of these in verses 6-11.

Verse 6 warns against lusting after evil things. Paul may have had in mind specific examples like the people lusting after the fleshpots of Egypt (Num. 11:4). The Israelites' entire history was a history of the people's tendency to lust after evil things, rather than seeking the things of God.

Verse 7 quotes Exodus 32:6, which describes what accompanied the worship of the golden calf. Their idolatry was not just bowing down before an idol; it included pagan revelry. Since Paul was warning against idolatry feasts in Corinth, this was a particularly apt Old

Testament example.

Verse 8 warns specifically against sexual immorality. Paul had in mind the sin of the people at Baal-Peor, recorded in Numbers 25:1-9. This sordid record tells how the Israelites committed sexual immorality with pagan women and how many were killed as punishment.

Verse 9 describes a time when the Israelites put the Lord to the test and were destroyed by snakes. Numbers 21:4-9 fits this description. The Old Testament emphasizes that they were testing the Lord by constantly complaining about God's provision for them. Paul was emphasizing a broader aspect of this principle: testing God by seeing how far one can press God's patience and mercy.

Verse 10 warns against murmuring, something the Israelites did repeatedly between Egypt and Canaan. Examples are in Exodus 15:24; 16:2,7; Numbers 14:2; 16:11,41.

Verse 11 enlarges on the basic premise of verse 6. Paul wrote that these Old Testament events were written for the admonition of God's people of all ages. As people of the new covenant, Christians have been privileged to know God's full revelation in Jesus Christ. The Old Testament must be read in light of this full revelation (Matt. 5:17-18; Heb. 1:1-2). If we so read it, the Old Testament contains many lessons for the New Testament people of God.

## II. Overcoming Temptation (1 Cor. 10:12-17)

### 1. Beware overconfidence (v. 12)

12 Wherefore let him that thinketh he standeth take heed lest he fall.

Verse 12 clearly reveals the source of Paul's concern in chapter 10. He feared that some of the Corinthians were overconfident about their ability to withstand temptation. They were guilty of presuming on their spiritual privileges as if their profession of faith and participation in the ordinances made them immune from falling into sin.

Paul was the great apostle of assurance in Christ. Verse 13 is one of many examples of an emphasis on the grace and faithfulness of God as the basis for true assurance (for other examples, see Phil. 1:6; Rom. 8:35-38). But Paul was careful to distinguish assurance from presumption. In fact, throughout his ministry he had to defend the gospel of grace from those who tried to use salvation by grace as an excuse to live in sin (see Rom. 6:1-4). Those who are truly free in Christ do not use their freedom to live ungodly, sinful lives (Gal. 5:13).

Verse 12 stresses that people are never so vulnerable to temptation as when they feel confident of their own ability to flirt with temptation and remain unscathed. As Proverbs 6:27 asks, "Can a man take a fire in his bosom, and his clothes not be burned?"

### 2. Take the way of escape provided by God (v. 13)

13 There hath no temptation taken you but such as is

**common to man: but God is faithful, who will not suffer you to be tempted above that ye are able; but will with the temptation make a way to escape, that ye may be able to bear it.**

This is one of the Bible verses that every Christian should have committed to memory. It is the classic Bible verse about resisting temptation. In the face of temptation, Paul assured his readers of the faithfulness of God. If we rely on ourselves, we cannot overcome temptation. If we rely on the faithfulness of our God we can. James 4:7 puts it well: "Submit yourselves, therefore, to God. Resist the devil, and he will flee from you." Unless you first submit yourself to God, resisting the devil is useless.

God shows His faithfulness in two striking ways: (1) He never allows us to be tempted beyond what we can endure with His help. (2) God always provides a way of escape so that we may bear temptation. This provides a surefire solution for the problem of temptation for those who will avail themselves of God's way of escape. Those who submit themselves to God and rely on His help will be shown the way of escape in each situation.

**3. Flee from idolatry (vv. 14-17)**

**14 Wherefore, my dearly beloved, flee from idolatry.**
**15 I speak as to wise men; judge ye what I say.**
**16 The cup of blessing which we bless, is it not the communion of the blood of Christ? The bread which we break, is it not the communion of the body of Christ?**
**17 For we being many are one bread, and one body: for we are all partakers of that one bread.**

The basic problem often is that some people don't really want to overcome temptation. Most don't intend to really get caught up in sin, but they want to carry on a sly flirtation with sin. This was the problem with some of the Corinthians. Later verses in this chapter show that some of them felt free to join in the pagan feasts to idols. Paul said that it was one thing to eat meat sacrificed to idols at home or in a normal social setting, but joining in pagan feasts was deadly (vv. 18-32).

Therefore, Paul told them to flee idolatry. He gave similar instructions in 1 Corinthians 6:18 about sexual immorality. The only proper Christian response to some activities is to flee from them. The Corinthians took pride in their wisdom; Paul said that a truly wise person would recognize the truth of what he wrote.

Why did Paul consider idolatry so dangerous? He recognized that idols were nothing in themselves, but he knew that idol worship opened people's lives to satanic influences in a variety of ways. He made this point in verses 18-21.

He laid the foundation for this point in verses 16-17. The Lord's Supper signifies a communion between believers and the crucified, risen Lord whom they worship. If the Lord's Supper means what it should, it signifies that believers are one with their Lord and with one another in His one body. Paul's point is that if partaking the Lord's Supper signifies such a communion, so do idol feasts bind revelers together with unbelievers under the influence of their evil lord, the devil.

## APPLYING THE BIBLE

"Rock of Ages."—One of the best-loved hymns of Christendom is Augustus Toplady's hymn, "Rock of Ages."

Toplady was curate of the Blagdom parish in Somerset, England, from 1762 to 1764. According to tradition, Toplady took shelter one day from a storm in Burrington Combe, and the place where he found refuge was a great cleft in a rock. Some authorities on hymns say that likely the tradition is not true. The story that Toplady's hymn was an expression of thanksgiving for deliverance from the storm seems first to have been started in 1850 by the then vicar of Blagdom.

Although one who visits Burrington Combe today will be shown the rock that inspired the hymn, this is not the most important thing. The most important thing is the Savior, our "Rock of Ages cleft for me," to whom it points.

**Yield not to temptation.**—A cowboy was converted on the frontier and signed a temperance pledge that he would not drink again. But he continued to tie his horse at the same hitching post in front of the hotel in which there was a bar. An older, wiser Christian brother noticed the young cowboy's habit and gave him this sage advice: "John, forgive me for intruding into your business. But I have learned some things along my Christian journey. Let me share a little bit of advice with you. You've just been saved and you believe you are strong in the Lord, and hopefully you are. But if you want to be sure not to fall into your old habits again, take my advice and change your hitchin' post."

It is not a sin to be tempted, but it is a sin to fall victim to the temptation. About this, John Dryden (1631-1700), the English poet, said: It is better to shun the bait than struggle in the snare.

**The great price of immorality.**—Sexual immorality is as old as the race. And, it seems it is far more widespread today than ever in our history. As a result of this sin, we have filled our land with unwanted pregnancies, venereal disease, AIDS, and ruined lives. Indeed, sexual immorality carries with it an expensive price tag.

How strikingly this is borne out by Alfred Lord Tennyson in "Romney's Remorse." George Romney, who died in 1802, was a well-known and popular London portrait painter. His best-known model was the beautiful Emma Hart, better known as Lady Hamilton, who was the mistress of Lord Horatio Nelson, Britain's greatest naval hero.

When Romney heard the great painter and teacher Sir Joshua Reynolds say that marriage spoiled an artist, as Romney's popularity soared he left his wife. But when the end came, old and broken in mind and health, Romney returned to his wife who cared for him until he died.

His wife forgave him and Tennyson pictured a forgiving wife trying to cheer Romney: "Take comfort, you have won the Painter's fame." Romney's sad answer was: "The best in me that sees the worst in me, and groans to see it, finds no comfort there."[1]

As Paul delves into the history of Israel in the wilderness, he shows how God punished them severely for their immorality: "Neither let us commit fornication, as some of them committed, and fell in one day three and twenty thousand" (v. 8). It is a warning most appropriate for our day.

**Missionary Hudson Taylor's humility.**—One of history's greatest missionaries was Hudson Taylor (1853-1905) who began his missionary work in China in 1853. He was the founder of the China Inland Mission which is still the largest "faith mission" that makes no direct solicitation for funds.

Two ladies who were visiting Shanghai when Taylor was there wondered if Taylor were ever tempted with pride. One of the ladies said she would ask Mrs. Taylor, and Mrs. Taylor replied she did not know but she would ask Mr. Taylor.

Taylor was surprised. "Proud about what?" he asked. And his wife replied, "Why proud about the things you have done?" Taylor immediately answered, "I never knew I had done anything." And it wasn't a false humility, for Taylor knew that God had done it all.[2]

## TEACHING THE BIBLE

▶ *Main Idea:* Resisting temptation means that we should beware of the dangers of flirting with temptation and should take the way of escape God provides.

▶ *Suggested Teaching Aim:* To lead adults to examine what Paul meant by resisting temptation, and to identify ways they can resist temptation and take the way of escape God provides.

### A TEACHING OUTLINE

1. *Introduce the lesson.*
2. *Lead members in a Scripture search.*
3. *Discover how to overcome temptation.*

**Introduce the Bible Study**

Use the illustration, "Yield not to temptation" in *Applying the Bible* to introduce the lesson. Point out the title of the lesson on the unit poster you made. Read the main idea of the lesson.

**Search for Biblical Truth**

Write *Warnings from the Scripture (1 Cor. 10:1-11)* on a chalkboard or a large sheet of paper. Ask a volunteer to read verses 1-5 while members listen for the Old Testament experience described (Num. 25:1-9). Use *Studying the Bible* to explain how Paul took an Old Testament event and gave it New Testament meaning. Point out that in spite of the great spiritual privileges, the first generation out of Egypt rebelled against God and was condemned to die in the wilderness.

Ask a volunteer to read aloud verses 6-11, and assign the following Scriptures to members to compare as the volunteer reads: (1) Numbers 11:4-6, (2) Exodus 32:6, (3) Numbers 25:1-9, (4) 21:4-9, (5) Exodus 15:24; 16:2,7. After 10:6-11 is read, ask the people to indicate which Old Testament verses Paul had in mind when he wrote the following: 10:6 (Num. 11:4); 10:7 (Ex. 32:6); 10:8 (Num. 25:1-9); 10:9 (Num. 21:4-9); and 10:10 (Ex. 15:24; 16:2,7).

Write on the chalkboard or large sheet of paper the following:

OVERCOMING TEMPTATION (1 Cor. 10:12-17)

1. Beware overconfidence.
2. Take the way of escape provided by God.
3. Flee from idolatry.

Ask a third of the class to look at verse 12, another third to look at verse 13, and the final third to study verses14-17. Ask the members to find the following: (1) What is the teaching in these verse(s)? (2) How can we apply this teaching to our lives?

Call for reports from the three groups. Be sure the relationship of the Lord's Supper to the idolatrous feasts is clearly understood. (See *Studying the Bible.*)

**Give the Truth a Personal Focus**

Refer to the illustration of the cowboy in "Introduce the Bible Study." Ask members to think of experiences in their lives with which they are flirting with temptation.

Distribute paper and pencils to all members. Tell them that they are the only ones who will see their paper. Ask them to review their spiritual lives to see if they need to flee from a certain practice or temptation. Read the following from *Studying the Bible:* "The basic problem often is that some people don't really want to overcome temptation. Most don't intend to really get caught up in sin, but they want to carry on a sly flirtation with sin."

If after a spiritual inventory they decided they do need to make a change, ask them to write the needed change or to write an expression of deep gratitude to God because they do not need to make a change. (This way, all members will be writing.)

Point out that God has made a way of escape, but we must do the fleeing. Urge members not to make a similar mistake as the Corinthians made, but to flee from anything that would compromise their faith. Ask them to list at least two steps they will take to flee the temptation. Close in prayer.

---

1. Adapted from Clarence Edward Mccartney, *Great Interviews of Jesus* (New York, Nashville: Abingdon Press, 1964), 21.

2. Adapted from Walter B. Knight, *Knight's Master Book of New Illustrations* (Grand Rapids: William B. Eerdmans Publishing Co., 1956), 515.

March
26
1995

# Dealing with Conflict

**Basic Passage:** 2 Corinthians 12—13
**Focal Passages:** 2 Corinthians 12:19-21; 13:5-13

Certain people in Corinth had made a vicious and sustained attack on Paul and on his right to call himself an apostle. They had accused him of being cowardly and weak. They even charged that he had misused the collection for his own advantage. They said that some of their own leaders were more closely allied with the true apostles than Paul. The embattled apostle had to defend himself for the sake of the gospel and for the welfare of the Corinthian church. Paul felt that his opponents would destroy the fellowship of the church as they tried to destroy him. He, therefore, set out to defend himself and to plead for the church to practice Christian peace and love.

**Study Aim:** *To commit to dealing with conflict in such a way that the church will be built up*

## STUDYING THE BIBLE

Because of the ridiculous claims of Paul's opponents, Paul was forced to boast of his own credentials and accomplishments; however, he boasted more of his dependence on God's grace than on anything he himself had done (vv.1-10). He reminded the Corinthians of the marks of a true apostle that were apparent in his ministry among them (vv. 11-13). He defended himself against the charge of using the collection for himself (vv. 14-18). Paul expressed his worst fears that some of the Corinthians were engaged in sins of divisiveness and immorality (vv. 19-21). He spoke of his coming visit and stated that he was ready for a showdown if that is what was required (vv.1-4). Rather than judging Paul, they ought to test the validity of their own moral and spiritual condition (v.5). Paul was ready for confrontation, but he prayed for reconciliation and building up of the church (vv. 6-10). Paul made a fervent appeal for Christian peace and love (vv. 11-13). His closing benediction invoked the blessing of God the Father, Son, and Spirit on them (v. 14).

### I. Defense of Paul's Apostleship (2 Cor. 12:1-18)

**1. Boasting of weaknesses, not visions (vv. 1-10).**—Paul had reluctantly become involved in a boasting contest with those in Corinth who professed more apostolic authority than he. Chapter 11:22-33 and chapter 12:1-10 make the same point using different illustrations. In 11:22-29, Paul listed the sacrifices he had made; but in 11:30-33, he closed with an example of his weakness. In 12:1-4, he told of an amazing vision; but in vv. 5-10, he told of his thorn in the flesh. Throughout both passages, Paul emphasized two things: First, he had been forced into a boasting contest, which he could easily win. Second, he preferred to boast of his weakness and thus magnify the grace and power of the Lord.

**2. Marks of a true apostle (vv. 11-13).**—Paul reminded his readers of his ministry in Corinth. He could not understand why they did not see and commend the obvious marks of his apostleship in what he did in Corinth.

**3. Defense against false charges (vv. 14-18).**—Paul reminded them that he had supported himself while in Corinth. He did not want to be a burden to them. Now some critics were saying that Paul's refusal of pay was just a shrewd cover-up for his plan to take advantage of them through the special offering (see 2 Cor. 8—9). Paul vigorously denied that he or any of his associates would do such a thing.

## II. Warnings and Concerns (12:19—13:10)

### 1. Warnings against sins (12:19-21)

19 Again, think ye that we excuse ourselves unto you? we speak before God in Christ: but we do all things, dearly beloved, for your edifying.

20 For I fear, lest, when I come, I shall not find you such as I would, and that I shall be found unto you such as ye would not: lest there be debates, envyings, wraths, strifes, backbitings, whisperings, swellings, tumults:

21 And lest, when I come again, my God will humble me among you, and that I shall bewail many which have sinned already, and have not repented of the uncleanness and fornication and lasciviousness which they have committed.

Did the Corinthians think that they were Paul's judges and that he was only trying to excuse or defend himself before his rightful judges? Paul was not standing before any human judges; he spoke and lived "before God in Christ" (see 1 Cor. 4:3-5). Paul wrote tenderly to them as "dearly beloved," for whom all his efforts had been directed toward their "edifying" or building up.

Although Paul wanted to deal only positively with those whom he loved, he feared that when he came, he and they would be at odds over what they were doing. He spelled out his worst fears by listing sins that might be in the church.

Verse 20 lists eight sins in four pairs. Each pair of sins are the kinds of sins that accompany strife and dissension among people. These same sins, which are found in barroom brawls, are also found when Christians fight among themselves. Verse 21 lists three aspects of sexual immorality, which were prevalent in pagan Corinth, but which also were practiced or condoned in the church (see 1 Cor. 5–6). Paul's lists of "works of the flesh" in Galatians 5:19-21 contains sins from both these lists.

**2. Possible need for discipline (13:1-4).**—If Paul's worst fears came true, he warned the Corinthians that the wrongdoers would need to be disciplined. And he made plain that he was ready to take the lead in following proper procedures of fair hearings. Some of them had accused Paul of being too weak to exercise such authority. He reminded them that the cross and resurrection of Jesus reflect both weakness and power. As one who lived in the spirit of the cross and power of the resurrection, Paul was by no means powerless.

**3. Test yourselves (13:5)**

> **5 Examine yourselves, whether ye be in the faith; prove your own selves. Know ye not your own selves, how that Jesus Christ is in you, except ye be reprobates?**

Verse 5 is among the strongest statements Paul ever wrote. Jesus taught His followers not to pass judgment on others; instead we need to be more aware of our own sins (Matt. 7:1). The Corinthians had been judging Paul and pronouncing him guilty of various weaknesses and sins. Paul challenged them to focus attention on themselves. They needed to make a rigorous moral and spiritual examination of themselves.

The word "prove" commonly was used of testing that results in approval. Thus Paul was hopeful that such a rigorous self-examination would prove that they were "in the faith" and that Jesus Christ was in them. However, the closing clause of the verse leaves open the possibility that they might fail the test.

What was Paul's purpose in raising such a grim possibility? He had the same purpose as Jesus did in passages like Matthew 7:18-21. The Bible clearly teaches a doctrine of assurance for those who truly know the Lord, but just claiming to know the Lord is not the sole basis for assurance. Although we are saved by grace through faith, not by human goodness, something is seriously wrong with a professing Christian who persistently practices the kinds of sins described in 2 Corinthians 12:20-21. In individual cases, only God knows whether such a person is terribly backslidden or has never truly known the Lord. In either case, the person needs to repent more than to draw life's next breath.

**3. Committed to building up (13:6-10)**

> **6 But I trust that ye shall know that we are not reprobates.**
> **7 Now I pray to God that ye do no evil; not that we should appear approved, but that ye should do that which is honest, though we be as reprobates.**
> **8 For we can do nothing against the truth, but for the truth.**
> **9 For we are glad, when we are weak, and ye are strong: and this also we wish, even your perfection.**
> **10 Therefore, I write these things being absent, lest being present I should use sharpness, according to the power which the Lord hath given me to edification, and not to destruction.**

These verses require some explanation. At first reading, the most puzzling thing is Paul's reference to himself as among the "reprobates." Specifically, what did Paul mean in verse 7 by "though we be as reprobate"? How could the goodness and honesty of the Corinthians result in Paul being considered a reprobate? The word literally means to fail to pass the test. In verse 5, Paul used it of the ultimate test of whether the Corinthians were truly in Christ. In verse 7, he used it in a more general sense of his failing to pass the test of being a powerful, decisive judge in the affairs of the Corinthian church.

Keep in mind the main subject in verses 1-10. Paul spelled it out in verses 1-4, and he repeated it in verse 10. Paul's critics had said he was weak. Paul told them that he was prepared to show his power if their sins called for decisive action. His point in verses 6-10 is his prayer that their self-examination would prove them to be true people of faith and love. If that happened, Paul would not need to exercise his disciplinary power, and it would not be put to the test. He would "fail the test" in the sense of never having to take the test. Their repentance would make such a test of his power unnecessary.

Nothing would please Paul so much as not being called on to exercise disciplinary power among sinful church members. He had always stood for truth, and nothing so benefits the truth as Christians living as they should (v. 8). He was willing to keep his reputation as "weak" if the only way to prove his strength was to face a situation of deplorable sin in the church. After all, his goal was their perfecting in faith and love (v. 9). Paul far preferred to apply the Lord's power to building up the church than to presiding over its destruction (v. 10).

## III. Final Words (2 Cor. 13:11-14)

### 1. Appeals and greetings (vv. 11-13)

11 Finally, brethren, farewell. Be perfect, be of good comfort, be of one mind, live in peace; and the God of love and peace shall be with you.

12 Greet one another with an holy kiss.

13 All the saints salute you.

Paul had by no means given up on the Corinthians. He called them "brethren" and addressed them with warm affirming words. Verse 11 is an appeal to unity of spirit in the Lord. If 2 Corinthians 12:20-21 listed several of the "works of the flesh" from Galatians 5:19-21, 2 Corinthians 13:11 uses key words from the "fruit of the Spirit" in Galatians 5:22-23. The verse is an appeal to practice peace and love, and a promise that "the God of love and peace" abides with those who do.

The custom of the day—and the custom in many countries in today's world—was for people to greet one another with a kiss on the cheek. In the early church, this was done: men kissing men, and women kissing women.

Paul sent not only his own greetings but also the greetings of the saints in other places. As a traveling missionary, Paul saw believers in many different places. He was able to help the believers in one church remember they were part of a larger fellowship of faith and love.

**2. Benediction (v. 14).**—The final verse in 2 Corinthians is a beautiful benediction that has been used throughout Christian history: "The grace of the Lord Jesus Christ, and the love of God, and the communion of the Holy Ghost, be with you all. Amen."

## APPLYING THE BIBLE

**Three types of people in the church.**—The late Gaston Foote was pastor of the First Methodist Church of Fort Worth, Texas. For a number of years he wrote an article carried regularly in the Fort Worth *Star Telegram* titled, "Footnotes." In one of those articles Foote said there are three classes of people in the church: those who make things happen, those who watch things happen, and the vast majority who have no idea what is happening.

Foote wrote that in the local church today, 10 percent make things happen—teach Sunday School, give, etc.; 40 percent watch things happen—they don't want to be tied down with any responsibility; and the rest have no idea of what is happening!

At Corinth, Paul found the same thing: Some of the Corinthian Christians were just watching what was happening; others were contributing to what was happening; but too many didn't know what was happening because they were preoccupied with bickering. These were the ones Paul sternly addressed in our lesson today.

**"The Church of the Holy Fidgets."**—Halford E. Luccock says there are many kinds of churches. One is preoccupied with the mechanics of the organization. Activities loom larger than love. It is "the Church of the Holy Fidgets," he says. Marked by busyness, it never gets down to the real reason for its existence.

He says in Chicago there is the other kind of church. Named St. Stephens, it is called "the Church at the End of the Road." And Luccock concludes that is a fitting location for a church. There are so many people at the end of life's road whose strength and hope are gone, it is there the church needs to be.[1]

Paul rebuked the Corinthian church because it was more "a church of holy fidgets" than it was "a church at the end of the road."

**The orange-peel syndrome.**—In 1911 Bobby Leach was the second man to go over Niagara Falls in a barrel. Then it was a raft. Finally, he parachuted from the bridge into the Niagara River. But, tragically, Leach died in England some years after his accomplishments at Niagara Falls when he slipped on an orange peel.

The church at Corinth was standing on "orange peels"—in danger of destroying its effectiveness. Paul listed some of these destructive attitudes in the church in 12:20-21. In 13:1-4 he warned that the wrongdoers needed to be disciplined. His concern was for the unity and strength of the church's witness in a pagan society.

**The assurance of salvation.**—John Wesley, a clergyman of the Church of England, was so zealous for Christ that he came to America as a missionary to the Indians. During a storm at sea, Wesley became very frightened and asked a Moravian standing nearby, "Are you not afraid?" The Moravian replied, "Why should I be afraid? I know Jesus Christ." Looking straight into the eyes of Wesley, he asked the young zealot, "Do you know Jesus?" and for the first time in his life it dawned upon Wesley that he did not personally know Jesus. He then asked himself the question, "I came to America to convert the Indians, but who will convert me?" After long searching, Wesley was saved on May 24, 1738, during a Moravian meeting in Aldersgate Street, London. As Martin Luther's preface to the Epistle to the Romans was being read, Wesley testified that his "heart was strangely warmed." For the next fifty years of his ministry, he emphasized salvation by grace through faith.

Martin Luther once said: "If you should knock on the door of my heart and ask, 'Who lives here?' I would not answer, 'Luther lives here; but Christ lives here.'" In 13:5, Paul issues the stern warning: "Examine yourselves, whether ye be in the faith."

## TEACHING THE BIBLE

▶ *Main Idea:* Paul's instructions for dealing with conflict indicate that believers must be committed to dealing with conflict in such a way that the church will be built up.

▶ *Suggested Teaching Aim:* To lead adults to examine Paul's instructions for dealing with conflict, and to commit themselves to dealing with conflict in such a way that the church will be built up.

### A TEACHING OUTLINE

*1. Relate the study to their lives.*
*2. Ask six questions that explain 12:19-21.*
*3. Explain the use of the word "reprobate."*
*4. Identify ways they can resolve church conflicts based on this passage.*

### Introduce the Bible Study

Ask members, Have you ever been in a church that had a conflict that upset the whole congregation and cause hurt to many people? Let several mention these but be careful not to let this part of the lesson go too long. Point out that the Corinthian church had its problems and the conflict threatened to destroy the new movement. Paul's way of dealing with the controversy will help us today.

### Search for Biblical Truth

Invite members to open their Bibles to 2 Corinthians 12:19. Read aloud the Main Idea above. Summarize "Defense of Paul's Apostleship" *(Studying the Bible)* to set the context for the lesson.

Ask the following questions on verses 19-21 and give members time to find the answers in their Bibles. Encourage those who have modern translations to use them: (1) To whom is Paul speaking in verse 19? (Corinthians) (2) What does the word "excuse" in verse 19 mean? (defend) (3) Instead of trying to defend himself to the Corinthians, what was Paul trying to do? (to build up the Corinthians) (4) Why did Paul want to build them up (v. 19)? (He was afraid when he came to visit them that he would find they were totally backslidden.) (5) What do you think Paul's statement, "I will be found unto you such as ye would not" (v. 20) means? (Paul was afraid if he found them so far from the Lord, he would be so harsh on them that they would not like it.) (6) What actions was Paul afraid he would find at Corinth (v. 20)? (eight sins in four pairs: debates [quarreling] and envyings [jealousy]; wraths [hot tempers] and strifes [factions]; backbitings [insults] and whisperings [gossip]; swellings [pride] and tumults [disorder]).

Ask members to turn to verse 6. Explain that the word "reprobate" appears in verses 6,7 and has the idea of "unable to stand the test" [Analytical Greek Lexicon, 7]. Read verses 6-7 by substituting *I* for "we" and *failure* for "reprobate." Use information in *Studying the Bible* to further explain these verses.

Briefly summarize verses 8-9. Ask members to paraphrase verse 10 to summarize Paul's argument. Point out that Paul's primary purpose in all of his actions and criticism was to build up the Corinthians. By letting them see the evil of their actions, they would turn to good.

Point out that verses 11-14 are Paul's final greeting. Ask someone to read the verses.

**Give the Truth a Personal Focus**

Write on a chalkboard or large sheet of paper: *Ways to resolve a church conflict.* Ask members to list ways Paul handled this conflict that would help them. Write these on the chalkboard or large sheet of paper. Encourage them to commit themselves to behave in such a way that the church will be built up and not torn down by their behavior.

---

1. Adapted from Halford E. Luccock, *More Preaching Values in the Epistles of Paul,* Vol. II (New York: Harper and Brothers Publishers, 1961), 217.

# Building Up the Body

**Basic Passage:** 1 Corinthians 12
**Focal Passages:** 1 Corinthians 12:4-20,26

The words "now concerning spiritual gifts" in 1 Corinthians 12:1 introduce a long discussion that extends through chapter 14. The fact that Paul devoted so much space to the subject shows its importance. Chapter 14 reveals the specific problem in the Corinthian church. Some members placed the gift of tongues above all other gifts. This created friction with those who didn't have this particular gift. Some of Paul's most memorable passages are in his larger discussion of spiritual gifts. Chapter 13, the famous "love" chapter, is included as is the picture of the church as the body of Christ in chapter 12.

**Study Aim:** *To learn how to exercise spiritual gifts in a way that honors Christ by building up His body*

## STUDYING THE BIBLE

Honoring Jesus Christ as Lord is a mark of being led by the Holy Spirit (vv. 1-3). Different spiritual gifts come from the same Spirit (vv. 4-6). The mark of true spirituality is to act for the common good of Christ and His church (v. 7). The same Spirit bestows a variety of gifts on different believers (vv. 8-11). The members of the body of Christ are one in Christ (vv. 12-13). Just as is true in the human body: each member of Christ's body is important (vv. 14-16), no one member is the whole body (vv. 17-20), and all members are interdependent (vv. 21-24). Because members of the body of Christ care for one another, each suffers or rejoices when another suffers or rejoices (vv. 25-26). Although all members do not have any one gift, some gifts provide more opportunities for building up the body of Christ; and no gift is so important as Christian love (vv. 27-31).

### I. Spiritual Gifts (1 Cor. 12:1-11)

**1. Honoring Jesus Christ (vv. 1-3).**—Heathen worshippers were sometimes carried away with wild outbursts. Christians may be carried away, but they must be sure it is by God's Spirit. The test is this: A person who is led by God's Spirit honors Jesus Christ by word and deed.

**2. Different gifts, the same Spirit (vv. 4-6)**

4 Now there are diversities of gifts, but the same Spirit.
5 And there are differences of administrations, but the same Lord.

6 And there are diversities of operations, but it is the same God which worketh all in all.

The gifts given may differ from one person to another, but the same Spirit distributes the gifts. This is the main point in the entire chapter. Paul emphasized this point by repeating the same basic idea three times in verses 4, 5, and 6.

Verse 4 speaks of the Holy Spirit as the source of and distributor of the differing gifts. Verse 5 speaks of the Lord, which in the New Testament usually refers to Jesus Christ, as the source and recipient of differing ways of using the gifts in service. Verse 6 speaks of the different manifestations of power at work, but emphasizes that the same God gives the power to exercise each gift.

Although verses 4-5 do not spell out a full doctrine of the Trinity, this is one of the biblical passages that forms the basis for our belief in one God who reveals Himself as Father, Son, and Spirit. This is how God has revealed Himself and this is how we experience Him: God above us to whom we pray, God revealed as a human being for our salvation, and God within us and among us.

**3. Test of true spirituality (v. 7)**

7 But the manifestation of the Spirit is given to every man to profit withal.

The "profit" is not personal profit, but the profit of the entire church. Everything in chapters 12—14 shows that their problem in Corinth was that each wanted to us individual gifts from God for personal benefit. Paul hammered away at the need to use spiritual gifts for the common good.

This is a test of true spirituality, which Paul developed in chapter 14. True spirituality always acts for the good of Christ and the church, not just for the benefit of the individual. "Spirituality" that focuses solely on one's own enhancement or enjoyment is not the biblical definition of the term.

**4. Charismatic gifts (vv. 8-11)**

8 For to one is given by the Spirit the word of wisdom; to another the word of knowledge by the same Spirit;
9 To another faith by the same Spirit; to another the gifts of healing by the same Spirit;
10 To another the working of miracles; to another prophecy; to another discerning of spirits; to another divers kinds of tongues; to another the interpretation of tongues:
11 But all these worketh that one and the selfsame Spirit, dividing to every man severally as he will.

Don't be confused by the heading title. Today we use the word *charismatic* differently than it is used in the Bible. The word for "gift" in verses 4, 9, 28, 30, and 31 translates a Greek word from which we get our word *charismatic.* The Greek word is closely kin to the Greek word for *grace.* Thus the word emphasizes that spiritual gifts are gifts of God's grace. The word in verse 1 is a different word, which is kin to the word *spirit.* Thus it emphasizes that these are gifts of the Spirit.

In verses 8-10, Paul listed several specific gifts. In the closing verses of the chapter, he gives another list. He also lists gifts in Ephesians 4:11. One impression from comparing the three lists is that Paul did not have one official list that contained all possible spiritual gifts.

"Wisdom" and "knowledge" have to do with insight into the meaning and application of the gospel. "Faith" is more than the faith common to all believers; this seems to have been the kind of faith that can move mountains (see 1 Cor. 13:2). It is closely related to the gift to heal and the gift to work other miracles. "Prophecy" was Spirit-led proclamations or predictions. "Discerning of spirits" was the ability to distinguish false teachers. "Tongues" were ecstatic utterances. "Interpretation of tongues" was the ability to explain someone's use of tongues. (See the session for April 9 for further discussion of the last two gifts.)

Throughout verses 8-11, the point of verses 6-8 is reemphasized: the same Spirit is the source of each of these different gifts.

## II. One Body—Many Members (12:12-31)

**1. One body (vv. 12-13)**

12 For as the body is one, and hath many members, and all the members of that one body, being many, are one body: so also is Christ.

13 For by one Spirit are we all baptized into one body, whether we be Jews or Gentiles, whether we be bond or free; and have been all made to drink into one Spirit.

Early in Paul's letter, he revealed that divisive pride was a major problem. It showed itself in arguing about leaders (1:10-12). It also showed itself in arguing about spiritual gifts. In both cases, Paul's basic argument against division was the unity of Christ with His people. For example, in verse 13, he asked, "Is Christ divided?" Paul made the same point in 12:12. Just as in the human body, one body consists of many members, so in Christ and His body.

The early church consisted of different kinds of people, as far as human distinctions go. Some were Jews, and others were Gentiles. Some were slaves, and others were free. But they had experienced the work of one Spirit. They had been "baptized into one body."

**2. Importance of each member (vv. 14-16)**

14 For the body is not one member, but many.

15 If the foot shall say, Because I am not the hand, I am not of the body; is it therefore not of the body?

16 And if the ear shall say, Because I am not the eye, I am not of the body; is it therefore not of the body?

The boasting of some members about their favored gifts tended to make people without those gifts feel inferior. They may have been tempted to think that they were not really in the same body because their gifts did not draw so much attention to themselves. Paul showed how ridiculous this would be in the human body. The foot may not seem as important as the hand, but both are part of the body. The ear may not seem as important as the eye, but both are members of the same body.

**3. One member is not the whole body (vv. 17-20)**

> **17 If the whole body were an eye, where were the hearing? If the whole were hearing, where were the smelling?**
> **18 But now hath God set the members everyone of them in the body, as it hath pleased him.**
> **19 And if they were all one member, where were the body?**
> **20 But now are they many members, yet but one body.**

Those who took pride in their own gift and looked down on the gifts of others were acting as if they were the whole body. Paul again used the comparison to the human body to show how ridiculous this would be. He asked his readers to picture a huge eye trying to function as if it were the whole body.

Paul hammered away at his main point. God is the One who set the members of the body of Christ in their places, just as He wisely designed the human body to have many members.

**4. Interdependence of members (vv. 21-24).**—Paul spelled out another implication of the analogy. Just as the members of the human body are mutually dependent, so are the members of the body of Christ. No part of the human body can say to another, "I don't need you." Neither can any member of the body of Christ say that to any other member.

**5. Christian togetherness (vv. 25-26)**

> **26 And whether one member suffer, all the members suffer with it; or one member be honored, all the members rejoice with it.**

One result of being in the same body is what the New Testament calls *koinōnia.* The word is usually translated *fellowship,* but it means more than we generally mean when we say "fellowship." *Koinōnia* means to be bound together by a common life. A family is one example of such a relationship. This explains why the New Testament often refers to the church as being a family of faith and love. The same idea of Christian togetherness is expressed in 1 Corinthians 12 by the comparison of the church to the human body.

The members of the body of Christ care for one another. Because of being bound together, anything that affects one member affects all members. If one member is going through a time of suffering, the other members suffer too. If one receives a special honor, the other members rejoice with the one honored. The same idea in verse 26 is expressed in Romans 12:15: "Rejoice with them that do rejoice, and weep with them that weep."

Verses 25-26 enlarge on what Paul wrote in verse 7. Each member acts for the profit of the whole body. How can a member do otherwise if the member really understands what it means to be part of the body of Christ?

**6. Seek the best gifts and a more excellent way (vv. 27-31).**—The closing words of the chapter, especially verse 31, anticipate the rest of Paul's discussion on spiritual gifts. To see what he meant by the "best gifts," see 1 Corinthians 14 and the comments in the session for April 9. To see what he meant by "a more excellent way," see 1 Corinthians 13 and the comments in the session for May 28.

## APPLYING THE BIBLE

**Jesus is Lord.**—Some literary scholars believe that *King Lear* was the most powerful of Shakespeare's tragedies. In *King Lear,* the Duke of Kent requests that he be allowed to serve the king. King Lear replies, "Dost thou know me, fellow?" "No, sir," the Duke of Kent replies, "but you have that in your countenance which I would fain call master."

Jesus spoke of Himself as "the son of Man," but after the resurrection the Christian community expressed its veneration for Him as the risen and ascended Lord by the use of the term "the Lord." The word means "owner," "Master," "Lord."[1]

Paul told the Corinthians (vv. 1-3), as our lesson writer points out, that "honoring Jesus Christ as Lord is a mark of being led by the Holy Spirit."

**Christians are to honor Christ.**—Mark Twain once told about a friend whose goal in life was to stand on Mount Sinai and read the Ten Commandments. Twain told the friend it would be better if he stayed at home and followed them! That's what Paul was telling these Corinthian Christians.

**Speaking in tongues.**—Among the gifts of the Spirit listed in this passage, none has been more divisive in Christendom than speaking in tongues (v. 10). Some New Testament scholars believe that the gift of tongues has been removed by the Holy Spirit and is no longer valid; others believe the gift of tongues continues today to be a valid gift of the Spirit. It appears to this writer that there is no evidence the gift of tongues is no longer a valid gift, although some say that it is not based on 1 Corinthians 13:13. However, too many zealous Christians over emphasize the importance of speaking in tongues when what they ought to do is control the one they have! There is no commandment in Scripture to seek the gift of tongues, but we are commanded to seek after and practice love (vv. 1-13; 14:1).

**Keepers of the lighthouse.**—For thirty-five years, Kate Walker kept the light burning in the lighthouse at Robins Reef lighthouse where the Atlantic flows into New York harbor. The government pensioned Kate in 1922 and she moved to Staten Island where she could see the light flashing across the dark waters. Kate confessed it was often hard and lonely at the lighthouse, but she stayed with it and tended the light because "Jake said to me, 'Mind the light, Katie. Mind the light!'" I had to be faithful to what Jake told me to do, Kate told a neighbor.

Jake was her husband. For three years Kate, Jake, and their two children lived all alone at the lighthouse. Every five seconds the lamp on top of the lighthouse revolved, flashing its signal to the incoming seamen to warn them of the long, dangerous reef that lay ahead of them. Then Jake took sick and had to be rowed by boat to the hospital two miles across the harbor. Ten lonely days and nights later Kate received word that Jake had died.

His last words to Katie before he was taken away were, "Mind the light, Katie. Mind the light!"[2]

Paul was telling the Corinthians that they were to "mind the spiritual light" Jesus had put within them.

**Love is the best gift of all.**—E. V. Hill, well-known black preacher from Los Angeles, tells about a black pastor being killed for associating with white people during the Watts riots in Los Angeles a number of years ago.

One night Hill got a phone call telling him that his car was the next to be bombed. The next morning Hill went out to see if his car was gone. And it was. A little later, his wife drove up in the car and Hill asked, "Why did you do this?"

"If your car was to be bombed," she replied, "I wanted to die, not you." What an example of true love!

## TEACHING THE BIBLE

▶ *Main Idea:* Paul declared that we should learn to exercise spiritual gifts in a way that honors Christ by building up His body.

▶ *Suggested Teaching Aim:* To lead adults to examine Paul's directives for building up the body, and to determine how they can exercise their spiritual gifts in a way that honors Christ.

### A TEACHING OUTLINE

1. *Identify the similarities and differences in spiritual gifts.*
2. *Draw a principle from Paul's three different listings of spiritual gifts.*
3. *See how pride is so useless because all the body is needed.*

### Introduce the Bible Study

Use the illustration "Jesus is Lord" *(Applying the Bible)* to introduce the lesson.

### Search for Biblical Truth

Write *Different* and *Same* on a chalkboard or a large sheet of paper. Ask members to open their Bibles to 1 Corinthians 12:4-6. Ask members to suggest what Paul said is different (gifts, administrations, operations) and what is the same (Spirit, Lord, God). Let them suggest other words for administrations (serving) and operations (working). Ask: What is the main point of these verses (and the whole chapter)? (different gifts but same Spirit distributes the gifts) Who is the "Lord" (12:4)? (in the New Testament Lord is usually Jesus) Who gives the power to exercise these gifts? (God) What do these verses show about Paul's belief in the Trinity? (They mention Spirit, Lord [Jesus], and God.)

Use *Studying the Bible* to share the meaning of "profit" (12:7). Organize the class in three groups. Ask group 1 to look at the list of spiritual gifts in 12:8-10, group 2 to look at 12:27-28, and group 3 to look at Ephesians 4:11. Ask someone from each group to read their Scripture aloud. After all Scriptures are read, ask what principle(s) members can draw from the fact that Paul's three lists are all different? (Paul did not have an "official" list of spiritual gifts.)

Prepare poster strips of the following outline:

ONE BODY—MANY MEMBERS

1. One body (12:12-13)
2. Importance of each member (12:14-16)
3. One member is not the whole body (12:17-20)

Assign these strips to the three groups and ask them to place them on the focal wall as they report. Ask group 1 to answer this question: What does verses 12-13 say about pride? (Since we are all one in Christ, no one has a right to be proud.) Ask group 2 to answer this question: What does verses 14-16 say about one gift being more important than another? (As all parts of the body are important, all gifts are important to the body of Christ.) Ask group 3 to answer this question: How does verses 17-20 emphasize that the body of Christ needs people with different gifts? (As human body would be unable to exist with only one member, even so would the body of Christ fail to exist with only one gift.)

Ask a volunteer to read verse 26. Point out that this verse describes how the body of Christ ought to function. Use *Studying the Bible* to explain Paul's concept of *koinōnia.*

### Give the Truth a Personal Focus

Distribute paper and pencils to members. Ask them to draw a line down the middle of the sheet and list their spiritual gifts on one side and how they have used these gifts to build up the body. Now ask them to pick one gift and list two or three ways they can use that gift even more to build up the church.

Close in prayer that this will be a growing time for all members.

---

1. See Vincent Taylor, *The Names of Jesus* (New York: Macmillan and Co. Ltd., 1953), 38-51.
2. Adapted from Margaret White Eggleston, *Seventy-five Stories for the Worship Hour* (New York: Harper and Brothers Publishers, 1921), 79-81.

# Growing Through Worship

**Basic Passage:** 1 Corinthians 14:1-33a
**Focal Passage:** 1 Corinthians 14:20-33a

First Corinthians 14 is the concluding chapter in Paul's discussion of spiritual gifts. In chapter 12, he introduced the subject and laid the foundation by describing the church as the body of Christ—one body with many members. His point was that all members of the church are as important and interdependent as the parts of the human body. He concluded the chapter by urging his readers to "covet earnestly the best gifts." Paul also spoke of "a more excellent way" (1 Cor. 12:31). In chapter 13 (which we shall study on May 28), Paul presented the more excellent way that transcends all the gifts—self-giving love. Having done that, he proceeded to describe in chapter 14 how to "covet earnestly the best gifts."

**Study Aim:** *To evaluate worship practices and experiences in light of guidelines in 1 Corinthians 14:1-33a*

## STUDYING THE BIBLE

Three broad guidelines for evaluating worship are given in 1 Corinthians 14:1-33a. These are stated in the three main points of the outline that accompany the exposition. Running throughout the chapter are specific references to several spiritual gifts: especially prophecy and tongues. Paul began by emphasizing that while the gift of tongues may build up an individual, prophecy builds up the church (vv. 1-5). Paul gave several examples to show that meaningless sounds don't build up the church (vv. 6-12); while intelligible speech does (vv. 13-19). Christians should be mature, not childish, in their thinking (v. 20). In one sense, tongues is a sign of judgment to those who refuse to believe (vv. 21-22). In another sense, however, only clear communication can lead unbelievers to faith (vv. 23-25). Every part of church worship should contribute to building up (v. 26). Specific guidelines should be followed about both the gifts of tongues and prophecy (vv. 27-31). Spirit-led worshipers are able to control how they act in public worship (vv. 32-33a).

### I. Worship Should Build Up the Church (14:1-19)

**1. Desire spiritual gifts that build up the church (vv. 1-5).—** Judging from what Paul wrote in 1 Corinthians 12—14, some Corinthians were using the gift of tongues as a badge of their superiority. Paul insisted that the only value of tongues was to the individual; while prophecy was a gift that helped build up (edify), exhort, and comfort the church.

**2. Meaningless sounds do not build up the church (vv. 6-12).**— Some people think the gift of tongues at Corinth was like the tongues at Pentecost (see Acts 2). That is, they think believers at Corinth spoke in foreign languages. Yet those who heard the tongues at Corinth were unable to understand what they heard; while the people who heard the tongues at Pentecost did understand. Paul compared the tongues at Corinth to hearing a bugle that sounded no specific call or played no specific melody. He also said it was like two foreigners trying to talk without an interpreter.

**3. Intelligible speech does build up the church (vv. 13-19).**— Understanding as well as emotion is essential in worship. Prophecy contributes to understanding. Although Paul could exercise the gift of tongues in private, in church he had rather speak five words that made sense than ten thousand words of meaningless sounds.

## II. Worship Should Communicate the Gospel to Unbelievers (14:20-25)

**1. Be mature, not childish in your thinking (v. 20).**

> 20 Brethren, be not children in understanding: howbeit in malice be ye children, but in understanding be men.

Children are usually more impressed than adults by what is showy and outwardly impressive. Adults tend to probe beneath the surface and to look for what is real and meaningful, not just showy. Exercising the gift of tongues in church was more outwardly impressive to those who judged things as children do. Meaningful speech was more impressive to mature worshippers.

**2. Recognize that some people refuse to believe (vv. 21-22).**

> 21 In the law it is written, With men of other tongues and other lips will I speak unto this people; and yet for all that will they not hear me, saith the Lord.
> 22 Wherefore tongues are for a sign, not to them that believe, but to them that believe not: but prophesying serveth not for them that believe not, but for them which believe.

On the surface, verses 21-22 seem to contradict verses 23-25. In verses 21-22, Paul spoke of tongues as a sign to unbelievers, not believers. In verses 23-25, he said that the use of tongues in worship drives unbelievers away; while prophecy wins them.

The clue seems to be that Paul was speaking of hardened unbelievers in verses 21-22. Verse 21 refers to the situation in Isaiah 28:11-13. The hardhearted Israelites were about to be delivered to foreign invaders who spoke a language they couldn't understand. For people who have hardened their hearts to the Lord, any message—

meaningless sounds or clear communication—is like a foreign language.

**3. Clearly communicate to unbelievers (vv. 23-25).**

> 23 If therefore the whole church be come together into one place, and all speak with tongues, and there come in those that are unlearned, or unbelievers, will they not say that ye are mad?
> 24 But if all prophesy, and there come in one that believeth not, or one unlearned, he is convinced of all, he is judged of all:
> 25 And thus are the secrets of his heart made manifest; and so falling down on his face, he will worship God, and report that God is in you of a truth.

The word "unlearned," which appears in verses 16, 23, and 24, probably refers to people who were interested in Christianity but who had not yet made a commitment to Christ. Paul asked his readers to imagine a worship service in which church members were speaking in tongues without an interpreter. What would happen if an interested but uncommitted person came in, or if an unbeliever visited for the first time? Paul said that the outsiders would think the Christians were crazy.

What would happen if the outsiders came to a service where the truth of God was clearly communicated? In such a setting, conviction would come to the heart of an outsider. Such a person would see himself as God sees him. He would recognize that God was present among the worshippers. He would fall down and worship God himself.

## III. Worship Should Be Spirit-led and Orderly (14:26-33a)

**1. Worship practices should build up the church (v. 26).**

> 26 How is it then, brethren? when ye come together, everyone of you hath a psalm, hath a doctrine, hath a tongue, hath a revelation, hath an interpretation. Let all things be done unto edifying.

In the early church, members shared publicly in church worship as the Spirit led them. Not all had the same gifts, but each exercised individual gifts in such a way as to benefit the entire congregation. Worshippers often used a biblical psalm in worship, but the word "psalm" had come to mean a hymn or song (see Col. 3:16). "Doctrine" is teaching. Notice that "a tongue" is mentioned only because "an interpreter" also is mentioned (see vv. 27-28). Paul kept hammering away at his main point: every activity done when the church meets for worship should build up the church, not just be a private devotion for one's worship.

**2. Follow guidelines for spiritual gifts in worship (vv. 27-31).**

27 If any man speak in an unknown tongue, let it be by two, or at the most by three, and that by course; and let one interpret.
28 But if there be no interpreter, let him keep silence in the church; and let him speak to himself, and to God.
29 Let the prophets speak two or three, and let the other judge.
30 If anything be revealed to another that sitteth by, let the first hold his peace.
31 For ye may all prophesy one by one, that all may learn, and all may be comforted.

In these verses Paul spelled out some specific guidelines about the use of tongues (vv. 27-28) and of prophecy (vv. 29-31) in public worship.

Since this is the only Bible passage that gives specific guidelines for tongues in public worship, churches that practice tongues should follow these clear instructions in verse 27: (1) Only two or three people should speak in tongues in the same service. (2) Each should go one at a time. (This is the meaning of "by course.") (3) Someone should interpret the tongues.

Just to be sure that no one misunderstood, Paul said in verse 28 that unless an interpreter was present, a person should not speak in tongues in public. Instead, let the person exercise that as an act of private devotion when alone with God.

Verse 29 speaks of two or three prophets in a service. The words "let the other judge" refers to the gift of discerning of spirits (see 1 Cor. 12:10). In the early church, most converts came from paganism and the truth of Christ had not yet been clearly understood. Those who discerned spirits were to be sure that prophets were speaking consistently with the revelation of God in Jesus Christ.

Verse 20 adds that if someone else receives a revelation from God, the first prophet should step aside for the other prophet. Verse 31 shows that by following these guidelines the prophets speak one at a time so that people learn and are comforted.

**3. Exercise God-inspired self-control (vv. 32-33a).**

32 And the spirits of the prophets are subject to the prophets.
33 For God is not the author of confusion, but of peace.

Verse 32 is sometimes understood as reinforcing verse 31. If this is its meaning, the point is that one prophet should be willing to subject himself to another by standing aside to let the other speak. More likely, however, verse 32 goes with verse 33. If so, the point is that each prophet has control of his own spirit. He is not out of control and thus unable to follow the guidelines Paul set forth.

The guidelines of verses 26-32 assume that each member of the church is able to control the exercise of spiritual gifts in public worship. The opposite of this would be if the Spirit so took control of a person's life that the person lost any control of his actions. This apparently was what some of the Corinthians were claiming. Judging from what Paul said, some of them excused their actions in public worship by claiming that they had no control over their actions. Paul's guidelines assumed that Spirit-filled people retain enough control of their actions that these guidelines can be followed.

Paul did not describe exactly what was happening with regard to spiritual gifts in the worship services of the Corinthian church. However, if we read between the lines, probably many of them were clamoring to speak with tongues. Often they all tried to speak at the same time. Sometimes no one was present to interpret the tongues. Thus Paul gave the general rule in verse 33: "God is not the author of confusion, but of peace."

## APPLYING THE BIBLE

**How to kill a church.**—In Cleveland, Ohio, one will find the Euclid Avenue Baptist Church if it is still alive! Financed largely by the Rockefeller family, John D. Rockefeller, Sr., gave most of the operating cost and $250,000 as a gift for the building, then his son gave another $250,000 in 1934. At one time the church had a membership of 2,000, but it had dwindled to 75 in 1956. A fair guess would be that it died from too much help from too few people. Nothing will destroy a church as quickly as poor stewardship on the part of the members.

**United, praying churches can change their world.**—The greatest movements of history have involved few people in comparison with the population. Alexander the Great conquered the world with an army of only 35,000 men. Genghis Khan started in his world conquest with only 200,000 men. Tamerlane conquered the world with 230,000 soldiers. The Communists took Russia with only 40,000. Yet the numbers of men in these combined armies that conquered the world at various times in history, cannot compare in size with the huge army of Christian men and women in our churches who serve as pastors, deacons, Sunday School teachers, and so forth. Why then do we not have a greater impact on our world? It is because of our lack of unity and commitment which also was the bane of the Corinthian church.

**The lone rangers in the church.**—Every church, including the church at Corinth, has its "lone rangers." They want to do their thing regardless of whether it contributes to the growth of the body of Christ (vv. 23-25). Most churches have considerably fewer than 50 percent of their resident members in any given worship service. Many of these people say, "I can worship just as well at home, by the lake, or on the golf course."

Robert Hastings suggests these people need a Do-It-Yourself Worship Kit! The kit contains:

*One portable, lightweight seat, shaped like a church pew.*

*Can be set up anywhere.*

*One small, paper-covered hymnal containing one dozen well-known hymns (words and music).*

*One harmonica—or mouth organ—to take the place of the church organ. (Frankly, you will find it difficult to play and sing at the same time. But you can master it, and after all there must be some challenge.)*

*One abbreviated New Testament with familiar selections designed to be read in less than one minute each.*

*One small offering plate—to be held in the left hand while putting coin in with the right. (Denomination of the coin is unimportant as you will get it back anyway.)*

*One brief sermon titled "What a Good Boy Am I." You will feel much better after using this sermon. It may be read aloud or silently.*

Those who have used the do-It-Yourself Worship Kit tell us they get an extra lift from their own service if, at the close, they rush to a mirror and shake hands with themselves. But this is optional.[1]

**The tie that binds.**—Dr. George W. Truett told about an old man visiting a well-known art gallery one day and gazing earnestly at a picture of Christ on the cross. Involuntarily, the man was so moved that he sighed quietly, "Bless Him! I love Him!" A stranger standing nearby overhead the old man. Taking the old gentleman by the hand, the stranger said, "Brother, I love Him, too." Then a third and a fourth person joined them and soon there was a small crowd standing before the picture and worshiping Him whom they adored. They were drawn together by their common love of the crucified Savior.[2]

The church at Corinth had a fellowship problem. They were so divided over the gifts of the Spirit that the fellowship was broken. Paul wrote to set things straight and to encourage the Corinthian believers, at all costs, to restore their fellowship in Christ with each other. Concentrating on the cross will sweeten the spirit of the most divisive church.

## TEACHING THE BIBLE

*Main Idea:* Growing through worship means that believers evaluate their worship practices to be sure they benefit themselves and build up others.

*Suggested Teaching Aim:* To lead adults to examine Paul's statements on worship, and to list ways their worship can benefit themselves and build up others.

### A TEACHING OUTLINE

1. *Overview the whole Scripture.*
2. *Make a poster and assignment slips to guide the study.*
3. *Lead members to examine the Focal Passage.*
4. *Determine the effectiveness of your worship.*

**Introduce the Bible Study**

Use the illustration "Lone rangers in the church" *Applying the Bible* to introduce the lesson.

**Search for Biblical Truth**

To overview the study, briefly review the material in the introduction to *Studying the Bible.* Read the main idea.

IN ADVANCE, copy the following outline on a chalkboard or a large sheet of paper:

1. Worship Should Build Up the Church (14:1-19)
2. Worship Should Communicate the Gospel to Unbelievers (14:20-25)
3. Worship Should Be Spirit-led and Orderly (14:26-33*a*)

IN ADVANCE, copy the following headings on slips of paper:

(1) Be mature, not childish in your thinking (14:20);
(2) Recognize that some people refuse to believe (14:21-22);
(3) Clearly communicate to unbelievers (14:23-25);
(4) Worship practices should build up the church (14:26);
(5) Follow guidelines for spiritual gifts in worship (14:27-31);
(6) Exercise God-inspired self-control (14:32-33*a*).

Summarize the first point on the outline by stating these three points: believers should desire spiritual gifts that build up the church; meaningless sounds do not build up the church; intelligible speech does build up the church.

Distribute the six slips of paper to six members or groups. Ask them to read and study their Scripture and answer the following two questions:

(1) What did this mean to Paul and the Corinthians?
(2) What does it mean to us today?

Be thoroughly familiar with the material in *Studying the Bible* so you can add information to their answers.

Call for the first report. Be sure you mention the following: children like the showy, but adults should look for what is real and meaningful.

Call for the second report. Be sure you point out how verses 21-22 does not contradict verses 23-25 because Paul was talking about hardened unbelievers in verses 21-22.

Call for the third report. Be sure you define "unlearned" as those persons interested in Christianity but who had not made a commitment to Christ.

Call for the fourth report. Be sure you define "psalm," "doctrine," and the "tongue . . . interpretation."

Call for the fifth report. Be sure you spell out the three guidelines for using tongues in public worship. Explain the role of the prophets in the worship service.

Call for the sixth report. Be sure you explain the two interpretations of verse 32 and Paul's guideline that Spirit-filled people retain enough control of their actions that these guidelines can be followed. Point out that verse 33 is the key to all worship.

**Give the Truth a Personal Focus**

Ask members to look at the broader picture of worship in the church and to list principles for worship in your church. If they are hesitant, suggest the three points of the outline you wrote on the chalkboard or large sheet of paper would be places to start. Ask: What is one way we should be built up after a worship service? What do we do that keeps the gospel from being communicated to unbelievers who come to our worship? What proof do we have that a worship service is Spirit-led?

Ask members to list ways worship can benefit themselves and build up others. List these on the chalkboard and close in prayer that the worship today will accomplish these.

---

1. Adapted from Robert J. Hastings, *A Word Fitly Spoken* (Nashville: Broadman Press, 1962), 90-91.

2. Adapted from George W. Truett, *Follow Thou Me* (Nashville: Broadman Press, 1932), 66.

April
16
1995

# Being a Resurrection People

**Basic Passages:** Luke 24:1-11; 1 Corinthians 15
**Focal Passages:** Luke 24:1-11; 1 Corinthians 15:12-17, 56-58

Some people maintain that actions, not beliefs, are what count. They also insist that beliefs have nothing to do with actions. This is not true. Take, for example, belief in Christ's resurrection. This belief affects how we act and think as Christians. The session for this Easter is based on passages from two great chapters about the resurrection—Luke 24 and 1 Corinthians 15. These passages show clearly why Christians believe in the resurrection of Christ. The passage also shows some of the differences that his belief makes in our lives.

**Study Aim:** *To explain why Christians believe in Christ's resurrection and to testify to differences this belief makes*

## STUDYING THE BIBLE

The reality of Christ's resurrection is based on the empty tomb (Luke 24:1-11) and on the appearances of the risen Lord (1 Cor. 15:1-11). Because some in Corinth denied the future resurrection, Paul showed that Christ's resurrection and Christians' resurrection are inseparable (vv. 12-19). Because Christ has been raised from the dead, death will eventually be totally destroyed (vv. 20-28). Christians are able to defy death because of their faith in the resurrected Lord (vv. 29-34). The resurrection body of believers will be a spiritual body designed for the new mode of future life (vv. 35-50). Because Christ gives us victory over sin, death, and the law, we give thanks and live with steadfastness and assurance (vv. 51-58).

### I. Reality of Christ's Resurrection (Luke 24:1-11; 1 Cor. 15:1-11)

**1. The empty tomb (Luke 24:1-11)**

1 Now upon the first day of the week, very early in the morning, they came unto the sepulcher, bringing the spices which they had prepared, and certain others with them.
2 And they found the stone rolled away from the sepulcher.
3 And they entered in, and found not the body of the Lord Jesus.
4 And it came to pass, as they were much perplexed thereabout, behold, two men stood by them in shining garments:
5 And as they were afraid, and bowed down their faces to

**the earth, they said unto them, Why seek ye the living among the dead?**
**6 He is not here, but is risen: remember how he spake unto you when he was yet in Galilee,**
**7 Saying, The Son of man must be delivered into the hands of sinful men, and be crucified, and the third day rise again.**
**8 And they remembered his words.**
**9 And returned from the sepulcher, and told all these things unto the eleven, and to all the rest.**
**10 It was Mary Magdalene, and Joanna, and Mary the mother of James, and other women that were with them, which told these things unto the apostles.**
**11 And their words seemed to them as idle tales, and they believed them not.**

Luke 23:55-56 describes how women watched where Jesus' body was placed and returned home to prepare spices. When they returned very early on the first day of the week, they found the stone rolled away. They went into the tomb and discovered that the body of Jesus was not there. Notice that they did not immediately believe; instead they were perplexed.

Two men in shining garments reminded them of Jesus' predictions of His coming death and resurrection (see 9:22; 18:31-33). When the women were reminded, they remembered the words of Jesus. They went and told the apostles what had happened. However, the apostles didn't believe the women. Instead they accused them of raving like crazy people.

According to the some skeptics, the disciples were expecting Jesus' resurrection so fervently that they saw someone whom they mistook for Jesus alive from the dead. This theory does not fit the facts. Luke 24:1-11 clearly shows that the disciples were not expecting Jesus to be raised from the dead. He had predicted it earlier, but they had not really understood (18:34). The women were going to anoint a dead body. Even when they found the tomb empty, they were perplexed. Angels had to remind them of Jesus' words. The apostles not only refused to believe, they ridiculed the women for their report. Thus the empty tomb alone was not convincing evidence that Jesus was raised from the dead. However, when it is placed with the appearances of the risen Lord, it testifies to the One who is living, not dead.

**2. Appearances of the Lord (1 Cor. 15:1-11)**—The heart of the gospel is the death, burial, and resurrection of Jesus Christ. Paul listed some of those who saw the Lord after His resurrection: Cephas, the twelve, over five hundred believers, James, all the apostles, and Paul himself. Christian belief in the resurrection of Jesus Christ is based on the testimony of these and other credible eyewitnesses. They didn't see someone else and jump to the conclusion that it was Jesus; they had to be convinced that the One whom they saw was indeed the Lord Himself.

## II. Reality of the Future Resurrection (1 Cor. 15:12-58)

### 1. Christ's resurrection and ours (vv. 12-19)

12 Now if Christ be preached that he rose from the dead, how say some among you that there is no resurrection of the dead?

Some in Corinth were denying the future resurrection of believers. This may mean that they were denying any kind of life after death. More likely, however, these people claimed to believe that Jesus was raised from the dead and that Jesus has raised believers from a life of sin to a new life. What they denied was a future resurrection of the body. Thus they probably were like those whose beliefs Paul condemned in 2 Timothy 2:18.

13 But if there is no resurrection of the dead, then is Christ not risen:
14 And if Christ be not risen, then is our preaching vain, and your faith is also vain.
15 Yea, and we are found false witnesses of God; because we have testified of God that he raised up Christ: whom he raised not up, if so be that the dead rise not.
16 For if the dead rise not, then is not Christ raised:
17 And if Christ be not raised, your faith is vain; ye are yet in your sins.

Paul built on the sure foundation of belief in the reality of Christ's resurrection to show that if Christ was raised from the dead, so shall Christians be raised from the dead. He did this in verses 12-19 by forcing the Corinthians to face the logical outcome of their denial of the resurrection of Christians. Denying the future resurrection is denying also the resurrection of Christ (v. 13). The two stand or fall together.

Paul identified three terrible consequences that would follow if Christ was not raised from the dead: (1) Christian preaching and Christian faith would be empty and false (vv. 14-15). (2) Christians would still be in their sins (vv. 16-17). (3) Those who have lived and died believing in Christ would have perished with no reality to their hope (vv. 18-19).

**2. The death of death (v. 20-28).**—But because Christ has been raised from the dead, Christians can be assured of their own resurrection. Christ is like the first fruits that guarantees the harvest. He reversed the process of death set in motion by Adam. Christ will finally have dominion over all things. "The last enemy that shall be destroyed is death" (v. 26).

**3. Defying death (vv. 29-34).**—Christians are able to stand in the face of death and defy it because of Christ's victory over death. Those without such hope often report to denying death, but mature Christians can take risks in the name of Christ because they know Christ has conquered death. Those without such hope often live only for the moment. Many today, as in Paul's day, have this philosophy:

"Let us eat and drink; for to-morrow we die" (v. 32).

**4. The resurrection body (vv. 35-50).**—Paul knew that many people rejected the idea of resurrection because they thought of the resurrection body as a flesh-and-blood body. Paul, therefore, described the resurrection body as a spiritual body, not a flesh-and-blood body. Just as God has made many different kinds of bodies, so He will make a spiritual body appropriate to the new situation. Paul did not answer all the questions we might ask about the exact nature of this spiritual body. Suffice it to say, it will be a body; and God will give us the body we need at the time we need it.

**5. Future resurrection and Christian hope (vv. 51-58)**

> **56 The sting of death is sin; and the strength of sin is the law.**
> **57 But thanks be to God, which giveth us the victory through our Lord Jesus Christ.**
> **58 Therefore, my beloved brethren, be ye steadfast, unmovable, always abounding in the work of the Lord, forasmuch as ye know that your labor is not in vain in the Lord.**

Verses 51-54 proclaim the final victory over death. Both the dead in Christ and living believers will be transformed when "death is swallowed up in victory" (v. 54). The very thought of this wonderful hope caused Paul to ask, "O death, where is thy sting? O grave, where is thy victory?" (v. 55).

Verses 56-57 give a twofold answer to the questions of verse 55. Verse 56 shows that sin, not death, is the real enemy. Death is only the fruit of sin. Paul often described the human condition as a state of slavery in which we are bound by sin, death, and the law (see Rom. 7:1-24). Sin separates us from God. The law condemns us as guilty. Death is the inevitable result of sin.

Verse 57 gives the second answer to the questions of verse 55. In spite of our sin, the condemnation of the law, and the wages of sin—death, Christians can defy death because Christ has defeated sin, death, and the law. Because we are in Christ, we have been saved from sin, freed from the condemnation of the law, and promised victory over death (Rom. 8:1-2). We cannot think of this deliverance without saying, "Thanks be to God, which giveth us the victory through our Lord Jesus Christ' (v. 57).

Verse 58 describes some of the countless ways this belief affects our attitudes and actions. This assurance of victory creates steadfastness. Earlier verses describe some of the consequences of not having this assurance (vv. 19,32).

Believers in Christ are described as "always abounding in the work of the Lord.'" Believers know that their work "is not in vain in the Lord." The word "vain" is the same word found in verse 14. It means "empty." Without the resurrection of Christ, all we preach and believe would be empty. Because He has shared with us His victory over sin and death, life in Christ has eternal meaning.

## APPLYING THE BIBLE

**The nearest way to go home.**—Hudson Baggett, editor of the *Alabama Baptist,* writes: "Cemeteries and tombstones remind us of death, but God's Word reminds us that the grave is the gateway to a greater life.

"A former school bus driver told the story of how he used to stop his bus to let a student off at a cemetery every day. The driver was puzzled as to where the young student lived. He noticed that he always went toward the cemetery when he got off the bus. He asked the young man and he replied, 'Going through the cemetery is the nearest way for me to go home.'

"Likewise, the dead in Christ go through the cemetery to their eternal home. This is the message of Easter" (1 Cor. 15:12-17).

**Easter means reunion.**—Ivan Turgenev (1818-1883) is regarded as one of Russia's three greatest novelists. He was the first Russian writer to win wide recognition outside Russia.

In his book *Fathers and Sons,* Turgenev tells about a father and mother whose only son had been killed in a war. They go out to the poorly kept cemetery to visit his grave. The weeds have grown up, the fence is down, the trees have fallen and been left where they fell. But there is one grave that is well kept, green and smooth as velvet. As the elderly couple stand holding hands, looking down on the green, flower-covered grave, they bow their heads in prayer: "O gracious Heavenly Father, grant that one day in thy homeland and in thine own eternity we three may be together again, and know each other and love each other and live down the centuries together. O God, please grant this one thing, that we may live together again."[1]

Easter means resurrection and reunion! Paul told the Corinthians that "If there be no resurrection of the dead, then is Christ not risen: And if Christ be not risen, then is our preaching vain, and your faith is also vain" (vv. 12-13). But Christ has been raised from the dead. Our hope for tomorrow is not empty and vain. Easter means reunion!

**The most encouraging words ever heard on earth.**—Newspaper cartoonist H. T. Webster relates that he amused himself one day by sending congratulatory telegrams to twenty of his friends. Although none of them had done anything outstanding for which to be congratulated, Webster sent each the one-word message, "Congratulations." And each, in turn, wrote Webster a thank-you note without questioning why the message had been sent.

Everyone needs encouragement. But there is no encouragement that measures up to the encouragement Easter brings. Based on fact and not fantasy, Easter's encouragement is fresh and new every morning as the presence of the living Lord overshadows the believer.[2]

The most encouraging news that has ever been heard on earth was the announcement of the angel: "He is not here, but is risen" (Luke 24:6).

**"Now he belongs to the ages."**—Abraham Lincoln, the sixteenth president of the United States, was shot on Good Friday, April 14, 1865, by John Wilkes Booth. Lincoln was sitting with his party in the presidential box at Ford's Theater when Booth quietly opened the door to the box and walked up behind the President. Just as Mary Lincoln took the President's hand in hers, Booth fired his small pistol at Lincoln's head. They carried the President across the street to a home owned by William Peterson, where Lincoln died the next morning at 7:22 a.m. Secretary of War Edwin Stanton, who had been kneeling by the President's bed, pulled down the shades on the windows and closed the half-opened eyes of Lincoln. Then Stanton said, "Now he belongs to the ages."[3]

Paul said in Romans 1:4 that Jesus "through the Spirit of holiness was declared with power to be the Son of God by his resurrection from the dead" (NIV). If He were only a Jew hanging on a cross that would be all He would be—nothing more. But having been raised from the dead, He now lives not only in heaven but in the lives of multiplied millions of believers around the earth. Truly, He belongs to the ages!

**The empty tomb.**—A Muslim and a Christian were talking one day and the Muslim said, "We Muslims have one thing you Christians do not have." "What is that" asked the Christian. "When we go to Medina, we find a coffin and know that Mohammed lived because his body is in the coffin. But when you Christians go to Jerusalem you find nothing but an empty tomb." "What you say is absolutely true," the Christian replied. "And that is what makes our religion different from yours. We serve a Lord who lives and a risen Christ."

## TEACHING THE BIBLE

▶ *Main Idea:* Being a resurrected people means that Christians believe in Christ's resurrection and testify to differences this belief makes.
▶ *Suggested Teaching Aim:* To lead adults to explain their belief in the resurrection, and to testify to differences this belief makes.

### A TEACHING OUTLINE

*1. Use posters to illustrate the lesson.*
*2. Use creative writing assignments to discover the attitudes of those who observed the first Easter.*
*3. Use a Scripture search to find what would have happened if Christ had not been raised from the dead.*
*4. Use a case study to apply the Scripture to life.*

**Introduce the Bible Study**

Use the illustration "The nearest way to go home," *Applying the Bible.*

**Search for Biblical Truth**

IN ADVANCE, draw a rectangle (approx. 6- by 12-inches) on a large sheet of paper. On this write *Reality of Christ's Resurrection.* Place this on the focal wall. Draw a pyramid (approx. 12 inches on each side) to fit on top of this. On this write *Reality of the Future Resurrection.* Be prepared to add this to the wall later.

Ask members to open their Bibles to Luke 24. Ask members to read silently verse 1-11. Call attention to the poster. Ask: What is the basis of Christ's resurrection? *(empty tomb, appearances of the Lord)* What did Christ's resurrection do for death? *(destroyed it)* How does the resurrection influence the way Christians approach death? *(They can defy it.)*

Distribute paper and pencils to all members. Ask members to choose one person around the tomb and write what they think that person must have felt when he or she discovered the empty tomb that first Easter morning. Let several volunteers read their descriptions. Ask members to turn to 1 Corinthians 15:12-17 and read these verses. While they are reading, place the pyramid on the wall, using the earlier poster as a foundation. Point out that Paul built on the sure foundation of belief in the reality of Christ's resurrection.

Ask members to find verses that support the following if Christ had not been raised from the dead: (1) Christian preaching and Christian faith would be empty and false (vv.14-15); (2) Christians would still be in their sins (vv.16-17); (3) those who have lived and died believing in Christ would have perished with no reality to their hope (vv.18-19).

Using the material in *Studying the Bible,* prepare a brief lecture on vv. 56-58. In this lecture cover the following points: (1) the dead in Christ and the living believers will be transformed when "death is swallowed up in victory"; (2) this assurance caused Paul to ask the question, "O death . . . where is thy victory?"; (3) give the twofold answer to the question in verse 56; (4) describe some of the countless ways this belief affects our attitudes and actions; (5) the meaning our life in Christ has because of this victory.

Ask members to turn their papers over and write an answer to this question. How does the future resurrection affect that way you live today?

**Give the Truth a Personal Focus**

Organize the class in two groups. Ask half the class to listen to the following case study as though Joshua and Kim were Christians and the other half to listen as though they were not Christians: Joshua and Kim had been out of college about five years. Both had good jobs and had steadily advanced up the corporate ladder in both of their companies. One day a coworker of Kim's was discovered to have cancer. The woman was only thirty-six years old. Kim was quite shaken, since the woman was only about ten years older than she.

Read the case study and ask the class to respond. Be sure members are able to testify to the difference belief in the resurrection makes in their lives when they face trouble. Close in a prayer of gratitude for what the resurrection means to us.

---

1. C. Roy Angell, *Rejoicing on Great Days* (Nashville: Broadman Press, 1968), 20.
2. J. B. Fowler Jr., *Illustrated Sermons for Special Occasions* (Nashville: Broadman Press, 1988), 17.
3. Ibid., 19.

April
23
1995

# Exercising Liberty Wisely

**Basic Passage:** 1 Corinthians 8
**Focal Passage:** 1 Corinthians 8

Eating meat sacrificed to idols is not an issue for Christians today. It was an issue for Christians in first-century Corinth. Paul dealt with the issue at length in 1 Corinthians 8:1— 11:1. In the session for March 19, we dealt with 1 Corinthians 10:1-17, which contains part of Paul's larger answer to questions about meat sacrificed to idols. In the session for May 7, we will deal with another part of the larger answer in 1 Corinthians 9. In today's Bible study, we will deal with the first part of Paul's answer, where Paul presented principles for dealing with the problem. The principles apply self-discipline and love to issues where personal liberty and rights are involved. Although meat sacrificed to idols is not an issue today, self-discipline and love apply to every issue of personal liberty or rights.

**Study Aim:** *To apply principles of self-discipline and love to issues of personal liberty and rights*

## STUDYING THE BIBLE

After introducing the issue, Paul presented the relationship between knowledge and love (vv. 1-3). He affirmed a basic article of Christian faith—belief in one God (vv. 4-6). Although some Christians saw no moral significance to food, others felt guilty about eating meat sacrificed to idols (vv. 7-8). When the former group exercised their liberty without regard for the consciences of the latter group, they sinned against their brothers and against Christ (vv. 9-12). Paul, therefore, resolved not to eat meat in circumstances that might harm a fellow Christian (v. 13).

### I. Issue: Meat Sacrificed to Idols (8:1-6)

#### 1. Knowledge and love (vv. 1-3)

1 Now as touching things offered unto idols, we know that we all have knowledge. Knowledge puffeth up, but charity edifieth.

2 And if any man think that he knoweth anything, he knoweth nothing yet as he ought to know.

3 But if any man love God, the same is known of him.

Part of 1 Corinthians consisted of Paul's answers to questions the Corinthians had asked in a letter. The letter is mentioned in 1 Corinthians 7:1. The first part of 1 Corinthians 8:1 shows that Paul was about to deal with one of the issues from their letter. They had questions about whether

Christians were free to eat meat that had been offered to idols.

Idol worship flourished in ancient Corinth, and it was accompanied by animal sacrifices. Generally only part of the animal was sacrificed. The rest was either eaten by the priests or sold. Much meat sold by butchers had been part of animals sacrificed to idols.

Christians confronted the issue in three main areas of life: (1) When they purchased meat, should they be concerned about serving it in their homes? (2) When invited out for a meal at which meat was served, should they eat whatever was served without asking questions? (3) Should Christians participate in feasts served in idol temples? Chapter 8 shows that the Corinthians did not agree about how to answer these questions. As in other areas—like leaders and spiritual gifts—they argued among themselves about meat sacrificed to idols. One group saw nothing wrong with eating the meat; therefore, they ate it with a clear conscience. The other group felt that eating such meat was sinful.

Those who ate with a clear conscience based their actions on what they knew. Since they knew that idols were not real, they saw nothing wrong with eating the meat. They felt that this knowledge had set them free from bondage to pagan superstitions. The words "we all have knowledge" were probably from their letter. At any rate, the words represented the claim of some Corinthians to have superior knowledge. Paul agreed that Christians possessed special knowledge, but he contrasted proud knowledge with humble love. The wrong kind of knowledge puffs people up with pride. By contrast, Christian love builds up. The word "edifieth" literally means "builds up."

Verse 2 shows that superficial knowledge is blind to how little one actually knows. We have a saying: "A little learning is a dangerous thing." Young people often go through a stage when they think they know more than their parents. Later most of them realize how little they really knew at that stage in their lives. A truly wise person is aware of how much more there is to know.

Verse 3 focuses on another crucial aspect of Christian knowledge. The basic knowledge for Christians is personal knowledge of God Himself, not knowledge of various facts about God. This basic knowledge is not something we achieve on our own. We do not discover God; God seeks us. He loved us before we responded to His love. He knew us and sought us before we came to know Him. The person who truly loves God has this basic knowledge of God, from which flows humility and love for others.

**2. One God or many? (vv. 4-6)**

**4 As concerning therefore the eating of those things that are offered in sacrifice unto idols, we know that an idol is nothing in the world, and that there is none other God but one.**

**5 For though there be that are called gods, whether in heaven or in earth (as there be gods many, and lords many,)**

**6 But to us there is but one God, the Father, of whom are all**

things, and we in him; and one Lord Jesus Christ, by whom are all things and we by him.

Returning to the issue introduced in verse 1, Paul emphasized that God is the one and only God. The pagan world professed to worship many different gods. Paul insisted that these so-called gods actually did not exist. At this point, Paul was agreeing with a basic premise of the group at Corinth that saw nothing wrong with eating meat sacrificed to idols. Both they and Paul believed that pagan gods were nonexistent.

Verse 5 may suggest something that Paul spelled out later in his larger discussion of this issue. In 1 Corinthians 10:14-21, Paul warned against demonic powers behind idol worship. In other words, the idols themselves were nothing, and the gods they represented were nothing; however, demonic powers used idol worship to influence people to evil actions. Although Paul made this point later, his primary point in verses 4-6 was that idols and pagan gods are nothing.

## II. Principle: Liberty Exercised in Love (8:7-13)

### 1. Food and conscience (vv. 7-8)

7 Howbeit there is not in every man that knowledge: for some with conscience of the idol unto this hour eat it as a thing offered unto an idol; and their conscience being weak is defiled.
8 But meat commendeth us not to God: for neither, if we eat, are we the better; neither, if we eat not, are we the worse.

Not all the Corinthians shared the knowledge Paul had just expressed. Before they were converted, they had been idol worshipers. Therefore, in their minds, eating meat sacrificed to idols was still associated by them with pagan worship of false gods. When such people ate meat sacrificed to idols, they did so with bad consciences. They felt they were sinning.

The words "meat commendeth us not to God" were probably in the letter from the Corinthians to Paul. These words expressed the view of those with the knowledge that idols are nothing. Based on this knowledge, they claimed that food is not a moral issue. Since idols and gods are nothing, food sacrificed to idols is no better or no worse than any other food.

Paul basically agreed with those who claimed that food is not a moral issue. In a dispute about ceremonial uncleanness, Jesus took the same position. The source of human evil is not in outward things like clean or unclean foods, but in the human heart (Mark 7:1-23). Paul's clearest statement of this principle is in Romans 14:17: "For the kingdom of God is not meat and drink; but righteousness, and peace, and joy in the Holy Ghost."

On the surface, the last part of verse 8 seems to agree with the group that saw nothing wrong with eating meat sacrificed to idols. But in light of verses 7-13, it appears that some of the Corinthians were flaunting their freedom to eat meat sacrificed to idols. Some of them even acted as if this exercise of their liberty made them better. Paul denied that eating the meat made people either better or worse.

**2. Liberty without self-discipline (vv. 9-13)**

**9 But take heed lest by any means this liberty of yours become a stumbling block to them that are weak.**
**10 For if any man see thee which hast knowledge sit at meat in the idol's temple, shall not the conscience of him which is weak be emboldened to eat those things which are offered to idols;**
**11 And through thy knowledge shall the weak brother perish, for whom Christ died?**
**12 But when ye sin so against the brethren, and wound their weak conscience, ye sin against Christ.**

Verses 9-12 constitute the heart of Paul's message to people who believed that eating meat sacrificed to idols did them no harm. Love demands that Christians consider the effect of their actions on others. Some actions may do us no personal harm, but the actions may harm others.

Those who ate meat sacrificed to idols placed a stumbling block in the path of those who thought this was a sin. It tempted them to go against their conscience. Going against one's conscience is morally and spiritually dangerous. Conscience is like a red light flashing at a railroad crossing. Someone may accelerate and try to beat the train to the crossing. The person may even succeed, but this may embolden him to keep going against the red light. Eventually this rash act will have terrible consequences. Going against one's conscience in one thing encourages a person to go against conscience in other things.

In verse 10, Paul gave an example. If a scrupulous person saw another Christian eating meat at a feast in an idol temple, he would be emboldened to do the same thing. The strong Christian's knowledge would then be the cause of the weak brother's ruin. Paul used strong language to describe the ruin: "stumbling block" (v. 9), "perish" (v. 11), "wound" (v. 12).

The strongest language is in verse 12. The strong brother sins against his brother. And if he sins against his brother, he also sins against Christ, who died for the brother. Christ is so identified with His people that sinning against one of them is sinning against Him (see Matt. 25:45; Acts 9:4-5).

**3. Commitment to self-discipline (v. 13)**

**13 Wherefore, if meat make my brother to offend, I will eat no flesh while the world standeth, lest I make my brother to offend.**

Paul stated his own commitment to self-discipline (compare Rom. 14:21). Paul finished dealing with this subject in 1 Corinthians 10:14—11:1. He saw nothing wrong with a Christian eating meat in a home unless a brother raised a question about it. If that happened, Paul advised that the meat not be eaten, lest the brother be offended. Paul also warned that eating meat in a pagan temple was potentially dangerous even to strong Christians. They opened their lives to demonic influence.

## APPLYING THE BIBLE

**The power of love.**—Doctors have discovered anew that, for an infant, love is an imperative. Premature babies who are regularly touched develop much better than those who are left alone. Retirees are now volunteering to help nurses late at night care for "preemies" in maternity wards. Sterilized, strong hands reach through the portholes of the incubator and tenderly stroke the soft back of a newborn baby. The hands literally perform a life-giving act and the tiny babies respond well to the caresses. The *New York Times* reported that "premature infants who are massaged 15 minutes three times a day gained weight 47 percent faster than those who were left alone in their incubators." The *Times* continued: "The massaged infants also showed signs that the nervous system was maturing more rapidly . . . . They became more active, more responsive to such things as a face . . . . Infants massaged were discharged from the hospital on the average of six days earlier."[1] Hospitals used to suggest that the less contact with premature babies the better, but now much and frequent touching is widely encouraged.

**The love of God.**—Years ago these anonymous words were found scrawled on the walls of a mental institution:

*Could we with ink the ocean fill,*
*And were the skies of parchment made,*
*And every stalk on earth a quill,*
*And every man a scribe by trade;*
*To write the love of God above*
*Would drain the ocean dry,*
*Nor could the scroll contain the whole,*
*Tho' stretched from sky to sky!*

Most of us recognize those words as the last verse to the well-known song, "The Love of God."

**Christian liberty has its limitations.**—The American schooner *Frost* arrived in Guam from Manila in 1856. The military surgeon on Guam recommended to the governor that the ship be quarantined for at least three days and that no passengers be permitted to disembark. The quarantine was requested because the body of a young man who had died of smallpox had been cast overboard from the *Frost* only the day before.

In spite of the obvious danger to the citizens of Guam, a very prominent citizen of the island named Silvistre Torres Palomo insisted on coming ashore and bringing his servant. The servant was the first of 3,644 people to die of smallpox or its complications in the epidemic that followed. This number who died was 43.5 percent of the population of Guam at that time.[2]

**A Christian's influence.**—One's influence never dies. Long after we are gone, the impact of our lives on others will live on. In some of the old bricks of Egypt and Babylon that have been exhumed, the print of a dog's foot has been found. The bricks were made thousands of years ago and put out to dry, and the dogs stepped on some of the wet bricks. Now, thousands of years later, their long-ago presence is still felt.

Paul Harvey once said on his national radio program that a certain criminal had all his fingerprints removed from his fingers so that he could pursue his life of crime without being detected. He went through a long, painful ordeal in order to accomplish nothing. Now he is all the more easily caught when he commits a crime because he is the only man *without* fingerprints! Our influence is like that. It cannot be stopped or silenced.

About Abel's influence it is written: "He being dead yet speaketh" (Heb. 11:4). The late R. G. Lee said: "Every telephone ring says that Alexander Graham Bell still lives. Every vaccination against disease says that Louis Pasteur still lives. Every cotton gin says that Eli Whitney still lives. Every airplane says that Orville and Wilbur Wright still live. And every light bulb burning says that Thomas A. Edison still lives."

## TEACHING THE BIBLE

▶ *Main Idea:* Exercising liberty wisely means that believers should apply principles of self-discipline and love to issues of personal liberty and rights.
▶ *Suggested Teaching Aim:* To lead adults to examine how wisely to exercise liberty, and to identify principles of self-discipline and love they can apply to personal liberty and rights.

### A TEACHING OUTLINE

1. *Prepare poster strips to guide the study.*
2. *Organize the class in two groups and make group assignments.*
3. *Use a case study to apply the lesson.*

**Introduce the Bible Study**

Use the illustration "Christian liberty has its limitations" *(Applying the Bible)* to introduce the lesson.

**Search for Biblical Truth**

IN ADVANCE, write the following outline on three strips of paper. Place the title on the focal wall. Organize the class in two groups and give each group one of the strips along with the additional questions below. Ask them to place the poster strip on the wall as they make their presentations. If you do not want to organize in groups, you can present the information in a lecture.

EXERCISING LIBERTY WISELY

I. Issue: Meat Sacrificed to Idols (8:1-6)

II. Principle: Liberty Exercised in Love (8:7-13)

**Group 1—**

Read 1 Corinthians 8:1-6 and be prepared to share the following information with the class: (1) Describe briefly the practice of idol worship and sacrifices in ancient Corinth. (2) How were Christians affected when it came to eating meat sacrificed to idols (when they brought meat at the market, when invited to dinner in another's home, when attending a feast of an idol)? (3) Describe the principle Paul established that, since other gods do not really exist, Christians should not have to worry about eating meat.

Develop a role-play that would state this principle in a modern setting.

**Group 2—**

Read 1 Corinthians 8:7-13 and be prepared to share the following information with the class. (1) Why would some people object to eating meat sacrificed to idols? (2) Explain the principle of love that Paul said overrode the right to eat whatever a believer wanted. (3) How does sinning against a fellow Christian cause the person to sin against Christ (v.12)? (4) Explain the principle of self-discipline (v.13).

Present a role play that would describe this principle of self-discipline in a modern setting.

**Give the Truth a Personal Focus**

Read the last half of the suggested teaching aim. Read the following case study and let members respond:

Greg had grown up in a Christian home and had been educated in a Baptist college. Greg had always been active in church. A friend returned from a trip to Southeast Asia and brought a small statue made from jade and gave to Greg. Greg displayed it prominently in his living room. One evening Greg hosted his Sunday School class in his home. A member who was from Southeast Asia and was also a new Christian saw the statue and pointed out to Greg that it was actually an idol. Greg said . . .

Ask: how do you know when to demand your rights and when to demonstrate self-discipline and love? Does this mean that if someone finds what you are doing to be objectionable that you are obligated to change your behavior? Why?

Read the main idea and close in prayer for wisdom and courage for members to function in today's world.

---

1. Charles Foster Johnson, "The Second Page," Second Baptist Church, Lubbock, Texas, p. 4, July 28, 1982.

2. Adapted from Curtis H. Tutterrow, *Proclaim Magazine*, April, May, June 1992. [From R. L. Haddock, *A History of Health on Guam* (Igana, Guam; Cruz Publications, 1973), 38.]

April
30
1995

# Caring for One Another

**Basic Passage:** 2 Corinthians 1:1-14
**Focal Passage:** 2 Corinthians 1:3-14

God teaches us many lessons in the school of life. Among these are lessons learned by passing through troubles. One of the lessons is that those whom God has helped can help others who are passing through trouble. This was one of the lessons God taught Paul. He shared that insight in many Bible passages, but nowhere more clearly than in the opening of 2 Corinthians.

**Study Aim:** *To testify how lessons learned in times of trouble equip us to care for one another*

## STUDYING THE BIBLE

Paul began by identifying himself and sending personal greetings to the Corinthian church (vv. 1-3). He praised the God of comfort (v. 3). He stated the principle that believers can comfort one another because they have been comforted by God (v. 4). Sharing Christ's sufferings leads to comfort and endurance (vv. 5-6). Christians share together in a fellowship of suffering and comfort (v. 7). Paul told of a time when he faced death (v. 8). From this he learned to place his hope in God for both life and death (vv. 9-10). God uses intercessory prayers to accomplish His purposes (v. 11).

Paul emphasized his sincerity in how he lived and in his relationship with the Corinthians (v. 12). Paul defended himself against false charges and affirmed his hope for mutual confidence between himself and the Corinthians (vv. 13-14).

### I. Greetings (1:1-2)

Paul emphasized that he was "an apostle of Jesus Christ by the will of God" (v. 1). He mentioned Timothy not because Timothy was coauthor, but because he wanted to remind the Corinthians that Timothy was a trusted coworker.

He addressed the letter to the church at Corinth and included all the saints in the province of Achaia. Paul had had a stormy relationship with the Corinthians. Much had happened since Paul wrote 1 Corinthians. Second Corinthians reveals that opposition had challenged his claim to be an apostle (10:7-10). Paul had made a painful visit to Corinth (2:1,5-8), had written a stern letter (2:3,9; 7:8,12), and eventually had received word that the church was ready to be reconciled to him (7:5-16).

He greeted them with the usual Jewish greeting of peace and the Christian greeting of grace.

## II. Mutual Comfort (1:3-7)

**1. Praise to the God of comfort (v. 3)**

3 Blessed be God, even the Father of our Lord Jesus Christ, the Father of mercies, and the God of all comfort.

This beautiful doxology contains three titles for God. Paul did not use these as definitions of God, but as titles addressed to God in praise. The first title emphasizes that we know God as Father through what God did in His Son Jesus Christ. God revealed Himself in human flesh and acted to save sinners through the life, death, and resurrection of Jesus Christ.

The other two titles emphasize the compassion of the Father and the comfort received from Him. The root of the word translated "comfort" appears repeatedly in verses 3-7, either in its noun or verb form. It is sometimes translated as "consolation" in the *King James Version.* This root appears in the word "Comforter," which Jesus used to refer to the Holy Spirit (John 14:16,26; 15:26; 16:7). The basic idea is "to be called alongside of someone to help." The help takes various forms: encouragement, exhortation, comfort, consolation. The title in verse 3 reminds us that God Himself is the ultimate source of all true comfort.

**2. Comforted and comforting (v. 4)**

4 Who comforteth us in all our tribulation, that we may be able to comfort them which are in any trouble, by the comfort wherewith we ourselves are comforted of God.

The same Greek word is translated two ways in this verse: "tribulation" and "trouble." The word originally carried the idea of pressure. Paul gave an example of this in his own life in verse 8. The word is general enough to apply to all kinds of troubles; although for early Christians, the troubles often took the form of persecution. This is the word Jesus used when he said, "In the world ye shall have tribulation: but be of good cheer; I have overcome the world" (John 16:33).

In many ways, verse 4 is the key verse in the whole passage. The message is clear: when a Christian has been comforted by God, the Christian develops the capacity to help others who need comforting. Some of life's most important lessons are learned in the school of hard knocks. This lesson is among the most important. This is one of the good things that God can bring out of hard times. Passing through trouble makes us sensitive to others who are passing through troubles of their own. Having experienced God's comfort, children of God can be used by God to comfort and encourage brothers and sisters.

**3. Suffering, comfort, and endurance (vv. 5-6)**

5 For as the sufferings of Christ abound in us, so our consolation also aboundeth by Christ.

6 And whether we be afflicted, it is for your consolation and salvation, which is effectual in the enduring of the same sufferings which we also suffer: or whether we be comforted, it

is for your consolation and salvation.

We often speak of the sufferings of Christ as the door to forgiveness of sins. The Bible also refers to sufferings of Christ that we share as we deny ourselves, take up our cross, and follow Him. Following Christ in the way of the cross involves us in suffering for His sake. Verse 5 reminds us that just as we share His sufferings, so we share His comfort. If we walk in the way of the cross, we experience also the power of the resurrection.

Verse 6 adds another word that often appears in passages about suffering and comfort. The word is "endurance." We glory in tribulations also: knowing that tribulation worketh "patience" (Rom. 5:3). "Patience" in Romans 5:3 is the same Greek word translated "enduring" in 2 Corinthians 1:6.

**4. Sharing together in sufferings and comfort (v. 7)**

7 And our hope of you is steadfast, knowing, that as ye are partakers of the sufferings, so shall ye be also of the consolation.

The word "partakers" is from the same root as *koinōnia,* which refers to the shared life of those who belong to Jesus Christ. Those who share this life are "partakers." The word is similar to our word "partner." Through Christ, we are partners in sufferings and in comfort. We are bound together as a family of faith and love. In such a family, when one member suffers, all members suffer (see 1 Cor. 12:26). We weep with those who weep and rejoice with those who rejoice (Rom. 12:15). In such a family, God often ministers to one family member through another family member. He uses us to help and care for one another.

## III. Testimony of Divine Deliverance (1:8-11)

**1. Despairing of life (v. 8)**

8 And we would not, brethren, have you ignorant of our trouble which came to us in Asia, that we were pressed out of measure, above strength, insomuch that we despaired even of life:

Paul referred to a threat to his life during his ministry in the Roman province of Asia. Paul spent several years in Ephesus, the main city of Asia (Acts 19:8-10). Acts 19:23-41 tells of a riot that resulted from Paul's work in Ephesus. Paul also wrote, "I have fought with beasts at Ephesus" (1 Cor. 15:32). We cannot be sure what specific life-and-death crisis Paul referred to in verse 8. As we know from passages like 2 Corinthians 11:24-28, Paul faced death many times. In this particular situation, Paul was so threatened that he "despaired even of life."

**2. Trusting in God (vv. 9-10)**

9 But we had the sentence of death in ourselves, that we should not trust in ourselves, but in God who raiseth the dead:
10 Who delivered us from so great a death, and doth deliver:

in whom we trust that he will yet deliver us;

In verses 4-7, Paul noted one good that can come from suffering. We can learn to help others who suffer. In verses 9-10, Paul testified to another good fruit of suffering. Difficulty and danger force believers to realize that their lives are in God's hand and to trust God to care for them in life or death.

Paul was face-to-face with death. He committed his way to the Lord. In that particular situation, the Lord delivered him from death. However, Paul knew he eventually would die. And he trusted the God who had delivered him *from* death many times to deliver him *through* death when he died.

**3. Power of prayer (v. 11)**

11 Ye also helping together by prayer for us, that for the gift bestowed upon us by the means of many persons thanks may be given by many on our behalf.

Paul did not ignore the power of the prayers of the Corinthians and others for him. God used their prayers to effect Paul's deliverance. Paul did not try to explain the mystery of prayer, but he believed strongly that God uses our prayers as He does our ministering and witnessing. Verse 11 reminds us that we should express thanks to God for His response to our prayers.

## IV. Mutual Confidence (1:12-14)

**1. Model for ministry (v. 12)**

12 For our rejoicing is this, the testimony of our conscience, that in simplicity and godly sincerity, not with fleshly wisdom, but by the grace of God, we have had our conversation in the world, and more abundantly to you-ward.

In defending himself against the false charges of some in Corinth, Paul revealed much about himself. Thus 2 Corinthians is one of his more personal letters. In verse 12, he gave a good summary of his life and ministry. He had a good conscience because he had served with sincerity. He had relied on the grace of God, not human wisdom. His daily life and his relationships with the Corinthians had been according to God's will.

**2. Testimony of mutual trust (vv. 13-14)**

13 For we write none other things unto you, than that ye read or acknowledge; and I trust ye shall acknowledge even to the end;
14 As also ye have acknowledged us in part, that we are your rejoicing, even as ye also are ours in the day of the Lord Jesus.

Some of Paul's critics claimed that his letters were obscure and sometimes dishonest (see v. 18). In verse 13, Paul denied the charge. He wrote to be read and understood, and he trusted that most of the Corinthians read and understood his letters.

The words "in part" in verse 14 show that Paul was aware that some in Corinth still criticized him. However, he hoped that when all stood before the Lord on the final day, they would rejoice in him just as he rejoiced in them.

## APPLYING THE BIBLE

**The God of comfort.**—The great English Baptist preacher Charles Haddon Spurgeon once preached a sermon titled "Songs in the Night." It was based on Job 35:11: "[He] giveth songs in the night."

It is a beautiful and comforting promise and parallels what Paul said about "the God of all comfort" in our lesson today (v. 3).

Oliver Cromwell (1599-1658) ruled England between 1649-1658 in the period known as the Commonwealth and Protectorate. In 1656, he declined to be crowned king.

As Cromwell lay dying, it was a stormy night and the wind howled and shook the house. To those gathered around him, Cromwell said, "Read to me from Paul's Letter to the Philippians." When they came to Philippians 4:12, "I can do all things through Christ which strengtheneth me," Cromwell said: "Stop just there. That was the word that saved me. When my son, Oliver, died, that was the word that saved me. When my heart was broken, that was the word that saved me. When sorrow swept down on our home like a black vulture, that was the word that saved me. When in one short hour all my sun was hid in midnight darkness, that was the word that saved me." God does not promise to deliver us from all shadows, but He does promise to strengthen and comfort us when the shadows surround us.[1]

**Truett's last written words.**—For forty-seven years George W. Truett served as pastor of the First Baptist Church of Dallas, Texas. After several months of agonizing pain, Truett died in July 1944. The last book he read was titled *With the Sorrowing,* and the corner of one page was turned down to mark his place. In the margin on that page, Truett had scribbled: "There shall be no more death, neither sorrow, nor crying, neither shall there be any more pain: for the former things are passed away."

In verses 8-10, Paul describes some of his sufferings for Christ and His cross. Paul's conclusion (v. 10) was that God does and will deliver us from death. It was his personal testimony to the comforting presence and grace of his Savior.

**Our source of comfort.**—In the foyer of Johns Hopkins University in Baltimore, facing the entrance to the hospital through whose doors multitudes pass every day with heavy hearts, stands a marble statue of Jesus. The Savior is leaning forward. His arms are outstretched as though He were reaching for those who are hurting. On the base of the statue are the Savior's words from Matthew 11: "Come unto Me, all ye that labour and are heavy laden, and I will give you rest" (Matt. 11:28).

**All have their problems and all suffer.**—Suffering and trouble are common to the human race. Job said: "Man that is born of woman is of few days, and full of trouble" (Job 14:1). Paul echoed that truth in our lesson today. But God's grace is sufficient for all our problems.

Sir Walter Scott, the greatest dramatic novelist of Scottish history, suffered from lameness. Abraham Lincoln lost his mother as a child and had to deal with poverty and the lack of a formal education. Theodore Roosevelt had a lifelong battle with asthma. Thomas A. Edison, history's greatest inventor, was almost totally deaf as an adult.

Robert Louis Stevenson had tuberculosis and he went to the South sea islands seeking health. But it never came and he died there. Helen Keller was both blind and deaf. Demosthenes, history's greatest orator, was born with a speech impediment. William Cowper, author of "There Is a Fountain" was forever playing with broken bones in his hands.[2]

As trouble is common to all of us, so the grace of God is available to each of us to handle those problems.

**God uses others to answer our prayers.**—The story is told about a man who became lost in the woods. He later described his experience to a friend and told how frightened he was and that he knelt down and prayed and asked for God's guidance.

The friend asked, "Did God answer your prayer?" And the man replied: "Oh, no! Before God had a chance to answer, a guide came along and showed me the path!"

Concerning prayer, Paul encouraged us to help each other "by prayer" (v. 11), and most of the time God will answer our prayers by sending someone along who can minister to our particular need.

## TEACHING THE BIBLE

▶ *Main Idea:* Caring for one another means that we can testify how lessons learned in times of trouble equip us to care for one another.
▶ *Suggested Teaching Aim:* To lead adults to examine Paul's instructions for caring for one another, and to identify ways they can use their experiences in time of trouble to care for others.

### A TEACHING OUTLINE

1. *Introduce the lesson.*
2. *Develop a lecture covering the material in Studying the Bible.*
3. *Involve members by asking them to identify strip posters.*
4. *Apply the Scripture by identifying how they can use their suffering to comfort others.*

### Introduce the Bible Study

Introduce the lesson by using the illustration "The God of comfort" *(Applying the Bible).*

### Search for Biblical Truth

IN ADVANCE: (1) prepare a lecture incorporating the material in *Studying the Bible;* (2) copy the following Focal Passage Headings on strips of paper, mix them up, and tape them to the focal wall where all can see them: Praise to the God of comfort; Comforted and comforting; Suffering, comfort, and endurance; Sharing together in sufferings and comfort; Despairing of life; Trusting in God; Power of prayer; Model for ministry; Testimony of mutual trust.

Ask members to open their Bibles to 2 Corinthians 1:3. Introduce the lesson by briefly summarizing the material in Greetings (vv.1-2) from *Studying the Bible.* Point out the nine poster strips. As members listen, ask them to select the title that best summarizes your lecture. When the correct heading is suggested, place the heading in the proper order and ask the person to read the verses from the Bible.

In giving your lecture, be sure you mention the following when you discuss these verses:

**1:3.**—the three titles for God and their meaning.

**1:4.**—define "tribulation" and point out the importance of this verse to the whole passage.

**1:5-6.**—the relationship between Christ's sufferings and comfort; define "endurance."

**1:7.**—define "partakers" and point out its relationship to *koinōnia.*

**1:8.**—describe some of the persecution Paul went through.

**1:9-10.**—point out the benefit that comes from our suffering and the trust Paul had in God.

**1:11.**—describe Paul's praying.

**1:13.**—point out how this verse summarizes Paul's life and ministry.

**1:13-14.**—point out that Paul denied being obscure and dishonest in his letters and hoped that they and he could rejoice when they stood before the Lord.

### Give the Truth a Personal Focus

Distribute paper and pencils to members. Ask members to draw a line down the sheet, dividing the paper in half. Label the left column *Pain* and the right column *Lessons Learned.* Ask members to list several events or experiences that caused them pain. In the right column ask them to list as many lessons learned from the experiences as possible.

When they have done that, ask several volunteers to share some of their experiences and the lessons learned. Then ask members to turn to a person near them and determine how they can take these experiences and use them to comfort someone else. Let them pray with their partner.

---

1. Adapted from Hudson Baggett, *The Alabama Baptist,* June 6, 1991, 2.
2. Adapted from J. B. Fowler, Jr., *Living Illustrations from History, Literature, and Life* (Nashville: Broadman Press, 1955), 112.

# Living in Christian Freedom

**Basic Passage:** 1 Corinthians 9
**Focal Passages:** 1 Corinthians 9:1-7, 19-27

First Corinthians 8:1—11:1 began with the subject of whether to eat meat that had been sacrificed to idols. In chapter 8, Paul set forth the principle of voluntarily giving up his right to eat such meat for the sake of weaker brothers who felt eating such meat was sinful. The general principle is giving up one's rights for the welfare of others. In chapter 9 Paul applied this principle to areas other than meat sacrificed to idols.

**Study Aim:** *To identify areas of life in which personal freedom of action should be given up for the sake of the cause of Christ*

## STUDYING THE BIBLE

In 1 Corinthians 9:1-18, Paul dealt with his right as an apostle to accept pay for preaching. First, he established his claim as an apostle (vv. 1-2) to rights enjoyed by others (vv. 3-6). He concentrated on the right to receive pay (vv. 7-14) and stated that he had not exercised this right in Corinth (vv. 15-18). Paul applied the same principle to how he adapted himself to various kinds of people in order to win them (v. 19). He applied the principle to Jews (v. 20), to Gentiles (v. 21), and to the weak (vv. 22-23). Paul compared himself to a runner in an athletic contest (v. 24). He practiced rigorous self-discipline for his own moral and spiritual well-being as well as for the needs of others (vv. 25-27).

### I. Forgoing the Right to Be Paid for Preaching (9:1-18)

**1. A true apostle (vv. 1-2)**

1 Am I not an apostle? am I not free? have I not seen Jesus Christ our Lord? are not ye my work in the Lord?
2 If I be not an apostle unto others, yet doubtless I am to you: for the seal of mine apostleship are ye in the Lord.

Some of the Corinthians disputed Paul's claim to be an apostle. Thus Paul asked a series of questions designed to defend his claim to be a true apostle. Apostles were a unique group of eyewitnesses of the risen Lord, whom He commissioned as apostles. Paul insisted that the Damascus Road experience was nothing less than an appearance of the risen Lord, who commissioned Paul as an apostle (see 1 Cor. 15:8-10; Acts 9:1-16; Gal. 1:11-17).

Paul also asserted that the Corinthians themselves were like an official "seal" of God on his work there. Paul said that if anyone should recognize him as an apostle, the Corinthians should.

**2. Forgoing apostolic rights (vv. 3-6)**

3 Mine answer to them that do examine me is this,
4 Have we not power to eat and to drink?
5 Have we not power to lead about a sister, a wife, as well as
other apostles, and as the brethren of the Lord, and Cephas?
6 Or I only and Barnabas, have we not power to forbear working?

The word "power" can mean "authority" or "right." Here it means "right." In verses 3-6, Paul listed three rights he had as an apostle. The right "to eat and to drink" may refer back to the right to exercise his freedom to eat meat sacrificed to idols, or it may look ahead to the right to have the church provide the means of purchasing food.

Verse 5 refers to the right of apostles to marry and to have their wives as well as themselves supported by those to whom they ministered. The other apostles did this, including Cephas, who was popular with many in Corinth. The brothers of Jesus did this. Did not Paul have the same right?

Verse 6 deals directly with what is implicit in verses 4-5 and explicit in verses 7-18. Apparently Paul and Barnabas were the only ones who had not exercised their right to financial support.

**3. The right to financial support (vv. 7-14)**

7 Who goeth a warfare any time at his own charge? who planteth a vineyard, and eateth not of the fruit thereof? or who feedeth a flock, and eateth not of the milk of the flock?

Paul used four facts to support his claim that Christian preachers had the right to expect financial support. First, he used three examples from daily life: the soldier, the vineyard planter, and the shepherd. Each is supported by others or by the fruit of his labor.

Second, Paul quoted Deuteronomy 25:4 to show that the ox was not muzzled when he trod the grain. Verses 8-11 maintain that God intended this principle be applied to pay for preachers. Third, Paul reminded his readers that priests in the temple lived from the sacrifices offered (v. 13). Fourth, Paul cited the teaching of Jesus. Verse 14 apparently refers to Luke 10:7, "The labourer is worthy of his hire."

In the midst of listing the four factors, Paul explained that he had not exercised his right to take pay from the Corinthians. We know that Paul did accept pay from the Philippian church (Phil. 4:15-16; 2 Cor. 11:9). Paul apparently felt that the situation in Corinth was such that taking money would hinder the gospel there (v. 12).

**4. Forgoing the right to financial support (vv. 15-18).**—Verses 15-18 provide insight into Paul's reasons for preaching. He said that he preached because God had called him to preach, not because he had chosen this on his own. Thus as an obedient servant of God, Paul had no choice about preaching; his only choice was whether to preach with pay or without pay.

## II. Adapting Himself to Different Kinds of People (9:19-23)

**1. Free, yet a slave (v. 19)**

19 For though I be free from all men, yet have I made myself servant unto all, that I might gain the more.

Like all Christians, Paul was free in Christ to exercise many rights and privileges; yet he had voluntarily chosen to make himself a servant of others in order to win people to Christ. Elsewhere Paul wrote, "Ye have been called unto liberty; only use not liberty for an occasion to the flesh, but by love serve one another" (Gal. 5:13). Paul had just given an example of this principle in his decision to forgo his right to financial support. In verses 20-23, he gave three examples of another application of the same principle: adapting himself to different people and groups for the sake of the gospel.

**2. Groups to which Paul adapted himself (vv. 20-23)**

20 And unto the Jews I became as a Jew, that I might gain the Jews; to them that are under the law, as under the law, that I might gain them that are under the law;
21 To them that are without law, as without law, (being not without law to God, but under the law to Christ,) that I might gain them that are without law.
22 To the weak became I as weak, that I might gain the weak: I am made all things to all men, that I might by all means save some.
23 And this I do for the gospel's sake, that I might be partaker thereof with you.

All three groups were represented in the Corinthian church. They had probably noticed how Paul tried to adapt himself to each group; and to some of them, Paul appeared to be wishy-washy. Paul maintained that a difference exists between compromise of truth and accommodation for the sake of truth.

Although Paul was a Jew, he was free from the law as a way of salvation and as a legalistic system governing all of life. However, when he was ministering to Jews, he did his best to respect their customs without compromising the gospel.

When Paul ministered to Gentiles who had no background in the Old Testament law, Paul did not enforce on them any unnecessary Jewish distinctives. When Paul said he was "without law," he did not mean that he was a lawless person. To the contrary, he was subject to the law of Christ with higher demands than Old Testament law.
The "weak" in verse 22 were the group described in 1 Corinthians 8:9. Paul tried to respect their scruples for the sake of their spiritual welfare. His actions were designed to show that he and the Corinthians partook the same gospel.

### III. Practicing Rigorous Self-Discipline (9:24-27)

**1. Christian life as a race (v. 24)**

24 Know ye not that they which run in a race run all, but one receiveth the prize? So run, that ye may obtain.

Paul compared the Christian life to a race. Be careful not to press the comparison beyond Paul's intention. He was not saying that only one person wins the prize in the race of life. His point was that every runner puts forth every effort to win.

**2. Importance of self-discipline (vv. 25-27)**

25 And every man that striveth for the mastery is temperate in all things. Now they do it to obtain a corruptible crown; but we an incorruptible.

26 I therefore so run, not as uncertainly; so fight I, not as one that beateth the air:

27 But I keep under my body, and bring it into subjection: lest that by any means, when I have preached to others, I myself should be a castaway.

"Striveth for the mastery" translates a Greek word that means "engage in an athletic contest." The fact that we get the word *agonize* from this word shows that the Greeks never gave only a half-hearted effort to such contests. Paul's point in verse 25 is that if athletes exert such efforts for a prize that perishes, how much more should we when eternal issues are at stake?

The word translated "temperate" means "to exercise self-control." All winning athletes practice self-discipline. Paul practiced rigorous self-discipline.

Verse 26 combines two sports: racing and boxing—both familiar to the Corinthians. Paul said that he did not run the race of life like a runner who had lost sight of the goal. His most vivid description of the effort he exerted is in Philippians 3:14. "I press toward the mark for the prize of the high calling of God in Christ Jesus."

Paul was not like a boxer who spent all his time boxing shadows. Paul described himself as the opponent in the boxing ring. Paul's struggle with himself was like a boxer landing blows on his own body. Paul did not mean that landing actual blows on one's body is spiritually beneficial. He was using a strong image to emphasize that Christians should do whatever it takes to be what God would have us to be.

Paul wanted his own life to be the best possible example for the new converts. He wanted always to practice what he preached. Therefore, he kept reminding himself and others that our real source of strength is in the Lord, not in ourselves (see 1 Cor. 10:12, 2 Cor. 12:9-10). He was realistic enough to realize that sinful actions by him would have devastating results for all concerned. Paul was not fearful that he might lose His eternal salvation, but he feared failing to be all that God wanted him to be. Paul had few of the concerns that most people have; his major concern was failing to be a faithful witness for Christ (compare Phil. 1:20 with Phil. 4:11-12).

## APPLYING THE BIBLE

**The minister's farewell.**—Where it came from I have no idea, but in my files I found an old clipping titled, "A Minister's Farewell." Here is supposedly what he had to say:

"Brothers and sisters, I come to say goodbye. I don't think God loves this church, because none of you have ever died. I don't think you love each other because I never married any of you. I don't think you love me because you have not paid my salary. Your donations are moldy fruit and wormy apples, and by their fruits shall ye know them.

"Brethren, I am going to a better place. I've been called to be chaplain of the state penitentiary. Where I go you cannot come. But I go to prepare a place for you."

The church at Corinth was a problem church for Paul. Read his two letters to the church and you will discover the multitude of problems that plagued the church. Paul's patience with them, no doubt, wore thin. But he kept his grace and good spirit and rather than telling them off in harsh language, he wrote to this problem church the sweetest love poem ever written: 1 Corinthians 13. That should tell us something about the attitude a pastor ought to have as he faces problems in his church.

**How the preacher makes his living.**—While he was still a boy, Nathaniel Hawthorne wrote to his mother: "I do not want to be a doctor and live by men's diseases, nor a minister to live by their sins, nor a lawyer and live by their quarrels. So I don't see that there is anything left for me but to be an author."[1]

If the preacher lives "by their sins," as young Hawthorne stated, then Paul had plenty by which to live as he ministered among the Corinthian believers.

**The preacher should be a selfless person.**—From 1875 until 1899, American evangelist Dwight L. Moody was America's chief evangelical spokesman. He was to his day what Billy Graham is to our day.

F. B. Meyer (1847-1929) was a British Baptist preacher known around the world in his day. About Moody, F. B. Meyer said: "It seemed as though he had never heard of himself!"[2]

Although Paul sounds somewhat brash at times in his writings to the Corinthians (vv. 1-2), he was, in fact, a selfless person. In his ministry which encompassed the ancient world, Paul gave himself without thought for himself.

**The preacher's personal life.**—Preachers ought to practice what they preach. English poet John Milton wrote: "A writer ought himself to be a true poem if he wishes to write well . . . in laudable things." Let it be added that the preacher, as well as the Christian in the pew, should be a "true poem" of the gospel if he is to serve his Master and the Master's people well.

**On paying the preacher.**—The father of President Woodrow Wilson was a Presbyterian minister. One day a man observed the Reverend Mr. Wilson riding in a shiny buggy drawn by a sleek, well-groomed horse. Noting that the preacher was shabbily dressed, the man remarked, "Mr. Wilson, your horse looks better cared for than you do." Responding to the remark, Brother Wilson replied: "Yes, that is right, for you see I take care of my horse and my church takes care of me."[3]

Dr. M. E. Dodd was pastor of the First Baptist Church of Shreveport, Louisiana. When he went to the church in 1912 the deacons asked Dodd what kind of salary he expected. "I never put a price on my services," Dodd said. "Pay me what you want to. But when you see me wearing ragged and slick clothing, and you see me getting thin-faced and the word comes that I owe every merchant in town, when you know that my children are not properly fed and clothed, then you will know it is time to give me more salary."[4]

The late J. D. Grey, who told the two stories cited above, wrote: "It is degrading to his high calling as a man of God when his congregation does not compensate him properly. Yet on the other hand, the preacher and his family must not be spendthrifts, trying, as one man once said about a friend, 'Living a champagne life on a Coca-Cola income.'"[5]

## TEACHING THE BIBLE

▶ *Main Idea:* Living in Christian freedom means that when necessary we will give up our personal freedom for the sake of the cause of Christ.

▶ *Suggested Teaching Aim:* To lead adults to describe Paul's principles of Christian freedom, and to identify areas of their lives in which personal freedoms should be given up for the sake of the cause of Christ.

### A TEACHING OUTLINE

*1. Identify the differences between compromising and accommodating for the truth.*

*2. Use the procedure Answers and Questions.*

*3. Identify personal freedoms members would forgo for the cause of Christ.*

### Introduce the Bible Study

Introduce the lesson by reading the illustration, "The minister's farewell" *(Applying the Bible).*

Ask, What is the difference between compromising truth and accommodation for the sake of truth? *(Truth can never be compromised; we can make allowances in some cases for the sake of truth. Paul did this by refusing to take money for his preaching from the Corinthians.)*

### Search for Biblical Truth

IN ADVANCE, prepare the following Answers and Questions. The object of this procedure is to let one half of the class first suggest the answers, and let the other half match up the appropriate question. On slips of paper write the numbered answers and the unnumbered questions. Give the answers to one group and the questions to another.

Ask the member with answer 1 to read the answer and then let the members with the questions suggest which question fits with the answer. After each Answer/Question, use the material from *Studying the Bible* to guide a discussion on the verse(s):

To whom did Paul refer when he said "are not ye my work in the Lord" and "the seal of mine apostleship are ye in the Lord"? (vv.1-2)

What rights did Paul claim for himself? (v.3-6)

What three areas of life did Paul cite in claiming the right to financial support: (v.7)

What contradicting terms did Paul use to describe himself? (v.19)

To what three groups did Paul adapt himself so he might win them to Christ? (v.20-23)

In what context had Paul mentioned the weak in an earlier lesson? (8:9)

What does an athlete strive to win? (9:24)

What does the word *temperate* mean? (v.25)

What two sports did Paul combine to make a point that Christians had to keep focused on the goal? (v.26)

Why did Paul keep his body under control? (v.27)

(1) To the Corinthians whom he had led to Christ.
(2) The right to food and drink and the right to marry.
(3) Going to war, planting a vineyard, and caring for animals.
(4) Free, yet a slave.
(5) Jews, Gentiles, the weak.
(6) Those who were offended by eating meat sacrificed to idols.
(7) First prize in a race.
(8) To exercise self-control.
(9) Running and boxing.
(10) So he would not be disqualified.

**Give the Truth a Personal Focus**

On a chalkboard or a large sheet of paper, write *My Rights*. Ask members to list personal freedoms they value highly. Now ask, Under what circumstances would you consider giving up these freedoms if it would benefit the cause of Christ? Ask members to turn to one or two members near them and devise a role play or skit that would show how this freedom could be given up for Christ's sake.

---

1. The Britannica Home University, Second Series (American Literature), 35.
2. Ian MacPherson, *The Burden of the Lord* (New York: Abingdon Press, 1965), 73.
3. Adapted from J. D. Grey, *Epitaphs for Eager Preachers* (Nashville: Broadman Press, 1972), 20.
4. Ibid.
5. Ibid.

# Working for Reconciliation

**Basic Passage:** 2 Corinthians 5
**Focal Passage:** 2 Corinthians 5:11-21

Second Corinthians is one of Paul's more personal letters. This is not because it was written to a coworker, but because it reveals so much about Paul himself. Because Paul had been criticized by some in Corinth, he felt led to speak very personally about his life and ministry. Therefore, as we study 2 Corinthians 5, we shall see much about Paul's faith, motives, ministry, and message. As we look at his inspired words, we can evaluate ourselves.

**Study Aim:** *To evaluate personal motives and ministry in light of what Paul wrote about his motives and ministry*

## STUDYING THE BIBLE

Paul contrasted the body as an earthly tent to the Christian's eternal home (vv. 1-8). He also soberly reflected on the reality of the judgment seat of Christ (vv. 9-10). Paul's sense of accountability to the Lord motivated him to be earnest and sincere in all he did (vv. 11-13). The love of Christ motivated him to live for the Lord, not himself (vv. 14-15). Every believer is a new creature, who sees all things from God's perspective (vv. 16-17). God has reconciled us to Himself and given us the ministry of reconciliation (vv. 18-19). We are ambassadors for Christ, calling people to be reconciled to God (v. 20). The basis for our salvation is the sinless Savior who died a sinner's death for us (v. 21).

### I. Life After Death (5:1-10)

**1. Earthly tent and eternal home (vv. 1-8).**—Paul compared the difference between life on earth and life in heaven to the difference between living in a tent and in a house. The house is more than just a well-built house; it is an eternal home prepared by God for His own. The tent is temporary. Paul stated his confident hope of an eternal home with God. He expressed a preference for being absent from this mortal body in order to be at home with the Lord. This passage represents Paul's yearning for heaven and home. Other passages represent the richness of Paul's earthly relationship with the Lord. For example, verse 5 refers to a believer's earthly experience of the Holy Spirit. Also later in this chapter, Paul wrote of already being a new creature in Christ (v. 17).

**2. Judgment seat of Christ (vv. 9-10).**—Although Paul was confident of his eternal home, he realized that he would stand before Christ to give an account of his life and work. Paul was determined to please the Lord by all he did.

## II. Motives for Ministry (5:11-15)

### 1. Sense of accountability (vv. 11-13)

11 Knowing therefore the terror of the Lord, we persuade men; but we are made manifest unto God; and I trust also are made manifest in your consciences.

12 For we commend not ourselves again unto you, but give you occasion to glory on our behalf, that ye may have somewhat to answer them which glory in appearance, and not in heart.

13 For whether we be beside ourselves, it is to God: or whether we be sober, it is for your cause.

There are two keys to understanding these verses: One is to tie them to verses 9-10. One of the motivating factors in Paul's life was the awareness that he would give account of himself to the Lord. Although Paul did not fear for his eternal salvation, he was afraid of coming before the Lord to answer for some sinful or unworthy word or deed.

The other key is to keep in mind that Paul's life and ministry had been under attack in Corinth. These verses, along with many others in 2 Corinthians (see especially 10—13), show that Paul was answering charges against him. Repeatedly, Paul had to defend himself. He hoped to "persuade" the Corinthians of his sincerity. God knew his heart and saw his sincerity; Paul hoped that they too would recognize the same thing (v. 11).

Knowing that his critics would twist his words and make it appear that he was only boasting, the apostle denied that he was engaging in proud boasting. People who glory only in appearances would naturally assume Paul was only boasting. Paul explained that he was giving his friends in Corinth the facts needed to defend him against his critics (v. 12).

Paul's critics twisted any of Paul's actions to make him look bad. If he was enthusiastic, they accused him of being crazy. If he spoke quietly, they accused him of lacking zeal. Paul said that whatever he did, he did for the sake of those to whom he ministered (v. 13).

### 2. Love of Christ (vv. 14-15)

14 For the love of Christ constraineth us; because we thus judge, that if one died for all, then were all dead:

15 And that he died for all, that they which live should not henceforth live unto themselves, but unto him which died for them, and rose again.

Paul also was motivated by the love of Christ. What Christ had done for him constantly shaped his attitudes and actions. The cross and resurrection are the basis for our salvation. Paul emphasized this a few verses later (see vv. 18-21). Verses 14-15 emphasize that the cross and resurrection are not only the door to the Christian life but also the motive and power for it.

Those who receive Christ experience the cross and resurrection in their lives. They take up their cross daily to follow Christ (Luke 9:23). They are crucified with Christ and raised to walk in newness of life (Rom. 6:3-4; Gal. 2:20).

Thus in one sense, Christ died so that we might not have to die; in another sense, He died so that we might die. We need not die the spiritual death that sin brings. We are empowered to die to sin and self as Christ Himself did. This is not something we can do on our own; it is possible because the crucified and risen Lord empowers us.

Many people have no real idea what life is all about. Verse 15 is one of the clearest statements of how Christians view the purpose of living. We no longer live for ourselves, which is the essence of sin; instead we live for the One who died and rose again for us.

**3. A new creature (vv. 16-17)**

> **16 Wherefore henceforth know we no man after the flesh: yea, though we have known Christ after the flesh, yet now henceforth know we him no more.**
> **17 Therefore if any man be in Christ, he is a new creature: old things are passed away; behold, all things are become new.**

Paul often described believers as being "in Christ." He is in us and we are in Him. He permeates all we are. As a result, we see everything from a new perspective. The words "after the flesh" mean "from a purely human point of view." Before he came to be in Christ, Paul saw things from a purely human point of view. He even looked at Jesus through worldly eyes only. Now in Christ, he sees Christ and everything differently.

Those in Christ are new creatures. In verses 1-10, Paul wrote of his confident hope of the eternal home in heaven. In verse 17, he showed that the new creation has already begun. People who know Christ are already part of God's new creation. The fulfillment is yet future, but the reality has already begun. As Paul wrote in verse 5, the Holy Spirit is like the earnest money that ensures final payment. Because we are already new creatures, we know that we shall share in the new heavens and new earth.

## III. Ministry of Reconciliation (5:18-21)

**1. Reconciled to God (vv. 18-19)**

> **18 And all things are of God, who hath reconciled us to himself by Jesus Christ, and hath given to us the ministry of reconciliation;**
> **19 To wit, that God was in Christ, reconciling the world unto himself, not imputing their trespasses unto them; and hath committed unto us the word of reconciliation.**

The New Testament uses many human experiences to describe salvation from different points of view: new birth, new creation, adoption, justification (a term from the courts meaning "acquitted"), redemption (a word from the slave market meaning "liberation at a price").

Verses 18-19 use a human experience common to most people. We know what reconciliation is on a human level. Two people are separated from one another by hurt and hostility. They may be willing to forgive one another by absorbing the hurt without trying to get even. This opens the way for them to be reconciled. If so, their relationship is restored.

Some, but not all characteristics of human reconciliation, apply to being reconciled to God. One big difference is that separation from God is the result of our sins, not anything God has done. In divine reconciliation, God Himself takes the initiative in seeking reconciliation with sinners. Jesus Christ was the Son of God who came seeking sinners and offering His life in atonement for human sin. Thus God in Christ absorbed the hurt of our sins in order to offer forgiveness and reconciliation to sinners. Verse 19 refers to forgiveness as "not imputing their trespasses against them."

God has also shown His love by calling His people to become His instruments in the work of reconciliation with those who are still estranged from God. Other Bible passages stress that those who are reconciled to God become reconciled also to others who have been reconciled to God. One requirement for effective witness to sinners is sweet fellowship among brothers and sisters in Christ (see Eph. 2:11-22).

**2. Ambassadors for Christ (v. 20)**

> 20 Now then we are ambassadors for Christ, as though God did beseech you by us: we pray you in Christ's stead, be ye reconciled to God.

An "ambassador" in Roman times was an official representative of the government in foreign lands. During wars, ambassadors were sent to enemies with terms of peace. The ambassadors represented and spoke for the emperor. Paul used this human situation to describe Christians as ambassadors for Christ. We offer God's terms of peace to those who have been separated from Him by sin. He speaks His message through human ambassadors. In His name, we plead with people to be reconciled to God.

Reconciliation is not some automatic process that takes place because someone hears the gospel. God offers reconciliation. He pleads with sinners. But the choice to accept Him is up to each person. Thus the plea, "Be ye reconciled to God."

**3. The sinless Savior (v. 21)**

> 21 For he hath made him to be sin for us, who knew no sin; that we might be made the righteousness of God in him.

Verse 21 affirms three basic facts about the good news. (1) Jesus lived a perfect life; He had no sin. (2) In His death, He was made to be sin for us. This doesn't mean that He became a sinner. It means that He died a sinner's death in every way. (3) As a result of His atoning death, when we accept Him, we are justified or made right with God. This is what Paul described at length in Romans 3:21—5:21.

## APPLYING THE BIBLE

**Alive with Christ.**—After young Willie Lincoln died, Abraham Lincoln was overcome by uncontrollable grief. Dr. Vinton, pastor of Trinity Church, New York, visited Lincoln and tried to comfort him. "Your son is alive in Paradise," Vinton said.

Lincoln had hardly listened to anything Vinton had said. But when

Vinton spoke about Willie being alive, Lincoln jumped up from the sofa and exclaimed, "Alive! Alive! Surely, you mock me."

"No, sir, believe me," said Dr. Vinton. "It is a most comforting doctrine of the church, founded upon the words of Christ Himself."

For some minutes Lincoln sobbed and repeated, "Alive! Alive!"

In verses 1-8 Paul expressed the same confidence. When our earthly "tabernacle" is "dissolved," Paul said "we have a building of God, an house not made with hands, eternal in the heavens" (v. 1). The verb "have" is in the present tense: we have it right here and now while we yet live. The guarantee of a heavenly home is ours today. As the great Greek scholar A. T. Robertson put it, "We possess the title to it now by faith."

**What an infidel told William Booth.**—William Booth, a Methodist preacher, was the founder of the Salvation Army. A passionate and compassionate preacher of the gospel, Booth once told about a conversation he had with an infidel.

"If I believed what you Christians say you believe about the coming day of judgment when all shall answer to God, and the lost shall be eternally separated from God, then I would crawl on my bare knees on crushed glass all over London night and day telling men and women to flee from the wrath to come."[1]

**No one shall escape the judgment.**—An article carried in the *Nashville Banner* several years ago told about the location of a secret camp in California known as Scott Meadows Club that sprawled over 712 acres in the rugged Cascades near the Oregon border. The whole idea of the secret camp was to provide a post-doomsday retreat for rich people who were willing to pay an initial fee of $12,800 plus $300 a year for a place in which to survive national anarchy, a nuclear attack, or other catastrophes.

In the main building was stored the hydrated food and the 20 people who were members of the camp were taught how to live on nuts, vegetation, and the meat of wild animals. The members were not allowed to reveal the location of the camp; and, if they did, they were expelled. Those interested in joining the camp were led to it blindfolded.

But there is no escaping the greatest catastrophe of all for the unsaved which is the day of judgment. Knowing this, Paul wrote: "For we must all appear before the judgment seat of Christ" (v. 10).

**Christ's work of reconciliation.**—There is an old story about a boy who left home because he couldn't get along with his father. The boy had a hard lot of it trying to make his way in the world and before very long he had all he could take. Writing to his mother, he told her he wanted to come home. "If father will let me come home," he wrote, "tie a yellow ribbon around the back gate post. When the train passes by, if I see the yellow ribbon on the gate post I will know it's all right to stop. If it isn't there, I will keep going."

As the train neared his hometown, the boy became fidgety and his nervousness was apparent. The man sitting next to the boy asked him what the problem was and the boy revealed why he was so nervous. "Please, mister," the boy pled, "we're getting near my home and I don't have the nerve to look out the window to see if the ribbon is there. Please look for me and tell me if it's there."

In a matter of minutes the train neared the boy's home, and the man exclaimed: "Son, you must look out the window now. There isn't one yellow ribbon on the gate post, but the whole fence is covered with yellow ribbons!"

The train stopped, the boy got off and had a joyous reconciliation with his father.

It is a homely story but it is true to the Scriptures. Reconciliation is possible only through the death, burial, and resurrection of the Lord Jesus.

## TEACHING THE BIBLE

▶ *Main Idea:* Working for reconciliation demands that we evaluate our personal motives and ministry in light of what Paul wrote about his motives and ministry.

▶ *Suggested Teaching Aim:* To lead adults to explain Paul's concept of reconciliation, and to evaluate their personal motives and ministry.

---

### A TEACHING OUTLINE

*Proofs of Reconciliation*

1. *We have been given a sense of accountability.*
2. *We experience the love of Christ.*
3. *We are made new creatures.*
4. *We are reconciled to God.*
5. *We are ambassadors for Christ.*
6. *We have a sinless Savior.*

---

**Introduce the Bible Study**

Use the illustration, "Christ's work of reconciliation," from *Applying the Bible.* Point out that God has provided many ribbons to indicate that He has provided reconciliation for us.

**Search for Biblical Truth**

IN ADVANCE, cut six yellow ribbons approximately 3- by-36-inches from yellow paper and write the following:

(1) A Sense of Accountability (5:11-13),
(2) Love of Christ (5:14-15),
(3) A New Creature (5:16-17),
(4) Reconciled to God (5:18-19);
(5) Ambassadors for Christ (5:20);
(6) The Sinless Savior (5:21).

Use the information in the opening paragraph of *Studying the Bible* to explain the personal element in this chapter. Point out that Paul used God's reconciliation of the human race as a pattern for believers to follow in being reconciled with each other.

Place the first ribbon on the focal wall and ask a volunteer to read verses 11-13. Briefly set the context by sharing the material in "Life after Death (verses 1-10)" *(Studying the Bible).* Ask members to open their Bibles to 2 Corinthians verses 11-13. Explain that there are two keys to understanding these verses: (1) Paul was aware that he would give an account of himself to the Lord; (2) since Paul's life and ministry had been under attack in Corinth, Paul was answering charges against him in these verses.

Ask half the class to study verses 11-13 to find support for the first key and the other half to find support for the second key. Explain how Paul's critics could twist Paul's actions to try to make him look bad.

Place the second ribbon on the wall. Ask a volunteer to read verses 14-15 aloud. Ask, How are the cross and resurrection the basis for our salvation? Ask members to explain this sentence: "In one sense, Christ died so that we might not have to die; in another sense, he died so that we might die." Ask, What significance does verse15 have for our Christian lives?

Place the third ribbon on the wall and ask a volunteer to read verses 15-17. Ask: What does the phrase "in Christ" (verse 17) mean in this verse? What does the phrase "after the flesh" mean? If we are new creatures after our conversion, how does this change the way we should live?

Place the fourth ribbon on the wall and read verse 18-19. IN ADVANCE, read the article on "Reconciliation," *Holman Bible Dictionary* (1168-1169) + (or in any other Bible dictionary) and be prepared to explain the background of the term. Distribute paper and pencils, and ask members to write their understanding of how God reconciled us to Himself.

Ask, What effects does reconciliation with God have on our relationships with others?

Place the fifth ribbon on the wall and ask members to read verse 20 silently. Write on a chalkboard or a large sheet of paper:

*Political* *Spiritual*

Ask members to list the responsibilities of an ambassador from the United States to a foreign country. Write these on the chalkboard. Then ask how many of these responsibilities would apply to believers as we are ambassadors for Christ.

Place the sixth ribbon on the wall and ask a volunteer to read verse 21. Ask members what basic facts this verse affirms about Jesus. Point out that our reconciliation with God is possible because of this sinless Savior.

**Give the Truth a Personal Focus**

Call attention to the yellow ribbons across the front of the room. Use these to urge any in your class who have not accepted Christ to do so. Ask those who are Christians if they need to be reconciled with anyone.

---

1. Adapted from J. B. Fowler, Jr., *Illustrating Great Words of the New Testament* (Nashville: Broadman Press, 1991), 103. [From Walter B. Knight, *Knight's Master Book of New Illustrations* (Grand Rapids: William B. Eerdmans Publishing Co., 1956), 351.]

# Sharing Blessings with Others

**Basic Passage:** 2 Corinthians 8—9
**Focal Passages:** 2 Corinthians 9:1-8, 10-15

The setting was the collection for the poor of Jerusalem that Paul was promoting among Gentile churches (see 1 Cor. 16:1-4; Rom. 15:25-27), The church at Jerusalem had many poor members (see Acts 6:1; 11:29; Gal. 2:10). Paul was anxious for the Gentile churches to send financial help for two reasons: (1) The Jerusalem church needed special help. (2) An offering from Gentile churches could help Jewish Christians realize that Gentile believers were true followers of the Lord. Paul had promoted the offering in his earlier contacts with the Corinthian church. Apparently the rift between them and Paul had delayed completing the offering. Now that reconciliation had taken place, Paul wanted the Corinthians to complete their part in the offering.

**Study Aim:** *To evaluate the degree to which we share the kind of contentment and generosity described by Paul*

## STUDYING THE BIBLE

Paul emphasized giving as a grace by telling the Corinthians of the sacrificial giving of the Macedonians (8:1-5). He challenged them to practice this grace by reminding them of the grace of the Lord (9:6-9). He set forth the principles of proportionate giving and sharing with the poor (8:10-15). Paul explained that Titus and two others would collect the offering at Corinth (vv.16-24). Paul had told the Macedonians of the eagerness of the Corinthians to participate, and he urged the Corinthians not to embarrass either Paul or themselves by not completing their part (9:1-5). Paul promised that God would give sufficient resources to those who practiced contentment and generosity (vv.6-10). Giving to the offering not only would meet human needs but also would bring glory to God (vv.11-15).

### I. The Grace of Giving (8:1-9)

**1. Example of the Macedonians 8:1-5).**—Paul, who was writing to Corinth from Macedonia (2 Cor. 2:12-13), told of the sacrificial giving of the Christians there. Macedonia was a Roman province in which were the cities of Philippi, Thessalonica, and Berea. The Macedonians had experienced afflictions of their own, but they gave generously to the collection for the poor in Jerusalem. Paul referred to this as "the grace of God bestowed on the churches of Macedonia" (8:1). Their secret was that they had first given themselves to the Lord.

**2. Example of Jesus (8:6-9).**—Paul exhorted the Corinthians to complete what they had begun. As they had abounded in other spiritual virtues, Paul appealed to them to "abound in this grace also" (v.7). Paul didn't command this, but appealed for them to show their love. He reminded them of "the grace of our Lord Jesus Christ, that, though he was rich, yet for your sakes he became poor, that ye through his poverty might be rich" (v.9).

## II. Principles of Giving (8:10-24)

**1. Proportionate giving (8:10-15).**—Reminding his readers that they had been ready a year earlier, Paul challenged them to complete the offering. He set forth the principle that a gift is acceptable "according that a man hath, and not according to that he hath not" (v.12). This was a restatement of the principle of proportionate giving from 1 Corinthians 16:2. Those who had the means to give would help those who did not. At other times, the situation might be reversed as to who prospered and who was in need. In either case, the same principle applied.

**2. Careful administration (8:16-24).**—Titus had earnest concern for the Corinthians; thus he was willing to work with them in completing the collection. Paul referred to two other unnamed brothers who would work with the Corinthians. Paul, who had been under attack at Corinth, was determined that every effort be made to avoid anyone accusing him of using any of the money for himself. Men of unquestioned honesty would administer the entire process.

## III. Reasons for Giving (9:1-15)

**1. Example for others (9:1-5)**

1 For as touching the ministering to the saints, it is superfluous for me to write to you:

2 For I know the forwardness of your mind, for which I boast of you to them of Macedonia, that Achaia was ready a year ago; and your zeal hath provoked very many.

3 Yet have I sent the brethren, lest our boasting of you should be in vain in this behalf; that, as I said, ye may be ready:

4 Lest haply if they of Macedonia come with me, and find you unprepared, we (that we say not, ye) should be ashamed in this same confident boasting.

5 Therefore I thought it necessary to exhort the brethren, that they would go before unto you, and make up beforehand your bounty, whereof ye had notice before, that the same might be ready, as a matter of bounty, and not as of covetousness.

Paul felt that promoting the offering in Corinth was unnecessary because a year earlier they had been eager to participate. He had even used the eagerness of the believers in the province of Achaia, where Corinth was, as a good example for the Macedonians. The Macedonians had responded so well to the challenge that in 2 Corinthians 9:1-5, Paul had used their sacrifice to challenge the Corinthians.

Paul planned to come to Corinth. Some Macedonians might come with him. He didn't want to have to eat his words about the eagerness of the Corinthians. This would embarrass Paul, not to mention the Corinthians themselves. Therefore, Paul felt it important to exhort Titus and the two other brothers (2 Cor. 8:15-24) about their task in Corinth. He wanted the Corinthians to have time to complete their part in the offering willingly, not as something they were forced to do.

**2. Contentment and generosity (9:6-8, 10)**

> **6 But this I say, He which soweth sparingly shall reap also sparingly; and he which soweth bountifully shall reap also bountifully.**
>
> **7 Every man according as he purposeth in his heart, so let him give; not grudgingly, or of necessity: for God loveth a cheerful giver.**
>
> **8 And God is able to make all grace abound toward you; that ye, always having all sufficiency in all things, may abound to every good work:**
>
> ...............................................
>
> **10 Now he that ministereth seed to the sower both minister bread for your food, and multiply your seed sown, and increase the fruits of your righteousness;)**

A farmer who was stingy in sowing seed would have a skimpy harvest. All things being equal, a farmer who scattered much seed would have a bountiful harvest. Paul applied this fact from agriculture to giving. The generous person, who sows many seeds of kindness will reap bountifully. The stingy person will reap little.

Giving is a very personal issue. Each person must make a deliberate decision about how much to give. No one should give because someone else forces the gift to be given. By the same token, when each person makes this personal decision, the giving should be generous. God loves those who give generously and who do it joyfully, not grudgingly.

Verses 8-10 contain a beautiful promise for those who give freely and generously. The promise is that generous people will be given by God all they need to continue to be generous in sharing with others. Returning to the sower, Paul said that those who scatter the seeds of generous giving will have bread for their tables and enough seed left to continue to sow the seeds of generous giving.

The key word is "sufficiency" in verse 8. The Greek word means "enough." A key question for each of us is, "What is enough?" In Philippians 4:11, Paul used this word to describe his contentment with little or much. Thus the promise is not that God will give us all we need to maintain a standard of living that allows self-indulgence. The promise is that God will give us all we need to do what He asks us to do.

**3. Glory to God (9:11-15)**

> **11 Being enriched in every thing to all bountifulness, which**

**causeth through us thanksgiving to God.**
**12 For the administration of this service not only supplieth**
**the want of the saints, but is abundant also by many**
**thanksgivings unto God.**
**13 Whiles by the experiment of this ministration they glorify**
**God for your professed subjection unto the gospel of Christ, and**
**for your liberal distribution unto them and unto all men;**
**14 And by their prayer for you, which long after you for the**
**exceeding grace of God in you.**
**15 Thanks be unto God for his unspeakable gift.**

Verses 11-15 give three fruits of generous giving. (1) The first part of verse 11 refers to the personal experiences of the one who learns to be contented and generous (see vv. 8-10). (2) The first part of verse 12 mentions the obvious result of meeting the needs of the poor in Jerusalem. Money can't buy everything, but it can buy some things: among them, food for the hungry. (3) The rest of the passage focuses on the glory that comes to God for the generous giving of His people.

Paul predicted what would happen if a generous offering from Gentile churches was received by the poor of Jerusalem. Everyone would give thanks to God for such a testimony to His grace. Verse 13 lists two things for which the Jerusalem saints would glorify God: (1) They would glorify God for the Corinthians' obedience to the gospel of Christ. (2) They would be grateful for such a generous gift that met their own desperate needs.

Verse 14 expresses Paul's hope for the entire project. He wanted the Jewish and Gentile Christians to express their oneness in Christ. Ephesians 2:11-12 is a more lengthy expression of this oneness in Christ. Paul wanted the Jerusalem Christians to pray for their generous Gentile brothers and sisters and to long for ways of expressing the grace of God that they all shared.

Verse 15 is Paul's exclamation of personal praise. As he contemplated the grace of God in Christ at work among Jews and Gentiles, the apostle thanked God for "his unspeakable gift." At the deepest level, Christ is the expression of God's gracious giving (see 2 Cor. 8:9). But Paul was also thinking of the work of the Spirit in bringing Jews and Gentiles to Him and thus making them brothers and sisters. The success of this offering would be a powerful expression of what God had done, was doing, and will do through Christ in the lives of Jews and Gentiles.

## APPLYING THE BIBLE

**Four men to take up the offering.**—Three little boys were bragging about their daddies. One of the fathers was a poet, another was a songwriter, and the third father was a preacher.

"My father writes a few short lines on paper, calls it poetry, and gets ten dollars for it," the first boy said.

"My daddy makes strange dots on paper, calls it a song, and gets twenty-five dollars for it," the second boy said.

Not to be outdone, the third little boy whose father was a preacher responded: "My daddy writes a sermon on a sheet of paper, gets up in his pulpit and reads it, and it takes four men to take up the offering!"

**He left it all.**—Zig Ziglar relates that someone in Dallas, Texas once asked how much money billionaire tycoon Howard Hughes left behind when he died. The Christian man who had been asked the question wisely replied, "He really left it all behind!" We need to keep in mind that no hearse ever pulls behind it a U-Haul trailer on the way to the cemetery! We have a responsibility to be good stewards.

**A cheerful giver.**—In verse 7 Paul wrote, "God loveth a cheerful giver." The word "cheerful" is a translation of the Greek work *hilaron.* According to *Thayer's Greek Lexicon*, the word means "cheerful, joyous, prompt to do anything." When a pastor looks at the offering plate on Sunday morning and sees the scanty gifts when his people have been blessed so abundantly, does he wonder about the "hilarity" and "promptness to do anything" demonstrated by his people?

**Money—god or master?**—Henrietta "Hetty" Green (1834-1916) was regarded as the wealthiest woman in the world at the time of her death. She inherited six million dollars from her father's estate and through investments saw it swell to an estimated one hundred million dollars at the time of her death. But apparently her money brought her few comforts and little joy. In the winter she would pad herself with newspapers to keep warm. After she read her morning paper, she resold it. Rather than buy a Pullman berth on a train when she traveled, she would sit up all night in the day coach to save a few dollars. She sorted out the white rags from the colored rags because the junk man paid a penny more a pound for the white ones. She hated to pay income tax, so she lived in cheap hotels in New York, under assumed names, so the government couldn't find her. When she was on her deathbed, the nurses were told not to wear white uniforms because old Hetty would have died of a seizure if she had suspected she was paying registered nurses' wages. You decide: Was money her god or her master?

**Joe Louis may have been the finest boxer in history.**—He turned professional in 1934 and won the heavyweight title in Chicago in 1937 when he knocked out James J. Braddock in the eighth round. Louis defended his title successfully twenty-five times, scoring twenty knockouts. During his lifetime, Louis earned nearly five million dollars in the ring, but he never had much to show for it and died virtually broke.

"When I die, I only want one word on my tombstone—'even.' The world don't owe me nothin', and I hope I don't owe it nothin'."

We will never die "even." The world may not owe us anything, but we owe the world and God who has abundantly blessed us more than we can ever repay. We can show our gratitude by being good stewards of what He has entrusted to us.

## TEACHING THE BIBLE

▶ *Main Idea:* Paul's plea for the Corinthians to share their blessings with others illustrates that we must evaluate the degree to which we experience the kind of contentment and generosity described by Paul.

▶ *Suggested Teaching Aim:* To lead adults to describe Paul's plea for the Corinthians to share with the Jewish believers in Jerusalem, and to evaluate the reasons for their generosity.

### A TEACHING OUTLINE

*1. To explain the offering Paul was taking for the saints.*
*2. Identify three reasons Paul suggested for generosity.*
*3. Examine why we give today.*

**Introduce the Bible Study**

To introduce the lesson, share the illustration, "Four men to take up the offering" *(Applying the Bible).*

**Search for Biblical Truth**

IN ADVANCE, write the following on a chalkboard or a large sheet of paper. Cover the points until you are ready to discuss them:

*Paul's Reasons for Giving*
*My Reasons for Giving*

1. Example for others
2. Contentment and generosity
3. Give glory to God

Use the material in *Studying the Bible* to explain the offering Paul was collecting for the poor Christians in Jerusalem. Ask members to open their Bibles to 9:1-5. Point out that one reason Paul wanted the Corinthians to give was so they would be an example to others. (Uncover the first point.) Give a brief lecture covering the following points:

(1) why Paul felt it unnecessary to promote the offering in Corinth;

(2) what Paul did to keep from embarrassing himself and the Corinthians.

Uncover the second point. Distribute paper and pencils. Assign every member one of the verses in 9:6-10 and ask them to paraphrase it. (If you have more than four members you will need to assign one verse to several members.) Allow time for writing and then ask several volunteers to read their paraphrases. Sum up this section by this sentence from *Studying the Bible:* "The promise is that God will give us all we need to do what He asks us to do."

Uncover the third point. Give a brief lecture in which you point out the three fruits of generous giving:

(1) the benefits one who learns how to be contented and

generous receives;

(2) the needs of the poor will be met;

(3) God is glorified when His people are generous.

Ask: What two things does v.13 suggest the Jerusalem Christians will praise God for because of the Corinthians generosity? *(obedience to the gospel; the generous gift)*

Ask members to look at v.15. Ask, Considering the context in which Paul made this statement, what different meanings can you think of to apply to God's "unspeakable gift"? *(Christ; work of the Spirit in bringing Jews and Gentiles together).*

**Give the Truth a Personal Focus**

Refer to the chart used earlier. Ask members to review the three reasons Paul gave for generous giving to determine how many of these reasons they would give for their generosity. Ask them to list other reasons that influence their generosity.

Close with a prayer that all would come to a deeper understanding of the need to be generous in sharing their resources.

# Expressing Love to All

**Basic Passage:** 1 Corinthians 13
**Focal Passage:** 1 Corinthians 13

For twelve weeks, we have been studying Paul's Corinthian letters. The study of 1 Corinthians 13 forms a fitting climax. The love that Paul described here was the answer for the problems that plagued the Corinthian church. Paul began 1 Corinthians by setting forth the basic problem and the basic solution. The problem was reliance on the world's self-seeking wisdom. The solution was the wisdom of God seen in the cross. Although Paul did not use the word *love* in that chapter, that is what he meant. In 1 Corinthians 12—14, Paul described the problems and solution for the Corinthians' disputes about spiritual gifts. In chapter 12, Paul described the variety of gifts in the one body of Christ. He concluded the chapter by mentioning a "more excellent way" that should permeate everything Christians do. Chapter 13 presents that more excellent way.

**Study Aim:** *To practice Christian love in all relationships*

## STUDYING THE BIBLE

The most eloquent speech without love amounts only to noise (v. 1). A person may practice the highest spiritual gifts, but is nothing without love (v. 2). Giving away everything and even giving up one's life gains nothing if done without love (v. 3). Love is described in terms of what it does and does not do (vv. 4-6). Love bears, believes, hopes, and endures all things (v. 7). Love lasts forever; while spiritual gifts are part of the earthly order (v. 8). Two examples illustrate differences between incomplete earthly experiences and the perfection of heaven: differences in knowledge between children and adults, and the difference between seeing face-to-face and seeing imperfect reflections in a mirror (vv. 9-12). Faith, hope, and love are eternal, but love is the greatest (v. 13).

### I. Necessity of Love (13:1-3)

**1. Speech without love (v. 1)**

> **1 Though I speak with the tongues of men and of angels, and have not charity, I am become as sounding brass, or a tinkling cymbal.**

One of the most ambiguous English words is *love.* Think how many different ways this word is used. The Greeks had a number of words to express different kinds of love. The Greek word in 1 Corinthians 13 is *agape.* Although rarely used by the Greeks, the Bible uses the word to describe the essence of God (John 3:16; 1 John 4:16). The word is also used to describe how followers of Christ are to act toward God and others. The idea is summed up in the Golden Rule (Matt. 7:12). Christian love is doing good for others without thought of personal gain and regardless of personal loss.

As we saw in the session on 1 Corinthians 14 (April 9), the gift of tongues was a source of pride for many Corinthians. If a person had that gift or if the person could speak like angels, the person would be making only so much noise if the speech was made without love.

**2. Spiritual gifts without love (v. 2)**

> **2 And though I have the gift of prophecy, and understand all mysteries, and all knowledge; and though I have all faith, so that I could remove mountains, and have not charity, I am nothing.**

Paul asked his readers to suppose that he had all the higher gifts: the gift of prophecy, which imparted special wisdom; the gift of knowledge, which gave him all knowledge; and the gift of faith, which enabled him to perform miracles comparable to moving mountains (see 1 Cor. 12:8-10). People might be impressed by such an apparently important person; but if he didn't have love, he would actually be nothing.

**3. Self-sacrifice without love (v. 3)**

> **3 And though I bestow all my goods to feed the poor, and though I give my body to be burned, and have not charity, it profiteth me nothing.**

The English word "charity" fails to capture the meaning of *agape,* just as the word "love" does. When we use the word "charity" today, we mean what Paul described as bestowing our goods to feed the poor. Paul used as extreme example of charity—giving away everything. Paul said that he could have such charity, but he would gain nothing if he didn't have *agape.* Paul then referred to the supreme act of self-sacrifice—giving one's life. We may wonder how anyone could practice such self-sacrifice without love. Keep in mind what Jesus taught in Matthew 6:1-18 about the importance of motives. He said that something is wrong with people who do good things in order for people to see and praise them. Of such people, Jesus said, "They have their reward" (Matt. 6:2,5,16). In other words, they acted in order to receive praise; when they received it, they received the only reward they would ever get. This is what Paul meant when he said that self-sacrifice without love "profiteth me nothing."

## II. Description of Love (13:4-7)

**1. What love does and does not do (vv. 4-6)**

4 Charity suffereth long, and is kind; charity envieth not; charity vaunteth not itself, is not puffed up.
5 Doth not behave itself unseemly, seeketh not her own, is not easily provoked, thinketh no evil;
6 Rejoiceth not in iniquity, but rejoiceth in the truth.

Rather than trying to define *agape,* Paul describes it by telling what it does and does not do. It is patient and kind, like God Himself (Ex. 34:6-7; Rom. 2:4). Love is devoid of the kind of jealousy that envies what others have. Love isn't puffed up with arrogant pride.

Love doesn't act in inappropriate ways. It doesn't focus its energies on advancing oneself. Love isn't touchy and easily offended. Love doesn't keep track of wrongs done by others (meaning of "thinketh no evil').

Love has nothing to do with evil. It doesn't practice it, condone it, or find smug satisfaction in the sins of others. Instead, love finds its joy in spreading and living the truth.

**2. How love overcomes (v. 7)**

7 Beareth all things, believeth all things, hopeth all things, endureth all things.

Love is both tender and tough. It overcomes by forbearing and forgiving others (Eph. 4:2,32). It believes the best of others; and even when others prove false, love remains hopeful. Such tenderness and toughness enable love to endure whatever happens.

## III. Excellence of Love (13:8-13)

**1. Outlasts spiritual gifts (v. 8)**

8 Charity never faileth: but whether there be prophecies, they shall fail; whether there be tongues, they shall cease; whether there be knowledge, it shall vanish away.

Keep in mind that Paul wrote this chapter to deal with disputes about spiritual gifts. In verse 8 he makes the point that love will outlast all the spiritual gifts. The exercise of one's spiritual gift is important for the present age. The body of Christ functions as each member performs its gift in harmony with the other members and their gifts (1 Cor. 12).

Paul was pleading in chapter 13 for each member of the body of Christ to see that love must permeate each person and the exercise of every gift. Without love, the gifts are nothing (vv. 1-3). In verse 8 he added another reason for focusing on love rather than on specific gifts. Love will outlast all the gifts. They are for this age only, but love is eternal.

**2. Partial versus complete (vv. 9-12)**

9 For we know in part, and we prophesy in part.

10 But when that which is perfect is come, then that which is in part shall be done away.

11 When I was a child, I spake as a child, I understood as a child, I thought as a child: but when I became a man, I put away childish things.

12 For now we see through a glass, darkly; but then face to face; now I know in part; but then shall I know even as also I am known.

In these verses, Paul explained why love outlasts spiritual gifts. Compared to the future, the things of this age are incomplete. Even at best, spiritual gifts share the incompleteness of other things of this age. For example, consider the gift of knowledge; one's knowledge is partial compared to the completeness of heaven. The same is true of the gift of prophecy. We prophesy in part based on our limited human understanding and experience.

The gifts are useful in this imperfect age. God uses people who submit their gifts to Him. But the time is coming when this age will give way to the future age of perfection and completeness. At that time, what is partial will give way to what is complete.

Paul used two illustrations from human experience. (1) A child has limited knowledge and understanding compared to an adult. In a sense, differences between earthly things and eternal things are like the differences between a person's understanding as a child and as an adult. (2) The mirrors of Paul's day were made of polished metal. The images were imperfect compared to seeing a person face-to-face. The things of this age are like looking at imperfect reflections in a mirror. Our knowledge in the future age will be like seeing face-to-face.

**3. Faith, hope, and love (v. 13)**

13 And now abideth faith, hope, charity, these three; but the greatest of these is charity.

The writers of the New Testament often mentioned these three qualities together. (See, for example, Rom. 5:2-5; Gal. 5:5-6; Col. 1:4-5; 1 Thess. 1:3; 5:8; Heb. 6:10-12; 1 Pet. 1:21-22). Earlier in 1 Corinthians 13, Paul showed how love believes all things and hopes all things (v. 7). Verse 13 is the most famous listing of these three basics of the Christian life.

Paul made two points in verse 13. The first point is that faith, hope, and love are eternal. They constitute who and what we really are. Most of what we call our own will pass away with this world and the present age, but who and what we are will outlast our death and the end of this world. Our physical possessions, for example, are only loaned to us for a while. We won't take them with us, but the way we use them shapes who we are—faithful and generous, or unfaithful and selfish. We will leave our possessions behind; but we will take with us either our generous spirit or our selfish spirit.

Thus faith, hope, and love rank at the top of the list of heavenly treasures that last forever (see Matt. 6:19-21). Our faith, hope, and love doubtlessly will find new modes of expression in the perfection of face-to-face experience with God. However, they will provide the building blocks for eternity.

Paul's second point is that love is the greatest of the eternal qualities. Perhaps Paul meant that love is greatest because it partakes of who God is. The Bible says, "God is love" (1 John 4:16); however, it never says, ""God is faith'' or "God is hope." Another aspect of this preeminence of love is that love inspires faith and hope (see v. 7).

## APPLYING THE BIBLE

**Love is more than a four-letter word.**—A young fellow was madly in love with a beautiful young lady. His attention to her was unending and his promises to her were abundant.

In a letter to her on one occasion, the young suitor wrote: "Mary, darling, I love you more than words can ever tell. I would climb the highest mountain for you. I would swim the widest sea for you. I would brave the fiercest blizzard for you. I would fight wild animals for you. I would die to protect your virtue. More than anything in this world, I love you . . . love you . . . love you."

At the close of the letter, he added: "I'll be over Thursday night and take you to dinner if it doesn't rain!"

Love is more than a four-letter word. It is more than eloquent talk (v. 1). It reaches out and embraces, lifts, ennobles, and strengthens everything it touches.

**Love finds a way.**—When German composer Felix Mendelssohn fell head over heels in love with the young woman who later became his wife, he wrote to his sister Rebecca for some advice.

"I am more desperately in love than I ever was in my life before, and I do not know what to do. I have not an idea whether she likes me or not, and I do not know what to do to make her like me. When away from her, I am always sad. O Rebecca! What shall I do?"

In our lesson today Paul said that love finds a way to express itself. Eloquent speech without love is empty. Spiritual gifts without love amount to nothing. Self-sacrifice without love is meaningless (vv. 1-3). Love will find a way to express itself in attitudes and actions.

Love is little—just four letters—but it helps everybody. It unlocks doors and opens hearts. It creates friendship and good will. Love inspires respect and confidence. Everybody loves love. Love is never boring. Love breaks no laws. Love costs nothing, yet it costs everything. Love is praised by everyone and condemned by no one. Love is useful every moment of every day and night. Love is courtesy even in the small things of life.[1]

**Robert E. Lee's kindness.**—In the opinion of some of us, America has never produced a Christian layman with finer qualities of character than those possessed by Confederate General Robert E. Lee. On one occasion, Jefferson Davis, the president of the Southern Confederacy, asked General Lee for his opinion of General Whiting.

"Whiting is an exceptionally qualified man," Lee replied. But a friend who was standing nearby and overheard the conversation reminded General Lee that Whiting had said some unkind things about Lee.

"Yes, I know what General Whiting has said," replied Lee, "but President Davis asked me my opinion of Whiting; he did not ask Whiting's opinion of me."[2]

**Love conquers all.**—John Keats, who wrote so much about love, missed it entirely when he said: "I can never understand why people rave so about love. It is nothing but a simple biological process."

Countless individuals have tried to conquer the world by force, but their efforts were successful only temporarily, if at all. Force destroys and wounds. It neither lifts nor heals. On the other hand, love and love alone can conquer the world. Although the ancient Roman army conquered the world of their day and kept it beneath their cleated sandals, they still knew the power of love. In their own language they wrote, *Amor omnia vincit.*

Meaning? Love conquers all.

Is that not what Paul is saying in verses 4-8?

Napoleon knew what he was talking about when he said: "Alexander, Charlemagne, and I built kingdoms upon force. Jesus Christ built upon love. Today no one would follow us, but millions would die for Jesus Christ!"

## TEACHING THE BIBLE

- *Main Idea:* Expressing love to all means that believers must practice love in all their relationships.
- *Suggested Teaching Aim:* To lead adults to describe Paul's "more excellent way," and to identify at least one relationship in which they will put love into action.

### A TEACHING OUTLINE

1. *Describe the necessity of love.*
2. *Examine the description of love.*
3. *Explain the excellence of love.*
4. *Identify a relationship where love is needed.*

### Introduce the Bible Study

Introduce the lesson by sharing this illustration: A young boy went to the lingerie department of a store to purchase a gift for his mother. He whispered to the clerk that he wanted to buy a slip for his mother but did not know her size. The baffled clerk asked if his mother were thin, fat, short, tall, or what. "Well," replied the youngster, "she's just about perfect." The clerk chose a medium size. A few days later, the mother came to exchange the gift. She needed a much larger size! Her son had seen her through eyes of love.

Ask, What differences would it make in our relationships if we saw through eyes of Christlike love and acted accordingly?[3]

**Search for Biblical Truth**

Organize the class in three groups and give them the following assignment:

**Group 1—**

Study verses1-3, The Necessity of Love. Define the use of love *(agape)* and paraphrase these verses. Be prepared to discuss the following: How do motives influence the results of our actions?

**Group 2—**

Study verses 4-7, The Description of Love. List the positive and negative traits of love and present a role play or case study illustrating one of these characteristics. Be prepared to discuss the following: How can love be tender and tough at the same time?

**Group 3—**

Study verses 8-13, The Excellence of Love. Describe what makes love more excellent than other gifts. Using a familiar hymn tune, write a hymn describing the excellence of love. Be prepared to discuss the following: How can we use our physical possessions that are impermanent to demonstrate the excellent of love?

Allow six to ten minutes for study and call for reports.

**Give the Truth a Personal Focus**

Distribute paper and pencils. Give them the following instructions:

(1) List five persons whom you feel fairly comfortable in the way you have expressed your love.

(2) List five persons you need to improve in your practice of Christian love.

(3) Circle one of these five for whom you will plan a special way of practicing Christian love.

---

1. Adapted from Virginia Ely, *Devotion for Personal and Group Worship* (Westwood, N.J.; Fleming H. Revell Co., 1960), 113.
2. Ibid., 109.
3. From *Bible Book Study for Adult Teachers,* October-December, 1991, 101.

# A Nation Turns to God

**Books from BROADMAN & HOLMAN for Studying and Teaching**

*Layman's Bible Book Commentary,* Volume 6
*The Broadman Bible Commentary,* Volume 3
*The Teacher's Bible Commentary,* Paschall and Hobbs
*Old Testament Survey,* Paul R. Howse
*The Heart of Hebrew History,* H. I. Hester
*Holman Bible Dictionary,* Trent C. Butler, ed.
*Atlas of the Bible Lands,* Harry Thomas Frank, ed.
*Pronouncing Bible Names,* W. Murray Severance
*How to Interpret the Bible,* Robert L. Cate
*Holman Bible Handbook,* David S. Dockery, ed.

## INTRODUCTION

This quarter's studies trace Israel's history from the death of Solomon to the fall of the Northern Kingdom in 721/722 B.C.

**Unit I,** "The Price of Power," focuses on the division of the kingdom after Solomon's death and on prophets like Elijah and Elisha. This unit describes how the abuse of power under Solomon and Rehoboam led to the division of the kingdom. The kings of the Northern Kingdom opened the way for false religion, which prophets like Elijah challenged. Elijah also challenged the injustices connected with the death of Naboth. This unit tells one episode from the ministry of Elisha—the lepers who told the good news about the lifting of the siege of Samaria.

**Unit II,** "The Approaching Judgment," includes warnings from the prophets Amos, Hosea, and Micah. Amos declared judgment on the sins of Judah and Israel. Amos condemned injustices in Israel and called for righteousness. Hosea's life gave him insight into God's love for unfaithful Israel. Hosea pleaded with Israel to receive God's love. Micah denounced greedy leaders in Judah.

**Unit III,** "The Judgment Arrives," deals with events in Judah and Israel during the period leading to Israel's fall. In a stirring vision in the temple, Isaiah was called as a prophet. He warned Judah of her sins. He used the fall of Israel to reinforce his warning to Judah. The end of Israel came at the hands of the Assyrians.

June
4
1995

# When Power Is Misused

**Basic Passage:** 1 Kings 11:26—12:24
**Focal Passages:** 1 Kings 12:6-11, 16-17

The misuse of power is one of the themes of human history. Each of us has power to act and to influence others. Some have great power to influence the lives of many people. Human nature is such that only with God's help can people wield power wisely and for the benefit of all concerned. Power is a great temptation for many people. The Bible gives many examples of the misuse of power and the terrible consequences that followed. Solomon and his son Rehoboam had great power, but their misuse of power eventually led to the division of the kingdom.

**Study Aim:** *To recognize the serious consequences that result from the misuse of power*

## STUDYING THE BIBLE

During the final years of Solomon's reign, Jeroboam became a focal point for unrest among the northern tribes (11:26-28). The prophet Ahijah predicted the division of the kingdom (11:29-39). Jeroboam was forced to flee to Egypt (11:40), where he remained until Solomon died (11:41-43). The northern tribes asked Rehoboam to redress their grievances (12:1-5). The older men advised Rehoboam to be a servant leader (12:6-7), but the younger men advised him to demand even more than Solomon (12:8-11). When the king acted on the advice of the young men (12:12-15), the northern tribes rebelled (12:16-20). Rehoboam heeded the advice of the prophet Shemaiah not to launch a civil war (12:21-24).

### I. Seeds of Dissension (11:26-43)

**1. Jeroboam—potential threat to Solomon (11:26-28).**—Solomon had sown the seeds of dissension by his harsh use of forced labor from the northern tribes. An able and ambitious young man named Jeroboam made the most of the dissatisfaction. Solomon unwittingly aided Jeroboam by promoting him to an administrative position.

**2. Ahijah's prophecy (11:29–39).**—The prophet Ahijah met Jeroboam and predicted the division of the kingdom. He signified this by tearing his new garment into twelve pieces and giving ten of these to Jeroboam. Ahijah made clear that the promise of God to David was being honored by allowing the house of David to continue to rule over all but the ten northern tribes. Ahijah promised Jeroboam that God would establish his house over the ten tribes on condition that Jeroboam would keep God's commandments (a condition that Jeroboam failed to meet).

**3. Flight of Jeroboam to Egypt (11:40).**—When Solomon became aware of Jeroboam's ambitions, Solomon recognized Jeroboam as a threat. As a result, Solomon gave orders for Jeroboam's death. Jeroboam fled to Egypt, where Pharoah Shishak protected him.

**4. Death of Solomon (11:41-43).**—After a checkered reign of forty years, Solomon died. His son Rehoboam became the new king, and the stage was set for the fulfillment of Ahijah's prophecy.

## II. Division of the Kingdom (12:1-24)

**1. Rehoboam hears Israel's request (12:1-5).**—Keep in mind the history of the kingdom up to this time. Saul had been the first king of Israel, but he reigned over little more than a loose confederation of tribes. During much of Saul's reign, David and many followers from his tribe of Judah were considered outlaws by Saul. After Saul's death, David was made king of Hebron; but initially he was not recognized as king by the northern tribes, who wanted to remain loyal to Saul's son Ishbosheth. Eventually the tribal leaders of all Israel recognized David as king (2 Sam. 5:1-5). Even during the latter years of David's reign, Sheba led an unsuccessful rebellion against David. At the beginning of Sheba's rebellion, the northern tribes followed Sheba ( 20:1-2).

David's authority was such that he was able to transfer reign over all Israel to Solomon. During Solomon's latter years, the ancient schism between north and south reappeared. Solomon's harsh policy of using forced labor greatly contributed to the discontent of the northern tribes (see 1 Sam. 8:16; 1 Kings 5:12-13). Therefore, when Rehoboam met with the people of Israel at Shechem, the issue quickly surfaced. This is what the Israelites meant in 1 Kings 12:4 when they complained about the "grievous service" and "heavy yoke" placed on them by Solomon. Since Jeroboam had returned from Egypt, his presence added to the volatility of the situation. Rehoboam asked for three days to consider their petition.

**2. Rehoboam receives counsel from older advisors (12:6-7)**

> 6 And king Rehoboam consulted with the old men, that stood before Solomon his father while he yet lived, and said, How do ye advise that I may answer this people?
>
> 7 And they spake unto him, saying, If thou wilt be a servant unto this people this day, and wilt serve them, and answer them, and speak good words to them, then they will be thy servants for ever.

The older men, who had been Solomon's counselors, advised Rehoboam to promise to be a servant leader. The text does not define all that the counselors meant when they advised the king to be "a servant unto this people." The word itself is the frequently used Hebrew word for *servant* or *slave.* The verb form of the same word is also used in verse 7, when the counselors told the king to "serve" the people.

At the very least, the old men were advising the king to announce a change in the harsh policy of Solomon. At the most, it would mean that the king would see himself not as a pampered autocrat to be served by his people, but as a king who would lead his people as a shepherd leads his sheep.

Some Bible students interpret verse 7 as a shrewd, deceptive promise. In other words, if emphasis is placed on the word "today," the older men were advising Rehoboam to make a kind of "campaign promise" that he never intended to keep after he had secured the full reins of power. The traditional interpretation is that the old men gave good and sincere advice. They had seen the problems created by the policy of Solomon's latter years. They knew that the north was a powder keg. Only a changed policy had any chance of keeping all the tribes loyal to Rehoboam.

**3. Rehoboam seeks advice of younger men (12:8-11)**

> **8 But he forsook the counsel of the old men, which they had given him, and consulted with the young men that were grown up with him, and which stood before him:**
> **9 And he said unto them, What counsel give ye that we may answer this people, who have spoken to me, saying, Make the yoke which thy father did put upon us lighter?**
> **10 And the young men that were grown up with him spake unto him, saying, Thus shalt thou speak unto this people that spake unto thee saying, Thy father made our yoke heavy, but make thou it lighter unto us; thus shalt thou say unto them, My little finger shall be thicker than my father's loins.**
> **11 And now whereas my father did lade you with a heavy yoke, I will add to your yoke: my father hath chastised you with whips, but I will chastise you with scorpions.**

Rehoboam was not only arrogant; he was stupid. Any person in touch with reality would have seen the wisdom in what the old men advised. Rehoboam, however, had already decided not to follow their wise counsel. Instead, he looked for someone who would advise him to do what he had already decided to do. His own cronies were just the group to do this.

Some rulers become totally out of touch with the common people. Some of this is inevitable, but many political leaders insulate themselves from the real world. Rehoboam had grown up in the sheltered, luxurious life of the palace. So had his friends.

The words of the petition from 1 Kings 12:4 were quoted by both Rehoboam (v. 9) and the young men (v. 10). They knew what the grievance was, but they showed little awareness that they really understood the words. The petitioners used the word "yoke." A yoke is what is placed on oxen. The Old Testament sometimes used it of the yoke that a conqueror placed on a conquered people (see Jer. 27:8, 11-12). The people's complaint was that Solomon had treated the northern tribes as conquered people.

The young men picked up on the word "yoke." They advised Rehoboam to tell the disgruntled Israelites that he was going to add to the heavy yoke placed on them by Solomon. They also told Rehoboam to tell the people that his little finger was thicker than his father's loins, which some translate as "waist." Also, he was to tell them that Solomon had punished them with whips, but he would punish them with scorpions. "Scorpions" were lashes that had spikes in them.

**4. Rehoboam answers the people harshly (12:12-15).**—After the three days had passed, Jeroboam and all the people came to Rehoboam to hear what he had decided. Rehoboam used the exact words that the young men had given him. He intended to intensify the harsh policy of Solomon toward them.

**5. Israel rebels against the house of David (12:16-17)**

> **16 So when all Israel saw that the king hearkened not unto them, the people answered the king, saying, What portion have we in David? neither have we inheritance in the son of Jesse: to your tents, O Israel: now see to thine own house, David. So Israel departed unto their tents.**
>
> **17 But as for the children of Israel which dwelt in the cities of Judah, Rehoboam reigned over them.**

The words of verse 16 reflect the rallying cry from Sheba's attempted rebellion against David (2 Sam. 20:1). The fact that this cry of an earlier generation was remembered shows that resentment against the house of David had been smoldering among the northern tribes. The meaning of the rallying cry was that the northern tribes felt that they did not belong to the house of David, nor did they have any inheritance in his territory. Instead, they had their own portion and inheritance. They were returning to their own inheritance. David's house, represented by Rehoboam and Judah, would have to go it alone, without any further help from the northern tribes.

Verse 17 shows that Rehoboam was left with only the people of Judah and any Israelites who lived in the cities of Judah.

Verse 18 gives further proof of how little Rehoboam was in touch with reality. He sent Adoram, the administrator of the forced labor, to speak to the northern tribes. Recognizing Adoram as the instrument of their grievous service, the Israelites stoned him to death. Convinced now that the northern tribes were in earnest, Rehoboam fled for his life.

The northern tribes chose Jeroboam as their own king, and this ended the period of the united kingdom and inaugurated the period of the divided kingdom. The Northern Kingdom was called Israel, and the Southern Kingdom was called Judah.

**6. Rehoboam advised not to attack Israel (12:21-24).** When

Rehoboam returned to Jerusalem, he gathered an army from Judah and Benjamin. His intention was to attack the northern tribes. A prophet named Shemaiah delivered God's message, which was not to fight the people of Israel. The people of Judah and Benjamin obeyed God and returned to their homes.

## APPLYING THE BIBLE

**The right use of power.**—The late George W. Truett relates that when William IV, king of England, died there was a young teenage girl spending the night at the palace. When she was awakened and told that she was now the queen of England, she immediately fell on her knees and asked God to give her guidance and grace in the years that were to follow.

Her name was Victoria, and she ruled England for sixty three years, from 1837 to 1901, the longest reign of any British monarch. When she came to the throne, the people had no respect for the throne, but under Victoria's powerful and gracious reign the throne was elevated to a position of respect and veneration. She literally became the symbol, and still is the symbol, of Great Britain's greatness.

How differently Rehoboam, the son of Solomon, who reigned after his father's death. He had great power but he used it selfishly and unwisely, resulting in the division of the kingdom (12:16-20).

**The Power to use power appropriately.**—Years ago, *Moody Monthly* magazine carried a brief story about the late Dr. George S. McCune who was a missionary to Korea.

One day a Korean said to McCune: "We have had a code of morals. We have known what we should do, but we did not have the power to do it. But when Jesus Christ came into our lives, we had power to do what was right."

Thus, we have in a brief statement here, why powerful people do not use their power in the right way. Only Jesus Christ in one's life can give sufficient wisdom as to how to use power.

**The abuse of power.**—Rehoboam had every opportunity to be a great king, but he abused his power. Contrast the way William Wilberforce used his power and the way Napoleon used his.

In 1779 Wilberforce led the first campaign in the British Parliament to abolish the slave trade in the West Indies. Although the bill failed, he persisted and a bill to end the slave trade passed the House of Commons in 1792. Wilberforce had power and influence, and he used them to benefit those who most needed help.

A contemporary of William Wilberforce was Emperor Napoleon of France. Although he has been called the greatest military genius of his time, he ran roughshod over Europe for nearly twenty years, spilling the blood of millions of people. As emperor, he controlled everything: the press, the police, foreign policy, and government at home. He was a talented and strong leader but his pride and self-centeredness brought grief to millions in Europe.

Like Rehoboam, Napoleon had the opportunity to use his power for good, but he was too full of Napoleon to do it!

**Who must influences you?**—John Wesley, the founder of the Methodist church, was greatly influenced by the Bible-loving Moravians. As a student at Oxford, he determined to have no companions except those who would help him live the life of faith and righteousness.

Voltaire, the French agnostic and talented writer, was greatly influenced by the Abbe de Chateuneuf, a priest who sowed the seeds of deism in Voltaire's young heart.

Augustine (A.D. 354-430) was the greatest theologian among the early fathers of the church. Wayward and immoral in his youth, Augustine was brought to Christ through the prayers and influence of Monica, his godly mother. Her influence on Augustine was immeasurable.

Justin Martyr, born about A.D. 100, was a Gentile who became a great power in the spread of Christianity in the second century. As his mind began to open, he investigated the teachings of the great philosophers to discover truth: Zeno the Stoic, Aristotle, Pythagoras, and Plato. But one day while he was out walking alone, an old man approached Justin and in their brief conversation planted the seeds in his mind that led him to Christ. Christianity, Justin Martyr concluded, contained the highest human wisdom.

Ezra Kimbell led Dwight L. Moody to Christ. Moody was a strong influence on Frederick B. Meyer, the great English theologian. Meyer came to the United States to preach and met and encouraged a young minister named Wilbur Chapman, who became one of America's great evangelists. Chapman chose as his associate a young professional baseball player named Billy Sunday who also became a great American evangelist. Sunday was preaching in Charlotte, North Carolina, and from that a prayer group was organized that met regularly to pray for revival. Their specific prayer was that another revival be sent by God to Charlotte that would have the power of the Billy Sunday revival of earlier years. In answer to their prayers, Mordecai Ham came to preach. And in that revival meeting, evangelist Billy Graham was saved.

It is important who influences us and whose counsel we follow. Would the division of Israel have come during Rehoboam's reign if he had sought the right counsel (12:6-7, 8-11)?

## TEACHING THE BIBLE

▶ *Main Idea:* Rehoboam's unwise actions demonstrate that serious consequences result when people misuse power.

▶ *Suggested Teaching Aim:* To lead adults to cxamine Rehoboam's misuse of power, and to identify ways they use their power properly.

## A TEACHING OUTLINE

*1. Identify Jeroboam and Rehoboam.*
*2. Organize two groups to study these two men.*
*3. Ask a series of questions to review the lesson.*
*4. Lead members to recognize their own power and how it can be abused.*

**Introduce the Bible Study**

To introduce the Bible study, share the following illustration: The French Revolution overthrew the French monarchy because the monarchy had gotten out of touch with the common people. People were hungry, but when they complained to Queen Marie Antoinette that they had no bread, she responded by saying, "Let them eat cake."

Point out that Solomon's son Rehoboam was just as insensitive to the needs of the people.

**Search for Biblical Truth**

IN ADVANCE, enlist two members to read the *Holman Bible Dictionary* or another Bible dictionary and prepare a report on Jeroboam and Rehoboam. Place a large sheet of paper on the wall with "Jeroboam" written on it; place one on the opposite wall with "Rehoboam" on it.

As members enter, ask them to go to the posters and write anything they know about these two men. Read what the members have written and then call on the two people assigned the reports. Fill in any information from *Studying the Bible* that members need to understand the background of this situation.

Organize the class in two groups. Ask group 1 to study 11:26—12:24 to find all the things Rehoboam did wrong. Let them suggest why they think he responded the way he did.

Ask group 2 to study 11:26—12:34 to find why Jeroboam rebelled against Rehoboam.

Allow six to eight minutes for study and then call for reports. After the reports, ask the following questions to review (answers are all found in *Studying the Bible*): What was the relationship between Jeroboam and Solomon? What was the relationship between Solomon and Rehoboam? Who was Ahijah and what was his relationship with Jeroboam? What was the basic reason the Israelites rebelled against Solomon and his son? What expression did the Israelites use to call Israel to separate and when had it been used before? What were the names of the two new nations? What tribes belonged to the Northern Kingdom? to the Southern? Who was Adoram and what did his death show?

**Give the Truth a Personal Focus**

Write the words *power* and *abuse* on a chalkboard or a large sheet of paper. Ask members to list some of the situations in their lives in which they have power. Point out that all of them have some power over someone else; no one is absolutely powerless. One possible response might be: parents over children. Write this under *power.* Other possible responses might be: boss over employee; teacher over student; voters over elected officials; customer over store. Encourage members to see that they do have some power. As members suggest responses, list these under the word *power.*

Now, ask, How can you abuse your power? Let members suggest ways parents can abuse their power over children. Then go down the rest of the list and let members suggest ways their power can be abused.

Let members suggest steps they can take to keep from abusing their power and to use it properly. Close in prayer that all will use their power properly.

---

1. *Oxford Dictionary of Quotations,* 2nd ed. (London: Oxford University Press, 1955), 329.18.

June
11
1995

# The Danger of False Religion

**Basic Passage:** 1 Kings 18
**Focal Passage:** 1 Kings 19:30-39

The people of Israel were tempted to participate in false religions. God had called them to worship Him alone and to show their faith by obeying His commandments. In other words, they were called to a distinctive faith and lifestyle. Baal worship provided a constant temptation to compromise their faith and way of living. From our perspective, we wonder what was appealing about worshiping idols. We need to realize that Baal worship promised a happy, fulfilling life; and that it made no moral demands. To the contrary, Baal was often worshiped through temple prostitution. The contest on Mount Carmel was a contest between the Lord God and the popular, materialistic religion of the day.

**Study Aim:** *To recognize the dangers of moral and spiritual compromise associated with false religions*

## STUDYING THE BIBLE

Elijah promised that the Lord was going to send rain (vv. 1-6). Elijah told Obadiah to summon Ahab to meet with him (vv. 7-16). Elijah challenged Ahab to summon the people and the prophets of Baal to Mount Carmel (vv. 17-19). On Mount Carmel, Elijah proposed a contest to help the people decide whether to serve God or Baal (vv. 20-24). The prophets of Baal tried unsuccessfully to get Baal to answer their prayers (vv. 25-29). Elijah repaired the altar of the Lord (vv. 30-32), prepared the sacrifice (vv. 33-35), and prayed (vv. 36-37). When fire came down from heaven, the people declared that the Lord is God (vv. 38-40). When Elijah prayed for rain (vv. 41-44), rains came (vv. 45-46).

### I. Preparation for the Contest (1 Kings 18:1-19)

**1. Promise of rain (vv. 1-6).**—As a background to 1 Kings 18, read 1 Kings 16:29—17:24. King Ahab was condemned as the worst of a bad lot of kings of Israel. The reason was that he not only continued Jeroboam's sin of calf worship but also married Jezebel and gave Baal worship official status. Elijah was a prophet who declared a drought in the name of the Lord. This drought thus was a blow at the claim of Baal to provide rain.

Chapter 18 begins in the third year of the drought with Elijah promising rain. Meanwhile, the drought had become so severe that Ahab and his servant Obadiah were searching for water for their animals.

**2. Elijah and Obadiah (vv. 7-16).**—Elijah met Obadiah and told him to inform Ahab that Elijah wanted to see him. Obadiah was afraid that by the time Ahab arrived, Elijah would be gone; then Ahab would punish Obadiah. Obadiah reminded Elijah how he had hid the Lord's prophets from Jezebel, who was killing prophets. Elijah promised to remain, and Obadiah went to get Ahab.

**3. Elijah and Ahab (vv. 17-19).**—When Ahab saw Elijah, the king called Elijah "he that troubleth Israel" (v. 17). Elijah replied, "I have not troubled Israel; but thou, and thy father's house, in that ye have forsaken the commandments of the Lord, and thou hast followed Baalim" (v. 18). Elijah then challenged Ahab to summon to Mount Carmel all the people of Israel and the prophets of Baal.

## II. Contest on Mount Carmel (1 Kings 18:20-40)

**1. Elijah's challenge (vv. 20-24).**—Mount Carmel was a ridge that provided a view of the Mediterranean Sea in one direction and a fertile plain in the other. Elijah confronted the people with the challenge to make a decision whether to serve the Lord or Baal. He warned them to quit trying to hold on to both. "If the Lord be God, follow him: but if Baal, then follow him" (v. 21). The people remained silent in the face of this dramatic call to choose.

Elijah contrasted himself as the only remaining prophet of the Lord with the 450 prophets of Baal who were there. Elijah proposed a contest. The people would provide two bulls. The prophets of Baal would choose one bull and sacrifice it, but not burn it. Elijah would do the same with the other bull. The prophets of Baal would pray to their god for fire, and Elijah would pray to the Lord. The people agreed with the proposal.

**2. Failure of the prophets of Baal (vv. 25-29).**—Since they were many, Elijah told the prophets of Baal to go first. After preparing the sacrifice, they prayed to Baal from morning to noon; but no answer came. Elijah began to taunt the prophets of Baal. He told them to cry louder because perhaps Baal was talking, traveling, or even sleeping. During the afternoon, the prophets of Baal became more frantic and began to cut their bodies with knives. When evening came, no answer had come.

**3. Repairing the altar (vv. 30-32)**

> 30 And Elijah said unto all the people, Come near unto me. And all the people came near unto him. And he repaired the altar of the Lord that was broken down.
>
> 31 And Elijah took twelve stones, according to the number of the tribes of the sons of Jacob, unto whom the words of the

Lord came saying, Israel shall be thy name.
32 And with the stones he built an altar in the name of the Lord: and he made a trench about the altar, as great as would certain two measures of seed.

Elijah called the people to gather round; he didn't want them to miss anything. He began by rebuilding the altar. The altar probably had been destroyed by orders of Jezebel in her effort to stamp out the worship of the Lord.

Elijah used twelve stones to rebuild the altar. To those familiar with their own history, this act would remind them of an earlier time when twelve stones were used to signify the twelve tribes of Israel as God's people (Josh. 4:1-9). All the people were surely aware of the twelve tribes, who were descended from Jacob, or Israel (as God had named him in Gen 32:28).

Often twelve called His people to remember their history. Remembering their history reminded the children of Israel that the Lord was their God, and they were His people. Although the twelve tribes were now split into two kingdoms, the twelve stones reminded the Israelites that they were part of God's covenant people.

**3. Preparing the sacrifice (vv. 33-35)**

33 And he put the wood in order, and cut the bullock in pieces, and laid him on the wood, and said, Fill four barrels with water, and pour it on the burnt sacrifice, and on the wood.
34 And he said, Do it the second time. And they did it the second time. And he said, Do it the third time. And they did it the third time.
35 And the water ran round about the altar; and he filled the trench also with water.

Elijah took great care with the sacrifice. The twelve barrels of water served several purposes. The water ensured that no spark or fire was already in the wood. The number twelve, like the twelve stones, was another reminder of the twelve tribes of Israel. Pouring out the water also had another purpose. It signified the earnest prayer for rain. Keep in mind that although fire was central to the contest, the ability to provide rain was the real issue at stake.

**5. Elijah's prayer (vv. 36-37)**

36 And it came to pass at the time of the offering of the evening sacrifice, that Elijah the prophet came near, and said, Lord God of Abraham, Isaac, and of Israel, let it be known this day that thou art God in Israel, and that I am thy servant, and that I have done all these things at thy word.
37 Hear me, O Lord, hear me, that this people may know that thou art the Lord God, and that thou hast turned their heart back again.

The prophets of Baal had taken most of the day. Elijah's prayer came at the time of the evening sacrifice. The law prescribed a sacrifice just before sunset (see Ex. 28:38-41; Num. 28:3-4). This was a traditional time for prayers (see Ezra 9:4-15).

Elijah's name means "the Lord is God." "Lord" here translates the personal name of the God who revealed Himself to Moses and entered into a covenant with Israel. Some translations use "Jehovah" or "Yahweh." The heart of Elijah's prayer was that the people of Israel would know that the true God is not Baal, but none other than the God of Abraham, Isaac, and Israel, the Lord who made a covenant with their forefathers at Mount Sinai.

This central prayer had two subsidiary parts. One was the prayer that the people would know that Elijah was a true prophet of the true God, and that he spoke the word of the Lord. Since Elijah was there as the representative of the Lord, seeing him as God's prophet would glorify God's name.

The final part of verse 37 was a prayer for the people's hearts to be turned back to the Lord. This would be the result of recognizing the Lord as the only true God.

**6. Elijah's prayer answered (vv. 38-40)**

> **38 Then the fire of the Lord fell, and consumed the burnt sacrifice, and the wood, and the stones, and the dust, and licked up the water that was in the trench.**
> **39 And when all the people saw it, they fell on their faces: and they said, The Lord, he is the God; the Lord, he is the God.**

The Lord answered Elijah's prayer by sending fire from heaven. It consumed the burnt offering. In addition, it consumed the altar and everything on it—not only the wood but also the stones. It even licked up all the water in the trench.

When Elijah earlier had challenged them to make a choice, the people had been silent. They continued to try to remain neutral and claim something from both religions—the ancient faith of Israel and the popular, new religion that seemed to promise so much for so little (v. 21). Now suddenly, they made up their minds. The dramatic miracle left no doubt who was God. Baal had done nothing. The Lord had consumed the sacrifice and the altar.

Elijah's prayer was answered. The people cried out, "The Lord, he is the God."

## III. End of the Drought (1 Kings 18:41-46)

**1. Prayer for rain (vv. 41-44)**—Apparently a festival followed the miracle. Elijah told Ahab to eat and drink because the prophet could hear the coming rain. Then Elijah went to the top of Mount Carmel and prayed to the Lord for rain. Each time he prayed, he sent his servant to a point where he could look out over the Mediterranean Sea. For six times, the servant saw nothing. On the seventh time, he saw "a little cloud out of the sea, like a man's hand" (v. 44). Elijah sent his servant to tell Ahab to get in his chariot and head for home because if he delayed the heavy rain might stop him.

**2. The rains came (vv. 45-46).**—As Ahab headed down the mountain to Jezreel, the sky "was black with clouds and wind, and there was a great rain" (v. 45). God's hand with laid on Elijah with such power that he outran Ahab's chariot down the mountain.

## APPLYING THE BIBLE

**"Israel's" first appearance in secular history.**—Since our lessons during this quarter deal with Israel, perhaps it would be interesting for you to know a bit more about Israel.

"Israel" means "ruling with God," as *Young's Analytical Concordance* defines it. *Holman Bible Dictionary* says Israel means, "God strives," "God rules," "God heals," or "he strives against God."[1]

The name was first used in Genesis 32:28 where God said to Jacob: "Thy name shall be called no more Jacob, but Israel: for as a prince hast thou power with God and with men, and hast prevailed."

According to Werner Keller, "Israel" first appears in secular literature in 1229 B.C. In the Cairo Museum there is a monument from a temple near Thebes commemorating the victory of Pharoah Merenptah (came to the throne in 1234 B.C.) over the Libyans. The hymn praising the pharaoh reads: "Canaan is despoiled and all its evil with it. Askelon is taken captive, Gezer is conquered, Yanoam is blotted out. The people of Israel is desolate, it has no offering. Palestine has become a widow for Egypt."[2]

Thus, the ancient nation of Israel is not only confirmed to have existed from sacred Scripture, but from secular literature as well.

**Sin's destructive power.**—French novelist Victor Hugo (1802-1885) tells in *The Toilers of the Sea,* about a man thrusting his arm down into a crevice in the sea to pull out a crab. Immediately, his arm was seized by something as strong as steel and as cold as ice. First, it wound its tentacles around the fisherman's arm. Then a second, third, and fourth tentacle wound itself around the man's chest. Soon, he was helplessly bound in tentacles he could not break.

Sin is like that. One sin is quickly followed by another sin and, as the conscience is deadened, other sins are committed and each tightens its grip upon the sinner. Finally, sin drags the sinner down to terrible destruction and eternal doom.[3]

**What is His name?**—Helen Keller was an inspiration to millions of people. She conquered both deafness and blindness and lived in a most-productive life.

When she was a child, an illness that was diagnosed as brain fever destroyed both her sight and hearing. She was not yet two years old when the tragedy struck her. Unable to see, unable to speak, and unable to hear, Keller was shut off from the world. But through the patience of her teacher, Anne Sullivan, Helen Keller was able to rise above many of her difficulties. From the time Keller was seven until Sullivan died, she was Keller's teacher and companion.

Sullivan feared she would never be able to teach little Helen about God, but when Helen was fourteen she placed her sensitive fingers upon the throat and lips of Sullivan as Sullivan slowly spelled "G-O-D."

It was a breakthrough. Helen's face lighted up and she exclaimed joyfully: "Oh, I am so glad you told me His name, for He has often spoken to me."[4]

Israel knew God's name and His great love for them, but their history was one of rebellion against that name and love. In our lesson today, Israel once again witnesses the great power of God in His victory over Baal (vv. 38-40).

## TEACHING THE BIBLE

▶ *Main Idea:* Worshiping false religious shows the moral and spiritual compromise that comes when worship of the true God is abandoned.

▶ *Suggested Teaching Aim:* To compare Baal worship and worship of Yahweh, and to identify ways they let false religion creep into their worship.

### A TEACHING OUTLINE

*1. Make a poster to guide you through the study.*
*2. Lead members to examine Elijah's victory on Mount Carmel.*
*3. Guide members to identify ways they can eliminate false religion in their lives.*

**Introduce the Bible Study**

To introduce the lesson, use the illustration from *Applying the Bible* entitled, "What is His name?"

**Search for Biblical Truth**

IN ADVANCE, make the following poster:

THE CONTEST ON CARMEL

1. The Sin:
2. The Prediction:
3. The Punishment:
4. The Proposal:
5. The Preparation:
6. The Plea:
7. The Answer:
8. The Result:

Using *Studying the Bible,* prepare a lecture in which you cover each of the points on the poster. Summarize "Preparation for the Contest" (18:1-19) to understand the background. Be sure you point out:

(1) Ahab's and Israel's sin was idolatrous worship of the agricultural god Baal; (2) Elijah declared that God controlled the elements, not Baal, and predicted a three-year drought; (3) for three years God punished Israel (the Northern Kingdom) by withholding rain. Ask members to suggest answers to fill in the poster. Their answers should correspond to the above numbered statements although they will be worded differently. Write members' suggestions on the poster.

Ask members to open their Bibles to 1 Kings 18:20-32 and find what Elijah proposed: (4) the prophets of Baal would ask Baal and Elijah would ask God for fire to consume a bull placed on an altar. Point out that the prophets of Baal failed to attract Baal's attention even though they pleaded all day long.

Ask members to read 18:33-35 and discover what preparation Elijah made for his sacrifice: (5) rebuilt the altar of twelve stones and poured twelve barrels of water over the offering. Point out the significance of the time of Elijah's sacrifice and of the twelve stones and the twelve barrels of water.

Ask members to describe Elijah's plea: (6) that the people would know God was the Lord and Elijah was His servant and that Israel would return to the Lord.

Ask members to read 18:38-40 and describe God's answer: (7) fire consumed the sacrifice, wood, stones, dust, and the water around the altar. Point out that as a result of this awesome demonstration, the people declared the Lord was their God.

Summarize "End of the Drought" (1 Kings 18:41-46) and ask members to describe the result of the contest: (8) the rains came and broke a three-year drought.

**Give the Truth a Personal Focus**

Ask: Why do you think God responded so dramatically on Mount Carmel? (people needed a dramatic lesson) Does God still respond as dramatically today? Why?

Point out that although God may not send fire from heaven, He has given us His Son and His Word by which we can judge the false religion in our lives. Ask them to suggest ways false religion in our lives. Ask them to suggest ways false religion creeps into their lives and what they can do to eliminate it. Point out that when we worship only God, we shall experience "showers of blessings" in our spiritual lives.

---

1. *Holman Bible Dictionary* (Nashville: Holman Bible Publishers, 1991), 722.
2. Werner Keller, *The Bible As History* (New York: William Morrow and Co., 1956), 154.
3. Adapted from J. B. Fowler, Jr., *Illustrating Great Words of the New Testament* (Nashville: Broadman Press, 1991), 168.
4. J. B. Fowler Jr., *Illustrating Great Words of the New Testament* (Nashville: Broadman Press, 1991), 64.

# When Justice Is Corrupted

**Basic Passage:** 1 Kings 21
**Focal Passages:** 1 Kings 21:1-4, 15-20

The Old Testament stresses faith in the one true God. It also emphasizes that faith in God must show itself in ethical actions. Rival religions like Baal worship made no connection between their devotion to Baal and any requirement of moral behavior. By contrast, the worship of the Lord God of Israel required that worshipers reflect the qualities of the God they worshiped. They were to be righteous in actions and merciful toward others. The kings of Israel as well as the people were held to this high standard. Much of the history of Israel and Judah consists of confrontations between sinful kings and the prophets who boldly spoke the word of God. The classic confrontation is recorded in 1 Kings 21.

**Study Aim:** *To understand why God pronounces such terrible judgments on those guilty of injustice*

## STUDYING THE BIBLE

Naboth refused Ahab's offer to secure his vineyard (vv. 1-4). Jezebel used royal authority to intimidate judges and bribe witnesses against Naboth (vv. 5-10). Justice was corrupted and Naboth was murdered through judicial action (vv. 11-14). Jezebel told Ahab to go take possession of the vineyard (vv. 15-16). The Lord directed Elijah to pronounce judgment on Ahab (vv. 17-19). Elijah confronted Ahab and pronounced judgment on him and his family (vv. 20-24). Ahab and Jezebel were both guilty of great abominations (vv. 25-26). Ahab humbled himself, and the Lord delayed the doom coming on his family (vv. 27-29).

### I. Injustice and Associated Sins (1 Kings 21:1-16)

#### 1. Ahab covets Naboth's vineyard (vv. 1-4)

1 And it came to pass after these things, that Naboth the Jezreelite had a vineyard, which was in Jezreel, hard by the palace of Ahab king of Samaria.

2 And Ahab spake unto Naboth, saying, Give me thy vineyard, that I may have it for a garden of herbs, because it is near unto my house: and I will give thee for it a better vineyard than it; or, if it seem good to thee, I will give thee the worth of it in money.

3 And Naboth said to Ahab, The Lord forbid it me, that I

should give the inheritance of my fathers unto thee.

4 And Ahab came into his house heavy and displeased because of the word which Naboth the Jezreelite had spoken to him: for he had said, I will not give thee the inheritance of my fathers. And he laid him down upon his bed, and turned away his face, and would eat no bread.

Jezreel and Samaria were cities in the Northern Kingdom. Samaria, the capital of Israel, had been built by Ahab's father, Omri (1 Kings 16:23-24). King Ahab had palaces in both Samaria and Jezreel. Naboth, a citizen of Jezreel, had a vineyard that adjoined Ahab's palace in Jezreel. Ahab wanted ownership of Naboth's vineyard. He told Naboth that he wanted it to use as a vegetable garden. Ahab offered to trade Naboth a better vineyard for the one adjoining his property. Ahab told Naboth that if he preferred, the king would pay cash for the vineyard.

Naboth refused to part with the vineyard, which was his inheritance from his forefathers. Not only was Naboth within his rights to do this; but he also was obeying the law of God about family ownership of the land. The law commanded that a family's land not be sold. The basis for this was the fact that the Lord owned all the land and humans were only trustees (Lev. 25:23). Based on this commandment, families were to make every effort to keep land within the family or to buy back land that somehow had been lost (vv.24-28). Thus Naboth was obeying God's law and seeking to protect the land inherited from his ancestors so he could pass it along to his descendants.

Ahab became sullen and angry because of Naboth's refusal. Like a spoiled child who didn't get his way, he went to bed, turned his face to the wall, and refused to eat.

**2. Jezebel's plot to get Naboth's vineyard (vv. 5-10).**—Such pouting attracted Jezebel's attention. When Ahab explained why he was angry, she asked him if he wasn't the king of Israel. Her implication was that if he acted as a king, he could have whatever he wanted. She told him to get up, eat, and be happy because she would give him Naboth's vineyard.

She wrote letters in Ahab's name and with his royal seal. The letters went to the elders and nobles in Jezreel. They were told to proclaim a fast for some unnamed crisis. They also were told to set Naboth "on high" (v. 9), which means in a place of honor. They were to hire two evil men to testify that Naboth had blasphemed God and the king. Since blasphemy was a capital crime under the law (Ex. 22:28; Lev. 24:16), the people of Jezreel then were to stone Naboth to death.

**3. Legalized murder of Naboth (vv. 11-14).**—The elders and nobles constituted the judicial system in a town. The law prescribed that judges be fair and impartial (Deut. 16:18). Their job was to dispense justice. Yet the judges in Jezreel carried out Jezebel's instructions to the letter. They well knew the price for offending the ruthless Jezebel. If they refused, they would be accused of disobeying a royal decree. So they could rationalize that they were not accountable because they were just following orders.

**4. Ahab in Naboth's vineyard (vv. 15-16)**

15 And it came to pass, when Jezebel heard that Naboth was stoned, and was dead, that Jezebel said to Ahab, Arise, take possession of the vineyard of Naboth the Jezreelite, which he refused to give thee for money: for Naboth is not alive, but dead.

16 And it came to pass, when Ahab heard that Naboth was dead, that Ahab rose up to go down to the vineyard of Naboth the Jezreelite, to take possession of it.

We know from 2 Kings 9:26 that all of Naboth's sons were executed with their father. The legal justification of this was the belief that an entire family partook of the guilt of the father (see, for example, Josh. 7:19-25). From Jezebel's point of view, the entire family had to be killed so no one would be left to claim the family land. Either the property of executed criminals was forfeited to the crown, or Jezebel found some other way to confiscate the property.

Jezebel told her husband that Naboth was dead and that Ahab was free to take possession of the vineyard. She stated Naboth's stubborn refusal to sell the vineyard as if he was somehow to blame for his fate. Probably she and her fellow conspirators rationalized that such stubborn refusal of a royal request constituted nothing less than blasphemy. And if he blasphemed the king, that was the same as blaspheming God.

## II. God's Judgment on Injustice (1 Kings 21:17-29)

**1. God's word to Elijah (vv. 17-19)**

17 And the word of the Lord came to Elijah the Tishbite, saying,

18 Arise, go down to meet Ahab, king of Israel, which is in Samaria: behold, he is in the vineyard of Naboth, whither he is gone down to possess it.

19 And thou shalt speak unto him, saying, Thus saith the Lord, Hast thou killed, and also taken possession? And thou shalt speak unto him, saying, Thus saith the Lord, In the place where dogs licked the blood of Naboth shall dogs lick thy blood, even thine.

The Lord told Elijah that Ahab the king was going from Samaria to take possession of the vineyard in Jezreel. The Lord gave Elijah the message to deliver to Ahab. The Lord told Elijah not only to confront Ahab with his sins but also to pronounce judgment on him. The dogs of Jezreel would lick the blood of Ahab where they earlier had licked the blood of Naboth. This was literally fulfilled in 1 Kings 22:38.

The Lord set in motion a process that eventually brought judgment to Ahab, Jezebel, and his entire family. We are not told about the others who participated in this judicial murder, but the same God must have dealt also with them for their sins.

How much did Ahab know about how Jezebel got Naboth's vineyard? We are not told how much he knew about what she did. Since she used his name and seal, he must have known something. The word of the Lord to Ahab makes plain that the Lord held him fully accountable for what Jezebel and the others had done in his name.

All of it of course started with Ahab coveting the vineyard of Naboth. Never underestimate the seriousness of the Tenth Commandment. Look at how many other Commandments were broken as a result of covetousness. The Sixth Commandment (murder), the Eighth Commandment (stealing), and the Ninth Commandment (bearing false witness) were all broken. Verse 19 accuses Ahab of killing Naboth and of stealing ("taken possession") his vineyard. The trial was based on a conspiracy and lies about an innocent man.

**2. Elijah pronounces judgment on Ahab (vv. 20-24)**

> **20 And Ahab said to Elijah, Hast thou found me, O mine enemy? And he answered, I have found thee: because thou hast sold thyself to work evil in the sight of the Lord.**

Imagine the scene described here. Ahab had been enjoying inspecting his new vineyard. Suddenly he looked up and saw Elijah. He greeted the prophet with a sneering question in which he referred to Elijah as his enemy. In their earlier confrontation during the drought, Ahab had called Elijah "he that troubleth Israel" (1 Kings 18:17). Now he saw Elijah not just as a troubler of the nation but also as his personal enemy.

In the previous confrontation, Elijah had accused Ahab of being the real troubler of Israel (v.18). Here he confronted Ahab with his sins, which he thought had been hidden. The double use of "found" by Ahab and Elijah reminds us of the biblical warning, "Be sure your sin will find you out" (Num. 32:23). The point is not just that the Lord sees our sins but also that something in the sin itself will bring judgment. It is the principle of reaping what we sow (Gal. 6:7-8).

Another striking phrase is "sold thyself." Ahab had sold himself to become a slave of his evil actions. Jesus spoke of sin as self-imposed slavery (John 8:34). Ahab had sold himself for a vineyard. Others have sold themselves for much less. Even if we were able to sell ourselves for the whole world, it would be a bad bargain (Matt. 16:26).

Elijah proceeded to tell Ahab that all his sons would be killed. His royal house would go the same way as the previous dynasties of Israel. The body of Jezebel would be eaten by the dogs of Jezreel.

**3. Sins of Ahab and Jezebel (vv. 25-26).**—No king's sins were worse than the sins of Ahab and Jezebel, who urged him on. Their abominations were comparable to the terrible sins of the Amorites whom the Lord cast out of Canaan.

**4. Ahab's humiliation and postponement of doom (vv. 27-29).**—The word of God had some effect on Ahab. He humbled himself in sackcloth. The Lord told Elijah that because Ahab humbled himself, the judgment on his sons would be postponed until his son's reign. Thus several years passed between Ahab's death and the deaths of Jezebel and Ahab's sons, but the bloody judgment eventually came (2 Kings 9–10).

## APPLYING THE BIBLE

**Covetousness is no little sin.**—Covetousness, which was Ahab and Jezebel's problem (vv. 1-4), is not a sin that God takes lightly. Its importance is magnified by the fact that it is lasted among the Ten Commandments (Ex. 20:17).

Virginia Ely has some things to say about covetousness that we need to hear:

1. It is idolatry (Eph. 5:5; Ex. 20:17).
2. It is never satisfied (Eccl. 5:10; Phil. 4:1).
3. It is inconsistent in Christians (Heb. 13:5).
4. It leads to injustice (Mic. 2:2).
5. It leads to foolish lusts (1 Tim. 6:9).
6. It leads to untruthfulness (2 Kings 5:20-27).
7. It leads to murder (Ezek. 22:12).
8. It leads to theft (Josh. 7:21).
9. It leads to poverty (Prov. 28:22).
10. It leads to family trouble (Prov. 15:27).[1]

Ahab and Jezebel's sin of covetousness was far-reaching and tragic. Look at what it cost them, Naboth, and others.

**The genius who looked like a thief.**—Dr. George A. Gordon, pastor of the Old South Congregational Church in Boston, was a very well-known minister in his day. On one of his early trips across the Atlantic, Gordon was assigned a cabin mate who was crippled, hunchbacked, and who looked like a deformed dwarf. Going to the purser, Gordon put all his valuables in the purser's hands and asked that they be locked up in the safe so they would not be stolen by his cabin mate. Much to Dr. Gordon's surprise, the purser told Gordon that his cabin mate had brought his valuables in a few minutes earlier with the same request.

Later, Dr. Gordon and the man, Dr. Charles Steinmetz, became the best of friends. The little, deformed, crippled man was neither a thief nor a robber. He became one of America's greatest scientists who is best remembered for his development of the theory of alternating currents and for experimenting with "man-made lightning."

Steinmetz, a Ph.D. from Germany, went to work for General

Electric where he spent the remainder of his career in research on electricity. They paid him a fabulous salary for that day only to "tinker around" and see what he could discover.

Appearances are often deceiving, as we well know. One doesn't know what Jezebel looked like—she may have been a strikingly beautiful woman. But we know about her character: at heart she was a thief, and she didn't hesitate to shed blood to get her way (vv. 5-14).[2]

**Greed brings death.**—There's an old Persian legend about a father who went on a long journey and left his son with a mirror to entertain himself. When the father returned, he discovered that the boy had starved to death looking at himself in the mirror. Moral: Self-centeredness and greed have tragic consequences.

Their greed and self-centeredness not only cost Naboth his life, but ultimately it cost Ahab and Jezebel their lives.

**Judgment day comes sooner than we think.**—A slick, Scottish lawyer rented a horse and either by accident or mistreatment killed the horse. When the owner learned about the death of his horse, naturally he was very upset and wanted to be compensated for his loss.

The lawyer asked the owner of the deceased animal if he would accept a promissory note. The man replied that he would be glad to do so, but the lawyer insisted that he be given time—too much time, in fact—to make restitution. The trusting farmer told the lawyer what he needed to hear. He drew up the proper papers indicating that the debt would be due and payable on judgment day. When the farmer saw he was being swindled, he took the matter to court and the judge ruled that the promissory note was valid and that the debt should, indeed, be paid on judgment day. He then decreed, "Judgment day is tomorrow!"[3]

Judgment day came for Ahab and Jezebel all too soon (vv. 17-29: 22:34-38; 2 Kings 9:30-37). Judgment upon sin comes upon all who do not repent.

## TEACHING THE BIBLE

▶ *Main Idea:* When justice is corrupted God pronounces terrible judgments on those guilty of practicing injustice.

▶ *Suggested Teaching Aim:* To lead adults to examine God's judgment on Ahab for taking Naboth's vineyard, and to correct injustices in their community.

### A TEACHING OUTLINE

*1. Make a chart to guide the study of the lesson.*

*2. Make an assignment to have a member summarize a Scripture.*

*3. Use DISCUSSION QUESTIONS to apply the Scripture material.*

*4. Identify how members can correct social injustices in their community.*

### Introduce the Bible Study

Begin the lesson by sharing the illustration "Judgment day comes sooner than we think" *(Applying the Bible)*.

### Search for Biblical Truth

IN ADVANCE, write the following on a chalkboard or a large sheet of paper:

WHEN JUSTICE IS CORRUPTED

| Character | Action |
|---|---|
| Ahab | |
| Naboth | |
| Jezebel | |
| Elijah | |

Ask members to open their Bibles to 1 Kings 21:1-4. Call for a volunteer to read these verses as members look for the following: (1) where the event took place (Jezreel); (2) the two characters involved (Ahab and Naboth); (3) what Ahab requested (Naboth's vineyard); (4) Naboth's response (refused because it was his family's land and the law forbade selling it), and (5) what was Ahab's response (sulked)? On the chart under "Ahab's Action" write: *coveted Naboth's vineyard.* On the chart under "Naboth's Actions" write: *refused to sell family land.*

DISCUSSION QUESTIONS: How important is your family's religious heritage? Why?

IN ADVANCE, enlist a member to summarize 21:5-14. Call on that person at this point. Add any additional information members may need from Studying the Bible. Under Jezebel's Actions on the chart write: *plotted to murder Naboth.*

DISCUSSION QUESTION: What kind of manipulation and ignoring of others' rights have you participated in to get your way? Summarize the material in *Studying the Bible* on 21:15-16. Under Ahab's Actions write: *possessed vineyard.*

DISCUSSION QUESTION: How willing have you been to benefit by the evil plans executed by someone else?

Ask members to read silently 21:17-20. Explain that Elijah's message came from God and that his prophecy came true literally (1 Kings 22:38). Under Elijah's Actions write: *confronted and condemned Ahab.*

DISCUSSION QUESTIONS: Do you think people take seriously the Tenth Commandment? Why? How significant a Commandment is it today?

### Give the Truth a Personal Focus

On a chalkboard or a large sheet of paper write at the top: *Society.* Ask members to suggest social injustices that are apparent in their community as you list these.

Ask: What do you feel is the responsibility of the church in dealing with these injustices? What is your personal responsibility? What can we do about one of these as a Sunday School class?

(You many need to appoint a ministry group to do some research and report back to the class next Sunday.)

Close with a time of prayer. Ask members to turn to someone near them and share a particular request they have so that God might use them this week to correct an injustice in their world. Let the members pray together in teams and then leave the room quietly without disturbing those still praying.

---

1. Adapted from Virginia Ely, *Devotion for Personal and Group Worship* (Westwood, New Jersey: Fleming H. Revell Co., 1960), 24-25.

2. Adapted from William L. Stidger, *There Are Sermons in Stories* (New York, Nashville: Abingdon-Cokesbury Press, 1942), 130-132.

3. Adapted from Walter B. Knight, *Knight's Master Book of New Illustrations* (Grand Rapids: William B. Eerdmans Publishing Co., 1956), 350-351.

# A Day of Good News

**Basic Passage:** 2 Kings 6:24—7:20
**Focal Passage:** 2 Kings 7:1-9

The Bible is a book of good news. The word translated *gospel* in many English translations literally means "good news." The good news of God burst with full glory in the coming, life, death, and resurrection of Jesus Christ (see, for example, Luke 2:10; Matt. 4:23; 1 Cor. 15:1-4; Rom. 1:16). This session contains a famous Old Testament verse about the importance of telling good news. The words were spoken by four unnamed lepers outside the besieged city of Samaria during the time of Elisha.

**Study Aim:** *To resolve to tell the good news of God's deliverances and blessings*

## STUDYING THE BIBLE

The Syrian army laid siege to the city of Samaria (6:24). The resulting famine produced conditions that shocked the king (vv.25-29). The king of Israel swore to kill the prophet Elisha (vv.30-31). The message of the king to Elisha showed the king's anger toward God (vv.32-33). Elisha predicted that by the next day conditions would have returned to normal in the city (7:1-2). Four lepers decided they had nothing to lose by going into the camp of the Syrians (vv.3-4). The lepers discovered an empty camp because the Lord had frightened the Syrians into flight (vv.5-7). The lepers ate, drank, and began looting the amp (v.8). The lepers, who began to feel guilty, decided to tell the good news to the people in Samaria vv.:9-11). The king suspected a trap but sent scouts, who reported that the Syrians had fled across the Jordan (vv.12-15). The people plundered the camp and Elisha's prophecy was fulfilled (vv.16-20).

### I. A City Under Siege (6:24—7:2)

**1. Samaria besieged by the Syrians (6:24).**—During this period of the history of the Northern Kingdom, their chief military enemy was the kingdom of Syria (see 1 Kings 20; 22; 2 Kings 5; 6:8-23). The Syrian king Benhadad sent his army against Israel and besieged Samaria, the capital of Israel.

A siege was a normal strategy of warfare in that day. Cities were built behind strong walls. Thus attackers were discouraged from a frontal assault. Instead, the invading army surrounded the city and waited until the city's provisions ran out.

**2. Terrible conditions during the siege (6:25-27).**—Samaria was not well-prepared to withstand a lengthy siege. Soon the people were reduced to starvation. The most disgusting kinds of food were being sold at exorbitant prices. Even worse, some of the people were resorting to cannibalism. As the king, probably Jehoram (1 Kings 22:40; 2 Kings 1:12-17), inspected the wall, a woman asked for his help. She told a horrible tale which revealed that mothers were eating their own children.

**3. The king's anger at Elisha (6:30-31).**—When he heard what the woman said, the king tore his clothes. The people saw that he wore sackcloth under his clothes, sackcloth being the traditional sign of mourning. Then the king swore to kill Elisha the prophet (see 2 Kings 2:1-20; 5; 6:8-23). Why did Jehoram want to kill Elisha? Second Kings 6:33 shows that the king blamed God for the siege. Since Elisha was the prophet of the Lord, the king felt that he had either caused the famine or had done nothing to deliver the people from it.

**5. The king's anger at God (6:32-33).**—The king sent a messenger to Elisha. The prophet, who was with the elders, predicted the coming of the messenger. Elisha said that the murderous king intended to behead him. When the messenger arrived, he delivered the king's message. The king blamed God for the siege and starvation, and he had given up any hope of divine deliverance.

**6. Elisha's prophecy of normal conditions (7:1-2)**

> **1 Then Elisha said, Hear ye the word of the Lord; Thus saith the Lord, Tomorrow about this time shall a measure of fine flour be sold for a shekel, and two measures of barley for a shekel, in the gate of Samaria.**
>
> **2 Then a lord on whose hand the king leaned answered the man of God, and said, Behold, if the Lord would make windows in heaven, might this be? And he said, Behold, thou shalt see it with thine eyes, but shalt not eat thereof.**

Elisha's response to the king's anger against God was to make a calm prediction about the return to normal conditions within a day. Contrast the conditions described in 7:1 with the conditions of 6:25. The inedible food would be replaced with flour and barley. The ridiculously high prices would return to normal.

The prophet didn't explain how this miracle would take place by the next day. Verse 2 reports the response of one of the king's officers to Elisha's prophecy. The officer said that Elisha's prophecy couldn't happen even if God made windows in heaven. Elisha then said that the officer would see the fulfillment of the prophecy but not partake of any of the food.

## II. The Siege Lifted by the Lord (7:3-20)

**1. Decision of four lepers (7:3-4)**

> **3 And there were four leprous men at the entering in of the gate: and they said one to another, why sit we here until we die?**
>
> **4 If we say, We will enter into the city, then the famine is in the city, and we shall die there: and if we sit still here, we die also. Now therefore come, and let us fall unto the host of the**

Syrians: if they save us alive, we shall live; and if they kill us, we shall but die.

Lepers were considered unclean by Jewish law. As a result, they were isolated from the rest of the community (Lev. 13:1-46). These four unnamed lepers thus lived outside the walls of Samaria. Their plight was bad enough under normal conditions. They lived mostly from the leftovers and garbage of the city. During a famine, there was no garbage.

They considered their options. As they saw it, they had three options. They could enter the city, stay where they were, or go to the camp of the Syrians. If they entered the city, they would starve with everyone else. If they stayed where they were, they would starve. If they went to the Syrian camp, one of two things might happen. The Syrians might feed them, or they might kill them. Since they were going to die anyway, a quick death at the hands of the Syrians seemed better than slowly starving to death.

**2. What the lepers discovered (7:5-7)**

5 And they rose up in the twilight, to go unto the camp of the Syrians: and when they were come to the uttermost part of the camp of Syria, behold, there was no man there.

6 For the Lord had made the host of the Syrians to hear a noise of chariots, and a noise of horses, even the noise of a great host: and they said one to another, Lo, the king of Israel hath hired against us the kings of the Hittites, and the kings of the Egyptians, to come upon us.

7 Wherefore they arose and fled in the twilight, and left their tents, and their horses, and their asses, even the camp as it was, and fled for their life.

At twilight the four lepers went toward the camp of the Syrians. When they reached the edge of the camp, the lepers were surprised to find no one there.

Verses 6-7 inform readers what had happened. The Lord had caused the Syrian army to hear what sounded like many chariots approaching. They concluded that the king of Israel had hired the Hittites and the Egyptians to swoop down upon the Syrians. This rumor caused the Syrians to panic and flee, leaving behind everything in the camp.

**3. Lepers looting the camp (7:8)**

8 And when these lepers came to the uttermost part of the camp, they went into one tent, and did eat and drink, and carried thence silver, and gold, and raiment, and went and hid it; and came again, and entered into another tent, and carried thence also, and went and hid it.

The hungry lepers were at first most interested in the abundance of food in the Syrian camp. They went into one tent and ate and drank their fill. Then they began to notice the gold, silver, and costly clothes in the tent. They loaded themselves down with this wealth, and took it and hid it.

Then they entered another tent and repeated the process of carrying out the silver, gold, and costly garments. They took these and hid them also.

**4. A day of good news (7:9-11)**

> **9 Then they said one to another, We do not well: this day is a day of good tidings, and we hold our peace: if we tarry till the morning light, some mischief will come upon us: now therefore come, that we may go and tell the king's household.**

After looting and hiding the contents of the second tent, the lepers began to feel guilty. As they talked about their feelings, they all agreed that what they were doing was not right. They had stumbled into an empty camp filled with food and unbelievable wealth. Although their first actions had been to eat their fill and hide some of the wealth, they remembered that the people of nearby Samaria were starving to death. The lepers had good news to tell. The people of Samaria could not have imagined any better news than they had to tell. Yet so far they had filled only their own stomachs.

These lepers knew enough about the religion of Israel to believe that one's sins will eventually find him out (Num. 32:23). The word translated "mischief" can mean either "iniquity" or "punishment for iniquity." Sin carries within itself the seeds of its own punishment. The lepers feared that if they delayed until morning, some punishment would come on them for their sin.

Notice that this was a sin of omission. They were not responsible for the starvation of Samaria. They themselves had harmed no one, but they had the means of helping starving people. Failing to tell the good news was a serious sin.

The application to sharing the Christian good news is obvious. We have found in Christ salvation and riches beyond compare. All about us people are perishing. We have good news to tell. Failing to tell the perishing of the Savior is a sin.

The lepers decided to do something about their good fortune and their guilt for not sharing it. They went and told the gatekeepers, who in turn told the good news to the servants to the king.

**5. Testing the good news (7:12-15).**—The king, suspecting a trick by the Syrians, thought that the Syrians planned an ambush. The king agreed to send scouts on the few horses remaining in Samaria. The scouts tracked the fleeing Syrians and the ground littered with discarded equipment. The scouts returned to say that the Syrians had fled beyond the Jordan River.

**6. Fulfillment of Elisha's prophecy (7:16-20).**—The starving Israelites rushed out and plundered the Syrian camp. As a result, food became so plentiful that by the next day the food and prices were exactly as Elisha had predicted. The king's officer who earlier had expressed such unbelief, lived to see the abundant food, but he did not live to eat of it. He was trampled by the crowds of people. Thus Elisha's prophecy was completely fulfilled.

## APPLYING THE BIBLE

**Telling the good news.**—Dr. Norman Vincent Peale, former pastor of the Marble Collegiate Church in New York City, was one of America's best-known ministers. The author of numerous books, including *The Power of Positive Thinking,* Peale was born the son of a Methodist minister in 1898.

Peale confessed that his preaching was begun "on shaky legs." Terrified at the thought of public speaking, Peale wired his minister father for help, and his father wired back: "Prepare your own sermons. Just tell the people that Jesus Christ can change their lives. Love, Dad."

That is the good news on which our lesson today focuses. This is "A Day of Good News" because Jesus Christ can and will change the life of one who trusts Him and walks with Him by faith.

**Who in the world was Benhadad?**—It will help us in our lesson today to know with whom we are dealing. Benhadad is used in the Bible both as a personal name and as a royal title. It means "son of Hadad." Hadad, a stormgod, was one of the gods of the Syrians. "The kings either bore a title, 'ben hadad,' son of the god, much like Israel's kings seem to have been called 'son of God' at their coronation (Ps. 2:7) and as emperors of Rome were called "caesars,' or Benhadad was the personal name of several kings."[1]

Although "Benhadad" is used in the Old Testament with reference to three Syrian kings, in 842 B.C. This Benhadad succeeded his father, King Hazael, as king of Syria.

**Do you want to know more about Samaria?**—Perhaps you know everything you want to know about Samaria, but for those who are interested here is some additional information from the *Holman Bible Dictionary:* While Benhadad was king of Syria, he besieged Samaria twice, both times unsuccessfully (1 Kings 20; 2 Kings 6). Samaria was forty-two miles north of Jerusalem and was the capital residence and burial place of the kings of Israel (1 Kings 16:23-28; 22:37; 2 Kings 6:24-30). After the Northern Kingdom (Israel) fell to Assyria in 721 B.C., exiles from many nations settled Samaria (Ezra 4:9-10). It was the only major city founded by Israel, the Northern Kingdom. Omri, Israel's sixth king, purchased the hill of Samaria for his royal residence. Israel's King Ahab, influenced by his wicked wife Jezebel, made this city the center for Baal worship (1 Kings16:29-33). Jezebel also had many prophets of Yahweh killed in Samaria (18:2-4). During the reign of Omri (885-874 B.C.), the name became identified with the entire region surrounding the city, the tribal territory of Manasseh and Ephraim. The name became synonymous for the entire Northern Kingdom (13:32).[2]

**Suffering cleanses and purges.**—It is inconceivable that one would think the gracious and gentle Heavenly Father gets any joy out of seeing His people suffer. Although sin always brings suffering, God uses it to cleanse and purge His people. As it was so in Israel's history, we have discovered it to be so in our lives as well.

Henry Drummond (1851-1897) was a Scottish evangelist probably best remembered for his marvelous little book titled *The Greatest Thing in the World.* It is a treatment of 1 Corinthians 13. Everyone ought to have a copy of it.

Sent to Africa by the African Lakes Company on a scientific assignment, Drummond saw suffering firsthand. He had never had any close contact with bereavement and had never been lonely. But in Africa he saw the graves of the heroes and heroines of the faith such as Mrs. David Livingstone. Then he fell sick and for a month, with the sun making his tent unmercifully hot and the clouds deluging him with rain, he despaired for his life.

When Drummond got back to Scotland, friends noticed gray in his hair and commented to him about it. "I've been in an atmosphere of death," Drummond would reply. But that terrible experience of personal suffering and seeing the suffering of Christ's servants in Africa colored the remainder of his life. It strengthened his faith. It broadened his mind. It mellowed and deepened his compassion. Through suffering, he learned what he would never have learned otherwise.[3]

## TEACHING THE BIBLE

▶ *Main Idea:* The lepers' declaration of good news demonstrates how we should share the good news of God's deliverance and blessings.

▶ *Suggested Teaching Aim:* To lead adults to examine how God delivered Israel from the Syrians, and to identify a way they will share the good news of Christ with one person.

### A TEACHING OUTLINE

*1. Sing a hymn about good news.*
*2. Organize the class in three groups to examine the Scripture.*
*3. List ways members can share the good news of God.*

**Introduce the Bible Study**

Introduce the Bible study by singing or reading the words to "Tell the Good News" (No. 566, *The Baptist Hymnal,* 1991).

Point out that today's lesson is entitled "A Day of Good News."

**Search for Biblical Truth**

IN ADVANCE, enlist a member to present the information in "Do you want to know more about Samaria?" *(Applying the Bible).*

Organize the class in three groups and make the following assignments. Allow time for study and then call for reports.

**Group I–**

INSTRUCTIONS: Read 2 Kings 6:24—7:20 and answer the following questions about the *king.*

(1) Who was king of Israel? *(probably Jehoram)*

(2) What was the capital city of the Northern Kingdom? *(Samaria)* [Call on the person enlisted to share the information on Samaria.]

(3) What political crisis threatened Israel? *(invasion by the Aram [AY ram] or Syrian army under Benhadad)* Locate Syria on a map.

(4) Why was the king angry with Elisha? *(The king blamed God for the siege—2 Kings 6:33—and Elisha was God's prophet.)*

(5) What threat did the king make against Elisha? *(to kill him)*

(6) What did the king's attitude toward God show? *(king had given up on divine deliverance)*

**Group 2–**

INSTRUCTIONS: Read 2 Kings 6:24—7:20 and answer the following questions about *Elisha.*

(1) How did Elisha know the king threatened to kill him? *(God revealed it)*

(2) What prediction did Elisha make about the end of the siege? *(would end in a day)*

(3) What sign did Elisha give that the siege would end? *(food would be sold at normal prices)*

(4) What prophecy did Elisha give to the king's advisor? *(would see the siege end but would not eat food)*

**Group 3–**

INSTRUCTIONS: Read 2 Kings 6:24—7:20 and answer the following questions about the *lepers.*

(1) How many lepers were there? *(four)*

(2) Why were they outside the city? *(shut out because of their disease)*

(3) What led them to the Syrian camp? *(decided possible slaughter by syrians better than certain starvation)*

(4) What did they find? *(Syrian army fled across Jordan)*

(5) What was the lepers' response? *(ate, looted, then told Israelites)*

(6) What happened when they told the king? *(King was skeptical but investigated; the people rushed out to the Syrian camp and trampled the king's advisor to death)*

### Give the Truth a Personal Focus

Ask, What good news do you know? List all the suggestions on a chalkboard or a large sheet of paper. Put an asterisk beside all those that deal specifically with God's deliverance and blessings. Ask members to suggest steps they can take to share this good news with others.

---

1. *Holman Bible Dictionary* (Nashville: Holman Bible Publishers, 1991), 165.
2. Ibid., 1224.
3. Adapted from Thomas Jefferson Villers, *The Hurry Call of Jesus* (Philadelphia: Judson Press, 1927), 57-58.

# Condemnation of National Wrongdoing

**Basic Passage:** Amos 1:1—3:2
**Focal Passages:** Amos 2:4-8; 3:1-2

We have been studying two of the greatest nonwriting prophets of Israel: Elijah and Elisha. Now we will begin a study of the four great eighth-century writing prophets: Amos, Hosea, Micah, and Isaiah. The first two directed their messages to the Northern Kingdom; the last two spoke primarily to the Southern Kingdom. All of them ministered in the final century of the life of the Northern Kingdom. Our focus in this session will be on the condemnation of national sins—especially Israel's sins—by Amos.

**Study Aim:** *To recognize the sins for which God brought judgment on Israel*

## STUDYING THE BIBLE

### I. Introduction to Amos (Amos 1:1-2)

Amos, a herdsman from Tekoa in Judah, was called to preach to the Northern Kingdom of Israel. He preached during the reign of Jeroboam II (787-746 B.C.). This was a period of superficial prosperity. The sins of this time contributed to Israel's final plunge toward ruin. Amos was a plainspoken man whom God called to pronounce judgment on Israel. The voice of God in judgment sounded to Amos like the roar of an angry lion.

### II. Sins of Other Nations (Amos 1:3—2:5)

**1. Sins of pagan nations (1:3—2:3).**—Many people like to hear about the sins of others. They especially like to hear about the sins of other nations. Amos captured the attention of his audience in Israel by condemning the sins of other nations. He began by condemning one at a time the sins of six pagan nations who were Israel's neighbors, and often Israel's enemies or competitors.

Amos condemned Damascus or Syria for their brutal treatment of captives in Gilead. They ran over their captives with threshing instruments, which were equipped with jagged iron spikes (1:3-5).

Amos condemned Gaza and the Philistines for selling into slavery an entire group of people (vv.6-8). Selling anyone into slavery was evil, but selling an entire nation was worse. No free people were left to continue the nation. Amos condemned Tyre and the Phoenicians for a similar crime, selling an entire people to Edom (vv.9-10).
Edomites, the descendants of Esau, were condemned for their

perpetual hatred against their brother, the descendants of Jacob (vv.11-12). Throughout their history, the Edomites did hateful things against the Israelites.

Amos pronounced judgment on the Ammonites, descendants of Lot, for atrocities against pregnant women during fighting in Gilead (vv.13-15). Amos condemned the Moabites, also descendants of Lot, for sacrilege against the bodies of the kings of Edom (2:1-3). Either they killed the kings and then burned their bodies, or they exhumed the bodies and burned them.

**2. Judgment against Judah (2:4-5)**

> **4 Thus saith the Lord; For three transgressions of Judah, and for four, I will not turn away the punishment thereof; because they have despised the law of the Lord, and have not kept his commandments, and their lies caused them to err, after the which their fathers walked.**
>
> **5 But I will send a fire upon Judah, and it shall devour the palaces of Jerusalem.**

All eight of the pronouncements of judgment in Amos 1—2 begin with the same formula about transgressions. The numbers are used symbolically. "Three" stands for enough, full, or complete. "Four" stands for more than enough. The point is not that each of these nations had committed only four transgressions. The point is that each nation had committed more than enough sins for God's patience to run out and for judgment to come. Amos did not claim to name all their transgressions, but he named one that was typical of many sins committed by each nation.

The sin of Judah was that the people despised the law of the Lord and turned to the lies of idolatry. The people of the six pagan nations had sinned against what should have been a common moral code of all nations. The Lord held them accountable for breaking that common moral code. How much more accountable were the people of Judah, to whom the Lord had given His law for moral guidance. If the pagan nations were guilty, how much more guilty were the people of Judah?

Amos did not name the time when the fires of judgment would sweep through Judah and Jerusalem. As it turned out, the fires came almost two centuries after the time of Amos; but come they did!

We are not told how the audience of Israelites responded as they heard Amos denounce the sins of their pagan neighbors and of Judah. Very likely, they greeted the prophet's words with smug approval. They were often enemies or at least rivals of all these nations, including Judah. They probably resented the holier-than-thou attitude of the people of Judah about having the sacred temple. By condemning the sins of others, Amos prepared the way for the condemnation of Israel's own sins. This was the part of the prophet's sermon that his audience didn't want to hear.

## III. Judgments Against Israel (Amos 2:6-16)

### 1. Israel's transgressions (2:6-8)

6 Thus saith the Lord; For three transgressions of Israel, and for four, I will not turn away the punishment thereof; because they sold the righteous for silver, and the poor for a pair of shoes.

7 That pant after the dust of the earth on the head of the poor, and turn aside the way of the meek: and a man and his father will go in unto the same maid, to profane my holy name:

8 And they lay themselves down upon clothes laid to pledge by every altar, and they drink the wine of the condemned in the house of their god.

When Amos condemned the other seven nations, the prophet named only one typical sin of each nation. However, when he condemned Israel, Amos listed a number of their sins. By doing this, the prophet was saying that Israel's many transgressions were far more than enough to call for divine judgment.

The word "sold" in verse 6 is often used in the Old Testament of someone being sold into slavery. For example, this was the word used when Joseph's brothers sold him as a slave (Gen. 37:27-28). Debtors who could not pay their debts were sometimes sold as slaves by their rich creditors. These particular debtors are referred to as "righteous." This means that their cause was righteous and that they were treated unjustly. Probably the rich creditors had used a position of wealth and power to influence everything to their own even greater profit.

The word "poor" in verse 7 is often translated "needy." It is a different word than the word "poor" in verse 8. The two words are often found together, generally in one of the many commandments not to oppress the poor and needy, but to care for them (Deut. 15:11; 24:14). In spite of such clear words from the Lord, some people not only sold the righteous for silver but sold the needy for as little as a pair of shoes.

The first part of verse 8 has puzzled Bible students. In what sense did the Israelites "pant after the dust of the earth on the head of the poor"? The point may be that the rich were so landhungry that they begrudged the poor even the dust that settled on their head. More likely, the point is that the rich rejoiced when the poor had dust on their head. Putting dust on one's head was a sign of grief in that day. Thus, a poor man in mourning often meant a man who was in dire economic straits. Predatory people saw the poor man's grief as their opportunity. They circled him like buzzards waiting for their prey to die.

Another way to describe the same sin is that they "turn aside the way of the meek." The "meek" is the righteous but poor person. His "way" refers to his case in court or his need for some other kind of help. When the meek sought the help of the greedy predators of their day, the meek were turned aside. Their needs and pleas were ignored. Actually their pleas were music to the ears of the greedy predators.

The last part of verse 7 may refer to a father and a son using a helpless young slave as their common concubine. Or it may refer to their participation in the sexual immorality that was part of Baal worship. Each had sex with the same woman. Either of these immoral practices would "profane" God's holy name.

Verse 8 describes sexual terrible sins. First of all, the Israelites were worshiping other gods. Second, they were practicing sexual immorality as part of this pagan worship. Third, they were using in pagan worship items taken from poor and needy people.

Debtors often gave garments as pledges that they would repay their debts. The law forbade a creditor keeping the cloak of a poor man overnight (Ex. 22:26-27). The cloak often served as his only cover against the cold of the night. Thus these immoral worshipers were also greedy predators who used the poor man's cloak to lie on during sexual immorality. Similarly, they bought wine with money collected in fines extorted from the righteous poor, when the poor were unjustly "condemned."

**2. God's acts of deliverance for Israel (2:9-11).**—Amos followed this terrible litany of transgressions with a reminder of how God had blessed Israel. He had brought them out of Egypt, led them in the wilderness, and driven out the Amorites so Israel could have the promised land. God had raised up prophets and Nazarites to guide the people.

**3. Sins and inescapable judgment (2:12-16).**—The Israelites had tried to get the Nazarites drunk and tried to silence the prophets. The burden of their sin had reached the breaking point. Judgment would be inescapable for the evildoers of Israel. The swift would not be able to outrun the coming judgment. The strong would not be able to deliver themselves from divine judgment.

## IV. Israel's Election and Responsibility (Amos 3:1-2)

> **1 Hear this word that the Lord hath spoken against you, O children of Israel, against the whole family which I brought up from the land of Egypt, saying,**
> **2 You only have I known of all the families of the earth: therefore I will punish you for all your iniquities.**

The people of Israel strongly agreed with the first part of verse 2. They cherished the fact that God had chosen them to be His people. However, they totally misunderstood what was involved in being God's people. They viewed it primarily as a special privilege that bound God to bless and protect them. They failed to hear what their own covenant obligations were.

God had already made plain through Amos 1:3—2:3 that God holds all nations accountable for basic human decency. He holds His own people far more accountable, exactly because they are His people. He called and blessed them in order that they might glorify His name by their words and deeds. When their actions instead profane His name, God will call His people to judgment.

## APPLYING THE BIBLE

**When God's patience runs out.**—Robert G. Ingersoll (1833-1899) was an American lawyer and politician. Also, for nearly thirty years, Ingersoll, who claimed to be an agnostic, attacked the Christian faith. Ingersoll is well remembered for his lectures in which he would hold up his watch and declare pompously: "God, if there is a God, strike me dead within five minutes." Carefully watching his watch as the minutes ticked away, Ingersoll would then declare he had proved there was no God. In response to Ingersoll's impertinence, Christian minister Theodore Parker said about Ingersoll's antics: "Does the gentleman think that he could exhaust the patience of the Eternal God in five minutes?"

God is patient and long-suffering with us sinners as the Bible clearly declares (Ps. 103). But as the lesson points out today, there is an end to the patience of God (2:4-5). God is always eager to forgive, but when that forgiveness is not sought and accepted judgment comes.

**Coming judgment ignored.**—Gaius Plinius Secundus, better known in history as Pliny the Elder, died in the eruption of the Italian volcano Mount Vesuvius in A.D. 79. He is best remembered in history for his thirty-seven-volume natural history which survives today.

When the volcano began to erupt, Pliny's Roman fleet—for he was an admiral—was anchored near Pompeii. As the billowing black smoke and ashes descended on Pompeii and Herculaneum, Pliny's friends begged him to flee for his life. But he refused and stayed to help the fleeing refugees. As the urgings continued, Pliny, unconcerned about his welfare, continued to say to his imploring friends: "It will be all right. It will be all right. It will be all right."

But it wasn't all right. If Pliny had listened to his concerned friends, he would have survived. But he didn't and died entombed in the molten lava that flowed down the sides of the rumbling mountain.[1]

Amos prophesied that God would not only judge the pagan nations surrounding Judah and Israel, but His judgments would also fall upon Israel and Judah unless they repented. They also waited too late.

**Good-bye, God!**—Aaron Burr (1756-1836) was vice president of the United States from 1801-1805 under President Thomas Jefferson. Both Burr's father and grandfather were presidents of what is now Princeton University. Burr's grandfather was the noted colonial preacher Jonathan Edwards. Burr was graduated from Princeton in 1772.

During his student days at Princeton, a great spiritual awakening swept the campus and Burr went to President John Witherspoon for spiritual counsel. Witherspoon discouraged Burr from getting too caught up in the "emotion" of the revival, and Burr made no public commitment to Christ. One account of what followed—whether true one cannot really know—relates that Burr went back to his dormitory room, threw open the window, and shouted out across the campus, "Good-bye, God!"

Aaron Burr finally came to a bad end. After having served as vice president and in the House of Representatives, Burr was defeated by Alexander Hamilton for the governorship of New York in 1804. Burr was so incensed by the defeat that he challenged Hamilton to a duel on July 11, 1804, and Hamilton was fatally wounded. Grand juries in both New Jersey and New York indicted Burr for murder, but he fled south before he could be arrested. Returning to Washington when Congress reconvened, Vice-president Burr presided over the term until it ended. Later, he was arrested in New Orleans for treason but was acquitted in 1807. He lived in Europe for awhile but returned to the United States in 1812 and lived under an assumed name, practiced law, and died in 1836.[2]

By their actions, both Judah and Israel lived out Burr's supposed statement, "Good-bye, God!" And tragedy followed in the wake of Judah and Israel's decision to live without regard to God's word and commandments.

## TEACHING THE BIBLE

▶ *Main Idea:* Amos' condemnation of national wrongdoing demonstrates that God judges those who disobey Him.

▶ *Suggested Teaching Aim:* To lead adults to examine the sins for which God judged Israel, and to identify and eliminate similar sins in their lives.

### A TEACHING OUTLINE

*1. Make an advanced assignment on the prophet Amos.*
*2. Identify the sins of Israel's surrounding pagan neighbors and Judah.*
*3. Identify Israel's sins.*
*4. Identify sins in their life similar to Israel's and ask God for His forgiveness.*

**Introduce the Bible Study**

Read Luke 12:48. Ask members if they would agree with that statement. Point out that this is the basis of today's lesson.

**Search for Biblical Truth**

IN ADVANCE, enlist a member to read "Amos," in the *Holman Bible Dictionary* or another bible dictionary and prepare a two- to three-minute report on Amos to introduce this lesson.

On a chalkboard or a large sheet of paper, write the following headings (Cover the last two titles with strips of paper until you are ready for them):

Sins of Neighboring Countries
Sins of Judah

Sins of Israel

Summarize "Sins of Other Nations" under *Studying the Bible.* Explain "three transgressions . . . and for four." On the poster under "Sins of Neighboring Countries" list each of the six nations and their sins. Do not take too much time with this step. Point out God's punishment. (fire)

Ask members to read Amos 2:4-5 and under "Sins of Judah" write "despised God's law." Point out that God's *fire* was going to fall on Judah as well as the pagan nations. (This came in 586 B.C., nearly two centuries later, when the Babylonians destroyed Jerusalem.)

Assign one verse from 2:6-8 to each member in the class. (If you have a small class, members will have more than one verse; if large, more than one member may have the same verse.) Ask them to read their verse and find the sin Amos condemned. List the sins under "Sins of Israel." Use *Studying the Bible* to explain what each of the sins was.

Ask all members to look at 3:1-2 and find the reason God was going to punish Israel. (God had brought them out of Egypt as His covenant people.)

Ask members to study 3:1-2 and develop a principle or guideline for our nation today. Allow a couple of minutes for study and then call for members' suggestions. List these on a chalkboard or a large sheet of paper. You may have several with different thoughts, but at least one of your principles should be similar to this: our acceptance of God's leadership and blessings in our lives gives Him the right to expect proper behavior from us.

**Give the Truth a Personal Focus**

Read the Suggested Teaching Aim. Ask: Has our church been blessed by God? Have we been blessed personally? Does God hold us accountable for our behavior in light of His blessings and leadership? (most certainly!) Remind them of Jesus' statement that He required more out of those to whom He had given much (Luke 12:48).

Distribute paper and pencils to all members. Read what you wrote under "The Sins of Judah." Remind members that God condemned Judah for not obeying His law. Next, let members summarize the "Sins of Israel." (social injustice and idolatry)

Ask members to examine their lives for evidences of sins similar to Israel's and Judah's. Allow two to three minutes for silent consideration. Ask members to use the back of their paper to list sins in their own life God condemns.

Close with a directed prayer. Ask members to bow their heads and close their eyes. Ask them to picture Jesus on the cross. Now picture Him coming off the cross holding His nail-scarred hands out toward them, asking them to let their behavior demonstrate what they say they believe.

---

1. Adapted from J. B. Fowler, Jr., *Illustrated Sermons for Special Occasions* (Nashville: Broadman Press, 1988), 33.

2. Ibid

# A Call for Justice and Righteousness

**Basic Passage:** Amos 4—5
**Focal Passages:** Amos 4:4-5; 5:18-24

One of the themes of Amos became a theme of many of the later prophets. The word of God through Amos expressed strong disapproval of participating in worship while also participating in mistreating other people in daily life. The prophet used strong language to express God's hatred of such superficial worship. No amount of fervent worship can substitute for treating other people right, nor can worship provide a cloak for sins against God and others. Amos also expressed God's fervent calls for justice and righteousness.

**Study Aim:** *To evaluate the genuineness of worship in light of daily practice of justice and righteousness*

## STUDYING THE BIBLE

Amos pronounced judgment on wealthy, self-indulgent women (4:1-3) and on empty worship practices of the Israelites (vv.4-5). The Lord had used a variety of natural disasters in a vain effort to lead the people to repent (vv.6-11). The impenitent people needed to expect to encounter God as Judge (vv.12-13). Amos summoned them to a vision of their nation's funeral (vv.1-3) and predicted nationwide mourning (vv.16-17). He repeatedly called them to seek God and live (vv.4-9, 14-15). Their self-indulgence and oppression of the poor sealed their fate (vv.10-13). Amos warned that the day of the Lord would be a day of darkness, not light for them (vv.18-20). The Lord had rejected their effusive worship practices (vv.21-23). He called for justice and righteousness (vv.24). He predicted the coming captivity (vv.25-27).

### I. Prepare to Meet Your God (Amos 4:1-13)

**1. Judgment against wealthy, self-indulgent women (4:1-3).**—Wealthy, self-indulgent women kept pressuring their husbands to provide drink and whatever else they wanted. Their husbands responded to this pressure by oppressing the poor and crushing the needy. God compared such women to fat cows who would be led into captivity with hooks.

**2. Judgment against empty worship (4:4-5)**

4 Come to Bethel, and transgress; at Gilgal multiply transgression; and bring your sacrifices every morning, and your tithes every three years:
5 And offer a sacrifice of thanksgiving with leaven, and

**proclaim and publish the free offerings: for this liketh you, O ye children of Israel, saith the Lord God.**

Bethel was the major worship center in Israel (Amos 7:13). A memorial to God's help was established at Gilgal when the Israelites entered the promised land (Josh. 4:19-24). The people were accustomed to being called to come to these places and to bring their sacrifices. Amos shocked the people by using a call to worship as a call to transgress or rebel against God.

They are called to bring sacrifices and tithes that went beyond what the law required (1 Sam. 1:3,7,21; Deut. 14:28), but such practices were used by religious pilgrims to express special devotion. The leaven in the brad was not what the law required, but the worshipers apparently felt that this could make their sacrifice more acceptable (Lev. 2:11).

What was wrong with their worship? Part of their problem was that they did it for the wrong reasons. This is implied in what the Lord said about their freewill offerings. They were called to proclaim and publish these "for this liketh you." They were like the Pharisees of Jesus' day, who performed acts of worship to be seen and praised by other (Matt. 6:1-18).

Their main problem, however, was that they thought their worship practices could substitute for helping the poor and even cloak their oppression of the poor. Emphasis on this theme throughout Amos makes this clear. Later verses spell it out even more than in 4:4-5 (see 5:7,14-15,21-24).

**3. Unheeded warnings (4:6-11).**—God had sent famine, drought, mildew, locusts, pestilence, war, and earthquake to try to lead the people to repent. The relentless theme of these verses is "yet have ye not returned unto me, saith the Lord" (vv. 6,8-11).

**4. Prepare to meet your God (4:12-13).**—Because the people ignored God's every effort to lead them to repent, nothing remained for them except to expect the Creator God to come as Judge.

## II. Foreseeing Israel's Funeral (Amos 5:1-17)

**1. Lamentations for fallen Israel (5:1-3,16-17).**—Amos 5:1-17 begins and ends with a vision of Israel's funeral. In an opening lamentation (vv. 1-3), Israel was compared to a dead virgin and to a city decimated by loss of life. The final lamentation (vv. 16-17) is a vision of nationwide mourning.

**2. Calls to life (5:4-9,14-15).**—God called Israel to seek Him and live. They were not to seek their places of worship, but to seek the Lord Himself. Verse 7 makes explicit the problem with their worship. They turned justice into something as bitter as wormwood, and they totally cast aside righteousness. Verses 14-15 make it even more clear: they were to seek good, not evil. Seeking good involves establishing justice in judicial proceedings and doing the right thing in daily life.

**3. Sins and judgment (5:10-13).**—The Israelites were so hardhearted that they hated anyone—like Amos—who rebuked their sins (compare 5:10 with 7:10-15). Verses 10-12, like 2:6-8, list Israel's prominent sins: luxury and self-indulgence, oppression of and extortion from the poor, perversion of justice through bribery.

## III. What the Lord Expects (Amos 5:18-27)

**1. The day of the Lord (5:18-20)**

18 Woe unto you that desire the day of the Lord: to what end
is it for you? the day of the Lord is darkness, and not light.
19 As if a man did flee from a lion, and a bear met him; or
went into the house, and leaned his hand on the wall, and a
serpent bit him.
20 Shall not the day of the Lord be darkness, and not light?
even very dark, and no brightness in it?

The "day of the Lord" is found often in the writings of the prophets. Amos was probably the first prophet to mention it. He apparently did not originate the term, but he did clarify the people's understanding of the day of the Lord. They saw the day of the Lord as a time when the Lord would be victorious. He would defeat and judge His enemies and save and bless His people. Amos used the word "desire" to describe how the Israelites viewed the day of the Lord. They said they would welcome it; they wanted the day of the Lord to come.

The people were right about the day and right that God's people ought to desire the coming of the day of the Lord. The problem was that they falsely assumed that they would be among God's people whom He would save and bless. They could point to God's choice of Israel as His chosen people, and they could point with pride to their devotion to worship. Based on this view of themselves, they thought of the day of the Lord as a day of light for them.

Amos had just described the funeral of Israel as a people who had sinned against God. Now he pronounced a divine woe on them for their false self-confidence. For them, the day of the Lord would be a day of deep darkness, not of light and brightness.

God compared Israel to a man who fled from a lion only to encounter a bear. God used another comparison of a man who leans against a wall in a house and is bitten by a snake. Both men thought they were safe only to discover they were not. The parables condemn false self-confidence. God's word through Amos had burst all their bubbles of false confidence. When they presumed on their status as God's chosen people, God told them that this fact only made them more accountable for their sins (3:2). When they took refuge in their pious acts of worship, God pointed to the inconsistency of their injustice and transgression (4:4-5; 5:5-7,21-24).

**3. Rejected worship (5:21-23)**

21 I hate, I despise your feast days, and I will not smell in your solemn assemblies.
22 Though ye offer me burnt offerings and your meat offerings, I will not accept them: neither will I regard the peace offerings of your fat beasts.
23 Take thou away from me the noise of thy songs; for I will not hear the melody of thy viols.

This passage reflects the varied worship practices of the Israelites of Amos' time. They had special feast days and other times of religious gatherings. They offered burnt offerings, in which the sacrifice was totally consumed by the fire. They had peace offerings, in which part of the sacrifice was eaten by the people. They used singing and a variety of musical instruments in their worship.

Speaking through Amos, God used strong language to describe how He hated and despised all of these supposed acts of worship. "I will not smell" reflects the idea that offerings were like a pleasing smell in the nostrils of God. God said that their offerings had no pleasing smell. God also used strong language about their music. Their songs were like so much "noise" that God wanted to be taken away from Him. God refused to listen to the sound of their viols (harps).

**3. Call for justice and righteousness (5:24)**

24 But let judgment run down as waters, and righteousness as a mighty stream.

Many Bible students consider this the key verse in Amos. The Lord had been condemning their injustice, oppression, and dishonesty. Now He told them what He expected of them. The word "judgment" means fair and right judgments in judicial proceedings, in other words, what we mean by the word *justice*. "Righteousness" is a more general word to describe doing the right thing.

These were the two qualities that God said they lacked (Amos 5:7). They are absolutely indispensable for God's people. No amount of religious activities can take the place of these. God used two pictures involving water to show what He wanted to happen. The first is a picture of justice being like a flood of water gushing down a dry stream bed. The other is a picture of a never-failing river of righteousness.

**4. Coming exile (5:25-27).**—God yearned for a time when the people had walked with Him, but realistically He knew their hearts had turned to other gods. The Lord pronounced the sentence of exile for Israel.

## APPLYING THE BIBLE

**Drenched in selfishness.**—The following anonymous poem pretty well sums up the attitude of foolish, selfish indulgence of which Amos accused the women of Samaria:

*I gave a little party this afternoon at three—*

*'Twas very small*
*Three guests in all*
*Just I, Myself, and Me.*
*Myself ate up the sandwiches*
*While I drank the tea,*
*And it was I*
*Who ate the pie*
*And passed the cake to Me.*[1]

The champion and defender of the poor, Amos lashed out at the moral and religious evils that prevailed in his day calling for justice to "roll down like waters, and righteousness like an everflowing stream" (5:24, NRSV). *Holman Bible Dictionary* says: "His word of judgment was severe for the 'first ladies of Samaria' who encouraged the injustice and violence of their husbands toward the poor." Amos calls those women "ye kine of Bashan." Translated into our vernacular, Amos called them "fat cows." To say the least, that's pretty strong preaching!

**When worship is empty.**—Author Archibald Rutledge tells about attending a church service where the enthusiasm was very exciting. Great passages of Scripture were read with the proper ministerial inflections, noble prayers were uttered, and psalms and hymns were quoted and sung with great fervor. Everyone, including Rutledge, felt it had been a great worship service.

But as they were leaving the church, Rutledge saw a wretched, bedraggled, old woman—rather wild-looking, as he put it—sitting against the churchyard fence weeping as though her heart were broken. Most of the worshipers exiting the church saw the poor woman and, no doubt, pitied her and had compassion upon her. But Rutledge relates that only one of "our great company" went to her, knelt over her, dried her tears, and comforted her. All were touched by the woman's needs, but only one person who had been worshiping God tried to do something about it.[2]

Love for God expresses itself in more than just formal worship. One does not worship God, regardless of how loudly the hymns are sung and how piously the Scriptures are read, until that worship translates itself into acts of compassion and love for others. And therein lay Israel's great sin.

**Not ashamed to sin, but ashamed to repent.**—Daniel Defoe, the author of *Robinson Crusoe,* ran away from home and went to sea as a young man. His father protested young Defoe's plans, and his mother wept. But Defoe was determined to have his way. On his very first voyage out, his ship was wrecked and young Defoe barely escaped with his life. He saw his foolishness and the bad choice he had made, but he was afraid to go back home because he knew his friends would make fun of him. Describing how he felt, Defoe said that people are not ashamed of sin, but they are ashamed to repent.

Theologian Augustus H. Strong defined repentance as "that

voluntary change in the mind of the sinner in which he turns from sin." Turning from sin always means turning to God, otherwise it is not genuine repentance.

**Not guilty by reason of insanity.**—Judge Barrington Parker ruled that John W. Hinckley, Jr., who attempted to assassinate President Ronald Reagan, was "not guilty by reason of insanity." The judge dismissed each of the thirteen charges for the reason stated. The trial is said to have cost the American taxpayers $2.5 million. The district attorney of Bell County, Texas, on hearing Parker's ruling, said that although the assassination attempt had been seen on television by one hundred and twenty-five million people, still the would-be assassin was declared not to be guilty.

Although sin has been described as spiritual insanity, Israel could not plead "not guilty by reason of insanity" because that is one plea God will not hear. When we sin we repent or suffer for it. No plea but a plea for mercy will stay God's hand of chastisement against the guilty sinner. Much to her sorrow, Israel learned this too late.

## TEACHING THE BIBLE

▶ *Main Idea:* Amos' call for justice and righteousness challenges adults to evaluate the genuineness of their worship in light of their daily practice of justice and righteousness.

▶ *Suggested Teaching Aim:* To lead adults to identify the practices of Israel to which God objected, and to evaluate the genuineness of their worship in light of their daily practice of justice and righteousness.

### A TEACHING OUTLINE

*1. Introduce the lesson by using an illustration.*
*2. Present a lecture covering the Focal Passage.*
*3. Use DISCUSSION QUESTIONS to apply the Focal Passage.*
*4. Lead members to evaluate the genuineness of their worship in light of the way they live.*

**Introduce the Bible Study**

Use "When worship is empty" *(Applying the Bible)* to introduce the lesson.

**Search for Biblical Truth**

IN ADVANCE, enlist a member to read the Scripture for you.

Make poster strips of the following and be prepared to put up strips as you discuss that section:

1. Judgment Against Empty Worship (4:4-5)
2. The Day of the Lord (5:18-20)
3. Rejected Worship (4:21-23)
4. Call for Justice and Righteousness (5:24)

Place the first poster strip on the focal wall and call on the enlisted member to read 4:4-5. Use *Studying the Bible* to present a brief lecture in which you cover these points: (1) the significance of Bethel and Gilgal; (2) how they used the leavened bread; (3) what Amos meant by "for this liketh you"; and how they tried to use their worship to cloak their oppression of the poor.

DISCUSSION QUESTION: What actions do you participate in that are contrary to your worship?

Place the second poster strip on the focal wall and call on the enlisted member to read 5:18-20. Using *Studying the Bible*, present the following lecture: (1) define the "day of the Lord"; (2) why Israel's understanding of the day of the Lord was wrong; (3) explain the two comparisons and their message.

DISCUSSION QUESTION: If the day of the Lord were suddenly to come at this moment, would you welcome it or despair? Why?

Place the third poster strip on the focal wall and call on the enlisted member to read 5:21-23. Using *Studying the Bible,* present the following lecture: (1) how the Israelites used burnt offerings; (2) what God meant by ""I will not smell"; (3) what God's attitude was toward their music.

DISCUSSION QUESTION: What do you think God's attitude is toward your church's worship services? your personal worship?

Place the fourth poster strip on the focal wall and call on the enlisted member to read 5:24. Using *Studying the Bible,* present the following lecture: (1) the importance of this verse to Amos; (2) the meaning of the words ""judgment" and ""righteousness"; (3) explain the two images of water; (4) explain that because Israel had not done this, God would exile them (5:25-27).

DISCUSSION QUESTION: Is a person a Christian who refuses to show justice and righteousness in his or her daily living?

**Give the Truth a Personal Focus**

Ask members to suggest elements of worship as you list them on a chalkboard or a large sheet of paper. (Among others: sincerity, reverence, meaningfulness, vitality, spontaneity.)

Ask, How does your life outside the house of worship validate what goes on in the worship? Distribute paper and pencils and ask members to write one thing they need to do to bring their life in line with their worship.

---

1. Benjamin P. Browne, *Illustrations for Preaching* (Nashville: Broadman Press, 1977), 118-19.
2. Archibald Rutledge, *Love's Meaning* (New York: Fleming H. Revell Co., 1943), 27.

# A Prophet Who Lived His Message

**Basic Passage:** Hosea 1:1—3:5
**Focal Passages:** Hosea 1:2-9; 3:1-5

God teaches us lessons through personal experiences. He taught Hosea a lesson so profound that the prophet shared this divine revelation. The prophet suffered through the unfaithfulness of his wife. The Lord used this personal experience to teach Hosea several great lessons about God and His people: (1) The relationship between God and Israel is like that of a husband and wife. (2) The sin of Israel was like unfaithfulness to a loving husband. (3) God loved unfaithful Israel.

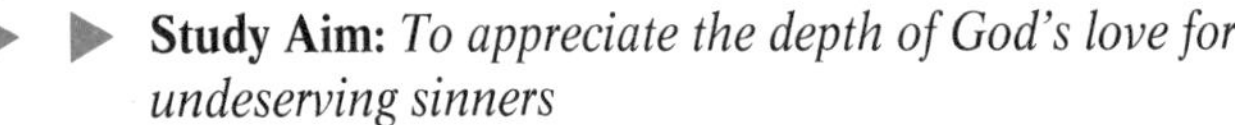
**Study Aim:** *To appreciate the depth of God's love for undeserving sinners*

## STUDYING THE BIBLE

God's word came to Hosea in the days of Jeroboam II (1:1). God told the prophet to marry Gomer, who proved to be unfaithful (vv.2-3). Their three children's names—Jezreel (vv.4-5), Loruhamah (vv.6-7), and Loammi (vv.8-9)—revealed specific messages about Israel's sin and divine judgment. In spite of Israel's sin, God promised hope for the future (vv.10—2:1). However, before israel could be restored, the nation must undergo the discipline of divine judgment (vv.2-13). Out of this would come a new beginning (vv.14-23). God told Hosea to love his unfaithful wife as God loved unfaithful Israel (3:1). Hosea paid the price to redeem Gomer (v.2). He restricted her for a time from relations with anyone (v.3). Israel would be deprived of national and religious supports as a step toward restoration under the Messiah (vv.4-5).

### I. The Prophet, His Wife, and Children (Hos. 1:1-9)

**1. The prophet (1:1).**—Hosea began his ministry during the reign of Jeroboam II of Israel (786-746 B.C.). Like Amos, he preached to the Northern Kingdom during a time of superficial prosperity. His ministry continued beyond Jeroboam's time, as Israel moved closer and closer to its doom at the hands of the Assyrians in 722 B.C.

**2. Gomer (1:2-3)**

2 The beginning of the word of the Lord by Hosea. And the Lord said to Hosea, Go, take unto thee a wife of whoredoms and children of whoredoms: for the land hath committed great whoredom, departing from the Lord.

3 So he went and took Gomer the daughter of Diblaim; which conceived and bare him a son.

The command sounds as if God told Hosea to marry a woman who was immoral and already had illegitimate children. Some interpreters, therefore, believe that Gomer was one of many temple prostitutes involved in Baal worship. They interpret this command as a symbol of God's love for sinners.

Many interpreters, however, believe that God would never have told one of His prophets to marry an immoral woman. "Wife of whoredoms" may mean a woman who had a bent toward sexual immorality, but she was not immoral when Hosea married her.

**3. Jezreel (1:4-5)**

4 And the Lord said unto him, Call his name Jezreel; for yet a little while, and I will avenge the blood of Jezreel upon the house of Jehu, and will cause to cease the kingdom of the house of Israel.
5 And it shall come to pass at that day, that I will break the bow of Israel in the valley of Jezreel.

When a son was born to Hosea and Gomer, the Lord gave the child a name that was prophetic. Jezreel was the name of a valley and a village. It was the site of Jehu's bloody extermination of Jezebel and the sons of Ahab (2 Kings 9:14—10:17). Although God used Jehu to bring judgment on the house of Ahab and to destroy many places of Baal worship, Jehu continued the sins of Jeroboam I by worshiping the calves at Bethel and Dan (2 Kings 10:18-31).

Hosea pronounced judgment not only on the house of Jehu but also on "the kingdom of the house of Israel." Judgment was coming on the entire Northern Kingdom. The house of Jehu came to an end with Zechariah (2 Kings 15:8-12). The nation itself fell not many years later when the mighty Assyrian Empire sent its armies to besiege Samaria. The fall of Samaria marked the end of the Northern Kingdom (2 Kings 17).

**4. Loruhamah (1:6-7)**

6 And she conceived again, and bare a daughter. And God said unto him, Call her name Loruhamah: for I will no more have mercy upon the house of Israel; but I will utterly take them away.
7 But I will have mercy upon the house of Judah, and will save them by the Lord their God, and will not save them by bow, nor by sword, nor by battle, by horses, nor by horsemen.

When a daughter was born to Gomer, God named her "Loruhamah," which means "not loved." The name of the daughter was to be a sign to Israel that God would not continue to show love to them if they continued in their sins. Later prophecies show that although God judged Israel, He continued to love her even beyond national judgment. By contrast, when judgment fell on Israel, Judah was spared. The

Assyrians attacked Judah after they conquered Israel, but the Lord delivered Judah from the Assyrians (2 Kings 19). Later Judah followed Israel in continual unfaithfulness to God, and was defeated by the Babylonians (2 Kings 25).

**5. Loammi (1:8-9)**

> 8 Now when she had weaned Lorhamah, she conceived and bare a son.
> 9 then said God, Call his name Loammi: for ye are not my people, and I will not be your God.

The third child, a son, was given a name meaning "not my people." This name held a chilling message for a people whose entire source of life was in God. Note the differences in how Hosea described the births of the three children. Of the first child, Hosea said that Gomer "bare him a son" (v. 3). Of the second, he wrote that she "bare a daughter" (v. 6). Similar words are used of the third child: she "bare a son" (v. 8). The word "him" is included in verse 3, but not in verse 6 or 8. Did Hosea deliberately omit any reference to either Loruhamah or Loammi being his children? If so, the names of the second and third children were signs not only of God's relationship with Israel but also of the deteriorating marriage of Hosea and Gomer.

## II. Judgment and Hope (Hos. 1:10—2:23)

**1. Hope for the future (1:10—2:1).** The themes of judgment and hope are interspersed in most of the prophets. Recalling God's past promises, Hosea foresaw a time when the symbolic names of Loruhamah and Loammi would be changed to Ruhamah and Ammi. Instead of being called "not loved," Israel would be called ""loved." Instead of being called "not my people," she would be called "my people."

**2. Judgment on unfaithfulness (2:2-13).**—These verses describe God's call to His wayward bride Israel. Israel looked to Baal, a fertility god to supply all the good things described in verse 5, but God would make the land like a wilderness. Thus deprived of the good things of life, Israel would return to her true Husband, the real giver of all good things. God would judge Israel bringing to an end her worship of Baal. This would be because Israel acted like an unfaithful wife who forgot her husband and went after other lovers.

**3. A New Beginning (2:14-23).**God would regain and renew His love for Israel. Israel would call God "Ishi," which means "my Husband." This would provide hope and a new beginning for the people and land of Israel.

## III. Love and Hope (Hos. 3:1-5)

**1. Loving as God loves (3:1)**

> 1 Then said the Lord unto me, Go yet, love a woman beloved of her friend, yet an adulteress, according to the love of the

Lord toward the children of Israel, who look to other gods, and love flagons of wine.

Throughout Hosea 1—3 is a intertwining of Hosea's relationship with Gomer and God's relationship with Israel. Sometimes one or the other is in view; at other times, both seem to be interwoven. The beginning of verse 1 clearly refers to Hosea and his wife. Hosea had married Gomer. She had proven untrue to her vows. She was an adulteress who had another lover. In spite of this, the Lord told Hosea to go again and love her.

The last part of verse 3 is crucial. The prophet might have asked how and why he was to try to reclaim his unfaithful wife. Anticipating these questions, the Lord explained that Israel had treated Him as Gomer had treated Hosea. The Israelites had gone after other gods and reveled in the worship practices of Baal.

**2. Love that redeems (3:2)**

2 So I bought her to me for fifteen pieces of silver, and for an homer of barley, and an half homer of barley.

Gomer had become the property of someone. She could have belonged to the master of the female prostitutes in the Baal temple. She could have been a slave on the block. She could have become the property of her lover. At any rate, reclaiming her required a ransom price. The amount shows two things: (1) The money amount of what Hosea paid was equal to the price of a female slave according to Exodus 21:32. (2) The fact that Hosea paid part in goods may indicate that he was a poor man.

**3. Love that disciplines (3:3)**

3 And I said unto her, Thou shalt abide for me many days; thou shalt not play the harlot, and thou shalt not be for another man: so will I also be for thee.

For a long unspecified period of time, Gomer would be required to go through a time of testing. She would be back under Hosea's roof. She would no longer have sexual relations with another man. The words "so will I also be for thee" probably mean that he would refrain from sexual relations with her during this testing period. Such a time was apparently needed to wean her away from her old life. At the same time, it gave both an opportunity to see if their love could be renewed. Love cannot be forced.

**4. Love that triumphs (3:4-5)**

4 For the children of Israel shall abide many days without a king, and without a prince, and without a sacrifice, and without an image, and without an ephod, and without teraphim:

5 Afterward shall the children of Israel return, and seek the Lord their God, and David their king; and shall fear the Lord and his goodness in the latter days.

God intended for unfaithful Israel to undergo experiences that would lead them to return to Him. All the supports of their national and religious life would be ended. They would have no king or prince after the nation fell. Their sacrificial system and places of religious memorial would be no more ("image" is "pillar," a place where a stone commemorated some act of God, as in Josh. 24:27). The "ephod" and "teraphim" were crude but popular forms for seeking God's will.

Verse 5 predicts a time when the children of Israel would seek the Lord and "David their king" (a reference to the Messiah). They "shall fear the Lord and his goodness in the latter days."

## APPLYING THE BIBLE

**God's leadership.**—William Cullen Bryant (1794-1878) is known as "The Father of American Poetry." A lawyer, naturalist, and traveler, one of Bryant's best-known poems, "To a Waterfowl," was called the "best short poem in the English language" by the great English author Matthew Arnold. As Clarence Macartney tells it, young Bryant left home one bleak autumn day, starting out to face the world. Lonely and homesick, sad and uncertain about his future, Bryant looked up as he traveled along and saw a waterfowl flying toward its winter home in the South. Young Bryant knew the bird was guided by God Himself, and it reminded Bryant that God would lead him as well. Out of this profound experience Bryant wrote:

*He who, from zone to zone,*
*Guides through the boundless sky thy certain flight,*
*In the long way that I must trod alone,*
*Will lead my steps aright.*[1]

**Trust Him when it's the hardest thing to do.**—Hosea found that trusting God was sometimes the hardest thing one has to do. Consider the grief Hosea brought on himself when he followed God's command and married Gomer. About trusting God when it's hard to do so, a poet wrote:

*Trust Him when dark doubts assail thee,*
*Trust Him when thy strength is small,*
*Trust Him when to trust Him simply*
*Seems the hardest thing of all.*[2]

**Israel's sin against God.**—Martin Luther, in a fit of anger, once exclaimed impulsively: "If I were God and the world had treated me as it has treated Him, I would have kicked the wretched thing to pieces long ago!" Since each of us is a sinner, we can be grateful that God does not take that attitude toward us.

For generations Israel had provoked God by her unfaithfulness, and her great sin against God is graphically pictured in 2:2-13. But in spite of Israel's sin, God continued to love Israel and expressed His love very dramatically in Hosea's love for Gomer. But to escape the wrath of God Israel must repent, and God constantly called the nation to forsake sin and be blessed by God (1:10). However, Israel refused to repent and return to God and shortly after Hosea's ministry ended the Assyrian captivity began.

**The costliness of love.**—Over two graves in a cathedral in England are the effigies of a knight of the Crusades and his lady. But the lady does not have a right hand. According to tradition the knight who lies buried in the cathedral was captured by Saladin, the Muslim conqueror in the war of the Crusades. The knight asked that his life be spared because of the lady in England who loved him, but Saladin scoffed, "She will soon forget you, and marry another." Tradition relates that Saladin then told the knight that if the lady would send evidence of her love for the knight—her right hand—Saladin would release him. When the lady in England received the letter, she promptly cut off her right hand and sent it to Saladin. When Saladin saw the hand, he quickly released the knight and sent him back home to his lover.[3]

The costliest thing in the world is love. And nowhere in Scripture is this more dramatically portrayed, except in the crucifixion of Jesus Christ, than it is in the patient love of Hosea for Gomer. It is a revelation of God's love for Israel—love that would pay any price to have Israel return that love to Him (3:1).

**The greatness of God's love.**—Charles Wesley, the younger brother of John Wesley, founder of the Methodist church, wrote approximately eight thousand hymns—three hymns a week for fifty-seven years. On the first anniversary of his conversion, Wesley wrote one of our most beautiful Christian hymns.

Remembering, perhaps, the remark of his Moravian friend Peter Bohler, "Had I a thousand tongues, I would praise Him with them all," Wesley wrote "O For a Thousand Tongues":

*O for a thousand tongues to sing*
*My great Redeemer's praise,*
*The glories of my God and King,*
*The triumphs of His grace.*

## TEACHING THE BIBLE

▶ *Main Idea:* God's use of Hosea's love for his wife demonstrates the depth of God's love for undeserving sinners.

▶ *Suggested Teaching Aim:* To lead adults to describe how Hosea's love for Gomer was used to describe God's love for Israel, and to describe their own relationship with God.

### A TEACHING OUTLINE

*1. Introduce the lesson with an illustration.*
*2. Use a guided Bible study to cover the focal passage.*
*3. Lead members to describe their relationship to God in terms of a marriage and determine one way to improve it.*

**Introduce the Bible Study**

Introduce the lesson by sharing "The costliness of love" *(Applying the Bible).*

**Search for Biblical Truth**

IN ADVANCE, enlist a member to read "Hosea" in the *Holman Bible Dictionary* or another Bible dictionary and give a two- to three-minute report on Hosea.

IN ADVANCE, make two large cards. On one write:

THE FAMILY

on the other,

THE LOVE

Place these on the focal wall to head two columns. On smaller cards write:

(1) Hosea (1:1)
(2) Gomer (1:2-3)
(2) Jezreel (1:4-5)
(3) Loruhama (1:6-7)
(3) Loammi (1:8-9).

Tape these to the backs of five chairs. On four other cards write:

(1) Loving as God loves (3:1)
(2) Love that redeems (3:2)
(3) Love that disciplines (3:3)
(4) Love that triumphs (3:4-5).

Tape these to the backs of four different chairs.

Ask members to open their Bibles to Hosea 1:1:9. Explain that the lesson today involves the story of a family. Ask a volunteer to read aloud verse 1. Ask the person with the card on which Hosea's name is printed to place it on the wall below *The Family.* Call for the report on Hosea from the enlisted number.

Ask a volunteer to read verses 2-3 and for the person with Gomer's name to place the card on the wall under Hosea. Use *Studying the Bible* to explain the two interpretations of "a wife of whoredoms."

Ask a volunteer to read verses 4-5 and for the person with Jezreel's name to place the card on the wall. Use *Studying the Bible* to clarify the following points about Jezreel: (1) the prophetic relationship of the name with the name of the valley; (2) the significance for Israel of Israel of Hosea's calling a child by this name.

Ask a volunteer to read verses 6-7 and for the person with Loruhamah's name to place the card on the wall. Ask: Who was Loruhamah's name to place the card on the wall. Ask: Who was Loruhamah [loh-roo HAH muh]? (Hosea's second child, first daughter) What does the name mean? (not loved) What did Hosea intend to communicate to Israel by naming his daughter this? (that God would no longer show love to them if they continued in their sin)

Ask a volunteer to read verses 8-9 and for the person with Loammi's [loh AM igh] name to place it on the wall. Explain the significance of this name for Israel.

Briefly summarize "Judgment and Hope" in *Studying the Bible.*

Point out that over against *The Family* of the Book of Hosea is *The Love.* Call on the four people in order to place the four descriptions of love on the wall under *The Love.* Ask a volunteer to read the verses and ask members to listen for the two levels of the story that run through these verses. Be sure they see Hosea's love for Gomer reflecting God's love for Israel. Use *Studying the Bible* to explain these verses.

**Give the Truth a Personal Focus**

Ask members to picture their relationship to God as a marriage. Ask them to listen as you read this list to see how they would rank their relationship with God: openness, intimacy, trust, loyalty, faithfulness. challenge them to pick one of these that needs improvement to work on this week. Write out one step they will take to accomplish this.

---

1. Adapted from Clarence Edward Macartney, *Macartney's Illustrations* (New York, Nashville: Abingdon-Cokesbury Press, 1945), 291.

2. Ibid., 34.

3. Walter B. Knight, *Master Book of New Illustrations* (Grand Rapids: William B. Eerdmans Publishing Company, 1956), 701.

# God's Love for Israel

**Basic Passage:** Hosea 11
**Focal Passage:** Hosea 11:1-9

Hosea is known as the prophet of love. He often used the Hebrew word for human love to describe God's love for His people. He also sometimes used the word that describes "steadfast love" or "covenant love." God gave Hosea special insight into the loving heart of God. This does not mean that Hosea was soft on sin. Like the other prophets, Hosea spoke strongly against israel's sins; but he saw the special anguish that sin caused God. Hosea 11 is one of the high points of Old Testament revelation because of what it reveals about the love of God.

**Study Aim:** *To recognize how God's love for Israel was like a parent's love for a wayward child*

## STUDYING THE BIBLE

God showed His love for Israel by calling the people as a child out of Egypt (v. 1). From the beginning, Israel sinned against the love of God (v. 2). God continued to show tender care for Israel (vv. 3-4). Because Israel was bent on sinning, God let His people reap the consequences of what they had sown (vv. 5-7). However, God's loving heart rebelled at the idea of giving up on Israel (vv. 8-9). Someday Israelites would return to the Lord (vv. 10-11). Meanwhile, Israel practiced lies and deceit (v. 12).

### I. The Father's Love for Wayward Israel (Hos. 11:1-4)

#### 1. God's call and love (v. 1)

**1 When Israel was a child, then I loved him, and called my son out of Egypt.**

The deliverance from Egypt was the formative event in Israel's history. The exodus plus the giving of the law at Mount Sinai were God's call to the children of Israel to be His own people. Hosea 11:1 describes this as an act of God the Father toward Israel, His son.

When the people of Israel tried to explain why God called them as His chosen people, they were forced to conclude that God chose them only because He loved them. God's calling of Israel could not be explained because of their greatness, for they were slaves in the land of Egypt. God's choice could only be explained because God chose to love them (Deut. 4:37; 7:7-8).

The New Testament reveals that God loves not only Israel, but also all people. He chose Israel to be missionaries of His love. Unfortunately, during most of their history, the Israelites interpreted God's calling only as a special privilege, not also as a responsibility.

**2. Israel's sin against love (v. 2)**

**2 As they called them, so they went from them: they sacrificed unto Baalim, and burned incense to graven images.**

Earlier God had described Israel as being like an unfaithful wife; here He described Israel as being like a wayward child. Although the Israelites heard God's loving call, they also heard the calls of Baal and other false gods. These, of course, were not real gods who could speak, but their worshipers spoke alluring words that tempted the Israelites to worship the false gods. The Israelites yielded to the temptations and sacrificed at the various Baal shrines and burned incense to graven images.

Some people think of God as a powerful tyrant, not as a loving Father. Thus they see sin as a brave rebellion against the tyranny of arbitrary authority. The truth is that God is a loving Father, and our sin is a sin against One who loves us. This is what makes sin so evil; it ignores and rejects the love of the Heavenly Father. No sin is so bad as a sin against love.

**3. God's care for Israel (vv. 3-4)**

**3 I taught Ephraim also to go, taking them by their arms; but they knew not that I healed them.**

**4 I drew them with cords of a man, with bands of love: and I was to them as they that take off the yoke on their jaws, and I laid meat unto them.**

Verses 3-4 add to the description of the Father's love from verse 1. Verse 3 describes three acts of love of a father for his child. First, God taught Israel to walk as a father teaches his son to walk. "Ephraim" was the largest tribe of Israel, and sometimes was used to refer to all Israel. The word "go" means "walk." Second, God took His people in His arms as a father carries and hugs his child. Third, God healed His children. Unfortunately, while the Father was healing His children, they ignored Him.

The first part of verse 4 uses words that describe the kind of bonds that bind God to His people. God did not bind them with chains or harsh bonds. He bound them with bonds of love. The last part of verse 4 seems to use the analogy of a farmer easing the yoke of his oxen so they might eat. Some bible students think that the Lord was still thinking of a father and children in verse 4. If so, the picture is of the tender care of a father feeding his children. "Laid meat unto them" means "gave them food."

## II. Love's Discipline, Anguish, and Hope (Hos. 11:5-12)

**1. Tough Love (vv. 5-7)**

**5 He shall not return into the land of Egypt, but the Assyrians**

shall be his king, because they refused to return.
6 And the sword shall abide on his cities, and shall consume
his branches, and devour them, because of their own counsels.
7 And my people are bent to backsliding from me: though
they called them to the most High, none at all would exalt him.

This is a sad commentary on the fate awaiting Israel. God was like a heartbroken parent who realized that he must allow his children to be accountable for their own decisions. The Israelites had chosen not to return to the Lord; therefore, they would return to a land of captivity. Their earlier captivity had been in Egypt; this captivity would be at the hands of the Assyrians.

The sword of judgment would come to their cities. The word "branches" may refer to the bars that protected their city gates or it may refer to their leaders. In either case, they would be destroyed. The people of Israel had listened to the wrong counsel or advice; as a result, judgment was coming.

Sadly, God admitted that His people had a bent toward turning from Him. The word translated "bent" usually means "hang." It was like saying they had a hang-up. The word translated "backsliding" means "turning back" or "turning away." A survey of Israel's history shows their tendency to keep turning from their God. Translators struggle with the last part of verse 8. The idea may be that although at the time of judgment, the people would cry out to God, it would be too late. Or the idea may be that although the prophets cried out to the people, none of them exalted God.

We speak today of "tough love" as a strategy sometime used by parents to try and help their wayward offspring. It involves withholding parental support and letting the children reap the consequences of their own choices and habits. Parents do this as an act of love in the hope that the discipline will cause the children to wake up to reality. Tough love may be tough, but it is done because of love.

In a sense, that is what God did with Israel. The fact that He allowed them to reap what they had sown was not a denial but an affirmation of His love. God could have made creatures with no choice except to serve Him, but such service would never have been done in love. Love must be freely chosen. In order to have the freedom to choose God, people must have the freedom not to serve God. When they do, they reap the consequences of an existence without God.

**2. Love that won't give up (vv. 8-9)**

8 How shall I give thee up, Ephraim? how shall I deliver
thee, Israel? How shall I make thee as Admah? how shall I
make thee as Zeboim? mine heart is turned within me, my
repentings are kindled together.
9 I will not execute the fierceness of my anger, I will not
return to destroy Ephraim: for I am God, and not man; the Holy
One in the midst of thee: and I will not enter into the city.

There is a difference between giving a person up to reap what he has sown and totally giving up on the person. Israel's sins and stubborn impenitence had reached a point where the judgment of verses 5-6 was inevitable. Did this mean that God had given up on Israel? Was this the end of God's plan to use His people as a means of redemption for the entire world? The fall of Israel and later of Judah looked on the surface as if God had given up on what He said when He called Abraham (Gen. 12:1-3). Hosea 11:8-9 shows that God was not giving up on His purpose of human salvation.

The four questions in verse 8 are the anguished cries of the Father against whom the people had sinned. He was asking Himself how He could possibly give up on His people.Admah and Zeboim were cities overthrown in the destruction of Sodom and Gomorrah (Gen. 19; Deut. 29:23). God asked Himself if He intended to utterly destroy Israel forever.

God's heart would not let Him give up on His plan and His people. God's heart recoiled within Him at the very thought. The Bible sometimes attributes to God human characteristics in order to communicate with human beings. When the Bible speaks of God changing His mind or "repenting," the Bible is not saying that God changes His purpose. The point is to help us identify as best we can with God's unfailing love. In other words, if we were God dealing with the rebellious Israelites, we would have given up on them long before this. God, however, did not give up on them. He is pictured as sharing the human temptation to wash His hands of them forever, but His heart would not allow Him to do this.

Instead of giving up on Israel, God chose not to totally destroy Israel forever. This did not mean that the judgment of verses 5-6 was not coming. It meant that God would continue His work and eventually His people would return (vv.10-11).

How can God do this? He can do it because He is the loving Heavenly Father, not a human being. Humans are shortsighted and impatient. God is farsighted and longsuffering.

**3. Israel's restoration (vv. 10-11).**—God's plan and purpose cannot be judged from a purely human point of view. "One day is with the Lord as a thousand years, and a thousand years as one day" (2 Pet. 3:8). Love is the foundation for hope. God predicted that eventually His scattered people would return unto Him.

**4. Israel's sins (v. 12).**—Verse 12 actually goes with chapter 12 more than with chapter 11. It returns to the theme of Israel's present sins for which they were about to be judged.

## APPLYING THE BIBLE

**The God of the second chance.**—Lou Gehrig (1903-1941) was one of America's greatest professional baseball players. He played in 2,130 consecutive games with the New York Yankees. Once, when Gehrig came to bat, it was the ninth inning and the winning runs were on second and third bases. New York was one run behind, and Gehrig knew that if he could get a hit it would mean a win for the Yankees. But the count against Gehrig was three balls and two strikes.

With the grandstands in an uproar, the pitcher threw a fast ball across the plate and the umpire called, "Strike three." Turning very slowly to the umpire, Gehrig said something and that was not like him. As the crowd went wild, thinking Gehrig was arguing with the umpire, the sports reporters rushed out onto the field and asked the umpire, "What did Lou say to you?" Smiling, the umpire called Lou back to home plate and said, "Lou, tell the boys what you said when I called that third strike on you."

Timid and embarrassed, Gehrig replied: "I said, 'Mr. Ump, I would give ten dollars to have that one back.' "

One of the reporters wrote up his story that evening for the sports page and he added: "There are people all over the world who would give ten dollars or ten thousand dollars to get just one minute back and for the privilege of changing something they said or did in that minute."[1]

Is there a road back? There is, for God is the God of the second chance. But even though that is true and we can come back and make a fresh start, the scars of our sins will forever remain.

Hosea pictures this love and grace of God in which He gives us a second chance. Although Israel had continuously rebelled against the love of God, again and again He gave them another chance (vv. 2-4). Thanks be to God! He is the God of the second chance.

**God's grace will cover our sins.**—Norwegian composer Edvard Grieg (1843-1907) once was staying at a small Norwegian hotel. There was a child there, not properly disciplined by his parents, who annoyed the guests by trying to play the piano. Although he had some musical training, his rendition of the classics was, to state it mildly, atrocious! The guests complained at the discordant sounds that irritated them, but little was done to correct the problem. But Grieg came into the room, sensed the situation and walking up behind the child who was seated at the piano bench, Grieg stretched his arms around the child and began to weave his beautiful harmonies around the discordant rendition of the child. What had been irritating suddenly became enjoyable because of the touch of the master's hands.[2]

Israel had rejected God's leadership and blessings. The people's rebellious attitude had produced discord, disharmony, grief to God, and national chaos. God would embrace Israel, forgive Israel's sins, and lead Israel into peace and joy if only the people would respond in repentance to Him. But the nation refused to do so even after the many warnings of the prophets, including Hosea.

**Love that won't let go.**—I once heard the late Dr. Gaston Foote tell about an experience he had when he was pastor of the First Methodist Church of Haskell, Texas. Foote's last pastorate was at First Methodist Church of Fort Worth, Texas.

Early one morning, Foote was walking back to the parsonage from downtown when he saw a young man lying by the side of the board sidewalk. He had been drinking and had been beaten into unconsciousness by his drinking friends. Recognizing the young man as the wayward son of one of Foote's widowed members, he picked the young man up and carried him to his mother's house. When she opened the door she gasped: "Pastor, take him into the bedroom and then get some clean towels and a basin of water, please." She sat down on the feather bed and Dr. Foote placed the boy on the bed, and she cradled his head in her lap as the blood oozed from his wounds onto her snow-white apron.

When Dr. Foote returned he saw the mother carefully pushing her son's blood-matted hair back out of his eyes and weeping audibly: "Oh, my boy, my boy, you never will let me love you when you're sober."

That was God's attitude toward Israel. But like the wayward son, Israel resisted the divine love.

## TEACHING THE BIBLE

▶ *Main Idea:* God's love for Israel demonstrates that God cares for us like a loving parent even when we disobey.
▶ *Suggested Teaching Aim:* to lead adults to examine God's love and judgment for Israel, and to list ways God shows His love and judgment today.

### A TEACHING OUTLINE

*1. Use a study group to describe the Father's love for wayward Israel.*
*2. Use a study group to describe love's discipline, anguish, and hope.*
*3. Let members list ways God shows His love and judgment to them.*

**Introduce the Bible Study**

Introduce the Bible study by sharing "The God of the second chance" in *Applying the Bible.*

**Search for Biblical Truth**

IN ADVANCE, copy on poster strips the seven sentences in the paragraph following *Studying the Bible* ("God showed His love . . ."). Tape these to the backs of seven chairs. These will be used to review the lesson.

Organize two groups and make the following assignments.

**Group 1—**

Read Hosea 11:1-4 and be prepared to portray the Father's love for His wayward son. You may present this in any manner you desire, but consider one of the following. What ever method you choose, be certain the class will understand the message in these verses.

1. Choral reading of the Scripture followed by a poster presentation of some of the difficult terms in the text.

2. Biblical skit in which two observers talk about what God is doing to Israel and what Israel is doing to God. You would convey all of the information in these verses.

3. Biblical simulation in which you present a television news cast in which an on-the-spot reporter interviews an Israelite man or woman, a government official, and a religious leader who describes God's love and the way the Israelites have rejected it.

You will have eight minutes for your study and four minutes for your presentation.

**Group 2—**

Read Hosea 11:5-12 and be prepared to portray love's discipline, anguish and hope. You may present this in any manner you desire, but consider one of the following. What ever method you choose, be certain the class will understand the message in these verses.

1. Choral reading of the Scripture followed by a poster presentation of some of the difficult terms in the text.

2. Biblical skit in which two observers talk about what God is doing to Israel and what Israel is doing to God. You would convey all of the information in these verses.

3. Biblical simulation in which you present a television news cast in which an on-the-spot reporter interviews an Israelite man or woman, a government official, and a religious leader who describes God's love and the way the Israelites have rejected it.

4. Role-play in which parents demonstrate tough love in a modern situation and then guide a discussion about how in the past God demonstrated this kind of tough love with Israel and us.

5. Monologue in which God talks about His feelings and love for Israel.

You will have eight minutes for your study and four minutes for your presentation.

Allow time for the study and then call for reports. Ask the seven people who have the poster strips taped to their chairs to read them. Use this time to fill in any of the gaps the groups may have left.

AS AN ALTERNATE, use the seven poster strips as a teaching outline. Place these strips on the focal wall and share information under each heading in *Studying the Bible.*

### Give the Truth a Personal Focus

Ask members to list ways God has shown His love and judgment in their lives. Challenge members to return to the Lord if needed; thank God for His wonderful love.

---

1. Adapted from C. Roy Angell, *Baskets of Silver* (Nashville: Broadman Press, 1955), 36.
2. Adapted from Benjamin P. Browne, *Illustrations for Preaching* (Nashville: Broadman Press, 1977), 154.

# Greedy Leaders Denounced

**Basic Passage:** Micah 1—3
**Focal Passage:** Micah 3:5-12

Some people think that the Tenth Commandment does not deal with a serious sin. Covetousness seems tame compared to murder, adultery, and stealing. The Bible, however, contains numerous warnings about the dangers of unbridled covetousness or greed. Jesus warned that covetousness can so preoccupy a person that he ends up missing life (Luke 12:13-21). Paul wrote that "the love of money is the root of all evil" (1 Tim. 6:10). Recently we studied how Ahab's coveting of Naboth's vineyard led him to break the Sixth, Eighth, and Ninth Commandments. Micah described what happens when the leaders of a nation allow greed to consume them.

**Study Aim:** *To define greed and identify its dangers*

## STUDYING THE BIBLE

Micah preached in Judah about the sins of Israel and Judah (1:1). He described God's coming and His pronouncement of judgment against Israel and Judah (vv.2-9). Micah spoke a lament over the coming ruin of Judean cities (vv.10-16). Micah attacked people who allowed their greed to lead them to acts of injustice (2:1-5). When critics told Micah to quit preaching such things, he only sharpened his attack (vv.6-11). Looking beyond the coming judgment, Micah predicted salvation for a faithful remnant (vv.12-13). Micah condemned leaders who acted as brutally as cannibals (3:1-4). He condemned prophets whose messages were determined by how much they received (vv.5-7). Micah was led by the Spirit to uphold justice (v.8). The leaders were guilty of injustice and brutality (vv.9-10). Political and religious leaders were easily bought with money (v.11a). Although they tried to claim God's protection, God's judgment was coming (vv.11b-12).

### I. Announcement of Coming Judgment (Mic. 1:1-16)

**1. Micah (1:1).**—Micah prophesied in Judah during the last quarter of the eighth century B.C. Some of his messages were directed against Israel just before their final defeat in 722 B.C., but most of his messages were directed toward Judah.

**2. God's coming in judgment on Israel and Judah (1:3-9).**—Micah described the Lord's coming with an indictment against Israel

(Samaria) and Judah. Israel's sins would bring destruction for the nation. Micah lamented the fact that Judah also would be judged.

3. **Lament over Judean cities (1:10-16).**—Micah quoted the beginning words from David's lament after the death of Saul. Then he proceeded to describe the judgment coming on the cities of western Judah.

## II. Micah's Preaching and the People's Response (Mic. 2:1-13)

1. **Judgment against greed and injustice (2:1-5).**—Micah told how greedy men laid awake at night scheming to add the land of the poor to their estates. God would judge them by allowing foreign invaders to take away their lands.

2. **Opposition to Micah's preaching (2:6-11).**—The greedy told Micah not to preach such things. His response was to condemn their sins even more pointedly. He said that they wanted preachers who would approve such sins as their use of strong drink.

3. **A word of hope (2:12-13).**—Micah predicted a time when the Lord would lead a faithful remnant of His people like a shepherd.

## III. Sins of Leaders and Their Punishment (Mic. 3:1-12)

1. **Leaders who acted like cannibals (3:1-4).**—Micah condemned leaders who knew nothing of real justice. Their actions were comparable to killing and eating the helpless people who were their responsibility.

2. **Prophets in name only (3:5-7)**

> 5 Thus saith the Lord concerning the prophets that make my people err, that bite with their teeth, and cry, Peace; and he that putteth not into their mouths, they even prepare war against him.
>
> 6 Therefore night shall be unto you, that ye shall not have a vision; and it shall be dark unto you, that ye shall not divine; and the sun shall go down over the prophets, and the day shall be dark over them.
>
> 7 Then shall the seers be ashamed, and the diviners confounded: yea, they shall all cover their lips; for there is no answer of God.

Micah was by no means the only prophet in the land. Apparently a number of people claimed to be prophets. Official prophets preached whatever the power structure wanted them to preach (see, for example, 1 Kings 22). Micah said that the prophets of his day were not spokesmen for God; instead they suited their messages to how much their hearers gave them. When the hearers fed them well, the prophets preached peace and prosperity. When their hearers did not feed them well, the prophets preached war and disaster.

Micah predicted that lying prophets and their complacent hearers would be condemned to the darkness they had created. Night would fall over the prophets. They would be disgraced before the people. They would cover their own lips because everyone would know that they had no word or vision from God.

**3. A true prophet (3:8)**

> **8 But truly I am full of power by the spirit of the Lord, and of judgment, and of might, to declare unto Jacob his transgression, and to Israel his sin.**

Micah contrasted himself with the prophets in name only. His message and power came from God. He upheld justice with strength. Micah condemned the sins of the leaders and people even when such a message was unpopular.

"Judgment" means "justice." The Old Testament concept of justice meant defending the rights of everyone, especially the helpless and oppressed. To stand for justice includes more than not being involved in injustices; it means to attack the unjust and to defend the rights of the oppressed (see Isa. 1:17).

**4. Leaders who misled (3:9-10)**

> **9 Hear this, I pray you, ye heads of the house of Jacob, and princes of the house of Israel, that abhor judgment, and pervert all equity.**
> **10 They build up Zion with blood, and Jerusalem with iniquity.**

Micah boldly condemned the political leaders. The prophet used strong words to describe the sins of the leaders. They not only did not uphold justice, they abhorred or hated it. They were the enemies of justice, which they were sworn to uphold. They perverted equity or fairness. Justice involves impartial treatment of all people. Even today, the statue of justice is blindfolded. But the leaders of Micah's day perverted or twisted fairness.

They were not slow to employ whatever method furthered their own cause. They built the city with the blood of the innocent. The blood could be shed from sudden violence or from slow, grinding exploitation. The whole structure of society was built on the misery and suffering of the helpless and oppressed.

**5. Money talks (3:11*a*)**

> **11 The heads thereof judge for reward, and the priests teach for hire, and the prophets divine for money:**

Micah named three groups of leaders who were charged with the welfare of all the people, especially the helpless and oppressed. He named the judges who decided legal disputes, the priests who taught the law of God, and the prophets who divined and delivered God's message. Micah accused each group of being bought. Each was for sale to the highest bidder. The judges did not decide cases based on truth and justice, but decided in favor of whoever could pay the biggest bribes. What the priests taught and the prophets preached depended on what people would pay to hear.

We have a saying, "money talks." This was true in Micah's day. Many people with money believed that everyone has his price. They used their money to buy whatever they wanted—legal or not, right or wrong. They used money as leverage to tilt the scales of justice in their favor. They were willing to pay priests and prophets as long as they said what the rich wanted to hear.

Part of the blame, therefore, was on those who were only too willing to use their wealth to get anything they wanted. A big part of the blame, however, was on those whose responsibility was to be honest, fair, and true. The judges were supposed to be impartial dispensers of justice tempered with mercy toward the poor and needy. Yet rather than being protectors of the innocent, they became perpetrators of injustice and exploitation. The priests and prophets were supposed to represent God; instead they represented the wealthy in perverting the truth and oppressing the helpless.

**6. False confidence (3:11*b*-12)**

> **11 yet will they lean upon the Lord, and say, Is not the Lord among us? none evil can come upon us?**
> **12 Therefore shall Zion for your sake be plowed as a field, and Jerusalem shall become heaps, and the mountain of the house as the high places of the forest.**

The exploiters were smugly self-confident. To make matters worse, they brazenly claimed that God was the source of their confidence. They claimed to lean on or trust the Lord to protect them as His people and Jerusalem as His holy city, wherein dwelt the sacred temple. They felt that they were safe because God would allow no evil to come to them.

Micah was one of the first prophets to predict the eventual ruin of Jerusalem. The prophet said that Jerusalem (Zion) would be plowed like a field and become only heaps of rubble. The temple stood on a mountain in Jerusalem. Micah predicted that the temple mount would become like any other mountain in the forest. In other words, the temple would be destroyed.

During Micah's ministry, Israel fell to Assyria and went into captivity. The Assyrians came into Judah threatening to do the same thing. They captured some of the cities of Judah and besieged Jerusalem. On that occasion, during the reign of Hezekiah and the prophecy of Isaiah, the Lord chose to deliver Jerusalem (2 Kings 18—19).

Very likely, when that happened, the people mocked Micah and claimed that God's deliverance of Jerusalem from the Assyrians proved He would always protect it and them from enemies. A century later, the prophet Jeremiah repeated the warning of Micah that unless

Jerusalem repented, the city would fall. The people of Jeremiah's day had even more smug false confidence than did the people of Micah's day.

Micah's and Jeremiah's prophecies came to pass when the Babylonians captured and destroyed Jerusalem and the temple (2 Kings 25). When God promises to do something, this doesn't mean that He's going to do it today, tomorrow, next year, or even within our lifetimes. However, God's word will come to pass in His own time and in His own way.

## APPLYING THE BIBLE

**God doesn't settle His accounts in October.**—Two farmer neighbors were talking across the fence one day about Christian matters. One farmer was a dedicated Christian, and the other one wasn't. The Christian farmer encouraged his unsaved neighbor to accept Christ, put Him first in everything, and be blessed as the result. The unsaved farmer said he didn't see any need in doing that since he was already doing quite well.

"See my fine field, heavy with grain and about ready to be harvested?" he asked. "I plowed the field on Sunday. I planted it on Sunday. I worked it on Sunday. And I plan to harvest it on Sunday. Why should I become a Christian? I'm doing quite well the way things are," he said.

The Christian farmer, with heavenly wisdom, congratulated the neighbor on his good crop then hastened to point out: "You need to keep in mind God does not settle His accounts in October."

Micah, addressing the sins of both Judah (Jerusalem) and Israel (Samaria) warned them that although God had been patient in bearing with their rebelliousness for generations, His patience was about exhausted (1:1ff). He would settle his account!

In "Retribution," Henry Wadsworth Longfellow wrote:

*Though the mills of God grind slowly,*
*Yet they grind exceeding small;*
*Though with patience he stands waiting*
*With exactness grinds He all.*

Israel and Judah found out much to their sorrow that although God's judgment is often slow in coming, it is certain.

**Greed always says, "More!"**—Count Leo Tolstoy (1828-1910) was one of Russia's most celebrated writers of fiction. His massive work, *War and Peace,* and *Anna Karenina,* are two of his best-known novels.

Tolstoy tells about a man who was told he could possess all the land around which he could walk between sunrise and sunset. Hungry for land and driven by greed, he walked faster and faster the farther he went. As the day wore on, the word that burned in his brain was, "more!" "more!" When the sun was low and his body was exhausted, he took off his shirt and boots to quicken his pace. Finally, as the sun fell behind the trees, he threw himself forward on the ground and reached out as far as he could with his fingers to possess just one more foot of land. And there they found him—dead!

Friends buried the greedy man in all the land he possessed at day's end: a strip six feet long and two feet wide!

**Preachers who do not preach.**—Sir William Blackstone (1723-1780) was an English judge and professor who won recognition for his *Commentaries on the Laws of England* which have had a great influence on many lawyers including Abraham Lincoln. Blackstone's work was the basis of legal education in England and America for many years and had a strong influence on the American colonies.

The eminent jurist enjoyed going from church to church in London to hear the various preachers. To nearly all the sermons he heard, Blackstone's comment: "I did not hear a single discourse which had more Christianity in it than the writings of Cicero." He said it would have been impossible to have discovered from the sermons whether the preacher were a follower of Confucius, Mohammed, or Christ.

About the kind of preaching to which they listened in his day, one Methodist convert who left the Church of England said that many of the sermons preached in the church of that day were in an unknown tongue to the common man.

But how much different was John Wesley who rescued England from dullness and incomprehension in preaching. He addressed the common man—those sick in bed, the prosperous, the prisoner, the mourning, the feasting—with his down-to-earth messages about Jesus in the language the people could understand.

**Longfellow's comments.**—After one Sunday morning worship service, American poet Henry Wadsworth Longfellow went home and wrote in his diary: "John Ware of Cambridge preached a good sermon. I applied it to myself."

## TEACHING THE BIBLE

▶ *Main Idea:* God's denunciation of Judah's greedy leaders demonstrates that God opposes greed and warns against its dangers.

▶ *Suggested Teaching Aim:* To lead adults to examine God's denunciation of Judah's greedy leaders, and to identify similar practices in their lives that God opposes.

### A TEACHING OUTLINE

1. *Use a chart to examine the focal passage.*
2. *Identify the greed in the lives of four leaders.*
3. *Identify the greed in their lives.*

**Introduce the Bible Study**

Use "Greed always says, 'More!' " *(Applying the Bible)* to introduce the Bible study.

## Search for Biblical Truth

IN ADVANCE, enlist a member to read "Micah" in the *Holman Bible Dictionary* or another Bible dictionary and prepare a two- to three-minute report on Micah to begin the search for biblical truth.

On a chalkboard or a large sheet of paper write the following. Do not copy the italicized phrases; they are suggested answers. Your answers may differ somewhat and still be correct.

SINS OF LEADERS AND THEIR PUNISHMENT

**Micah 3**

| Leaders | Sin | Punishment |
|---|---|---|
| Prophets (5:7,11*c*-12) | *Saying what people want to hear* | Condemned to darkness; Jerusalem destroyed |
| Politicians (3:9-10) | *Twisted justice* | Jerusalem destroyed |
| Judges (3:11*a*,12) | *Bribes* | Jerusalem destroyed |
| Priests (3:11*b*,12) | *Teach what people want to hear* | Jerusalem destroyed<br>Jerusalem destroyed |

Call for a volunteer to read 3:5-7,11*c*-12 as members listen for the sins of the prophets and the punishment God promised.

Point out that even though Micah was a prophet, he was not like these false prophets. Ask members to read verse 8 and tell how Micah differed from the false prophets. (full of Spirit, upheld justice)

Call for a volunteer to read verses 9-10 as members listen for the sins of the politicians and government officials.

Call for a volunteer to read verse11a as members listen for the sins of the judges and priests. Point out that what bothered Micah as much as anything else was their saying they leaned on or trusted the Lord as they did their evil.

Share the information from *Studying the Bible* (the last three paragraphs) about the fall of Jerusalem.

## Give the Truth a Personal Focus

Ask members to share ways people today can and do commit similar sins. Point out the greed behind them. Then ask, What evidence of greed do you see in your life?

As members suggest evidences, write these on a chalkboard or a large sheet of paper.

Ask: What difference do you expect in God's response to greed in the twentieth century A.D. as compared to his response in the eighth century B.C.? What steps do you need to take to eliminate greed from your life?

Remind members of the opening illustration from Tolstoy and point out that in the final analysis a burial plot is all the land any of us will have.

Close in prayer that members would be honest with themselves and with God about their greed and take serious steps to correct it.

# Isaiah's Call and Message

**Basic Passages:** Isaiah 6; 1
**Focal Passages:** Isaiah 6:1-8; 1:14-17

We have studied passages from three of the four eighth-century prophets. For the next three weeks we will study passages from the fourth and most famous of this group. Amos and Hosea preached in the Northern Kingdom, and Micah and Isaiah preached in the Southern Kingdom. In our Bibles, Isaiah is the first of the prophetic books. This is not only because of the length of the book, but also because of its importance. In this lesson, we will look at the call of Isaiah and a sample of his messages to Judah.

**Study Aim:** *To summarize Isaiah's call and his basic message*

## STUDYING THE BIBLE

### I. Isaiah's Call (Isa. 6:1-13)

**1. Vision of God (6:1-4)**

> 1 In the year that king Uzziah died I saw also the Lord sitting upon a throne, high and lifted up, and his train filled the temple.
>
> 2 Above it stood the seraphims: each one had six wings; with twain he covered his face, and with twain he covered his feet, and with twain he did fly.
>
> 3 And one called unto another, and said, Holy, holy, holy, is the Lord of hosts: the whole earth is full of his glory.
>
> 4 And the posts of the door moved at the voice of him that cried, and the house was filled with smoke.

Hosea 1:1 dates the preaching of Isaiah during the reigns of four kings of Judah, extending roughly over the last half of the eighth century B.C. Isaiah 6:1 dates his call during the year that King Uzziah died. Uzziah, also called Azariah, had a long, prosperous reign. For the most part, he did what was right in the sight of the Lord. However, he failed to root out idolatry and became a leper in his old age (2 Kings 15:1-7). The death of a great leader is a traumatic experience for many in a nation. Thus, Isaiah may have been particularly open to a word from the Lord at this time.

As Isaiah grieved over the death of an earthly king, he saw a vision of the eternal King (see v. 5). He saw the Lord sitting on a throne. The train of his royal garments filled the temple. Very likely, Isaiah was in the Jerusalem temple when he saw this vision, but he saw much more than a worshiper could see with his eyes in the Jerusalem temple. Isaiah caught a glimpse of the heavenly temple.

The angelic seraphim praised God by crying to one another the words of verse 3. As they did, the foundations shook and smoke filled the temple. The word "holy" has a twofold meaning: (1) For one thing, it means that God is different from and exalted above human beings. (2) "Holy" also means that the Lord is righteous in who He is and what He does.

**2. Confession and cleansing (6:5-7)**

> **5 Then said I, Woe is me! for I am undone; because I am a man of unclean lips, and I dwell in the midst of a people of unclean lips: for mine eyes have seen the King, the Lord of hosts.**
>
> **6 Then flew one of the seraphims unto me, having a live coal in his hand, which he had taken with the tongs from off the altar.**
>
> **7 And he laid it upon my mouth, and said, Lo, this hath touched thy lips; and thine iniquity is taken away and thy sin purged.**

The vision of the Holy God brought to Isaiah a deep sense of conviction. He saw himself as "undone," a word meaning "lost" or "ruined." In the white hot glow of God's holiness, Isaiah was deeply aware of his sins. Isaiah was particularly aware of the uncleanness of his lips and the lips of his countrymen. He had heard the continual praises of the seraphim, and he realized how differently he had used the gift of speech. Perhaps he had been saying things that were wrong; more likely he had only been going through the motions of praising the Lord.

As Isaiah confessed his sins, one of the seraphim touched his lips with a live coal from off the altar. The angelic being then spoke words of assurance to Isaiah. The searing hot coal had cleansed his lips. As a result, his sin and guilt were forgiven and taken away.

**3. Call and response (6:8)**

> **8 Also I heard the voice of the Lord saying, Whom shall I send, and who will go for us? Then said I, Here am I; send me.**

For the first time in the vision, Isaiah heard the Lord Himself speaking. The scene is a kind of heavenly court or council, where God and His angels were assembled to pass judgment on Judah for her sins. Isaiah heard the Lord asking who should be sent to Judah.

At this point, Isaiah probably had no clear understanding of the mission for which God needed someone. To his credit, Isaiah volunteered. When we compare Isaiah's response with that of other Bible people whom the Lord called, Isaiah stands out. People like Moses (Ex. 3—4) and Jeremiah (Jer. 1) offered excuses why they should not be sent to fulfill the Lord's call. By contrast, Isaiah volunteered.

**4. Commission (6:9-13).**—When Isaiah said he would go, the Lord said, "Go" (v. 9). The commission of the prophet is stated in a way that sounds as if God made the people reject His message. The Old Testament sometimes states the result of God's call to sinners as if their rejection and judgment were what God wanted to happen. Other Bible passages make clear God's love for sinners. What is inevitable is judgment on those who reject. Thus God told Isaiah that most would reject His word through the prophet.

### II. Isaiah' Message (Isa. 1:31)

**1. Indictment of an impenitent nation (1:1-9).**—After introducing Isaiah, the heavens and earth were called to hear God's indictment against His rebellious children. Although God had sent disasters to warn the nation, the people continued to remain impenitent. Only divine restraint had kept God from treating them like Sodom and Gomorrah.

**2. Hypocritical religion (1:10-15)**

> **14 Your new moons and your appointed feasts my soul hateth: they are a trouble unto me; I am weary to bear them.**
> **15 And when ye spread forth your hands, I will hide mine eyes from you: yea, when ye make your many prayers, I will not hear: your hands are full of blood.**

A few weeks ago we studied a passage from Amos that sounds like this passage from Isaiah (see Amos 5:18-24). Both Amos and Isaiah used strong words to describe how God hates hypocritical worship. Isaiah 1:10-15 mentions most of the features of Hebrew worship: many sacrifices, numerous visits to the temple at the various appointed times, spreading out of hands in prayer to God.

Notice how God reacted to their worship practices. God said that he had had more than enough of their sacrifices and took no pleasure in them (v. 11). He called their incense "an abomination" (v. 13). He could not bear their solemn assemblies (v. 13). God "hated" their feasts, which had become a "trouble" that he "was weary to bear" (v. 14). God said that when they spread out their hands in prayer, He would not hear (v. 15).

Some scholars think that prophets like Amos and Isaiah opposed the sacrificial system and temple worship. However, a more likely explanation is that they opposed not formal worship in the temple, but hypocritical worship anywhere. Both Amos and Isaiah judged true worship not on the basis of what happened in the temple but on what happened in the daily lives of worshipers.

Although the people said the right words in prayer and used the right motions, their hands were "full of blood" (v. 15). Verses 10-15 are closely related to verses 16-17. Taken together, the passage shows that God condemns those whose worship fails to carry over into how they treat other people. Not only were they failing to help needy people, but they built their fortunes on the blood of the helpless and needy. This is similar to Micah 3:9-10 from last week's lesson.

**3. Call to repentance and service (1:16-20)**

16 Wash you, make you clean; put away the evil of your doings from before my eyes; cease to do evil;
17 Learn to do well; seek judgment, relieve the oppressed, judge the fatherless, plead for the widow.

As Isaiah had experienced divine cleansing from sin when he confessed his sins, he called the sinful people to be washed and become clean. This would come when they put away their sins, in other words, when they ceased to do evil. Thus verse 16 is one of many Bible verses that call sinners to repent or turn away from sin. Repentance includes godly sorrow for sin, but it must also involve stopping the sin.

Verse 17 states the positive side of repentance. Those who truly repent become obedient to God. Being obedient meant learning to do right and seeking justice in all their actions. Remember that "judgment" means "justice," treating others—especially the helpless and oppressed—with fairness and compassion.

In order not to be misunderstood, verse 17 mentions three groups who needed justice: the oppressed, orphans, and widows. The Old Testament is filled with commands for people of faith to take care of and defend widows, orphans, and the oppressed. God often reinforced this commandment to Israel by reminding them that they had been helpless and oppressed in Egypt (for example, see Deut. 24:17-18).

People of faith were expected not just to help an occasional needy person but also to defend the helpless and oppressed against those who would exploit them. The words "relieve" and "judge" call for ensuring justice for the oppressed and the fatherless. The word "plead" means to plead the case for widows when people threaten to take advantage of them. Widows were an especially vulnerable group in ancient society. Godly men of influence in the community were expected to look out for their needs. Unfortunately, as in the case of the Pharisees condemned by Jesus, some outwardly religious men "devour widows' houses" (Mark 12:40).

Isaiah 1:18 is one of the Bible's most beautiful promises. God calls sinners to repent and to be totally cleansed of their sins. If they repented and obeyed God, they would live (v. 19). If they continued to rebel, they would be "devoured with the sword" (v. 20).

**4. Judgment and hope for Jerusalem (1:21-31).**—Like most of the prophets, Isaiah's message was a mixture of judgment and hope. These two themes are intertwined in the closing verses of Isaiah 1. Jerusalem had become a harlot. Her leaders loved bribes and denied justice to orphans and widows (vv. 21-23). God predicted that the wicked would be destroyed, but He held out hope for a future righteous Jerusalem (vv. 24-31).

## APPLYING THE BIBLE

**"Sweet are the uses of adversity."**—Isaiah speaks about "the treasures of darkness" (Isa. 45:3). The darkness often brings out the best in us. The fruit sorrow finally produces is always the sweetest. As Shakespeare put it: "Sweet are the uses of adversity." When sorrow is conceived within us, tragedy and heartache follow. But as with the birth of a child, "joy comes in the morning." Sorrow often awakens a love within us that, in turn, sustains us in life's darkest hours. Remember Tennyson's moving words from "In Memoriam":

*I hold it true whate'er befall;*
*I feel it, when I sorrow most;*
*'Tis better to have loved and lost*
*Than never to have loved at all.*

Isaiah, the princely preacher, loved King Uzziah. But Isaiah loved and lost. But, my, what sweet fruit came from his sorrow for isaiah testifies: "In the year that king Uzziah died I saw also the Lord sitting upon a throne, high and lifted up, and his train filled the temple" (6:1).

**The boy who looked into heaven.**—In his book *Man in Black,* singer Johnny Cash tells about the death of his brother Jack in 1944. The family lived in Arkansas and times were hard. Jack was working on Saturdays cutting fenceposts and cleaning up around the school's agricultural building, earning $3.00 each Saturday. As Jack was working, he was pulled into the large saw he was using and was severely injured.

The doctor told the family there was no chance for Jack to live, but Mr. and Mrs. Cash and the other children continued to pray that God would spare Jack's life.

Early on Sunday morning Jack came out of his coma. Looking around he asked his mother, "Why is everybody crying over me? Mamma, don't cry over me. Do you see the river?" Mrs. Cash replied that she didn't see any river. Jack then asked, "Mamma, can you hear the angels singing?" When Mrs. Cash said she couldn't hear the angels singing, Jack replied, "But Mamma, you've got to hear them." And, as the tears rolled down Jack's cheeks, he told his mother: "Listen to the angels. I'm going there, Mamma. What a beautiful city. And the angels are singing. Oh, Mamma, I wish you could hear the angels singing." And with that, he slipped away to be with Jesus.[1]

When King Uzziah died, Isaiah looked into heaven and he describes what he saw in 6:2-4.

**Isaiah's call.**—Rowland Hill (1744-1833) was one of England's great evangelical leaders. A gifted preacher, Hill served a large congregation at Surrey Chapel in London.

There is an interesting story about a returned missionary to Russia who was visiting in the home of an English Congregational minister. The minister had a grandson and the visiting missionary and the little boy soon struck up a warm friendship. One day as they were concluding family worship, the missionary said he was convinced the boy would preach some day in the pulpit of Rowland Hill. He gave the boy a shilling and made him promise that when that day came he would lead the congregation to sing William Cowper's hymn, "God Works in a Mysterious Way His Wonders to Perform."

The years went by and the minister's grandson, now fifteen years of age, was on his way to church in Colchester one cold, snowy winter day. But the weather was so cold the boy decided to stop at the nearest church. Entering the Primitive Methodist Church on London's Artillery Street, the boy listened as an unlearned layman arose to speak in the absence of the minister who did not show up. For his text he read from Isaiah 45:22: "Look unto me, and be ye saved, all the ends of the earth." Only a few worshipers were present, but the boy felt as though God were speaking directly to him, and that morning the boy was saved.

His name was Charles Haddon Spurgeon who preached for thirty years in the great Metropolitan Tabernacle in London. Millions of copies of his sermons were circulated worldwide and he had probably the greatest impact on the world of the kingdom of God of anyone in the nineteenth century.

As Spurgeon was called to his divine work of spreading the gospel through a unique experience, so was Isaiah called. Read about his call in 6:8. It was a quiet call to his troubled heart, but that call was destined to shake the world.[2]

## TEACHING THE BIBLE

▶ *Main Idea:* The description of Isaiah's call and early message illustrates that God calls His people to holy living.

▶ *Suggested Teaching Aim:* To lead adults to examine Isaiah's call and early message, and to determine areas of their lives they need to have cleansed so they can offer themselves to God for service.

### A TEACHING OUTLINE

*1. Use an illustration to introduce the lesson.*

*2. Use a personal assignment and creative writing assignments to understand Isaiah's vision.*

*3. Lead members to role-play an application to the lesson.*

**Introduces the Bible Study**

Share the illustration, "Isaiah's call" in *Applying the Bible.*

**Search for Biblical Truth**

Explain that we have studied three of the four great eighth-century prophets. Today we will study about Isaiah, the fourth and greatest of the four men.

IN ADVANCE, enlist a member to read "Isaiah," from the *Holman Bible Dictionary* or another Bible dictionary and be prepared to present a two- to three-minute report on Isaiah to begin the search for biblical truth.

Distribute paper and pencils to all members. Call for a volunteer to read 6:1-8. Ask members to pretend that they are reporters for the *Jerusalem Journal* and to write a news story about what Isaiah saw and experienced. Encourage them to describe what they saw, felt, smelled, and heard. Call on several to read their accounts.

Ask: What was so special about Isaiah's call? (saw the Lord) What political event likely brought about the experience? (death of Uzziah) What was Isaiah's reaction to the vision? (saw himself as unclean) what was the significance of the angel's touching his lips with a coal? (cleansed him)

Point out that Moses and Jeremiah offered excuses when God called them; Isaiah actually volunteered even though he did not know what God was calling him to.

IN ADVANCE, write the following on a chalkboard or a large sheet of paper. Cover the second point until you are ready to use it.

1. Hypocritical religion (1:10-15)
2. Call to repentance and service (1:16-17)

Ask members to scan 1:10-15, and describe the evidences of hypocritical religion mentioned in these two verses. (in general superficial worship; in specific, such things as meaningless sacrifices, attending the temple services, burning incense, observing festivals without living holy lives)

Uncover the second point and ask a volunteer to read verses 16-17. Ask, What one thing does God want His people to do? (learn to do well) With what three groups were they to demonstrate their holy living? (those of society who had no one to care for them—oppressed, orphans, and widows)

**Give the Truth a Personal Focus**

Write on a chalkboard or a large sheet of paper: *Here am I; send me.* Enlist two members to present a role-play about what this would mean in their life if they truthfully made this statement to the Lord. (This could be in any of many areas: giving, willingness to serve, willingness to be a witness at work, missions—home or abroad, long-term or short-term.) While they prepare their role-play, distribute paper and pencils. Ask members to list those areas of their lives in which they need to have God cleanse them so they will then be ready to say, "Here am I; send me."

Do not force anyone to share, but if members wish, let them volunteer. Call for the role-play. Close in prayer that all the members would catch a vision of God and respond to His holiness.

---

1. Adapted from Johnny Cash, *Man in Black* (Grand Rapids: Zondervan, 1975), 40-48. See also J. B. Fowler, Jr., *Illustrating Great Words of the New Testament* (Nashville: Broadman Press, 1991), 70-71.

2. Adapted from Henry Alford Porter, *Toward the Sun Rising* (Nashville: Broadman Press, 1947), 81.

# When a Nation Is in Danger

**Basic Passages:** Isaiah 7; 2 Kings 16
**Focal Passages:** Isaiah 7:2-6,10-17

One of Isaiah's early prophecies was delivered to King Ahaz at a critical time in the life of Judah. The message called Ahaz to trust in the Lord; and when he refused, the word of the Lord warned of coming judgment. Part of the message to Ahaz received its ultimate fulfillment far beyond the time of Ahaz and Isaiah. Isaiah 7:14 is quoted in Matthew 1:21-23 as fulfilled in the birth of Jesus. The challenge of studying the passage is to see both how the message spoke to Ahaz and the crisis he faced and how it received ultimate fulfillment in Jesus Christ.

**Study Aim:** *To recognize the immediate and ultimate fulfillment of God's message spoken by Isaiah to Ahaz*

## STUDYING THE BIBLE

Ahaz was one of Judah's most evil kings (2 Kings 16:1-4). When he was attacked by Syria and Israel, Ahaz appealed to Assyria for help (vv.5-9). Ahaz even brought an Assyrian altar into the temple (vv.10-20). Ahaz and the people of Judah were terrified of the Syrian-Israelite invasion (Isa. 7:1-2). God sent Isaiah to challenge the faltering king to trust God and not fear harmless enemies (vv.3-9). When Ahaz refused God's offer of a sign, Isaiah accused him of wearying the God of Isaiah (vv.10-13). God then gave Ahaz a sign of coming deliverance from Syria and Israelùa sign with its ultimate fulfillment in the birth of Jesus (vv.14-17). God warned Ahaz that the Assyrians would be used to judge Judah as well as Syria and Israel (vv.17-25).

### I. Reign of Ahaz, King of Judah (2 Kings 16)

**1. The evil acts of Ahaz (vv. 1-4).**—The father (Jotham, 2 Kings 15:32-38) and grandfather (Uzziah or Azariah, 2 Kings 15:1-7) of Ahaz had been basically good men. Ahaz, however, was an evil man. He practiced the idolatry of the kings of Israel. So great was his evil that he even offered his son as a sacrifice to pagan gods.

**2. Appeal to Assyria for help (vv. 5-9).**—The Assyrian Empire was the dominant power of the day. Rezin, king of Syria, and Pekah, king of Israel, wanted Ahaz to join them in opposing Assyrian influence. When Ahaz refused, Rezin and Pekah sent their armies to besiege Jerusalem. Ahaz took the fateful step of appealing to Assyria for help. Ahaz sent silver and gold from the temple to Tiglath-pileser, king of

Assyria. The Assyrians attacked Damascus, capital of Syria, killed Rezin, and took the Syrians into captivity.

**3. Appeasing the Assyrians (vv. 10-20).**—Ahaz took further steps to appease the Assyrians. He made a copy of an Assyrian altar in the temple and worshiped at the altar. He made other changes in the temple of the Lord, designed to appease the Assyrians.

## II. Isaiah Speaks God's Word to Ahaz (Isaiah 7)

### 1. Ahaz's fear of Syria and Israel (vv. 1-2)

> **2 And it was told the house of David, saying, Syria is confederate with Ephraim. And his heart was moved, and the heart of his people, as the trees of the wood are moved by the wind.**

Verse 1 records the attack of Rezin and Pekah on Jerusalem. Verse 2 records the fear that Ahaz and the people of Judah had of the two invading armies. Their fears were like trees stirred by a strong wind. "Ephraim" was the largest tribe of the Northern Kingdom and was sometimes used to refer to Israel as a whole.

### 2. God's word through Isaiah (vv. 3-9)

> **3 Then said the Lord unto Isaiah, Go forth now to meet Ahaz, thou, and Shear-jashub thy son, at the end of the conduit of the upper pool in the highway of the fuller's field;**
>
> **4 And say unto him, Take heed, and be quiet; fear not, neither be fainthearted for the two tails of these smoking firebrands, for the fierce anger of Rezin with Syria, and of the son of Remaliah.**
>
> **5 Because Syria, Ephraim, and the son of Remaliah, have taken evil counsel against thee, saying,**
>
> **6 Let us go up against Judah, and vex it, and let us make a breach therein for us, and set a king in the midst of it, even the son of Tabeal.**

Isaiah was told by the Lord to take his son and meet Ahaz. Isaiah found Ahaz inspecting the water supply for the besieged city. The name of Isaiah's son means "a remnant shall return." Since the Lord had instructed Isaiah to take this son with him, apparently the child's name held some message for Ahaz. The name signified both judgment and hope: judgment that most of the nation would not survive and hope that some would be saved.

Verse 4 clearly states God's message to Ahaz in the crisis he was facing. He was to practice quietness that comes from trust in the Lord, and not to continue being afraid and discouraged. God reinforced this message by comparing Rezin and Pekah (son of Remaliah) to smoldering stubs of firewood. Their threatening words sounded fiery; but they were all smoke, with no fire.

Verses 5-6 contain their fiery words. They intended to invade Judah, partition it, and place on the throne some one they would choose. God assured Ahaz that this would never happen (v. 7). God told him that his enemies would be destroyed (vv. 8-9*a*). If Ahaz would stand firm in faith, He would continue to stand (v. 9*b*).

**3. Ahaz refuses a sign (vv. 10-13).—**

> 10 Moreover the Lord spoke again to Ahaz, saying,
> 11 Ask thee a sign of the LORD thy God; ask it either in the depth, or in the height above.
> 12 But Ahaz said, I will not ask, neither will I tempt the Lord.
> 13 And he said, Hear ye now, O house of David; Is it a small thing for you to weary men, but will ye weary my God also?

The Lord told Isaiah to tell Ahaz to ask for a sign. Signs were sometimes given to confirm a word from the Lord. For example, the Lord gave signs to Moses to confirm the call of Moses, and promised to give signs to confirm Moses' words to the Egyptians (Ex. 4:17). Thus God promised to give a sign to Ahaz of the truth of His promise to deliver Judah from Rezin and Pekah. God placed no limit on the sign that Ahaz might ask.

Ahaz refused to ask for a sign. He said that he didn't want to test the Lord by asking for a sign. Ahaz was probably thinking of Deuteronomy 6:16, which Jesus quoted when He was tempted to jump from the temple (Matt. 4:7; Luke 4:12). The big difference was that the devil was tempting Jesus to presume on God's power, and God Himself was challenging Ahaz to ask for a sign. So Ahaz was just using this as a hypocritical way of pretending to obey when actually he had already decided to disobey.

Isaiah's response to Ahaz shows what Isaiah thought of this pious fraud. Ahaz had said that he didn't want to test the Lord by asking for a sign. In essence, Isaiah said that Ahaz tested God's patience by his pious attempt to hide his basic failure to trust the Lord. Ahaz had been testing Isaiah's patience, but now he was wearying God. Ahaz had been challenged to ask a sign from "the Lord thy God" (v. 11). However, in verse 13, Isaiah asked Ahaz, "Will ye weary my God?" Notice the word "my." No longer did Isaiah consider the Lord to be the God of Ahaz.

**4. The Lord gives a sign (vv. 14-16)—**

> 14 Therefore the Lord himself shall give you a sign; Behold, a virgin shall conceive, and bear a son, and shall call his name Immanuel.
> 15 Butter and honey shall he eat, that he may know to refuse the evil, and choose the good.
> 16 For before the child shall know to refuse the evil, and choose the good, the land that thou abhorrest shall be forsaken

**of both her kings.**

Verse 14 is quoted in Matthew 1:23 as ultimately fulfilled in Jesus Christ, "God with us," born to the virgin Mary. Isaiah 7:14 takes its place along with other passages of Isaiah that pointed forward to Jesus. Isaiah 7:14 refers to His birth, Isaiah 9:6-7 announces His accession to His throne, and Isaiah 11:1-7 pictures His righteous reign.

The difficulty in the passage is not in identifying the ultimate fulfillment but in identifying the immediate fulfillment. Verses 15-17 make clear that the birth of the child of verse 14 was to be a sign to Ahaz in the crisis he faced. The mention of "butter and honey" (v. 15) seems to refer to the diet of a recently weaned child. The words about refusing evil and choosing good refer to a child who is mature enough to decide for himself about good and evil. In other words, before the child attained the age of accountability, the enemies of Ahaz—Syria and Israel—would lose their kings—Rezin and Pekah. Verse 16 was fulfilled when the Assyrians defeated Israel (2 Kings 15:29) and Syria (16:9).

Old Testament events sometimes had an immediate application that foreshadowed a more ultimate fulfillment in the New Testament. Apparently Isaiah's words in verse 14 referred first of all to a child about whose birth Ahaz would know. Many Bible students think the child was of the royal line. Many have suggested that Hezekiah may have been the child (2 Kings 18:1-8). Whoever the child was, Isaiah said that his birth was a sign of God's abiding presence with His people and of His promise to deliver them from their enemies. This child foreshadowed the unique One born of a virgin who is "God with us" and who came to save us from our real enemy—sin (Matt. 1:21-23).

**5. Judgment on Judah (vv. 17-25)—**

> **17 The Lord shall bring upon thee, and upon thy people, and upon thy father's house, days that have not come, from the day that Ephraim departed from Judah; even the king of Assyria.**

Although God promised to drive away the Syrians and Israelites, He predicted judgment coming to Judah. The historical background in 2 Kings sheds light on why and how this happened. Ahaz showed his lack of faith in God by sending to Assyria for help against Syria and Israel. He even brought Assyrian worship into the temple (Ch.16). Assyria eventually utterly defeated Israel (17:1-5). When they did, the Assyrians ravaged much of the land of Judah and besieged Jerusalem (18:13-35).

Isaiah 7:17 predicted a time of trouble for Judah comparable to the trauma felt when the northern tribes left Judah. The mention of the "king of Assyria" must have struck terror into Ahaz. No invaders were so brutal and inhuman as the Assyrians. Yet because of the sins of Ahaz and others in Judah, they were going to be attacked by these vicious barbarians. They would come on Judah like swarms of stinging insects (vv. 18-19). The land would be shaved as if by the Lord's razor in the hands of the king of Assyria (v. 20). The people would be reduced to a subsistence diet (vv. 21-22). The land would become a land of thorns and briers (vv. 23-25).

## APPLYING THE BIBLE

**What's wrong with the world?**—The world is in a mess as any thinking person would confess. The world's ills are given various names: fundamental disharmony; a basic bias toward evil; our evolutionary legacy; the inevitable evolutionary results from our alleged animal ancestry; the pains suffered by the race as it grows up; ad infinitum! But the Bible cuts through all the fancy jargon of intellectual diagnosticians and simply says the trouble with the world is this: S-I-N. As Ian MacPherson put it so vividly: The world's problems are so dreadful that an omnipotent God could only save it by dying for it.[1]

Things haven't changed any. They are the same today as they were in the days of Ahaz. The idolatry practiced by King Ahaz led people away from God. His sin was great and so was his judgment.

**The loyalty we owe others.**—C. K. Chesterton (1874–1936) was respected English poet and essayist who was very prominent in England during his lifetime. Chesterton wrote: "We are in a small boat on a stormy sea, and we owe each other a terrible loyalty. Ahaz, wrapped up in himself, forgot the loyalty he owed to the people who called him king. And the tragedy that followed brought Judah to her knees.

**Who is your best friend?**—In his book, *The Amazing Results of Positive Thinking,* Dr. Norman Vincent Peale tells about automobile Henry Ford. Ford and a friend were having lunch together one day when Ford asked his luncheon guest, "Who is your best friend?" After the man had named several people whom he considered to be his best friends, Ford wrote on the tablecloth: "Your best friend is he who brings out the best that is within you."[2]

**Four kinds of courage.**—For twenty-five years, Lord Moran was Winston Churchill's personal physician. Moran knew the horrors of war and both the fear and courage of the British people during their gravest crisis. Moran said there are four degrees of courage in men and women: Those who do not feel fear; those who feel fear but never show it; those who feel fear and show it but carry out their assignment; and those who feel fear, show it, and shirk their responsibilities.
In what category would you put King Ahaz? Terrified when Judah was threatened by Syria and Israel, Ahaz was told what to do by Isaiah, God's prophet. But Ahaz steadfastly refused to be obedient (Isa. 7:1-13). Ahaz was a wicked, weak, do-nothing king whose fear, which was rooted in disobedience toward God, was one of the factors that hastened Judah's destruction.

**He didn't listen to the masters voice.**—Near Jerusalem during World War I, a flock of sheep was blocking the road over which some Turkish soldiers were traveling. As the sheep were being roughly driven away by the soldiers, the shepherd who fallen asleep on the hillside on the warm spring day suddenly awakened. Seeing the sheep scattered all over the hill and valley, he knew he could not round them up by himself so he did what any good shepherd would do: standing on the side of the hill, he put his hands to his mouth and called loudly to his sheep. Hearing the call, the sheep paused, listened carefully, observed it was a familiar call, and rushed as quickly as they could to surround their master. According to Jesus, it is the nature of sheep to listen and heed the voice of their master (John 10).

Unlike the sheep, King Ahaz did not listen to the voices of the Master. When Isaiah the prophet told Ahaz what God required Ahaz to do, he refused.

## TEACHING THE BIBLE

▶ *Main Idea:* The description of Ahaz' response to God's word promises that we can trust God to fulfill His promises to us.
▶ *Suggested Teaching Aim:* To lead adults to analyze Ahaz's response to God's promise, and to trust God's intervention in a crisis in their lives.

### A TEACHING OUTLINE

*1. Introduce the lesson by using an illustration.*
*2. Examine the background of Isaiah 7.*
*3. Analyze the immediate and the final fulfillment of Isaiah's prophecy.*
*4. Determine how God can solve crises today in their lives or the lives of others.*

**Introduce the Bible Study**

Use "Four kinds of courage" in *Applying the Bible* to introduce the Bible study.

**Search for Biblical Truth**

IN ADVANCE, prepare the following chart on a chalkboard or a large sheet of paper:

GOD'S PROMISE TO ISAIAH

To Ahaz:

To Us:

To understand the background of this passage, briefly summarize I. Reign of Ahaz, King of Judah (2 Kings 16) (or IN ADVANCE enlist a member to do this).

Ask members to open their Bibles to Isaiah 7:2. Explain that Judah was being attacked by the two allied armies of Syria and Israel (the

Northern Kingdom). Ask, what image describes the fright of the people? (shaking like trees in a wind)

Ask: What was God's message to Isaiah? (take his son and tell Ahaz not to fear)

Ask a volunteer to read Isaiah 7:10-13. Ask: What did God tell Ahaz to ask for? (a sign) What was Ahaz' response? (refused because he had already decided not to trust God)

Ask a volunteer to read Isaiah 7:14-16. Refer to the chart you had written earlier. Ask members to search verse 14 to see what sign Isaiah promised Ahaz God would send.

Point out that the difficulty is not in identifying the ultimate fulfillment of this sign. The ultimate fulfillment was Jesus Christ. Matthew 1:23 affirms this. The difficulty in this passage is in identifying the immediate fulfillment.

Use *Studying the Bible* to explain how the prophecy offered hope to Ahaz. Fill in the chart as members suggest answers. Add information from Studying the Bible as you explain this near and far fulfillment.

Read Isaiah 7:17 and point out the ultimate punishment God promised Judah.

**Give the Truth a Personal Focus**

Remind members that God intervened in Israel's history and that He still intervenes today. Ask, How can God intervene in the following crises? (1) A man lost his job and his wife is in the hospital delivering their first child (God could use people to minister to the couple); (2) a family with a teenage daughter is going through a crisis.

Point out that God does intervene all the time in our lives but that He often does it by using His people. Encourage members to let God intervene in a crisis in their lives and to let God use them to help solve a crisis in someone else's life.

---

1. Adapted from Ian McPherson, *The Burden of the Lord* (New York and Nashville: Abington Press, 1960), 24-25. (See J. B. Fowler, Jr., *Illustrating Great Words of the New Testament* [Nashville: Braodman Press, 1991, 166-67.]),

2. Norman Vincent Peale, *The Amazing Results of Positive Thinking* (Englewood Cliffs, N.J.: Prentice-Hall Inc., 1959), 64.

# Judgment Comes on Israel

**Basic Passages:** Isaiah 9:8—10:4; 5
**Focal Passages:** Isaiah 5:8-12,18-23

The ministry of Isaiah coincided with the final years of the Northern Kingdom. Although the prophet addressed himself to the Southern Kingdom, some of his words dealt with the sins and judgment of the Northern Kingdom. The purpose of these warnings was to call Judah to repentance. This is true of Isaiah 9:8—10:4. Some of Isaiah's prophecies applied to the children of Israel, whether in Israel or in Judah. This is true of Isaiah 5.

**Study Aim:** *To identify sins that brought judgment on Israel and to evaluate to what degree these sins are practiced today*

## STUDYING THE BIBLE

Isaiah 9:8—10:4 contains four sections, each ending with the words, "For all this his anger is not turned away, but his hand is stretched out still" (9:12,17,21; 10:4). Each section shows God's wrath against specific sins: arrogant pride (9:8-12), sinful leaders (vv.13-17), chaotic strife (vv.18-21), injustice and exploitation (10:1-4). Isaiah 5 begins with the song of the vineyard (vv.1-7). Then comes a series of six woes with interspersed words of judgment. The woes deal with greedy landgrabbers (vv.8-10), drunken carousers (vv.11-12), guilty mockers of God (vv.18-19), the morally depraved (v.20), the self-sufficient (v.21), drunken exploiters (vv.22-23). The words of judgment are in Isaiah 5:13-17,24-30.

### I. The Outstretched Arm of God's Judgment (Isa. 9:8—10:4)

**1. Judgment on arrogant pride (9:8-12).**—The Northern Kingdom responded to disasters with arrogant pride that they could rebuild better than before. God continued to raise up enemies in a vain attempt to lead them to repentance.

**2. Judgment against sinful leaders (9:13-17).**—When Israel hardened their hearts, God sent judgment on their political and religious leaders. Unfortunately the national judgment also would fall on the people, whom the leaders had led astray or exploited.

**3. Judgment of chaotic strife (9:18-21).**—The final years of Israel's history were filled with social chaos and political anarchy (2 Kings 15:8-34). God's wrath allowed the Israelites to act ruthlessly toward one another and toward Judah.

**4. Judgment against injustice and exploitation (10:1-4).**—The rich and powerful wrote laws that allowed them to exploit the poor, needy, widows, and orphans. These greedy exploiters would have nowhere to flee when God's wrath fell.

## II. Song of the Vineyard (Isa. 5:1-7)

Isaiah put a parable into the form of a song. He sang of a friend who had lavished great care on his vineyard only to have it bear wild, bitter grapes. The friend decided to quit taking care of the vineyard and to allow the weeds to take it over. The singer asked the listeners if the vineyard owner was right in taking this action. Only at the end of the song did Isaiah reveal that God was the vineyard owner and Israel the vineyard.

## III. Pronouncement of Woes and Judgment (Isa. 5:8-30)

**1. Woe to greedy landgrabbers (5:8-10)**

> 8 Woe unto them that join house to house, that lay field to field, till there be no place, that they may be placed alone in the midst of the earth!
> 9 In mine ears said the Lord of hosts, Of a truth many houses shall be desolate, even great and fair, without inhabitant.
> 10 Yea, ten acres of vineyard shall yield one bath, and the seed of an homer shall yield an ephah.

Ancient Israel was an agricultural society in which land was a family's most valued possession. The law of God to Israel was designed to keep each family's land. No land was to be permanently lost to a family because human owners are only temporary tenants of what belongs to God (Lev. 25:23; see also vv.13-17,24-28).

In spite of God's clear commands, the rich and powerful people of Isaiah's day tried to add as much land as possible to their vast holdings. Isaiah wrote that each acted as if he wanted to buy up all the land and become king of the world. Although Isaiah does not mention their methods here, Micah 2:1-2 shows how greedy people laid awake at night devising schemes to rob the poor of their land.

Judgment was coming on greedy landgrabbers. The homes of the rich and famous of Israel would become desolate. Their lands would not produce enough crops to make a profit. Ten acres of vineyard would produce only one bath (about five or six gallons). A homer of seed (10 bushels) would produce an ephah (1 bushel).

**2. Drunken carousers (5:11-12)**

> 11 Woe unto them that rise up early in the morning, that they may follow strong drink; that continue until night, till wine inflame them!
> 12 And the harp, and viol, the tabret, and pipe, and wine are

**in their feasts: but they regard not the work of the Lord, neither consider the operation of his hands.**

The Bible takes a consistent stand against drunkenness. Two of the six woes in Isaiah 5 deal with this sin. Isaiah condemned those who got an early start in the day with their drinking and continued into the night. Their drinking was part of their entire approach to life. These people lived to party; and—like their modern counterparts—they couldn't conceive of a party without music and alcohol.

What's wrong with "having a good time"? This is how many then and now would excuse their actions. The last part of verse 12 focuses on one thing that is wrong with drunken carousing. Such people have no place for God in their lives. God is often disregarded and disrespected by words and deeds.

**3. Coming judgment (5:13-17).**—The people and leaders of Israel would go into exile (v. 13). Death is pictured like a hungry animal with jaws open to devour the great ones of Jerusalem (v. 14). Thus are the haughty proud always humbled by the exalted Lord (vv. 15-16). The animals left in the land would graze among ruins (v. 17).

**4. Guilty mockers of God (5:18-19)**

**18 Woe unto them that draw iniquity with cords of vanity, and sin as it were with a cart rope.**

**19 That say, Let him make speed, and hasten his work, that we may see it: and let the counsel of the Holy One of Israel draw nigh and come, that we may know it!**

The third woe was pronounced on people who haul the load of their heavy sin like an animal straining to pull a cart. The word "vanity" means "lies" or "deceit." They may think they are fooling everyone, including God; but they are only deceiving themselves. Sin has a numbing quality about it. People are deceived into thinking they are really living, when actually they are struggling with a heavy burden. They try to convince themselves and others that they are really free, when actually they are slaves of their own sins.

Nothing so shows their spiritual slavery as their mockery of God. Skeptics and spiritually confused people in every age have said much the same thing as is quoted in verse 19. The mockers in Isaiah 5:19 defiantly called on God to prove Himself by doing something that would prove to them that He is really God. Those who dare God to prove Himself show both their unbelief and their foolhardiness. When the time comes for God to show Himself to such people, they will face Him as Judge (see Amos 5:18-20).

**5. The morally depraved (5:20)**

**20 Woe unto them that call evil good, and good evil; that put darkness for light, and light for darkness; that put bitter for sweet, and sweet for bitter.**

Isaiah condemned people whose consciences no longer worked.

They had practiced so long at calling evil good and good evil that they no longer could tell the difference. People like that can't let their conscience be their guide because their consciences has become seared as with a hot iron (1 Tim. 4:2).

This verse shows that moral relativism is only a new name for an ancient condition. Recent surveys show that many people don't believe in moral absolutes. According to them, everything is relative. Whether something is right or wrong depends on the situation and the person. Everyone is supposed to be free to do his or her own thing, and society assumes that whatever a person chooses to do is all right. What the Bible calls evil is pronounced good by some people. What the Bible calls spiritual darkness is called enlightened living.

**6. The self-sufficient (5:21)**

> **21 Woe to them that are wise in their own eyes, and prudent in their own sight!**

This woe is closely related to the preceding one. Having forsaken God and His word as standards for conduct and truth, people act as if they are gods themselves. When the serpent tempted Adam and Eve, he lured them with the promise of godlike wisdom of good and evil (Gen. 3:5).

We only fool ourselves when we overrate our own wisdom. Such people are wise "in their own eyes." They may even fool a few others for a while, but they don't fool everyone and they never fool God. This doesn't mean that we have no wisdom or worth. Our wisdom and worth come from God's creation and redemption, not from setting ourselves up as little gods.

**7. Drunken exploiters (5:22-23)**

> **22 Woe unto them that are mighty to drink wine, and men of strength to mingle strong drink;**
> **23 Which justify the wicked for reward, and take away the righteousness of the righteous from him!**

Isaiah gave a vivid description of the kind of people who take such pride in their drinking and in their ability to mix drinks. They were called "heroes at drinking wine" and "champions at mixing drinks" (NIV). This is the second of the six woes about the misuse of alcohol. Taken together, these two woes focus on two reasons why the Bible condemns drunkenness: (1) Verses 11-12 point out that alcoholic intoxication reveals an absence of any vital relationship with God. (2) Verses 22-23 point to how drunkenness hurts people.

Alcohol numbs moral sensitivities. No wonder that criminals and evildoers often fortify themselves with alcohol before they act. The sins described in verse 23 are familiar sins of eighth-century Israel. The rich and powerful were perverting the justice system so that they got their way while the righteous person was defrauded or punished. Everyone who planned and perpetrated the injustice did so over a drink—usually more than one drink.

**8. Inevitable judgment (5:24-30).**—What awaits such sinners? The judgment of God would fall on those who have rejected His law and spurned His word (vv. 24-25). God would summon the fierce and relentless invaders to be the instruments of His terrible judgment (vv. 26-30).

## APPLYING THE BIBLE

**Ruined by greed.**—Sir James M. Barrie (1860-1937) was a famous Scottish writer. His best-known play was Peter Pan.

One of his short plays, *The Will*, which is only thirty minutes long, tells about a young, married couple who went to the lawyer's office to draw up their will. Happy and looking toward the future with bright eyes, they wanted to be sure their business was in order so that each would be taken care of in the event of the death of the other. Philip Ross, the husband, has inherited some money and in one, brief sentence in the will he leaves everything to his wife. Lovingly, she protests that she is the sole beneficiary. She wants him to include his cousins and a needy convalescent home. The lawyer, impressed by their unselfishness, teasingly tells them they are a ridiculous couple. "But don't change," he urges.

They come back twenty years later to rework their will. They have prospered, and their estate is sizable. The husband alone could handle the changes in their will, but his wife wants to be sure he doesn't do anything foolish. They don't talk about "our money;" rather, it is "my money." They finally reach a bitter agreement arrived at only after much agitation.

Twenty more years have passed and now it's Sir Philip Ross. Knighted and sisty-five years of age, he comes in alone. His wife has died and their children have turned out to be no good. All provisions in the previous will are canceled and all the relatives are left without a shilling. Sadly, Ross confesses as he paces the floor angrily, that he has no friends to whom to leave his money. Against the advice of his lawyer Ross leaves his sizable inheritance to his enemies, adding the phrase, "With my curses."[1]

Our lesson today points out (5:8-10) that the sin of greed runs rampant across the land. Enough is not enough! Driven by their love of money, the wealthy want more and more, all at the expense of the poor. Isaiah's words here are reminiscent of those in Micah 2:1-2. Israel's sin is America's sin. Take note that the greed of American Christians is glaringly revealed in our disobedience to bring the tithes and offerings to the storehouse as He commands (see Mal. 3).

**A serpent in the cup.**—An ancient king, so the story goes, was destroying himself with alcohol. His best friend was his doctor, and the doctor was much concerned about the king's health and the nation's welfare. Hoping to shock the king into changing his ways, the doctor had a silversmith craft a small silver serpent and fasten it to the bottom of the king's favorite wine cup. Not long after the strange request was finished, a servant drew the king a cup of wine and he eagerly emptied it. It was then he saw the serpent in the bottom of the cup and cried out in alarm, "There is a serpent in my cup!" The wise doctor replied, "Your Majesty, there is a serpent at the bottom of every cup of wine."

The late Dr. R. G. Lee called drinking "slop which makes children afraid of their fathers and makes wives to dread the home-coming of husbands, and make men, as Edgar said in 'King Lear,' to become false of heart, bloody of hand, and to be hog in sloth, wolf in greediness, dog in madness, lion in prey."[2]

Lee then adds: "Man, in ways various, changes corn into hiccough-producing hooch." Paraphrasing a familiar Mother Goose rhyme, Lee wrote:

*Jack and Jill*
*Went up the hill,*
*To get some bootleg licker,*
*Jack went blind*
*and lost hid mind—*
*And Jill is even sicker.*[3]

What evil has brought more heartache and ruin to our beloved land than alcohol? The answer: Nothing! (See also 5:22-23.)

## TEACHING THE BIBLE

▶ *Main Idea:* God's judgement on Israel illustrates that God holds people accountable for their sins.
▶ *Suggested Teaching Aim:* To lead adults to identifty the sins that brought judgement on Israel, and to evaluate to what degree they practice these sins.

### A TEACHING OUTLINE

1. *Introduce today's lesson by sharing an illustration on greed.*
2. *Lead members to identify the six woes for which God condemned Israel.*
3. *Organize members in six groups to find the relevance of these six woes.*
4. *Lead members to evaluate the extent that these six sins are present in their life.*

**Introduce the Bible Study**

Introduce the study by telling the illustration, "Ruined by greed," from *Applying the Bible.*

**Search for Biblical Truth**

IN ADVANCE, place the following posters on the wall around the room: Isaiah 5:3-10; Isaiah 5:11-12; Isaiah 5:18-19; Isaiah 5:20;

Isaiah 5:21; Isaiah 5:22-23.

As members enter, ask each person to go to one of the posters (try to have the class organized in six equal groups). Ask them to find the Scripture and above the Scripture reference write a *woe* condemning the person(s) mentioned in the Scripture. (Headings should be similar to the following: Greedy landgrabbers (vv.8-10); Drunken carousers (vv.11-12); Guilty mockers of God (vv.18-19); Morally Depraved (v.20); Self-Sufficient (v.21); Drunken exploiters (vv.22-23).

Call for their reports. Use the material in the introduction to *Studying the Bible* to summarize the bacground material. Then ask each gorup to develop a case study, role play, or drama to show the modern relevance of the woes. Call for reports.

DISCUSSION QUESTIONS: Which of these woes does our nation need to hear the most? Why?

**Give the Truth a Personal Focus**

Read the six woes from the posters. Ask members to evaluate their own lives to determine the degree that they are practicing these sins today? Remind members that God's inevitable judgement will fall today just as it fell in the eighth-century B.C.

Close in prayer of confession and enouragement that members may confess their sin and repent from it.

---

1. Adapted from J. Wallace Hamilton, *Ride the Wild Horses!* (Old Tappan, N.J.: Fleming H. Revell Co., 1962), 57-58.
2. Robert G. Lee, *Lord, I Believe* (Nashville: Broadman Press, 1927), 23.
3. Ibid.

# The End of a Nation

**Basic Passage:** 2 Kings 17:1-23
**Focal Passage:** 2 Kings 17:6-14

The Jewish people consider their Scriptures to consist of three major divisions: Law, Prophets, and Writings. What they call Prophets include many of what we call Books of History. One reason for this is that the stories of prophets like Nathan, Elijah, Elisha, and others are in our so-called Books of History. Another reason is that these books record history from a moral and spiritual point of view. A good example of this prophetic history is 2 Kings 17:1-23. This passage tells of the fall of the Northern Kingdom to the Assyrians, but it explains the moral and spiritual reasons for the fall.

**Study Aim:** *To describe the fall of the Northern Kingdom and to explain why it fell*

## STUDYING THE BIBLE

The Assyrians attacked Israel when King Hoshea sent tribute to Egypt instead of Assyria (vv. 1-5). After a three-year siege, Samaria fell and the Israelites were taken into captivity (v. 6). Israel fell because the people sinned against the Lord who had delivered them from Egypt (v. 7). They adopted the pagan worship and ways of other nations (v. 8). Throughout their history, sin and idolatry pervaded the land (vv. 9-12). God sent prophets to call the people back to Him (v. 13). When the people rejected God's word (vv. 14-17), God's wrath fell on Israel (v. 18). Judah continued for a while longer before a similar fate overtook her (vv. 19-20). In retrospect, the sin of Jeroboam I at the beginning of Israel's history exerted a continuing evil influence (vv. 21-23).

### I. Fall of the Northern Kingdom (2 Kings 17:1-6)

**1. Last years (vv. 1-5)**—The long reign of Jeroboam II was the last period of political stability for Israel (2 Kings 14:23-29). The prophets Amos and Hosea exposed the sins behind the facade of prosperity. The final years of Israel were filled with political chaos. After a short reign, Jeroboam's son Zechariah was assassinated by Shallum (15:8-12). Shallum was killed by Menahem (15:17-22). Menahem's son Pekahiah was killed by Pekah (15:23-26), who in turn was killed by Hoshea (15:27-31). Of the four kings between Jeroboam and Hoshea, only one died a natural death.

The final years of Israel coincided with the rising power of the Assyrian Empire. Assyria's aggressive actions are mentioned several times in 2 Kings. During the reign of Menahem, Israel was forced to pay tribute money to Assyria (15:19-20). Pekah joined Rezin of Syria in rebelling against Assyria. In reprisal, Assyrian armies captured many cities in Israel and carried people away as captives (v.29). The Assyrians also captured Damascus and carried its people into captivity (16:10). Hoshea withheld tribute from Assyria and began to send it to Egypt, Assyria's chief rival (17:1-4). As a result, Shalmaneser of Assyria invaded Israel, imprisoned Hoshea, and began a three-year siege of Samaria (v. 5).

**2. Fall of Samaria (v. 6)**

> **6 In the ninth year of Hoshea the king of Assyria took Samaria, and carried Israel away into Assyria, and placed them in Halah and in Habor by the river of Gozan, and in the cities of the Medes.**

History reveals how brutal the Assyrians were. Torture, execution, and terror were freely employed in their conquests. Their policy of dealing with survivors was to uproot defeated nations from their homeland and to scatter them. Other defeated nations in turn were resettled in lands from which people had been uprooted. Verse 6 describes the areas into which the Israelite survivors were scattered. Later the Assyrians brought captive people from five different areas to resettle the region vacated by the departure of the Israelites (v.24).

## II. History of Sin and Idolatry (2 Kings 17:7-12)

**1. Sinned against the Lord (v. 7)**

> **7 And so it was, that the children of Israel had sinned against the Lord their God, which had brought them up out of the land of Egypt, from under the hand of Pharaoh, and had feared other gods.**

Verses 1-6 summarize the political and historical facts of Israel's fall. Beginning with verse 7 is a lengthy explanation of the moral and spiritual factors in Israel's fall. The prophets who interpreted Israel's history looked behind the outward circumstances and saw that the real reason for Israel's fall was Israel's persistent sin against the Lord.

Israel's call to be God's special people came after the Lord's deliverance of them from Egyptian slavery. God gave them His law and entered into covenant with Israel at Mount Sinai. In describing how they left Egypt, Moses and later prophets never referred to it as an escape. It was not an escape engineered by Moses and carried out courageously by a liberty-loving people. It was a divine deliverance. The Lord "brought them up out of the land of Egypt." Shortly after accepting God's covenant, they built a golden calf. This became the pattern of their history.

**2. Compromised their distinctive faith and way of life (v. 8)**

8 And walked in the statutes of the heathen, whom the Lord cast out from before the children of Israel, and of the kings of Israel which they had made.

God called Israel to a distinctive faith and way of life. They were to worship the Lord as the one and only God, and they were to be holy as the Lord is holy. After they settled in the promised land, the Israelites were tempted to compromise their faith and way of life by adopting pagan worship and immorality. They worshiped other gods, and they practiced the immoral ways associated with pagan life.

After Jeroboam led the northern tribes to split away from Rehoboam and Judah, Jeroboam built two places of worship so that the people would not be tempted to go to the temple in Jerusalem. Jeroboam set up calves at Bethel and Dan (1 Kings 12:25-33). The people were supposed to worship God at these places, but the prophets condemned this as idolatry (see vv. 21-23).

**3. Sin and idolatry pervades the land (vv. 9-12)**

9 And the children did secretly those things that were not right against the Lord their God, and they built them high places in all their cities, from the tower of the watchman to the fenced city.

10 And they set them up images and groves in every high hill, and under every green tree:

11 And there they burnt incense in all the high places, as did the heathen whom the Lord carried away before them; and wrought wicked things to provoke the Lord to anger:

12 For they served idols, whereof the Lord had said unto them, Ye shall not do this thing.

Not only did the people worship the calves at Bethel and Dan, but they also followed the pagan practice of using a variety of local pagan shrines. Baal worship was often done at local shrines or sanctuaries located on hills or near large trees. These pervaded the land—located in rural areas and in cities.

The Second Commandment expressly forbade making graven images. This follows logically from the First Commandment to worship the Lord only (Ex. 20:3-4). People who used images in worship doubtlessly claimed to be using them as aids in worshiping the Lord. No man-made image of God can reveal God. Images inevitably become associated with idolatry and all its related sins.

## III. Rejection and Judgment (2 Kings 17:13-18)

**1. Prophets (v. 13)**

13 Yet the Lord testified against Israel, and against Judah, by all the prophets and by all the seers, saying, Turn ye from your evil ways, and keep my commandments and my statutes,

according to all the law which I commanded your fathers, and which I sent to you by my servants the prophets.

God's response was to send prophets to speak His word. During this quarter we have studied six of the prophets whom the Lord sent to speak His word. Four of these spoke to the Northern Kingdom: Elijah, Elisha, Amos, and Hosea. Micah and Isaiah spoke to the Southern Kingdom. Although each of the kings is listed in 1 and 2 Kings, the key figures are the prophets. With few exceptions, the kings were evil influences on the nation. The prophets persistently preached to kings and people.

Prophets called the people to repent, which involved turning from idolatry and sins; and they called repentant people to obey the commands of the Lord. The call to repent testifies to the mercy of the Lord and to His willingness—even His eagerness according to prophets like Hosea—to forgive and renew His people.

**2. Rejection (vv. 14-18)**

14 Notwithstanding they would not hear, but hardened their necks, like to the necks of their fathers, that did not believe in the Lord their God.

Israel fell not because the people sinned, but because they continued to reject God's repeated pleas for them to repent. They stiffened their necks like stubborn animals who refuse to obey the driver. Many of them would have argued with the description in verse 14, which charges that they "did not believe in the Lord their God." Many of them thought of themselves as believers, but their actions denied the reality of their professed faith.

Their idolatry was a flagrant breaking of their covenant with God. They became as empty and false as the idols they worshiped (v. 15). They worshiped not only the two calves but also "all the host of heaven, and served Baal" (v. 16). They even became so depraved that some of them offered their children as sacrifices to their idols (v. 17).

**3. Rejection (v. 18)**—Verse 18 shows that the writer had come full circle from verse 6. Verses 7-18 explain the real reason for Israel's fall to Assyria. The people had rejected the Lord. After persistent pleas for them to repent, they continually rejected God. His wrath was expressed by leaving them to reap what they had sown.

## IV. Judah's Plight Foreshadowed (2 Kings 17:19-20)

Judah was following closely behind Israel in their sins. The spoilers of Judah waited in the shadows to bring ruin. Although this came over a century later, it did come (2 Kings 25).

## V. Evil Influence of Jeroboam's Sin (2 Kings 17:21-23)

Jeroboam, the first king of the Northern Kingdom, built the two calves at Bethel and Dan. The recurring theme of all later kings of Israel was that each walked in the sins of Jeroboam. Thus Jeroboam set in motion a sin that influenced not only his own generation but succeeding generations, and which brought final ruin to his nation.

## APPLYING THE BIBLE

**Recognizing that we are sinners.**—George Whitefield (1714-1770) was a well-known English evangelist who made several trips to the American colonies. He was a friend of John and Charles Wesley.

On one occasion, Lady Huntington invited the Duchess of Buckingham to go with her to hear Whitefield preach. The duchess rebelled: "It is monstrous to be told that you have a heart as sinful as the common wretches that crawl on the earth—it is highly offensive and insulting."

American evangelist Dwight L. Moody (1837-1899) was preaching in Chicago and went to the city jail to visit the prisoners. In one cell he found two prisoners, each of whom declared false witnesses were responsible for their imprisonment. In another cell he found a convict who said he was only an accomplice to the crime for which he was convicted and that the one really guilty had escaped. In the last cell he visited, Moody found a man crying desperately over his sins.

Facing sin honestly and confessing it fully is hard to do. Theologian Augustus H. Strong, who relates these experiences of Whitefield and Moody, says that the true repentance over sin does not ask, "What will my sin bring to me?" but, "What does my sin mean to God?"[1]

God's complaint against Israel is stated in verse 7: "The children of Israel had sinned against the Lord their God, which hath brought them up out of the land of Egypt, from under the hand of Pharaoh, and hath feared other gods." But they would not face and forsake their sins.

**Groping along without a guide.**—English author Owen Meredith (1831-1891), the pen name of Edward Robert Bulwer-Lytton, was both a poet and diplomat. Describing a godless, purposeless, guideless life, Meredith wrote in "Lucille":

*Down the path of a life that led nowhere he trod,*
*Where his whims were his guides, and his will was his god,*
*And his pastime his purpose.*

Referring to Meredith's poem, Thomas J. Villers says it reminds him of a man about whom President Leland Stanford, founder of California's Stanford University, once spoke. As he was driving down one of California's long, hot highways, Stanford passed a tramp with a bundle thrown over his shoulder. Stanford thought himself selfish not to pick up the tramp since there was a vacant seat in the car so he stopped, backed up, and asked the man, "Would you like to ride? Slowly the man replied, "No, I don't think I need to ride since I ain't goin' no place and ain't in no hurry to get there."

Villers concludes the paragraph with the statement that following

Christ as one's Guide gives life a glory and makes of that life a mission rather than a career.[2]

**The unsinkable ship.**—The *Titanic* was christened at Southampton, England, as the unsinkable ship, on April 10, 1912. While the ship was being built at the Queen's Island shipyards in Belfast, Ireland, many visitors came to watch. One of the visitors, a Catholic priest, noticed that someone had scribbled a blasphemous phrase on the starboard bow of the Titanic, and he requested it be erased because misfortune, he believed, would befall a ship with such a blasphemous inscription. But his concern was laughed at and the phrase was left on the ship's bow.

Four days out of Southampton, the *Titanic* struck a partially submerged iceberg. As water poured in, the ship was abandoned by all who could find room in the lifeboats. There were more than two thousand two hundred people on board but only seven hundred eleven of them survived. And the blasphemous phrase went to the bottom of the Atlantic still on the bow of the Titanic.

Did the blasphemous phrase have anything to do with the sinking of the ship? Probably not, but the doom of both Israel and Judah was the direct result of their blasphemous attitude toward God (17:13-18).

## TEACHING THE BIBLE

▶ *Main Idea:* The description of the end of the nation Israel warns that God holds His people accountable for their actions.
▶ *Suggested Teaching Aim:* To lead adults to explain why the Northern Kingdom fell, and to identify sins in their lives that bring God's displeasure

### A TEACHING OUTLINE

*1. Review the quarter by filling in a poster.*
*2. Use a series of questions to explain why the Northern Kingdom fell.*
*3. Use a chart to identify the similarity of Israel's sins and our sins.*

**Introduce the Bible Study**

To introduce the Bible study, share "Recognizing that we are sinners" from *Applying the Bible.*

**Search for Biblical Truth**

IN ADVANCE prepare the following poster as a review of this quarter. Do not copy the italicized information.

THE NORTHERN KINGDOM

Date founded: *922 B.C.*
First king: *Jeroboam I*
Capital city: *Samaria*

Religious headquarters: *Bethel, Dan*
Nation's sin: *worshiped other gods*
Last king: *Hoshea*
Attacking army: *Assyria*
Date destroyed: *721 B.C.*

Ask members to fill in as much of the above poster as they can; add what they are not able to provide.

On a map locate Samaria and the general location of Halah and Habor in the country of the Medes (17:6). Explain the Assyrian practice of removing captives and settling them in foreign countries to keep them from rebelling. Explain that this is what happened to the Ten Tribes of Israel.

Use the following questions to analyze why the Northern Kingdom fell:

(1) What claim did God have on Israel (v.7)? *(delivered them from Egypt)*

(2) What did God find most objectionable in the nation's behavior (v.8)? *(worshiped gods of the people the Lord had driven out of Canaan)*

(3) What were some of the pagan practices Israel adopted (vv.9-12)? *(built high places, worshiped in groves, burned incense, worshiped idols)*

IN ADVANCE ask a member to read "High Places" in the *Holman Bible Dictionary* or another Bible dictionary and explain the significance of these worship centers.

(4) What method did God use to try to get the people to repent (v.13)? *(prophets)*

(5) What was Israel's response to God's prophets (v.14)? *(would not listen)*

**Give the Truth a Personal Focus**

On a chalkboard or a large sheet of paper write **Israel** on the left and **Today** on the right. Ask members to list all the sins of the Northern Kingdom they can think of. Write these down the left side of a chalkboard under **Israel**. Then ask them how many of these same sins our nation is committing today. Write the modern counterpart under **Today**. Ask, What did God do to Israel? Write *Destroyed!* over the column of Israel's sins. Ask, What will God do to our nation if we continue to sin?

Ask members to look at the list of sins and mentally to identify any sins on the list that they have in their lives that bring displeasure to God. Close with a time of confession and repentance that God would forgive and give them a new opportunity to serve Him.

---

1. Augustus H. Strong, *Systemic Theology* (Philadelphia: Judson Press, 1909), Vol. III, 832.
2. Adapted from Thomas Jefferson Villers, *The Hurry Call of Jesus* (Philadelphia: Judson Press, 1927), 51.

## INDEX

The following index gives the lesson date on which a particular passage of Scripture has been treated in *Broadman Comments* from September 1989 through August 1995. Since the International Bible Lessons, Uniform Series, are planned in six-year cycles, the lessons during any six consecutive years include the better-known books and passages on central teachings. Thus, anyone who has access to the 1989-95 volumes of *Comments* can use this index to find a discussion of almost any part of the Bible he or she may be interested in studying.

### Genesis



### Exodus



### Leviticus



### Numbers



### Deuteronomy



### Joshua



### Judges



### 1 Samuel

## Luke



## John



## Acts

## Romans



## 1 Corinthians



## 2 Corinthians



## Galatians



## Ephesians



## Philippians



## Colossians



## 1 Thessalonians



## 2 Thessalonians



## 1 Timothy

January
15
1995

SPECIAL EMPHASIS

# Protecting the Helpless

**Basic Passages:** Genesis 1:28*a*; Exodus 1:15—2:10; Dueteronomy 18: 10*a*; Psalm 139:13-15; Matthew 18:10,14; 19:14-15*a*
**Focal Passages:** Genesis 1:28*a*; Deuteronomy 18:10*a*; Psalm 139:13-15; Matthew 18:10,14; 19:14-15*a*

Many churches observe Sanctity of Human Life Sunday. This session is designed for use in Sunday School on that Sunday. Bible passages have been selected for study in order to see some of the biblical principles that undergird the emphasis on sanctity of human life. The Bible passages selected for study for this particular session emphasize Bible teachings about "Protecting the Helpless." Although some of these passages do not apply directly to protecting the unborn, the principles do apply to them.

**Study Aim:** *To discover biblical teachings about caring for and protecting the helpless so that we can oppose abortion*

## STUDYING THE BIBLE

God's command to be fruitful and multiply shows that husbands and wives are cocreators with God of new life (Gen. 1:28*a*). God's creative power and wisdom are at work as life is formed within a mothers's womb (Ps. 139:13-15). God's response to Pharaoh's order to kill infants shows God's concern for the newborn and His use of people to mediate His care (Ex. 1:15—2:10). Jesus taught that God loves and cares for little ones (Matt. 18:10,14). God strongly condemned the heinous practice of child sacrifice (Deut. 18:10*a*). By word and deed, Jesus showed His love for little children and encourgaged adults to bring little children to Him (Matt. 19:14-15*a*).

### I. God Is the Creator and Parents Are Cocreators with God of Human Life (Gen. 1:28*a*; Ps. 139:13-15)

**1. Cocreators of life with God (Gen. 1:28*a*)**

**28 And God blessed them, and God said into them, Be fruitful and multiply.**

The early chapters of Genesis contain foundational principles of God's plan for human beings. After describing God's creative work for the rest of creation, Genesis 1:26-28 describes His creation of human beings. He created them in His own image, capable of fellowship with him. He commissioned them to be trustees for Him over the rest of creation. God also commissioned human beings to be "be fruitful, and multiply."

God is the Creator of all things, who commissioned human beings to be cocreators with Him of other human beings. Genesis 2:18-25 shows that this command to procreate was given to a man and a woman whom God had joined together. God ordained marriage as the appropriate expression of the one-flesh union of a man and a woman. Thus God ordained marriage as the foundation for mutual love and for procreation. God's plan is that every child that comes into the world have a father and a mother who love each other and who love the child they have brought into the world.

As we are trustees for God over all His creation, a man and a woman are special trustees for God of the life that He has created as a result of their union. Children are gifts of God; they belong to Him. Parents are only trustees in God's name.

**2. God's creative work in new life (Ps. 139: 13-15)**

> **13 For thou hast possessed my reins: thou hast covered me in my mother's womb.**
>
> **14 I will praise thee; for I am fearfully and wonderfully made: marvellous are thy works; and that my soul knoweth right well.**
>
> **15 My substance was not hid from thee, when I was made in secret, and curiously wrought in the lowest parts of the earth.**

In a prayer, the psalmist expressed awe at God's complete knowledge of him (vv.1-6), His inescapable presence with him (vv. 7-12), and His creation of him (vv. 13-16). "Possessed my reins" means "made my inner parts." The psalmist marveled that God's knowledge of him began even before his birth. God was at work creating him in his mother's womb.

Psalm 139 is a prayer that often breaks into praise as in verse 14. The psalmist praised God for all His works, but he was particularly impressed that he himself was so "fearfully and wonderfully made." Our expanded knowledge of the universe and of the human body can only enhance our feelings of wonder and praise.

Verse 15 further celebrates in poetic form the prior knowledge and creative power of God. The psalmist's "substance" or "frame" was not hid from God; to the contrary, God was at work in creating him in the "secret" or "hidden" state while he was still in his mother's womb. The reference to the "lowest parts of earth" or "the womb of the earth" is a poetic way of referring again to the mother's womb (compare Job 1:21).

When Genesis 1:28a is read with Psalm 139:13-15, we see that as cocreators with God, the responsibility of parents begins before the child is born. As cocreators with God and trustees of this new life, parents are accountable fo what promotes the health and well-being of the life being formed by God within the womb. Viewed from this biblical perspective, anything parents do to harm the unborn child is wrong. Abortion would be the worst that parents could do.

## II. God Wants to Care for and Protect Children (Ex. 1:15-2:10; Matt. 18:10, 14)

**1. Protection of the newborn (Ex. 1:15-2:10).**—This passage describes the efforts of Pharaoh to destroy newborn Hebrew males and the concern of God to protect them. God worked through the midwives to spare many infants whom the midwives had been ordered to murder. God blessed the midwives for their faith and courage (vv.12-21). Then Pharaoh ordered the total population to cast every male Hebrew child into the river (v.22). Exodus 2:1 tells the familiar story of how God preserved Moses as an infant from Pharoah's order. In the case of the children spared by the midwives, God mediated His care and protection through people. In the case of Moses, God used Moses' mother, his sister, and even Pharaoh's daughter.

**2. God's concern for children (Matt. 18:10,14)**

> **10 Take heed that ye despise not one of these little ones; for I say unto you, That in heaven their angels do always behold the face of my father which is in heaven.**
>
> **14 Even so it is not the will of your Father which is in heaven, that one of these little ones should perish.**

Read the entire passage in Matthew 18:1-14. Little children are mentioned in verses 2-5. "Little ones" are mentioned in verses 6,10,14. Verse 14 follows one version of the parable of the lost sheep (vv. 12-13). Thus in verse 10 Jesus seems clearly to have had little children in mind. In verse 14 He seems to have broadened the meaning of "little ones" to include others who are helpless and in need.

One commentator suggests that Jesus meant what we mean when we refer to "little people." This includes children and also includes others who are often overlooked, neglected, or exploited.

How does God feel about "little ones'? Jesus left no doubt about this. In verse 10, He warned against neglecting or abusing little ones. He said, "Their angels do always behold the face of my father which is in heaven." The Bible gives some tantalizing glimpses into the ministry of angels, but much mystery remains. The message of verse 10 seems to be that children have guardian angels. These guardian angels of little ones have God's full attention as they represent the needs of little ones. This is a powerful way of affirming God's constant concern for little children. In verse 14, Jesus said that the will of the Father is that none of these little ones perish.

Human society has a sorry record of reflecting the Farher's concern for little ones. In ancient times, unwanted babies were often "exposed." That is, they were left helplessly to die or to be used by someone for evil purposes. This custom is practiced in some countries today. Our own record is not much better. Neglect and abuse of children often makes the news; more often it does not. Many helpless children are mistreated by those who have the power to treat the children as they choose.

Although these passages do not mention unborn life specifically, surely the principles about God's care for little ones after birth apply also to little ones before birth. Unborn life is even more helpless than little ones after birth.

### III. God Cares for and Protects the Helpless in Society and Expects Us to Do the Same (Deut. 18:10*a*; Matt. 19:14-15*a*)

**1. Child sacrifice (Deut. 18:10*a*)**

> 10 There shall not be found among you any one that maketh his son or his daughter to pass through the fire.

A frequent theme in the Old Testament is God's command for his people to care for the widows, orphans, strangers, and poor among them (see Deut. 24:10-22). These were the helpless groups of ancient society, and God commanded His people to care for the helpless in His name.

Deuteronomy 18:10a reflects an even more heinous sin than neglecting the needs of the helpless. It reflects the horrible practice of child sacrifice. A similar prohibition is found in 12:31: "Thou shalt not do so unto the Lord thy God: for every abomination to the Lord, which he hateth, have they done unto their gods, for even their sons and their daughters they have burnt in the fire to their gods."

This verse comes from a passage in which Moses was describing pagan religion. Pagans practiced child sacrifice to show their devotion to their gods and to secure the favor of their gods.

Deuteronomy 18:9-14 prohibits pagan practices that were used to try to gain special understanding or to influence events. Thus those who offered their children as sacrifices hoped to influence the pagan god to grant them some special favor.

Israelite law made child sacrifice a capital offense (Lev. 20:2-5). In spite of its heinous nature, it was sometimes practiced by Israelites. In fact, two of Judah's worst kings did it: Ahaz (2 Chron. 28:3) and Manassah (2 Kings 21:6).

**2. Jesus and children (Matt. 19:14-15*a*)**

> 14 But Jesus said, Suffer little children and forbid them not, to come unto me: for such is the kingdom of heaven.
> 15 And he laid his hands on them.

These two verses are from a familiar passage often used in teaching little children of Jesus' love for them. As we adults study it, the passage reminds us that we are accountable for showing the love of the Lord to little children. We are especially accountable for bringing little children to Jesus.

Verse 13 shows that the parents were right in wanting to bring their children to Jesus and the disciples were wrong to forbid them.

The Bible is clear in its teaching about the need for parents and the adult generation to teach little children about the Lord.
This is clear in such Old testament passages as Deuteronomy 6:4-9. Even more familiar is Paul's admonition to fathers, "And ye fathers,

provoke not your children to wrath: but bring them up in the nurture and admonition of the Lord" (Eph 6:4).

## APPLYING THE BIBLE

**Man/woman, the crown of creation.**—William Gladstone (1809-1898), was one of England's most-famous political leaders. He was also an outstanding lay leader of the Church of England. About the creation of man, Gladstone said that man is the crowning wonder of creation and the study of man and his nature is the noblest study one can make.

It is interesting to observe how the Holy Spirit, speaking through Moses, described the first five stages in creation. Looking at His creation, God said it was "good." But after He had made man, God said it was "very good." This teaches us that not only is man special in God's creative act, but he is also special to God.[1]

**"Fearfully and wonderfully made."**—On this special day when we are observing Sanctity of Human Life Sunday, we need to rediscover the precious value and uniqueness of human life.

According to cardiologists, the average human heart may pump as much as 36.8 billion times in a year. If you live out your threescore and twenty years, your heart will beat no fewer than 2.5 billion times. The human brain, which weighs about 35 ounces, contains between 30 and 50 billion cells. It has estimated that the number of possible circuits in the brain is greater than the number of atoms in the universe.

One writer has suggested that if the cells of the brain were only worth a nickel each, and if each connection those cells makes is worth only one penny, the value of the human brain would exceed one quintillion dollars. That's one billion dollars times one billion dollars or a one with 18 zeroes after it! Indeed, the psalmist wrote: "I will praise thee; for I am fearfully and wonderfully made" (Ps. 139:14).[2]

**Known before we were born.**—For years now, especially since Roe versus Wade in 1973, abortionists have contended that life does not begin until birth. This, however, is not the position of the psalmist. Referring to God knowing the fetus in the womb before birth, the psalmist exclaims in verse 15: "My substance was not hid from Thee, when I was made in secret, and curiously wrought in the lowest parts of the earth." God knew us in the womb as a vibrant, living, worthwhile creation. How presumptuous and wicked it is, therefore, that human life in the womb is valued so little that millions of abortions are performed in the United States simply as a matter of birth control.

**"What might that baby have become?"**—About the time the Civil War ended, a black baby was born near Diamond Grove, Missouri, to a slave mother. John Bentley was hired by the slaveholder to find the baby and his mother and bring them back. Several days later, Bentley returned with only the baby and he barely alive. When the slaveholder asked where the baby had been found, Bentley replied that he found the baby being cared for by "some womenfolk" near Conway, Arkansas, adding, "He ain't worth nothin'."

But the baby grew up to be the greatest black scientist in American history. When the boll weevil destroyed the South's cotton crop year after year, this black scientist told farmers to plant peanuts, sweet potatoes, etc. Then he created products from the peanut—more than three hundred of them—to make their product profitable. From the sweet potato he developed more than one hundred eighteen products. And from the pecan he developed more than seventy-five products.

His name was George Washington Carver, the very one about whom Bentley had said, "He ain't worth nothin'."

What if the child had been aborted before his birth? What might that baby have become who will be aborted today in the United States?

Remember what Ethel Waters, the black singer, had to say about it all: "God don't make no junk."[3]

**Are the children all right?**—Napoleon attacked Vienna in 1805, the shells fell all over the city. One hit a schoolroom, destroying the walls and blowing out all the windows. Inside that schoolroom was an eight-year-old boy named Franz who was practicing on the piano. Terrified, he fell to the floor and hid his face in his arms. As he was trembling in terror, he heard the reassuring voice of his schoolmaster calling through the debris: "SchubertùFranz Schubert, are you all right, my lad?"[4]

Benjamin P. Browne, who told the story in his book, *Illustrations for Preaching,* added: "Somehow in these days of hurt and terror to childhood, Christian teachers must be constantly in the spirit of calling through the blasted ruins of our days, 'Mary, John, are you all right?' We must remember that children can be hurt and frightened by more things than bombs."[5]

## TEACHING THE BIBLE

▶ *Main Idea:* The Bible's teachings on protecting the helpless demonstrate God's concern for the helpless before and after birth.

▶ *Suggested Teaching Aim:* To lead adults to describe God's desire to protect the helpless, and to identify ways they can protect the helpless before and after birth.

### A TEACHING OUTLINE

*1. Use life situations to introduce the study.*
*2. Organize in small groups to examine the Scripture and write principles for protecting the helpless.*
*3. Apply the principles to ways members can protect the helpless.*

**Introduce the Bible Study**

Read the following life situations and ask members to respond: Bill and Leah had been married for fifteen years when the doctor discovered that Leah was pregnant. They had married late in life and had been told they could never have a baby. The doctors warned that the baby had a good chance of a physical/mental handicap because of some medication Leah had taken before she knew she was pregnant. When Bill and Leah heard the doctor's report they came by to see you and you said . . .

Bill and Judy had been dating steadily all winter and spring. When their high school prom came, they attended, and, like so many other couples, stayed out all night. Later, Judy discovered she was pregnant. She had a scholarship to attend the state university and Bill was going into thee Army on a ROTC scholarship. Judy called and asked to see you. When she explained the circumstances to you and asked what she should do, you said . . .

**Search for Biblical Truth**

IN ADVANCE, make a poster of the following outline. Leave room to write a principle under each heading.

1. Cocreators of life with God (Gen. 1:28*a*)
   Principle:
2. God's creative work in new life (Ps. 139:13-15)
   Principle:
3. God's concern for children (Matt. 18:10, 14)
   Principle:
4. Child sacrifice (Deut. 18:10*a*)
   Principle:
5. Jesus and Children (Matt. 19:14-15)
   Principle:

Cut the above poster apart. Organize the class in five groups (groups may have only one person). Give each group one of the poster strips and ask them to do two things: (1) explain the Scripture and (2) develop a principle from the Scripture that would relate to the sanctity of human life, particularly to protecting the helpless.

Call for a report from each group. As groups report. ask them to tape their poster strip on the wall and write their principle under it.

**Give the Truth a Personal Focus**

Ask a member to read the principles above. Ask, based on these principles, what can we do to protect the helpless? (Be sure opposition to abortion is listed.) Close in prayer that God would make them all sensitive to ways they can protect the helpless.

---

1. Adapted from Herschel H. Hobbs, *The Origin of All things, Studies in Genesis* (Waco, Texas: Word Books, 1975), 25.
2. Adapted from J. B. Fowler Jr., *Illustrating Great Words of The New Testament* (Nashville: Broadman Press, 1991), 119.
3. Ibid., 120
4. Adapted from Benjamin P. Browne, *Illustrations for Preaching* (Nashville: Broadman Press, 1977), 90.
5. Ibid.